Higher Education Administration for Social Justice and Equity

Higher Education Administration for Social Justice and Equity empowers all administrators in higher education to engage in their work—to make decisions, hire, mentor, budget, create plans, and carry out other day-to-day operations—with a clear commitment to justice, sensitivity to power and privilege, and capacity to facilitate equitable outcomes. Grounding administration for social justice as a matter of daily work, this book translates abstract concepts and theory into the work of hiring, socialization, budgeting, and decision-making. Contributed chapters by renowned scholars and current practitioners examine the way higher education administration is organized, and will help readers both question existing structures and practices, and consider new and different ways of organizing campuses based on equity and social justice. Rich with case studies and pedagogical tools, this book connects theory to practice, and is an invaluable resource for current and aspiring administrators.

Adrianna Kezar is Dean's Professor for Higher Education Leadership at the University of Southern California and Director of the Pullias Center for Higher Education, USA.

Julie Posselt is Associate Professor of Education at the University of Southern California and Research Director of the California Inclusive Graduate Education Network, USA.

Higher Education Administration for Social Justice and Equity

Critical Perspectives for Leadership

Edited by

Adrianna Kezar and Julie Posselt

NEW YORK AND LONDON

First published 2020
by Routledge
52 Vanderbilt Avenue, New York, NY 10017

and by Routledge
2 Park Square, Milton Park, Abingdon, Oxon, OX14 4RN

Routledge is an imprint of the Taylor & Francis Group, an informa business

© 2020 Taylor & Francis

The right of Adrianna Kezar and Julie Posselt to be identified as the authors of the
editorial material, and of the authors for their individual chapters, has been asserted
in accordance with sections 77 and 78 of the Copyright, Designs and Patents Act 1988.

Library of Congress Cataloging-in-Publication Data
A catalog record for this title has been requested

ISBN: 978-1-138-35166-0 (hbk)
ISBN: 978-1-138-35168-4 (pbk)
ISBN: 978-0-429-43514-0 (ebk)

Typeset in Minion
by Newgen Publishing UK

To Bill and Estela, for academic careers dedicated to advancing more equitable, just leadership of higher education

CONTENTS

List of Contributors   x

Foreword   xvi
ROBERT J. STERNBERG

Preface   xx

Acknowledgments   xxiv

Chapter 1   Introduction: A Call to Just and Equitable Administrative
             Practice   1
             ADRIANNA KEZAR AND JULIE POSSELT

Part I Setting and Shifting Priorities   19

Chapter 2   Renewing and Revitalizing Shared Governance: A Social
             Justice and Equity Framework   21
             ADRIANNA KEZAR AND JUDE PAUL MATIAS DIZON

Chapter 3   Choose Wisely: Making Decisions With and For Equity
             in Higher Education   43
             JULIE POSSELT, THERESA HERNANDEZ, AND
             CYNTHIA D. VILLARREAL

Chapter 4   Elevating Equity through a Strategic Finance Approach:
             Empowerment as the Goal   67
             CHRISTOPHER M. MULLIN

Chapter 5   Practitioner Reflection: Working in Topsy-Turvy Higher
             Education Environments   82
             VASTI TORRES

Part II Human Resources   91

Chapter 6   Rethinking Mentoring: Integrating Equity-Minded Practice
             in Promoting Access to and Outcomes of Developmental
             Relationships   93
             KIMBERLY A. GRIFFIN

Chapter 7   Reconceptualizing "Merit" and "Fit": An Equity-Minded
             Approach to Hiring   111
             ROMAN LIERA AND CHERYL CHING

Chapter 8   Social Justice and Collective Bargaining in Higher
             Education: Untangling the Issues   132
             DANIEL J. JULIUS

Chapter 9   Practitioner Reflection: Leading for Social Justice in
             Enrollment Management and Policy   146
             JEROME A. LUCIDO

Part III Accountability and Data   157

Chapter 10   Leadership for Equity-Minded Data Use Toward Racial
             Equity in Higher Education   159
             ALICIA C. DOWD AND BRANDEN D. ELMORE

Chapter 11   An Examination of Anti-Sexual Harassment Policies and
             Practices: Legal Administration for Socially Conscious
             Campuses   176
             JEFFREY SUN

Chapter 12   Practitioner Reflection: Feeding the Data Hungry: The Role
             of the IR Professional in Ensuring Social Justice and Equity in
             Higher Education   196
             JENNIFER L. IVIE

Part IV Culture and Structure   207

Chapter 13   Navigating Neoliberal Organizational Cultures: Implications for
             Higher Education Leaders Advancing Social Justice Agendas   209
             SAMUEL D. MUSEUS AND LUCY A. LEPEAU

Chapter 14   Developing Equitable Work–Life Policies on Campus:
             The Importance of Addressing Power and Hierarchy   225
             JAIME LESTER

Chapter 15   Words Matter: Social Justice and Policy Discourses in Higher
             Education   238
             MAGDALENA MARTINEZ AND DEANNA COOPER

Chapter 16   Practitioner Reflection: Equity-Minded Leadership
             Perspectives for Community Colleges   251
             LUCA E. LEWIS

Index   265

CONTRIBUTORS

Cheryl Ching is assistant professor of leadership in education at the University of Massachusetts Boston. A qualitative researcher, she examines how institutional actors, organizational conditions, and the design of policies advance and/or constrain equity, particularly for low-income, racially minoritized students. She received the 2017 Bobby Wright Dissertation of the Year Award from the Association for the Study of Higher Education for her study on how a community college in California made sense of and enacted "equity." Her work has appeared in *Educational Policy* and *The Review of Higher Education*.

Deanna Cooper is a doctoral student in the Higher Education program at the University of Nevada, Las Vegas. She is an Air Force veteran who holds a Master of Science degree in National Resource Strategy, with an emphasis in supply chain management, and a Master of Science degree in Logistics and Business Management. Her research principally focuses on higher education policymaking and governance at state and local levels.

Jude Paul Matias Dizon is a doctoral student and Provost's Fellow in the Urban Education Policy Program, Rossier School of Education. Jude Paul's research interests focus on racialization and racism in higher education from an organizational perspective. Prior to graduate school, Jude Paul worked in multicultural affairs and taught courses in Asian American Studies.

Alicia C. Dowd is a Professor of Education, Senior Scientist, and Director of the Center for the Study of Higher Education in the Department of Education Policy Studies at the Pennsylvania State University. She currently serves as the associate editor of the *Review of Educational Research* (RER), a top-ranked journal in the field of education. An action researcher, Dowd's scholarship generates knowledge about organizational change toward racial equity in higher education. She is the author (with Estela Mara Bensimon) of *Engaging the "Race Question": Accountability and Equity in U.S. Higher Education* (Teachers College Press, 2015). Dr. Dowd holds the PhD, Master of Education, and Bachelor of Arts degrees, all awarded by Cornell University, where she studied the social foundations of education, labor economics, and curriculum and instruction.

Branden D. Elmore is a PhD candidate in the Higher Education program at the Pennsylvania State University. His current research interests include identity negotiation among senior-level minority administrators at predominantly white institutions; issues in equity and access; and the use of narrative inquiry methods, discourse analyses and critical race theory to further interrogate the concept of institutional work. Prior to his doctoral studies, Branden accepted a McNair Scholar fellowship to conduct research focused on crisis communication and the response from university administrators to a campus-specific racially charged crisis. Branden received his Bachelor's degree in Communication Studies with a certificate in Professional Writing from Fayetteville State University, as well as a Master's degree in Communication, Public Relations and Organizational Communication from the University of Cincinnati.

Kimberly A. Griffin is Associate Professor at the University of Maryland and the Editor of the *Journal of Diversity in Higher Education*. Prior to becoming a faculty member, she served as a higher education administrator and student affairs professional, working in undergraduate and graduate admissions, promoting diverse and hospitable learning environments, and new student orientation. Professor Griffin is a recognized scholar in the area of higher education access and equity research. Throughout her career, she has contributed to multiple projects that examine the diverse experiences of Black students and faculty, the impact of campus climate, and how mentoring relationships influence student and faculty success. Much of her current work focuses on graduate training in STEM and increasing diversity and inclusion in the faculty.

Theresa Hernandez is a research assistant at the Pullias Center for Higher Education and a Dean's Fellow in the Urban Education Policy PhD program at USC Rossier School of Education. She studies participation in equity, diversity, and inclusion work on college campuses in order to improve work toward transforming higher education for racial, gender, and other intersecting forms of equity. Hernandez completed her Bachelor's in comparative ethnic studies with a sociology focus at Columbia University and earned her Master's degree in higher and postsecondary education from Teachers College.

Jennifer L. Ivie is Director of Institutional Research & Assessment at Tulsa Community College. Dr. Ivie earned her PhD in Quantitative Psychology with an emphasis in educational measurement and psychometrics from the University of Kansas. She has served in multiple roles from full-time faculty, to leading faculty professional development, to leading the office of institutional research. Her research focuses on developmental education placement, student success, issues with transfer from community colleges to universities, and teaching evaluation.

Daniel J. Julius is a Visiting Fellow at the School of Management at Yale University. Most recently he was Senior Vice President and Provost at New Jersey City University and Adjunct Professor in the Higher Education Program at New York University. He has been an affiliated faculty member at Cornell University, ILR School, a Visiting Scholar at the University of California, Berkeley and an adjunct faculty member at Stanford University and at the University of New Hampshire. Dr. Julius has served as the Academic Vice President/Provost in three state institutions/systems, a Land Grant system, private liberal arts university and comprehensive state university. He has also been the vice president or senior director responsible for collective bargaining in California and Vermont state university systems, and the University of San Francisco. He has been a long-term employer consultant on collective bargaining for the University of California, and postsecondary systems in numerous states. He is a former President of the College and University Personnel Association (now CUPA/HR) and the Academy for Academic Personnel Administrators. Dr. Julius has edited over 20 books and published 90 articles, book chapters, reviews and monographs and made over 170 presentations. He earned a Master's and doctorate at Columbia University and completed a postdoctoral fellowship at the Center for Organizations Research at Stanford University.

Adrianna Kezar is Dean's Professor for Higher Education Leadership at the University of Southern California and director of the Pullias Center for Higher Education. Dr. Kezar is a national expert of leadership, governance, change, student success, equity and diversity, and the changing faculty in higher education. Kezar is well published with 19 books/monographs, over 100 journal articles, and over 100 book chapters and reports. Recent books include: *Envisioning the Faculty of the 21st Century* (Routledge, 2016), *How Colleges Change* (Routledge, 2013), *Enhancing Campus Capacity for Leadership* (Stanford Press, 2011), and *Organizing for Collaboration* (Jossey-Bass, 2009). She is the project director for the Delphi Project on the changing faculty and student success and oversees a $7 million study of the Thompson scholars learning community research study.

Lucy A. Lepeau is Associate Professor of Higher Education and Student Affairs at Indiana University and Associate Director for the National Institute for Transformation and Equity (NITE). Prof. LePeau has produced over 50 publications and presentations on approaches educators take in academic affairs and student affairs partnerships to create more equitable campus environments, organizational change, and improved student affairs teaching and practice. She has published in journals such as *The Review of Higher Education, The Journal of Higher Education,* and *The Journal of College Student Development.* She was a recipient of the 2018 IU Trustees Teaching Award and Emerging Scholar award from ACPA-College Student Educators International.

Jaime Lester is a professor in the Higher Education Program at George Mason University. Prof. Lester holds a PhD from the University of Southern California's Rossier School of Education. The overarching goal of her research program is to examine organizational change and leadership in higher education. Her more recent research on learning analytics and pedagogy in computer science is funded by the National Science Foundation (#1444789 and #1821589) and Google. The aim of this research is to create and promote new data-driven evidence to promote changes in pedagogy, instructional practice, and leadership decision making. Prof. Lester has over 50 peer-reviewed journal articles and other academic publications. Her work appears in all the major journals of the discipline. She also has many books on learning analytics in higher education, gendered perspectives in community colleges, family-friendly policies in higher education, ways to restructure higher education to promote collaboration, non-positional leadership, and workplace bullying.

Luca E. Lewis is the Vice President for Student Services at Whatcom Community College in Bellingham, Washington. Dr. Lewis brings over 16 years of higher education experience and is a nationally recognized transformative community college leader with a demonstrated track record of development and implementing effective and sustainable equity strategies in a postsecondary setting. He has consulted with numerous institutions and facilitated hundreds of workshops and trainings on equity-minded leadership, strategic planning, and change management.

Roman Liera is a Postdoctoral Research Associate at the University of Southern California. His research focuses on the organizational constraints faculty encounter in their efforts to institutionalize racial equity in policies and practices. His work has been published in *Education Policy Analysis Archives* and *The Journal of Higher Education.*

Jerome A. Lucido is Professor of the Practice and Executive Director of the Center for Enrollment Research, Policy, and Practice at the USC Rossier School of Education. Previously, he served as the chief enrollment officer at the University of Southern California, the University of North Carolina at Chapel Hill, and the University of Arizona. He is the author of numerous book chapters and articles and founder of the first Master of Education program in Enrollment Management and Policy at a research university. Dr. Lucido has played a leading national role in initiatives to improve access for low-income and underrepresented students and in the research, design, and execution of effective and principled college admission and enrollment management practices.

Magdalena Martinez is an assistant professor in the School of Public Policy and Leadership, College of Urban Affairs, at the University of Nevada, Las Vegas and Director of Education Programs with The Lincy Institute. Her research centers on issues of social justice, education policy, Latinx population, and women in policy-making. She regularly provides expert testimony (K-12 and postsecondary) on education policy issues and is involved in numerous efforts to build capacity through education research and policy.

Christopher M. Mullin serves as director of Strong Start to Finish (SSTF), an initiative supported by the Education Commission of the States. Prior to serving in this role, he was the executive vice chancellor of the Florida College System, assistant vice chancellor with the State University System of Florida and program director for policy analysis at the American Association of Community Colleges. He earned his doctoral degree in higher education administration, as well as his Bachelor's degree, from the University of Florida. He also holds a Master of Education degree from Teachers College of Columbia University.

Samuel D. Museus is Professor of Education Studies at the University of California, San Diego (UCSD) and also serves as Founding Director of the National Institute for Transformation and Equity (NITE). Prior to joining UCSD, he taught at Indiana University Bloomington, the University of Denver, the University of Hawaii at Manoa, and the University of Massachusetts Boston. His research agenda is focused on diversity and equity, transforming systems to be more inclusive and equitable, and college student outcomes.

Julie Posselt is Associate Professor of Education at the University of Southern California and a 2015–2017 National Academy of Education/Spencer Foundation postdoctoral fellow. Her research examines institutionalized inequities in selective sectors of higher education, and organizational efforts to advance equity and inclusion. Prof. Posselt is the author of *Inside Graduate Admissions: Merit, Diversity, and Faculty Gatekeeping* (Harvard University Press, 2015), and additional research is published in leading education and sociology journals. She is PI and Director of the California Consortium for Inclusive Doctoral Education and the Inclusive Graduate Education Network Research Hub. Prior to joining USC, she taught at the University of Michigan.

Jeffrey Sun is Professor of Higher Education, Affiliate Professor of Law, and Department Chair. Dr. Sun's research examines the extent to which policy instruments or other legal actions (e.g. government mandates, judicial decisions, and legally binding, negotiated agreements) advance or inhibit the academic operations through college teaching, learning, and knowledge creation. This stream rests heavily on concepts of civil rights and civil liberties, particularly on topics regarding free speech and Title IX, and he has been published in venues such as *Cardoza Law Review, Education Law Reporter* (Westlaw), *Journal of College & University Law, Review of Higher Education, Teachers College Record*, and the *University of Pennsylvania Journal of Constitutional Law*. In addition, Dr. Sun has four books and has been awarded over $11 million as the Principal Investigator and Project Director for numerous federally sourced grants and contracts.

Vasti Torres is a professor in the Center for the Study of Higher and Postsecondary Education (CSHPE) at University of Michigan. Previously she was the Dean of the College of Education at the University of South Florida and Director of the Center for Postsecondary Research (CPR) at Indiana University. Her research focuses broadly on the success of underrepresented students. She has been the Principal Investigator for several grants and works with several community college initiatives. In 2019 she begins her term as Vice President for Division J: Postsecondary Education for the American Educational Research Association (AERA). She was the first Latina president of a national student services association—ACPA. She served as a Fulbright Specialist in South Africa. Dr. Torres is a graduate of Stetson University and holds a PhD from the University of Georgia.

Cynthia D. Villarreal is a research assistant at the Pullias Center for Higher Education and a Rossier Dean's Fellow in the Urban Education Policy PhD program at USC Rossier School of Education. Her research brings a critical lens to organizations to understand the impacts of race and culture on issues of equity.

FOREWORD

ROBERT J. STERNBERG, CORNELL UNIVERSITY

Here is a headline from Yale University Communications: "Yale Class of 2022 sets record for socioeconomic diversity and yield."[1] "Well, that's good news!" any reasonable reader might think. But here is a report from the *New York Times:* "The median family income of a student from Yale is $192,600, and 69% come from the top 20%."[2] To be more specific, the average income percentile, according to the story, is 82. In all, the *New York Times* story relates, 3.7% of the students come from the top 0.1% of the income distribution, 19% from the top 1%, 45% from the top 5%, 57% from the top 10%, 69% from the top 20%, and 2.1% from the bottom 20%. So, if the Class of 2022 at Yale set records, given the past record of the university, that's not much to brag about. To the extent that the current admissions system was originally designed to create equity in a system formerly favoring the rich and powerful, the system, and indeed, the entire Zeitgeist of the university, has failed rather miserably—unless one cares little or not at all about equity with respect to parental income distribution. Would that the problem were only with admissions. There are serious problems of equity in all aspects of university administration—hiring, promotions, decisions regarding programmatic issues, and budgetary decisions of all kinds are only a few examples. For example, 13 senior professors at Yale all walked out simultaneously, because of inadequate resources, from a program designed to promote the teaching of ethnicity, race, and migration studies.

I chose Yale not because of hostility but rather because of affection toward it. I was an undergraduate there and a faculty member for 30 years. Moreover, I was one of those from a first-generation college family. Neither of my parents graduated from high school. My father sold buttons in a second-floor walkup in Newark, New Jersey, and my mother was a housewife. But I was the rare exception. Most people like me had no shot at an elite college, much less Yale. Moreover, Yale is not much different from other Ivy League schools and indeed from elite and not-so-elite schools in general. But then, a year at Yale costs $66,445,[3] way beyond the means of all but the richest families in the United States. And this level of tuition is fairly typical of private universities in the United States, including my own, Cornell (average cost, $65,494).[4] It gets worse. Yale is one of only five universities that are need-blind,[5] meaning that, if one is admitted, one's full financial need is covered. But for all the rest of the thousands of colleges and universities in the United States, one's admission, or at least one's ability to attend a university, is limited by one's financial situation, meaning that tremendous numbers of students either will not be able to attend the college or university of their dreams, even if they are admitted, or if they do, they will sink into years and possibly a lifetime of debt that will drag them down throughout the years of their adulthood.

It does not have to be this way. In addition to being a professor at Cornell, I am also an honorary professor at the University of Heidelberg, one of the top universities in Germany. If you get in, it's free, as it is at the other German public universities (and almost all are public). Free public higher education is common in Europe and elsewhere. The United States appears to be doing something—actually, a lot of things—wrong. What we are doing wrong and what we might do better is the subject of this book.

The book is edited and written by a group of distinguished scholars but the book is aimed at practitioners as well as scholars and has reflection pieces by those who are immersed in the practice of higher education. The point of view of the book is that social justice and equity are possible in higher education but that, at present, they are often sorely lacking.

Administrators hold considerable influence to improve the odds that students from underserved backgrounds can not only obtain access to higher education, but succeed when they do enroll. But traditional ways of thinking about administration are failing miserably at achieving these goals. A new mindset toward leadership is needed, and it should pervade all of the activities that come with leadership: decision making, budgeting, using data, mentoring, policy-making and more.

When one reads about a "social justice and equity" perspective, one may be tempted to dismiss the book as the product of an extremist, far-left-leaning group of scholars who shout down speakers whose views do not correspond to their own. Let me say therefore from the start that this unfortunate stereotype is *not* the perspective of this book. Rather, the book is true to its mission. Higher education in the United States is *not* equitable and does *not* help the country to achieve anything approaching social justice. If you come from the lower-income percentiles, your college prospects are vastly different than if you come from the upper-income percentiles, as the Yale figures demonstrate and other comparable figures also would show. Moreover, the problems do not end with admissions or financial aid—or the lack thereof. The problems students experience continue once enrolled in college, especially in an elite college. Students are more likely to struggle under decisions and policies made by administrators who do not have an equity and social justice perspective. Such individuals are less likely to hire diverse faculty to serve as role models, to allocate resources to appropriate support programs, and to create decision-making structures that include student voices to inform policy.

Many (although certainly not all) underrepresented minority students, students from low-income families, and students from rural backgrounds, among others, fail to acquire in their secondary schooling not only the academic knowledge and skills, but also the tacit (unspoken) practical knowledge and skills that are necessary for success in college, or at least in the more competitive colleges. So, students from such backgrounds may be admitted in small numbers to elite colleges, or admitted without adequate financial aid, but with a huge albatross around their necks. Rarely have administrators examined how the systems in place to run universities account for this albatross. They need so much compensatory work that it is difficult for them fully to succeed, even if the colleges have various token programs aimed at helping such students. The result often is alienation and the phenomenon of those students hanging out together because they do not fit in with the students from more privileged backgrounds—and often are unwelcomed by them.

It's worse than that. I spent almost a decade of my life in upper university administration—as a dean, provost, and briefly, president. The reward system could not be clearer. Sure, the pursuit of academic excellence and diversity gain adequate, sometimes more than adequate lip service. But in the end, American colleges and universities today, unlike the colleges and universities of times past, have become corporate—they judge your administrative expertise largely (although certainly not exclusively) by the money you bring in. It's not as ill-intentioned or even evil as it sounds: Today, as readers of this book probably know, many small and not-so-small colleges are going under. They just do not have the financial wherewithal to survive in a very tough environment in which the federal government and especially the states are decreasing their contributions to higher education. Moreover, unlike in probably any other country, administrators need to raise money not only for academic programs, but also for athletic teams, glitzy student centers, extensive extracurricular programs, and many items that are irrelevant to the university's academic mission. Even those administrators who genuinely want to focus on equity and social-justice considerations may find they are doing so on their own time, because the rewards for performance so much more lie with money raised than with academic leadership. Universities find themselves in permanent fundraising mode, and other aspects of administration may get short shrift, as they must when a university's mission is threatened by lack of funds.

We in the United States live in a society that is tearing itself apart. Moreover, as Warren Buffett recently said, "There's class warfare, all right, but it's my class, the rich class, that's making war, and we're winning."[6] Recent tax cuts have benefited the rich and the rising stock market of the last few years has benefited only those who can afford significant exposure to stocks. For the large majority of people in the United States, the strong economy has held little or no benefit.[7] Our system too often perpetuates an existing socioeconomic class structure and even leads desperate parents, in some cases, to cross the line from being helpful to possibly being criminal.[8] Our society cannot continue this way indefinitely and at some point, it will break rather than merely bend.

Higher education can and should play a vital role in helping our society to achieve equity and social justice, and that starts with how we run our colleges and universities. Right now, as this book points out, it is not doing a very good job. But the book also points out how it can do a much better job. We need to start doing better, not next year or next month, but now. Our time may be running out. The current trend, at least in the United States, is increasingly hostile toward immigrants, often even legal ones, and members of minority groups. I am confident you will find the essays in this book as provocative, edifying, and practically useful as I did as you learn how colleges and universities can do much more to create within their gates the same equity and social justice that many of us would like to see permeate our society.

NOTES

1 https://news.yale.edu/2018/08/23/incoming-class-2022-sets-record-socio-economic-diversity-and-yield

2 www.nytimes.com/interactive/projects/college-mobility/yale-university

3 www.google.com/search?client=firefox-b-1-d&q=how+much+does+a+year+at+Yale+cost%3F

4 www.google.com/search?client=firefox-b-1-d&ei=FlOlXI-wI4ef_Qar1beIBg&q=how+much+does+a+year+at+cornell+cost%3F&oq=how+much+does+a+year+at+cornell+cost%3F&gs_l=psy-ab.3...94269.97958..98121...6.0..0.102.1307.13j2.....0...1..gws-wiz......0i71j35i304i39j0i7i30j33i10.8QxsgiEbCSE

5 www.google.com/search?client=firefox-b-1-d&q=is+cornell+need+blind+in+admissions%3F

6 www.goodreads.com/quotes/123058-there-s-class-warfare-all-right-but-it-s-my-class-the

7 www.washingtonpost.com/business/2018/12/13/benefits-this-strong-economy-have-not-reached-all-americans/?utm_term=.e26146ee2d49

8 www.nytimes.com/2019/04/03/us/felicity-huffman-lori-loughlin-college-admissions-scandal.html

PREFACE

PURPOSE

This book fills a critical gap in the literature about administration in higher education. It stems from our own search for an administration course text that brings an equity and social justice lens to common areas of administrative practice, and which directly addresses how administrative work must be mindful of systems of power and privilege. Existing books on social justice or equity in administration are written for staff members designated to lead specific units' diversity or equity efforts, such as chief diversity officers, cultural directors, or vice presidents for multicultural affairs. This group is a small fraction of the overall administrative workforce in colleges and universities, however, and for higher education institutions to become more equitable and more just, all administrators should approach all of their work with mindfulness about how it aligns with—or falls short of—these values.

We envision *Higher Education Administration for Social Justice and Equity: Critical Perspectives for Leadership* to empower administrators of all types in higher education to engage in their work with critical thinking, with a clear commitment to justice, with sensitivity to power and privilege, and with capacity to facilitate equitable outcomes. We frame administration for social justice as a matter of daily work—work in which anyone likely has room for reflection and growth. Through it, practitioners can more readily translate what are often considered abstract concepts into everyday activities like hiring, supervision, budgeting, and decision-making. We believe all practice should be grounded in values and principles, and our opening chapter explores ethical and value propositions necessary for such grounding.

AUDIENCE

The intended audience for this book is current and aspiring educational practitioners—administrative, faculty, and staff—in higher education. For current administrators, we imagine a range of individuals will be interested in its content: presidents and provosts; leaders in academic affairs such as deans and department chairs; student affairs practitioners; and unit and department heads across functional areas ranging from admissions to business operations to human resources. For aspiring administrators—graduate students in higher education—this will also be an important resource in learning administrative practices that do not simply reinforce the status quo. This text will be an excellent administration and leadership textbook in higher education programs and resource for practicing administrators.

ORGANIZATION OF THE BOOK

The introductory chapter of the book sets a foundation by reviewing historic and organizational barriers to equity, current challenges, and a framework for equity and justice in higher education administration grounded in seven practices: clear definitions of equity and justice; mindful administrative practice; wisdom in judgment; critical consciousness about power; knowledge of self and positionality; student centeredness; and routinizing equity.

The book is then divided into four parts that encompass core administrative work: setting and shifting priorities; human resources; accountability and data; and culture and structure. Within each of these parts are two or three chapters by scholars that examine specific areas of administrative practice. Each part ends with a short reflection by an administrator working in this area of practice. For example, the first part, on setting and shifting priorities, reviews shared governance, budgeting, policy, and decision making. Then, in Chapter 5, Vasti Torres writes about her time as dean at the University of South Florida and how she made decisions and policies aimed at change and the challenges in the environment she faced pursing goals of justice and equity.

The chapters by scholars in each part re-envision key areas of administrative practice with a justice and/or equity lens. The reflective chapters by practitioners that close out each part are synthetic, describing how the lived experience of administrative work is to simultaneously engage in multiple areas of practice—hiring, governance, and decision-making—rather than one specific area alone. Administrators from different institutional types and in different positions describe how they dynamically enact their roles and implement the domains of practice described in earlier chapters. Each chapter ends with a set of questions and additional resources.

The content of each chapter speaks to common sets of questions—one set for scholars and another for practitioners—but with common themes of power and privilege, the practical work and ethical implications of socially just administration, and resilience in the face of these challenges. The chapters by scholars on specific areas of administrative practice were guided by the following questions:

1. How are power and privilege inherent to or part of this practice?
2. What assumptions should administrators question about this area of practice as it currently exists?
3. How can social justice and equity mindedness be embedded in this area of practice?
4. What new values can be associated with this practice so that it can meet the goals of social justice?
5. How can power and privilege be negotiated or changed as part of this practice?
6. What challenges—practical, political, social, or resource-driven— may emerge while attempting to shift this area of practice?
7. What ethical considerations should practitioners be aware of or consider?
8. How is the student part of administrative considerations and practice?

The reflective chapters by practitioners were guided by the following questions:

1. What does socially just administration look like for you day-to-day in your work?
2. What was your journey to socially just administration? If this is something you always gravitated toward what were some early influences?
3. What are the most important lessons you can share about trying to execute socially just administration?
4. What challenges have you faced? How have you negotiated power dynamics and/ or ethical dilemmas?
5. How do you remain resilient?
6. How have you embedded social justice and equity into your own practice and how have communicated and worked to integrate these values into those you work with?

We also invite readers to use these questions to reflect on their own professional practice on an ongoing basis.

DISTINCTIVE FEATURES

As noted above, this is the first book on higher education administration in which all chapters consider what it means to engage in the work with and for justice and equity, and provide guidance to that end. We see great potential in explicitly bringing that lens to a plethora of areas of administrative practice. Practically, we hope it will serve as both a textbook to support new administrators' socialization and training, as well as a resource for reflection and professional development among those already working in administrative roles. Reflecting these dual goals, chapters conclude with pedagogical tools such as questions for reflection and discussion, but the book is designed with narrative and readability in mind.

Another distinctive feature of this text is that it is both practical and theoretically informed. In terms of being concrete and practical, authors include numerous examples and case studies to help practitioners explore and utilize the concepts discussed within areas of practice. However, the book is also philosophical and theory-based, with authors drawing on the best available literature to inform practical recommendations with which readers can wrestle.

The book is also unique in bringing together the voices of scholars and practitioners, side by side. Two authorial voices are present: the expertise of scholars of higher education who examine administration from the standpoint of research literature and from critical theoretical perspectives. Reflections of current administrators, on the other hand, draw upon their lived experiences. They possess an undercurrent of wisdom about the challenges and strategies toward social justice and equity, and the ways that power and privilege play out within campuses. Whereas texts typically have one focus or the other, leaving either theory or real-life practice of administration on the margins, bringing these types of knowledge into dialogue with each other can move readers toward a more integrated understanding.

The dynamic social context and pervasive, persistent inequities of higher education demand that even the most experienced leaders see themselves as learners and engage that role accordingly. Change is possible when leaders throughout our campuses begin to mindfully aim administrative work toward social justice; when we acknowledge how injustices and inequities are institutionalized in existing policies and practices; when we interrogate power structures; and when we work collectively to re-envision these structures by integrating the knowledge of theory with the wisdom of experience. We hope this book is a useful tool in that endeavor.

ACKNOWLEDGMENTS

We gratefully acknowledge Monica Raad, Diane Flores, and student employees in the Pullias Center for Higher Education, for their excellent administrative support in the development of the book. We thank our editor Heather Jarrow for enthusiastic support of this project from start to finish.

1

INTRODUCTION

A Call to Just and Equitable Administrative Practice

ADRIANNA KEZAR AND JULIE POSSELT

This book is a call for justice and equity in higher education administration. Most of the classic textbooks for courses in administration in higher education do not explicitly examine issues of power and privilege, and few are anchored in values of social justice or equity. Meanwhile, general higher education administrative books about being a dean, department chair or business officer also rarely speak to the values that can and should underlie these roles. Books aimed at social justice and equity in higher education, on the other hand, typically do not address administrators in common roles such as department chairs, deans, division heads, and assistant directors, an exception being student affairs. Those books are typically aimed at staff members in positions centered specifically on diversity or equity efforts, such as chief diversity officers, cultural directors, or vice presidents for multicultural affairs (Williams, 2013). It is our contention, however, that *all* administrators have the potential to use their roles to create equity and encourage greater justice.

This book aims to address this gap with readings that will empower educational practitioners of all types in higher education to engage in their work—to make decisions, hire, mentor, budget, create plans, and carry out other day-to-day operations—with sensitivity to power and privilege and with capacity to facilitate equitable and just outcomes. Its chapters illustrate (1) how the practical activities and daily choices made by administrators, faculty, and staff are associated with value propositions and (2) the potential for improving administrative practice through a clear examination of these value propositions along with ongoing self-reflection. Presently, the few books that do address social justice and leadership tend to present the issue in terms of broad principles and abstractions—separate from daily practice (Dugan, 2017; Theoharis, 2007). By contrast, we position administration for social justice as a matter of daily work so that practitioners can more readily translate these abstract concepts into their responsibilities.

In this chapter, we illustrate how historical and current influences have shaped current administrative processes, and we lay out a framework for equitable and just administrative practice that rests on six principles. We begin by describing how historical structures and cultures in higher education have long privileged the powerful and disenfranchised marginalized groups, and how prevailing neoliberal culture on campuses runs counter to social justice and equity commitments. Our framework then begins by defining what we mean by equity and social justice—two important terms often used without precision and defined quite differently in the literature over time. Additionally, we have asked our chapter authors to define how they conceptualize these terms so that our meaning is well articulated in this volume. We then move to outlining a framework for administrative work through mindfulness and wise decision-making that can lead to equitable and socially just practice by explicit development of a critical consciousness of power and putting students at the center of administrative work. We end by exploring what it means to routinize this type of administrative practice and the complexities involved in such work.

Briefly, however, we want to acknowledge implicit notions that may prevent some readers from a deeper engagement with this text if not addressed. Administrators reading this might be thinking, "Well, surely I am for just and fair decisions" and thus presume a book like this will add little value to their current thinking. We want to be clear that we are not suggesting administrators are not committed to justice, but rather that the environments that most work within and their standard operating practices (as we discuss below) often do not promote justice. Thus, administrators often find themselves pressured to make compromises misaligned with their ideals of justice and equity. What is more, even the most skilled administrators are human, and like all humans, have biases that may run counter to equity and justice. Without clear processes in place, we are more likely to make unjust decisions, given our biases and environmental pressures. To sum, we believe administrators are not lacking an ethical or moral compass, but that there are very real threats to keeping our actions and decisions aligned with it.

Other readers may be thinking higher education has gone too far with social justice, that it compromises freedom of speech, debate, critical thinking, or academic freedom. Some news reports have (mis)characterized social justice as antithetical to these important traditions of open thinking on our campuses, but we find this argument a straw man and an attempt to delegitimize the equity aims our institutions of higher education are uniquely positioned to fulfill. Campuses can, do, and must hold social justice, academic freedom, and critical thinking in balance. Our book offers guidance to administrators in achieving this balance. Our view of social justice in this volume is capacious and expansive and we believe addresses many of these critiques. The process of mindfulness that we argue for will prepare administrators to combat the more baseless critiques of social justice.

HISTORIC AND ORGANIZATIONAL BARRIERS TO EQUITY

Today's sociopolitical conditions in higher education present clear challenges to equity and social justice; these conditions continue higher education's history of conferring social status and privileges to groups who already have it and allowing (or even facilitating) injustices (Cabrera, 2014; Wilder, 2013; Kezar, 2010). As an enterprise, higher education institutions were largely founded to support the intellectual development and career opportunities of elites, and wealthy white men have had disproportionate access until recently. Resources have been inequitably distributed through public policy, providing the least resources to community colleges that serve low-income, first-generation, and minority students and most to research universities that serve mostly privileged students (Gumport & Bastedo, 2001). Slaves built the earliest campuses on land taken from indigenous peoples, making colleges some of the biggest beneficiaries of Euro-American expansion.

Within universities, too, the organization of higher education over time has established power asymmetries that impede socially just and equitable processes outcomes. To maintain their market share and attract financial resources, campuses have pursued prestige through research and athletics, oftentimes de-emphasizing teaching and learning and undergraduate education (Kezar, Chambers, & Burkhardt, 2005). Public research universities have undermined their historic mission of providing access to in-state students of modest means by shifting enrollment priorities to international and domestic out-of-state students (Jaquette, Curs, & Posselt, 2016). Resources often flow on campuses to prestigious departments and colleges such as business schools, while schools of so-called "pink collar occupations" like social work, nursing, and education receive limited funds and support. The unequal distribution of resources and prestige has led to the dissolution of key areas of study and weakening of others that are essential to a liberal arts education and critical thinking needed for democratic development.

Longstanding organizational divisions and hierarchies also pose barriers to equity. Presidents ran institutions as autocratic tyrants until the development of disciplines led to greater autonomy over curriculum and instruction for departments and their faculties in the early twentieth century, and faculty demanded input into decision making in the 1930s. Tensions between administration and faculty interests remain today in many colleges and universities, hindering the effective collaboration through which more equitable outcomes might be achieved. This tension is reflected in the division between academic and student affairs (Kezar & Lester, 2009). On many campuses, academic affairs has been siloed from and privileged over student affairs. Administrators in training also need to be aware that this division, and the historical tendency to accord academic affairs more status than student affairs, renders decisions that do not always support students' success. This same hierarchy also exists with other divisions and roles (auxiliary services, technology, and administrative support) generally being subordinate to the academic core or divisions that are revenue-generating such as alumni affairs, research, or development.

A third way in which campuses have historically organized in ways that undermine social justice is through their relationship with their local communities. Studies of "town and gown" show how campuses have often exploited surrounding neighborhoods. They engage communities mainly opportunistically, such as for service learning or for campus resources (i.e. cultural events) and rarely give back to these same communities. In cities, it is not uncommon for universities to participate in gentrification, buying up land to expand the campus, replacing independent businesses with franchises that will be friendly to the student population, and pushing people out of their homes and communities. Our brief discussion here only scratches the surface of the ways that inequities, exploitation, and hierarchies are woven into the fabric of higher education as an enterprise and institution. Transformation of structures and cultures is necessary, compelling the need for fresh vision about administration.

ADMINISTRATORS' NEOLIBERAL PSYCHIC PRISON

Especially since the 1980s, economic principles have emerged as the driving value system for many administrators, derailing social justice goals that emerged in the 1960s to 1970s (Slaughter & Rhoades, 2004; Kezar, Depaola, & Scott, in press). While social justice has never been a dominant value system on campuses, there have long been seeds of this perspective in the notion of higher education as a public good. And in the 1960s and 1970s, social movements played out on campuses across the country, pushing administrators to consider policy consistent with social justice values. This was followed by a backlash of neoliberalism in the 1980s. Neoliberalism is the philosophy and system of political economy aimed at marketizing and privatizing public goods, and of pushing corporate values and practices onto public institutions (Slaughter & Rhoades, 2004). It privileges a market-based, capitalist mindset and economic drivers for public and government-based institutions. Campus cultures are increasingly fueled by two neoliberal trends, which tend to work in opposition to the social justice and equity approaches we describe in this book.

First, the neoliberal value system driving campuses focuses on revenue generation, finances more generally, efficiency, and technocratic concerns and solutions (Slaughter & Rhoades, 2004). A more corporate orientation to campus operations has become prevalent, reflected in actions ranging from outsourcing, contingent labor, and declining worker benefits and support, to treating students as customers, downsizing less profitable majors, and commercialization of research. New opportunities on campus are also being approached through a more corporate mindset: from curricular decisions (i.e. vocationalize the curriculum or move to revenue-generating online programs) to student development (i.e. partner with a business offering advertising to students in order to fund an initiative). Campus administrators face unprecedented pressures around cost-cutting and revenue generation given the decline in public finances, but also the general perception that higher education is not cost-effective. There is more need to justify financial decisions, and financial scrutiny increasingly drives behavior. Campus leaders are also increasingly being pushed to technological solutions and technocratic ways of operating through data analytics and modes that appear to offer neutral and efficient answers to problems. A focus on efficiency, cost/revenue generation, and technology solutions have typically subordinated principles and practices aimed at social justice and equity.

Second, the neoliberal psyche presses educational practitioners to perceive that they have little time and must make decisions immediately, thus limiting two key strategies for democratic decision-making: reflection and dialogue. These pressures run counter to the value placed on reflection and dialogue by scholars of social justice, such as Paulo Freire. Administrators report being more harried and in a constant state of crisis, running from one emergency to another. The culture on campuses supports and rewards quick decisions and efficiency in decision making as well. Promotions are awarded to administrators who are decisive. This neoliberal notion of time is articulated as part of a productivity model, but it can also be seen as a way to prevent administrators from thinking independently or acting with intentionality. Indeed, it has been argued that part of the power of neoliberalism is its ability to create an environment in which alternative positions cannot be considered. Social justice and equity may not be inherently opposed to neoliberalism, but the spread of this psyche has made it more challenging to raise and get attention to these perspectives. They may be thought of as luxuries rather than as foundations.

Through the chapters in this book, educational practitioners are challenged to resist the neoliberal psyche—to see and step out of its value system. We wish to empower administrators to see that a neoliberal way of operating is neither necessary nor desirable, but rather a deceptive and troubling fiction. Campus leaders can embrace a different value system that centers on social justice and equity, and can redefine how they go about the practice of administration guided by an ethic of wisdom and mindfulness. They can shed this neoliberal psyche, but it will require a conscious and deliberate re-orientation to administrative work. It starts by acknowledging that tacitly you have absorbed a value system that is so prevalent that it can be difficult to even recognize. Revenue generation, efficiency, technology, and marketing/branding need not define the values for administrative work. And indeed, if they continue to, higher education will lose its soul.

A FRAMEWORK FOR EQUITY AND JUSTICE IN HIGHER EDUCATION ADMINISTRATION

Most higher educational practitioners do not begin their careers intending to conduct their work in ways that undermine equity or student opportunities. Without an alternative to the neoliberal mindset, however, it can become all too easy to slip into such modes of action and decision making. Here, and in the chapters that follow, we propose a framework for administrators who wish to use their jobs to create equity and justice. It consists of seven key components, which are elaborated in the remainder of this chapter:

1. Clear definitions of equity and justice
2. Mindful administrative practice
3. Wisdom in judgment
4. Critical consciousness about power
5. Knowledge of self and positionality
6. Student centeredness
7. Routinizing mindfulness and wisdom

CLEAR DEFINITIONS OF EQUITY AND JUSTICE

One challenge for educational practitioners is developing, articulating, and enacting views of equity and justice that are both targeted enough to address the real needs of specific populations and the social hierarchies in which they are embedded, but also expansive enough to reach across multiple hierarchies. As editors, our own view of social justice and equity for the purposes of this volume is multifaceted and multi-dimensional, encompassing race, gender and gender identity, social class, sexual orientation, and religion, and others as the needs of specific contexts demand. We also recognize that forms of justice may be interrelated, such as environmental and social justice. We strive for a capacious approach, one that accommodates multiple dimensions of equity and justice, and which is inclusive to the diverse population of students and other stakeholders of higher education today. Both our own frame and those of the book's chapters, admittedly, are US-centered.

Shared understandings and explicit definitions of guiding principles are critical for effective action. Here, philosophies of justice and action are useful in providing focus and priorities. Many modern theories of justice fall short because profound social inequalities that the theories eschew are actually reinforced through the theoretical tenet of "equal opportunity" as a condition of justice. Equal opportunity does not go nearly far enough in the United States, where the opportunity structure neither serves nor includes people from all backgrounds equally well. Rather, it tends to best serve the interests of groups who created it (e.g. people who are wealthy, men, white, and/

or Christian). Equal opportunity to such an opportunity structure will never get us to equal outcomes—much less to justice. Indeed, profound inequality—both in society as well as within higher education—manifest injustice at a systemic level.

Taking up this critique, Martha Nussbaum contended that there can be no justice without opportunity for full inclusion, whether we are discussing cooperation among nation-states or among institutions and people within a country (Nussbaum, 2011). Inclusion, in this view, paves the way for equality. Working with economic philosopher Amartya Sen, Nussbaum insisted human development that facilitates full inclusion in society—not economic development—should be the focus of how we theorize justice and create just social policy (Nussbaum & Sen, 1993). They identified ten human capabilities necessary for humans to flourish and reach their potential (life; bodily health and integrity; senses; emotion; thought; practical reason; affiliation; relationships with other species; play; and control over one's environment) (Nussbaum, 2011).

Institutions and their structures have a special duty to promote these human capabilities, according to Nussbaum, and educational institutions in particular play a crucial role. In a 2004 lecture at Oxford University, she argued that institutions are both "made by people," who have a moral responsibility to one another, and that institutions have functional advantages in protecting and facilitating the equitable development of these capabilities. They can act voluntarily to address collective action problems better than individuals can. We can see this in the legitimacy accorded to decisions with the stamp of a faculty senate's or board of trustees' approval vs. positions that appear to be pushed by individuals. Institutions can also better accommodate issues of fairness and maintain the utilitarian logic that one should strive to maximize common welfare above one's own. The knowledge and skills of higher education leaders matter much from this angle, as arbiters of what our institutions stand for and as champions of policy that reflect those values.

These philosophies lend support for conceptualizing equity and justice not only in the numerics of representation and outcomes, but also in the processes by which we run our day-to-day affairs. For example, we should not only look at the presence or absence of certain groups in our student bodies and faculties, but also what their lives, satisfaction, and well-being are like. It means we should take into account not only the financial bottom-line, but the ethics of our budgeting practices. And it means that even professionals might not be judged only on their productivity, but on their engagement in learning about how their work can be more equitable. As educators, equity and justice mean not just pointing our goals toward, but actually embodying the developmental goals that have historically anchored the educational enterprise. Doing so will require mindfulness, we argue, and centering equity and justice as principles.

Consistent with this view, a model of equity-mindedness in higher education has been developed and propagated by the Center for Urban Education at the University of Southern California. It "refers to the mode of thinking exhibited by practitioners who call attention to patterns of inequity in student outcomes." It has five components. Equity-minded practice should be (1) mindful of the evidence base for a given issue and (2) conscious of race and the social and historical contexts of typical practices, which often reinforce patterns of exclusion and privilege. It should also be (3) focused on institutional explanations for inequities in outcomes and (4) mindful that strategies must engage with the systemic nature of inequality, rather than reinforcing student-level deficit narratives. As a result of this, equity-minded practice is (5) able to generate new practices that advance equity in the administrative or educational process under consideration, whether it is syllabus design, budgeting, hiring, or others. Mindfulness with respect to equity underlies all of these, and as we will add, *wisdom* where ethics may seem lacking and *attention to power and students* where they are so often taken for granted.

MINDFUL ADMINISTRATIVE PRACTICE

As noted earlier, neoliberalism's invasion of the administrative psyche is the principal way that it has become so dominant within modern organizations (Kezar et al., in press). To move toward socially just and equitable administration, therefore, requires a new mindset and work to be mindful as an administrator. Mindfulness as an administrator involves the slowing down of thought and engagement in reflection as a precursor to administrative practice (Lazar, 2005). Mindful administrators are more likely to explore the ethics of the situations in which they find themselves. They are more likely to seek out more information before making decisions or acting and more likely to see the uncertainty and potential flaws in their positions and those of their colleagues.

Mindfulness and wisdom, which we discuss next, are closely related but distinct. Mindfulness is more a way to approach a process whereas wisdom suggests specific ways to approach practice (Lazar, 2005). Therefore, as an example, an administrator may slow down his/her thinking about an upcoming hiring decision and come to some new insights from this slowing down process—for example, deciding that a candidate interviewed does not fit with her values around accountability. However, wisdom would go further, bringing in a set of considerations (discussed below) which entail examining not just personal concerns and interests but also broader issues such as departmental needs for the hire and environmental considerations—the need to think about the future direction of the field and ethical considerations for more diverse candidates.

Mindfulness also suggests reflecting upon and learning from past decisions and actions—both one's own and others'—and reflecting on what went wrong, with the goal being to recognize decisions and actions that lead to inequalities and thus to remedy the situation in the future. Mindfulness also reduces focus on past or existing structures, in order to free a thinker to be more creative and imagining new possibilities. This ability to free oneself from existing frameworks is important, as much of our current structures reflect inequalities, and a dearth of alternatives to the status quo is often cited as an excuse not to change. Of course mindfulness flies in the face of neoliberalism's pull to make quick decisions, based on corporate values and privileging institutional interests. Our chapter authors include both scholars of higher education and current higher education administrators; they describe how they navigate current environments while being mindful and invoking wisdom, conducting administrative practice in ways that have more integrity, sometimes successfully and other times not. We'd be slavishly bad bureaucratic managers without mindfulness—without recognizing how much of administrative work involves subtle judgments that affect our actions and which affect how we respond to others and their actions.

WISDOM IN JUDGMENT

Wisdom is a natural companion to mindfulness, in that mindful practice makes room for wisdom in judgment instead of privileging the speed with which one makes judgments. Current decision-making frameworks, which are summarized in Chapter 3 by Posselt, Hernandez, and Villarreal, rarely produce outcomes consonant with social justice and equity because the criteria and process pay too little attention to power, to the collective good, and to justice for marginalized people and groups. Moreover, decisions are rarely carried out with empathy, emotional sensitivity, and/or ethical principles. Our discussion of wisdom here will review its role in administrative practice, broadly, before proceeding to two areas of focus—attention to power and attention to students—that we believe will shape and enhance wisdom in administration today.

An emerging body of literature has developed in organizational studies and leadership on practical wisdom and wise decision-making. Part of the impetus for this literature has been concern over the past few decades about short-term, unethical decisions, driven mostly by technical concerns of goals and outcomes with dire and unfortunate circumstances. The literature traces how under capitalist regimes, wisdom's long tradition was suppressed in favor of reactive, short-term, and self-interested decision making. Wisdom focuses on what is good for the collective, in the long term, in weighing a multitude of factors, being sensitive to the interests of others and emotionally connected, that enables, empowers or brings resilience to others, and what is moral or ethically appropriate (Sternberg, 1990). It is considered a dispositional skill that requires ongoing work of reflection.

What, exactly, is wisdom? We adopt Sternberg's definition of wisdom taken from his balance theory: "as the use of one's intelligence, creativity, common sense and knowledge and as mediated by positive ethical values toward achievement of a common good through a balance among (a) intrapersonal, (b) interpersonal, (c) and extrapersonal interests, over the (a) short and (b) long terms to achieve a balance among (a) adaptation to existing environments, (b) shaping of existing environments, and (c) selection of new environments" (Sternberg, 1998). Sternberg elaborates on this definition, saying it does not over-rely on facets of knowledge or experience that are the focus of earlier definitions of wisdom. Balance speaks not just to the areas that are drawn upon in terms of evaluating and making judgments, but also to weighing personal considerations alongside others. At its core, wisdom is about balancing many interests that exist, even when we are not aware of how many interests are at stake; part of wisdom is pushing oneself to see broader interests that should be weighed. Balance also relates to long-term and short-term interests and considerations of the environment. Our decisions often reflect a bias to short-term interests, but wisdom seeks to enlarge the circumstances we weigh. Additionally, judgments are always made within environments/contexts and have an impact on those environments as well. Attention to context and culture is also critical to wisdom. As Sternberg notes, wisdom in one setting might be impractical or dangerous when transferred to another, and one is often better able to make wise decisions if one is more familiar with a context. The last consideration in balance relates to weighting. Sternberg notes: "the balance in the balance theory of wisdom does not mean that each interest, consequence, or response is weighted equally. The relative 'weightings' are determined by the extent to which a particular alternative contributes to the achievement of the common good" (www.robertjsternberg.com). It is also important to note that wisdom is tacit, developed through experience, practice and making judgments and is a form of practical intelligence. Wisdom is certainly something that can be learned, but takes time, experience and reflection—these are practices described throughout this volume.

Similar to Sternberg's definition, much of the organizational wisdom literature suggests that wisdom draws on many sources for guiding judgments, appeals to a broader collective good, entails moving beyond personal interests, and considers context. Nonaka and Takeuchi (2011) note that "wise leaders exercise political judgment by understanding the viewpoints and emotions of others, gleaned through everyday verbal and nonverbal communication" (p. 65). Similarly, when Nonaka and Toyama (2007) refer to "distributed practical wisdom" and a practice to "pursue common goodness," they allude to a collective sensitivity; judgments should be aligned with a broader notion of good that takes into account the broadest set of interests (p. 371). Wisdom suggests a process of deliberation in which we appreciate others' interests, are sympathetic and move beyond our narrow interests and perceptions. We echo this call for and need for wisdom to drive the judgments that underlie everyday decisions, not the more technocratic and capitalist concerns of goal attainment and self-interest.

What constitutes appropriate balancing of interests, response to the environment, and even the common good hinges on values and knowledge. Values, therefore, are an integral part of wise thinking. Attention to power begs the question of "whose values?" Although different major religions and other widely accepted systems of values may differ in details, they seem to have in common certain universal values, such as respect for human life, honesty, sincerity, fairness, and enabling people to fulfill their potential. The development of wisdom is thus beneficial because the judgments it yields can improve our quality of life and conduct. Knowledge can and indeed must accompany values. People need knowledge to draw upon in rendering judgments—knowledge of human nature, of life circumstances, or of strategies that succeed and those that fail. Although knowledge is necessary for wisdom, it is not sufficient for it. Merely having knowledge (and even less sufficient information) does not entail its use in judging rightly, soundly, or justly.

Wisdom as a principle leads us to our other principles below that serve collective interests (rather than just those in power and with privilege) and in particular in education to making students a part of decision-making. Wisdom also notes the importance of moral and ethical reasoning, which pave the way for orienting toward notions of justice and equity.

In following the precepts of wisdom, administrators may consider: How have I considered the broadest collective good in my decisions? Have I imagined how various groups are affected by my decision? Have I been empathetic to the needs of others, particularly minoritized interests? Have I weighed various interests, perspectives, values, and factors? Will this decision support and empower others? Have I considered the appropriate ethical factors? How have past decisions using this approach rendered equity and social justice, or not? What are the possible long-term effects of this decision? Have I examined the long-term and short-term consequences and considered the context of the decision?

CRITICAL CONSCIOUSNESS ABOUT POWER

Within organizations of all sorts, power is a constant that serves to organize relationships and processes—usually in ways that support hierarchies and inequalities instead of empowerment and workplace democracy. Without administrators being constantly vigilant about power, its misuse, and the interlocking systems of power associated with identities and social statuses, unequal power dynamics (i.e. power asymmetries) are likely to be present, either on purpose (i.e. directly) or as the result of a blindspot (i.e. indirectly). And as Paulo Freire points out, those traditionally in power do not have a monopoly on power; therefore, merely getting traditionally marginalized groups into positions of power does not automatically change inequalities and produce justice. Freire points out how marginalized groups tend to oppress others once they have power, for once one obtains power, one is often blinded to one's own privilege. Vigilance and self-reflection can break down the cycle of oppression and inequality.

In addition to disparate power held among groups with particular social identities, unequal power dynamics are demonstrated in many campus structures today, including the power asymmetry between academic and student affairs, mentioned earlier. Staff have long been invisible on campus. They are generally not included in shared governance on campuses and their work and accomplishments are ignored. A university may see the financial value in outsourcing its custodial work, for example, but miss the ways that this will disproportionately affect the university's staff of color. Administrators have built up enormous fiefdoms of staff and often the signal of administrative prestige is how many individuals report to or work for an individual, leading to a bloat in staffing as administrators jockey for power by expanding their empires. Budgets have soared for administration over the last few decades while shares of budgets dedicated to instruction—historically, the primary goal of institutions—have gone down. Faculty who have long enjoyed power on campuses are now being disempowered through policies that make faculty contingent and part-time.

In this text, most chapters point to the role of power. Kezar and Dizon's chapter on shared governance explores these historic and current power inequalities as they relate to shared governance. Griffin's chapter on mentoring also points to how relationships on campus often do not work to empower and how complicated mentoring can be in terms of disrupting existing power networks on campus. Posselt, Hernandez, and Villarreal define power in terms of influence over decision making and incorporate it into their decision-making framework. While these are just a few examples, they demonstrate how power operates to position people into hierarchies and how resources are unequally distributed. Lester's chapter on work–life policies, such as women being able to stop the tenure clock for family responsibilities, illustrates how taken-for-granted policies like timelines to tenure make it more challenging for women to succeed as faculty. Liera and Ching's chapter on hiring similarly reflects how traditional hiring processes favor traditional work trajectories, which tend to favor white men. From admissions, to work–life balance, to hiring and more, every campus policy and practice needs to be interrogated as they are not neutral and will—unless altered—favor those traditionally in power.

Socially just leadership means being aware of the way that power shapes administrative structures and culture—and working to dismantle these structures when power operates oppressively. Our policies and practices are not neutral. For example, even ostensibly race-neutral policies rarely are race-neutral in practice. Common structures and administrative processes are raced, gendered, classed and built on systems that favor certain groups over others (Acker, 1990; Posselt, 2016). Thus, in addition to general power inequalities, it is important to be conscious of other factors—race, gender, class, and other social identities that have long been disempowered in our social systems.

And while we call leaders to examine and interrogate systems of power, in the context of US higher education, race and racism must be foregrounded. As a form of discrimination, it has proven one of the most pernicious and destructive forms in this society and its institutions—including education. Dismantling racialized structures within higher education warrants greater attention by leaders aimed to create equity and social justice. Particularly for those who hold white identities, this work will also require dedication to learning about the various manifestations of racism, working effectively across race and ethnicity, and doing the personal work to examine one's own biases and complicity in systems of racial oppression.

Questions that critically conscious administrators may ask themselves include: Have I considered how power is operating in this situation? Have I considered how historic, structural inequalities are affecting this policy, practice, program process, structure or decision? Have I considered how current neoliberal pressures around neoliberalism—efficiency, cost control or corporate values—might be implicated in the way we are making a decision or engaging in a process/practice? Have I explored how my administrative practice and this decision shapes different racial groups, woman, low income, etc.? Have I considered how my administrative practice might be raced, gendered, classed, etc.?

KNOWLEDGE OF SELF AND POSITIONALITY

In order to act in ways that reflect and encourage social justice and equity, educational practitioners need to have an awareness of their own privilege and positionality. Power is institutionalized and embedded within our social and organizational structures, and is also personal and experiential. As Foucault reminds us, power is relational and embedded in every social interaction. Thus, it is deeply embedded into administrative practice, as will be described. But to reduce these interactions to process or practice could strip it of its personal and individual quality. This is where positionality is important to personalize power and to also connect it to practice and interactions.

In terms of positionality, we follow the principles offered by scholars such Collins (2002) that our social identities and backgrounds shape our experiences and viewpoints, particularly with respect to power and the conditions and means by which it is used/abused. Awareness of our own identities and the related matrix of privileges and disempowerment enables perspective-taking, as well as empathy and solidarity in the pursuit of judgment and wisdom. Self-knowledge also attunes us to our potential for biases and other cognitive blinders, as well as areas in which we have assets and resources we may draw upon to expand opportunities where it is inequitably distributed. Thus, administrative practice informed by social justice demands self-reflection. Several of our chapter authors reflect on their own backgrounds to model how this can be conducted and how it can inform and shape wise practice. As co-editors, we also strive for reflexiveness about our positionality and how it informs our work. For example, we acknowledge that as white scholars striving to be effective allies with communities of color, that we will always lack a full understanding of the challenges that faculty, staff, and students of color experience. We each try to embed ourselves in historical understandings and to be in relationships and collaborations with scholars of color who will challenge us, correct misperceptions, and more broadly enhance our awareness—critical precursors to working in solidarity. We also recognize that we have received unwarranted privileges as a result of our race and our socioeconomic status, as well as from being born in a country of wealth and status. As women, we have experienced gender-related discrimination of various forms and have been overlooked for opportunities and negatively judged when not living up to a male norm; nevertheless, the relative privilege that comes with being white women carries a serious responsibility to continuously check our understandings for bias and misunderstanding, and to speak up where and when we can about the miscarriages of justice throughout society.

STUDENT CENTEREDNESS

If we take Nussbaum's view that the development of capabilities that enable human flourishing is a foundation of justice, then higher education institutions can further social justice by putting students at the center of administrative actions and decisions. Students are too often not a central factor in practice and judgments at most institutions. As a prime example of this, at our own institution, the University of Southern California, the university's president and upper leadership privileged finances, alumni giving, and institutional reputation over student protections, needs, and development. A sexual predator working as a campus gynecologist was allowed to abuse thousands of students over decades. Such values and this type of decision making have long-lasting, negative consequences for real people and for institutions, and they must be challenged. Students, their learning, and their well-being must drive our collective administrative practice.

McNair, Albertine, Cooper, McDonald, and Major (2016) offer a vision for organizing campuses around students in their book *Becoming a Student-Ready College*. They call on administrators to reject a student-deficit model for understanding outcomes, and call for creating a new culture of leadership focused on student success. To that end, they interrogate how campus staff, faculty, and administrators often bemoan that students are not ready for college. They then turn this assumption on its head to ask how colleges can serve the students who come to college and, as institutions, become student-ready. In this book, we elaborate on these ideas by challenging our existing institutional structures and cultures and asking how they represent historic inequalities and injustice, and how leaders might push to rectify these underlying organizing principles. We also are aware that many administrators worry that today's students have been turned into consumers. When we speak about attention to students we are not calling for or supporting their commodification, but rather centering them within our institutions as learners and as democratic agents.

To that end, educational practitioners can ask themselves questions such as: How are students' interests related to decisions I am making? Are students a focus of the process, program or policy I am developing? How will students (from various backgrounds) be shaped by this practice? What needs of students are being compromised in the interests of protecting other values? Are student voices included in key decisions? Which students? How could new initiatives better center student learning, well-being, and/or development?

ROUTINIZING MINDFULNESS AND WISDOM

To create an alternative administrative mindset means not only resisting the forces of efficiency, revenues, and prestige, but also creating new habits of mind that are conducive to student interests and to remediating power asymmetries that operate throughout the academy. In the interest of creating new habits of mind, the last facet of our framework for just and equitable administrative practice is routinizing mindfulness and wisdom in administrative work and decision making (Aarts, Verplanken, & Van Knippenberg, 1998). At first mindfulness is quite necessary to develop critical consciousness about power; to have an awareness of how structures and cultures tend to be raced, gendered, and classed in ways that disempower traditionally marginalized groups; and to foreground values of social justice and equity. As discussed earlier, mindfulness can also facilitate the development of wisdom in professional judgment. Over time, wisdom and a collectivist orientation become an automatic or routine way of thinking and can happen without the conscious practice of mindfulness. As an automated way of thinking, leaders hold the potential to operate more seamlessly. However, mindfulness is essential for starting the process and for sharpening skills in and dispositions for wisdom. In their essay "Leading with Soul and Spirit," Bolman and Deal (2002) discuss how practiced reflection leads to wisdom that is essential to leadership with integrity. They describe embracing wisdom as part of reclaiming a more multifaceted way to lead that draws on past traditions and cultures through received knowledge, spiritual insights, creativity, intuition, emotional intelligence, and experience.

One of the dangers of automated thinking—and a major reason that mindfulness is important—is that decisions about equity and justice can often be complex. As Julius's chapter demonstrates, when it comes to collective bargaining and unions, workers' rights and support may be at odds with student interests. Unions have not examined their own discriminatory practices. Processes that may seem democratic and inclusive may not always follow these principles over time. Interests may not be easily resolved and come into conflict. Routinization will make inclusive practice common and normal, but the complexity of decisions and changing context for what counts as inclusive practice means that routines need to be checked and analyzed from time to time, making mindfulness a necessary tool in the long run.

One practical way to routinize mindfulness and the collectivist orientation that is central to wisdom is developing a habit of referring to data rather than acting on instinct or assumptions. As Chapter 10 highlights, when disaggregated by race and gender, for example, data more easily reveal implications of current practices for equity, and enable leaders to anticipate the outcomes of possible policy directions. Yet research from organizational learning and knowledge management underscore how data use is just one component of learning processes and good decisions. Good decisions are more than review of data. They involve careful interpretation processes that bring in experience, values, and reflection on past decisions, as well as understanding obtained through weighing multiple factors and through empathy and emotions. While equity-minded data use is increasingly important to administrative practice, we cannot count on data to clarify all administrative challenges.

Just as wise decisions involve accounting for a variety of types of input, wise leadership means accounting for a variety of identities among students, faculty, staff, and other stakeholders. Attending to race or gender does not absolve us of attention to the inclusion of LGBTQ or low-income students, for example. To ameliorate the effects of racist practice and yet turn a blind eye to engrained sexism within one's office, for example, hardly squares with wise leadership. We may never be fully conscious of all the equity issues at stake in a decision or in one's practice, further impelling the need to routinely and continuously re-examine one's own assumptions and practices. Given the inequalities and hierarchies in which all of us operate, we need to consider how our default choices and instincts might be motivated by the very frameworks we want to challenge.

We recommend that administrators ask themselves the following questions as they routinize considerations of equity and justice: Is my decision or practice based on my latest or old patterns of thinking? Have I considered equity and justice in a multifaceted way? If there are competing equity and justice interests, have I examined several tools to weigh these interests including data, conversation, outside perspectives? Can I provide examples of decisions and practice from this last week or month that reflect new thinking patterns of equity and justice?

In conclusion, we asked chapter authors to consider a series of questions that we see are part of a social justice and equity mindset—questions that we hope you will also use to reflect on your past, current, and upcoming administrative practice.

1. How is power and privilege inherent or part of this practice?
2. What assumptions should administrators question about this area of practice as it currently exists?
3. How can social justice and equity mindedness be embedded in this area of practice?
4. What new values can be associated with this practice so that it can meet the goals of social justice?
5. How can power and privilege be negotiated or changed as part of this practice?
6. What challenges—practical, political, social, or resource-driven—may emerge while attempting to shift this area of practice?

7. What ethical considerations should practitioners be aware of or consider?
8. How is the student part of administrative considerations and practice?

Additionally, we feel confident that you will be inspired by the thinking in this volume by scholars and practitioners of administration. And we hope that you will begin or move farther along on your journey toward more equitable and socially just administrative practice.

REFERENCES

Aarts, H., Verplanken, B., & Van Knippenberg, A. (1998). Predicting behavior from actions in the past: Repeated decision making or a matter of habit? *Journal of Applied Social Psychology, 28*(15), 1355–1374.

Acker, J. (1990). Hierarchies, jobs, bodies: A theory of gendered organizations. *Gender & Society, 4*(2), 139–158.

Bolman, L. G., & Deal, T. E. (2002). Leading with Soul and Spirit. *School Administrator, 59*(2), 21–26.

Cabrera, N. (2014). Exposing whiteness in higher education: White male college students minimizing racism, claiming victimization, and recreating white supremacy. *Race Ethnicity and Education, 17*(1), 30–55.

Collins, P. H. (2002). *Black Feminist Thought: Knowledge, Consciousness, and the Politics of Empowerment.* New York: Routledge.

Dugan, J. P. (2017). *Leadership Theory: Cultivating Critical Perspectives.* San Francisco, CA: John Wiley & Sons.

Gumport, P. J., & Bastedo, M. N. (2001). Academic stratification and endemic conflict: Remedial education policy at CUNY. *The Review of Higher Education, 24*(4), 333–349.

Jaquette, O., Curs, B. R., & Posselt, J. R. (2016). Tuition rich, mission poor: Nonresident enrollment growth and the socioeconomic and racial composition of public research universities. *The Journal of Higher Education, 87*(5), 635–673.

Kezar, A. (Ed.) (2010). *Recognizing and Serving Low-Income Students in Higher Education: An Examination of Institutional Policies, Practices, and Culture.* New York: Routledge.

Kezar, A., Chambers, T. C., & Burkhardt, J. C. (Eds.) (2005). *Higher Education for the Public Good: Emerging Voices from a National Movement.* San Francisco, CA: Jossey-Bass.

Kezar, A., Depaola, T., & Scott, D. (in press). *Academic Labor in Transition.* Baltimore, MD: Johns Hopkins University Press.

Kezar, A., & Lester, J. (2009). *Organizing Higher Education for Collaboration: A Guide for Campus Leaders.* San Francisco, CA: Jossey-Bass.

Lazar, S. W. (2005). Mindfulness research. *Mindfulness and Psychotherapy,* 220–238.

McNair, T. B., Albertine, S., Cooper, M. A., McDonald, N., & Major Jr., T. (2016). *Becoming a Student-Ready College: A New Culture of Leadership for Student Success.* San Francisco, CA: John Wiley & Sons.

Nonaka, I., & Takeuchi, H. (2011). The wise leader. *Harvard Business Review, 89*(5), 58–67.

Nonaka, I., & Toyama, R. (2007). Strategic management as distributed practical wisdom (phronesis). *Industrial and Corporate Change, 16*(3), 371–394.

Nussbaum, M. (2011). *Creating Capabilities: The Human Development Approach.* Cambridge, MA: Harvard University Press.

Nussbaum, M., & Sen, A. (Eds.) (1993). *The Quality of Life.* Oxford: Oxford University Press.

Posselt, J. R. (2016). *Inside Graduate Admissions: Merit, Diversity, and Faculty Gatekeeping.* Cambridge, MA: Harvard University Press.

Slaughter, S. A., & Rhoades, G. (2004). *Academic Capitalism and the New Economy: Markets, State, and Higher Education.* Baltimore, MD: Johns Hopkins University Press.

Sternberg, R. J. (Ed.) (1990). *Wisdom: Its Nature, Origins, and Development.* Cambridge: Cambridge University Press.

Sternberg, R.J. (1998) A balance theory of wisdom. *Review of General Psychology, 2,* 347–365.

Theoharis, G. (2007). Social justice educational leaders and resistance: Toward a theory of social justice leadership. *Educational Administration Quarterly, 43*(2), 221–258.

Wilder, C. S. (2013). *Ebony & Ivy: Race, Slavery, and the Troubled History of America's Universities (First US ed.)*. New York: Bloomsbury Press.

Williams, D. A. (2013). *Strategic Diversity Leadership: Activating Change and Transformation in Higher Education*. Sterling, VA: Stylus Publishing, LLC.

PART I

SETTING AND SHIFTING PRIORITIES

2

RENEWING AND REVITALIZING SHARED GOVERNANCE
A Social Justice and Equity Framework

ADRIANNA KEZAR AND JUDE PAUL MATIAS DIZON

INTRODUCTION

Policymaking is an important part of administrative practice and defines the rules for most activities on campus ranging from admissions, to hiring, to curriculum, to research, to financial allocations, to partnerships. Truly every aspect of campus life is governed by policies that are accepted as ways of conducting work, often with little critical examination. In this book, we urgently recommend that policies need critical examination in relationship to equity and just outcomes. For example, are our policies around admissions fair? Is our tenure clock policy fair? Are our criteria for curriculum review fair? Other times we may have fair and equitable policies but they are not followed. For example, adjunct faculty are typically hired by department chairs outside the affirmative action policies that are meant to guide campus decisions. Many chapters in this book examine particular policies and our hope is that you will begin to question the underlying principles and values of institutional acts, as well as explore who truly benefits. When we determine policies need to be changed, created, or better implemented we turn to our policymaking processes.

In higher education, shared governance is a set of principles used to determine the structure in which many policies have been crafted. Shared governance is the policy process which brings together faculty and administrators to collaboratively make decisions with different levels of delegated authority. The structures of shared governance vary from faculty senates working with administrative cabinets and task forces, to campus-wide senates that include faculty and administrators. What is unique about shared governance is the set of principles that define it rather than a specific structural configuration; these principles were codified in a joint statement in 1966 (described in detail in the next section) and revised slightly over time.

In this chapter we explore policymaking processes and how they may be made more socially just and equitable. We first explore the history of shared governance to establish context about policymaking processes that govern campuses. Then we describe the decline of shared governance, which has led to an environment in which socially just and equitable decisions are even more in peril than in the past. We next provide a vision for ways to alter traditional shared governance to make it more reflective of process that can lead to equitable ends. Throughout, we describe examples of how this new form of governance can be enacted.

A note on socially just and equitable governance: We believe there is an opportunity for collective leadership with involvement from all levels of the campus community. By re-distributing power in the model we describe below, policies can be crafted which correct power imbalances and the resulting disenfranchisement and exploitation of faculty, staff, and students. It is important to point out that most campus leaders believe that policies they enact are in some way fair, impartial, merit-based, and sometimes egalitarian. At the very least, many procedures and decisions are not made in overt bias. However, our processes do not allow us to hear enough voices which can point out flaws and the failings of the status quo. Tenure policies are an ideal example. Within the existing framework of equality and merit, traditional tenure policies can be read as fair. The same timetable for everyone means that everyone is given the same amount of time to earn job security. However, tenure policies do not take into account systemic biases which negatively impact women disproportionately. Thus, we acknowledge current leaders may be trying their best within the accepted notions of an objective, equal opportunity, merit-based system. We argue for a new set of values to define shared governance.

SHARED GOVERNANCE IN RETROSPECTIVE

Governance in the United States has always focused on including and balancing multiple perspectives. Colonial institutions of higher education included a board to represent community interests (usually made up of members of the community) that was invested with authority to provide an external check on presidents and faculty (Lucas, 1998). This system of vesting authority in an external board continued throughout the history of higher education in the United States. Shared governance became the ideal in the last century, emerging as faculty leaders became frustrated by powerful presidents that made decisions that were seen as capricious and unfair by not only internal stakeholders but also by journalists at the time. Faculty began to mobilize nationally through their disciplinary societies with similar stories of unfair firings, misuse of funds, and intrusion into research and teaching as conservative presidents intervened on progressive era faculty who were fighting against child labor and minimum wages. They felt faculty needed greater control over institutional decisions so such unjust and wrongheaded decisions were not made and to create policies that could enshrine protections and guidelines for appropriate behavior.

These faculty wrote what became a groundbreaking document—the American Association of University Professors and Association of American Universities Joint Statement on Academic Freedom and Tenure (1944)—that established an expectation that faculty would receive lifetime employment (i.e. tenure) in order to protect them from arbitrary decisions from administrators or boards and to ensure they had academic freedom to pursue research on topics they believed critical and to teach materials they saw fit. Shared governance was also raised as a core principle of being a professional. Faculty argued that having input on their working conditions was paramount as they would know best when it came to decisions about teaching and learning for example. While policies reflecting the vision of shared governance began to be implemented at many campuses following the publication of this report, the practice was not made a norm until the 1966 Association of Governing Boards, American Association of University Professors, American Council on Education (AGB/AAUP/ACE) Joint Statement on Shared Governance, which noted the importance of faculty and students to campus policymaking processes. The 1966 Statement gained more traction than earlier articulations of shared governance based on the collaborative development across AGB/AAUP/ACE; this joint effort bolstered shared governance as an ideal and principle. The statement outlined the rationale for shared governance, including that faculty have invaluable expertise that should be brought into decision-making processes. The statement also designated what decisions faculty should be delegated authority in (i.e. around teaching and learning, faculty hiring, student issues) and areas for their involvement in joint policymaking. The Statement notes: "a college or university in which all the components are aware of their interdependence, of the usefulness of communication among themselves, and of the force of joint action will enjoy increased capacity to solve educational problems" (p. 1). A core principle of this Statement is the inescapable interdependencies of boards, administrators, and faculty—no one constituency can effectively govern the institution as they each have important expertise necessary for strong decision-making. And shared governance has taken many different forms over time. Tierney and Minor's (2003) study of shared governance found about half of institutions (47%) follow a fully collaborative or collegial model; about another 26% followed a distributed model where each group has authority for certain decisions; and the remaining 27% followed a consultative model where faculty input was sought but faculty had no authority over final decisions.

Shared governance became an ideal. The 1960s and early 1970s was the heyday for when the most institutions enacted shared governance as a norm, which is perhaps not coincidental as these were times of broader struggles for racial and gender justice, civil rights, democratic participation, and questioning of control and power structures. However, not all institutions adopted it even in the heyday—for example, community colleges often did not. And already in the 1980s shared governance structures were beginning to be eroded as governing boards and presidents began modifying constitutions to provide less authority to faculty and centralizing decisions.

Recent studies reveal that shared governance has been on the decline on many campuses. Faculty report having less input and involvement in campus governance and having key responsibilities (i.e. budget, planning) taken away with administrators taking over more unilateral control (Schuster & Finklestein, 2006). Systems that once adhered more closely to the principles of shared governance have shifted to more top-down governance structures in which administrators take greater responsibility for more policymaking and fewer responsibilities are delegated to academic departments and faculty (Slaughter & Rhoades, 2004). This shift in authority for campus decision-making is indicative of neoliberal trends that have taken hold in higher education, the emergence of which Barrow (1992) traces to the intersection of two structural shifts in economic developments in the mid-1970s: a resurgence of global competition and a shift to a post-industrial economy (also known as the knowledge economy). As noted in the introductory chapter, neoliberalism refers to the philosophy that privatization (being run by corporations and business) of public operations that have traditionally been run by government, such as medicine or prisons, better serves the public interest (Slaughter & Rhoades, 2004). The simultaneous privatization of higher education and its commodification as a globalized services sector have heightened competition and creation of new markets. Pressure for individual success in the workplace to serve market interests have eroded communal, democratic goals. The logic of individual decision-making and the opening up of higher education to private interests and profit-making have given market forces greater influence over governance structures (Robertson & Dale, 2013).

This philosophy is at the heart of recent trends toward new managerialism on college and university campuses, in which corporate-like practices of management have replaced more collegial and shared approaches to governance. New managerialism, coupled with academic capitalism, in which campuses focus on revenue generation through marketing and other business practices (Slaughter & Leslie, 1997; Slaughter & Rhoades, 2004), have created a landscape in higher education in which universities are increasingly managed by administrators who do not engage faculty and staff in governance procedures and shared decision-making, and who are driven by market forces to focus more greatly on revenue generation and the bottom-line. This push toward new managerialism fosters campus environments in which faculty are at odds with administration over the core mission of their institutions, and faculty have less of a voice in campus decision-making, particularly in the United States (Cummings & Finkelstein, 2009).

Higher education as a public good is at stake when shared governance is weakened as the multiple voices needed to reflect the interests of the public good are lost. Pusser (2006) argues "we have long relied on a narrow definition of the public good produced in postsecondary education, one that increasingly privileges economic development over citizenship training, establishing common values, and democratic participation" (p. 12). Organizational decisions which promote prestige and profit may be valorized, but consequently "institutions are then criticized because they do not respond to state and public needs that call for centralization" (Tierney, 2006, p. 8). Gaining a competitive edge in the market sacrifices accountability in producing research relevant to public needs and developing citizens to think critically and participate in a democratic society. Scholars have proposed some ideas to reverse this trend, which include returning higher education to its status as a public sphere "where inclusiveness, discourse, identity development, knowledge production, and politics combine to enhance democracy" (Pusser, 2006, p. 19). In the public sphere of higher education, faculty, staff, students, administration, and local communities meet and dialogue to co-determine how the university can best serve the public. For this to happen, governance must "give way to contest, collaboration, and consensus.... [ensuring] that no single group controls the institution, a practice that is a time-honored tenet of responsible trusteeship" (Pusser, 2006, p. 20). Inclusion and equal participatory power among stakeholders can shift the neoliberal trend in higher education and restore its role as a public good. As noted in the introduction to the chapter, we are aware that administrators are often engaged in work that is arguably aimed at important socially just outcomes such as increasing college completion and student success and to be more efficient with scarce public resources. Some of the neoliberal goals being promoted and pressured on administrators' agendas might also support equity. It is clear that many board members that support these goals clearly believe they do. What these efforts among boards or policymakers are often missing is input from those on the ground about how efforts to promote student completion might compromise learning and student outcomes. The overall efforts are not misguided in their general direction, but in not seeking enough input and being too top-down in development, they end up missing their social justice and equity goals. This is the key differentiation between the social justice and equity aims we promote versus the neoliberal process that is inherently top-down in nature and not built on broad interests and voice.

In the following sections we argue not just for a return to the historical democratic values and principles long associated with shared governance in its ideal form, we also push for an even bolder form of shared governance that extends its core values around democratic input, the inclusion of multiple perspectives, transparent communication, and joint, collective action as healthy for policy processes. This may seem like an overly idealistic concept given that shared governance is under attack and barely visible in its robust form on many campuses. Others have argued that a return to shared governance is not possible given the entrenchment of neoliberalism (Talburt, 2005). But cracks in the neoliberal governance system as revealed in recent scandals at prominent research universities are shining a light on the problems of top-down, centralized governance without any checks and balances and without campus community members' input. Penn State University, Michigan State University, and the University of Southern California (PSU, MSU and USC) are all very visible cases of where a breakdown in shared governance has led to catastrophic results. The recent highly publicized scandals at these institutions are the end result of individual administrators prioritizing institutional reputation over student protection from sexual assault. Keeping egregious ethical and policy violations private rather than utilizing the normal channels of employee misconduct and sanctions led faculty, staff, and students alike to convey judgments of no confidence in senior leadership. It is these recent examples that provide the evidence that change is needed and neoliberal governance structures have failed.

TRANSFORMING SHARED GOVERNANCE

While we acknowledge the historic values of shared governance, we also recognize that a new approach must deal with the complexity of college campuses today that face more regulation, greater external pressures, declining funding, and need to adjust to integrating new technologies, a more diverse student body, and a multitude of new challenges. A new model needs to work effectively within a much larger and changing enterprise—one that necessitates more timely decisions, can facilitate dialogue between increasing and multiple stakeholders, and includes more groups in a single process. Current structures and processes need to be re-examined within the new environment, while maintaining the original principles of shared governance. Philosophical principles, such as including diverse viewpoints and involvement of those directly affected by policies, should shape efforts forward. A re-commitment to democracy in higher education governance and policymaking will help shift colleges and universities back into positions of "democratic spheres" (Giroux, 2002, p. 450). What we recommend in this section is a new process to democratize governance moving forward. Faculty, staff, and students can neither ignore the undeniable hold of state and market interests (even in the face of the excessive market forces that have resulted in the horrendous case examples at MSU, PSU, and USC) nor hold on to traditional structures (e.g. certain articulation of a senate) if they do not operate effectively for integrating higher education's increasing number of voices and interests. If the goals of higher education are changing, the only way it will succeed is to actively engage all voices in governance to ensure success, both in student learning and securing financial health for institutional survival.

One of the most difficult challenges of creating such a model is the exacerbation of power inequalities in more recent years. Faculty have been de-professionalized and moved on to semester-to-semester appointments; staff are largely silenced by the administration in order to meet the entrepreneurial goals of the university rather than the needs of students; and students themselves have been reduced from learners to customers (Rhoades, 1996; Slaughter & Rhoades, 2004). The neoliberal environment has created a destabilizing unbalance and de-emphasis of academic values. Without re-professionalizing faculty and staff on campuses and recognizing their value, the creation of any shared governance process is likely on shaky ground. It is simply too easy for market and state voices to dominate in this new era. Engaging students as stakeholders where their voice has weight, rather than passive customers or neglecting their concerns to the point of protest, will help reposition the university as a site of dialogue and citizenship development. It will take leadership among those with authority to ensure redistribution of power and inclusion, coupled with grassroots leadership among faculty, staff, and students to regain their voice and create positive sustained change.

A SOCIAL JUSTICE AND EQUITY-BASED MODEL FOR SHARED GOVERNANCE

We have synthesized scholarship on ethics, governance, leadership, and education to present a shared governance model centered on social justice and equity. Socially just shared governance is predicated on full and equal participation of all campus stakeholders in a policymaking process that is "democratic and participatory, inclusive and affirming of human agency and human capacities for working collaboratively to create change" (Bell, 2007, p. 2). Intended outcomes include the equitable redistribution of power and resources to meet the unique needs of historically marginalized members of the campus as well as the public community, including the mitigation of any negative social impact due to institutional actions.

The social justice change we advocate for is expansive: altered power dynamics, equitable outcomes, and a commitment to social responsibility. We reconfigure shared governance as a "continuous ethico-political action that is related not only to the self but also to others" in order to achieve collective accountability and action for the interests of the most marginalized on campus (Alakavuklar & Alamgir, 2018, p. 35).

Social justice and equity are the focal point of the model in order to both anchor the institution's shared governance processes and direct its outcomes toward fairness and social responsibility. We draw upon Byrne-Jimenez and Orr's (2013) following questions to evaluate the presence (or absence) of social justice: social justice for whom, social justice by whom, social justice how, and social justice for what. The social justice and equity-based model for shared governance responds to these critical questions (Figure 2.1). *Conscious public commitment* by campus stakeholders is a necessary first step in shifting campus ethics (social justice by whom). Altering power dynamics in decision-making requires *widening the circle* of participation to include and redistribute power among marginalized segments of the campus community (social justice by whom and for whom). *Transformative discourse* sets in motion collaborative dialogue and problem-solving (social justice how). Concrete changes are enacted through *dynamic institutionalization*, a continuous revisiting and revision of policies and practices (social justice how). Reflection upon one's biases and whether actions are consistent with stated social justice and equity goals underlie each

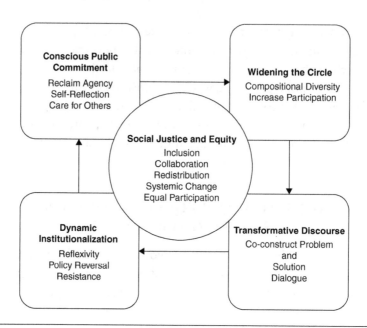

Figure 2.1 Social Justice and Equity-based Model of Shared Governance

component (social justice for what). In practice, shared governance is a continual process of revisiting goals, assumptions, and values in order to make progress. Thus, while we discuss each component separately we recognize they interrelate.

In the following section we will articulate each of these areas in detail. We start with a short vignette that tries to capture what this would look like if executed but it cannot capture all the details that the rest of the chapter articulates. But we hope it helps in starting to foster an understanding of governance that can and should evolve. In their review of safety protocol, administration recently implemented a new policy requiring university identification to enter all campus libraries. Cultural student organization officers recognized that while the policy is intended for safety, students of color may feel uncomfortable in having to interact with campus police officers to study or check out a book. Student government leaders talked with one another and learned no student input was considered. They also recognized youth and other local community residents were now unable to utilize the campus libraries, which they previously were able to access (*conscious public commitment*). Several student organizations hosted a joint community meeting to discuss the new ID policy (*transformative discourse*), which then led to a public form with community residents to publicly document instances of exclusionary and discriminatory encounters with campus police (*widening the circle*). Students delivered the compiled set of negative police encounters with a demand to end the library ID policy to the university president and vice president of student affairs (*conscious public commitment*). At the same time, concerned faculty on the academic senate invited students to speak on the issue during the upcoming meeting (*widening the circle*) and passed a resolution recommending new safety policies be developed with campus and community feedback (*dynamic institutionalization*). In response, the vice president for student affairs reached out to the president of the undergraduate student government to form a committee of student affairs unit directors and student leaders to examine the policy (*widening the circle*). The committee was able to put the policy on hold until they reached a recommendation (*dynamic institutionalization*). Throughout the next few months, the committee engaged in serious study of the ID policy, its potential unintended consequences, and crime statistics for the area (*transformative discourse*). In one of the final meetings, the committee walked through its recommendations to the president. The president then deliberated with key administrators, which resulted in an amendment to the policy: rather than an ID to enter the library at all times, an ID is only required after 9pm (*dynamic institutionalization*). The amendment maintains community access and implements the additional safety protocol during late-night hours to ensure student safety.

CONSCIOUS PUBLIC COMMITMENT

Critical scholars suggest that ethical organizational change begins with the self, which can then be mobilized collectively to shift organizational identity (Alakavuklar & Alamgir, 2018; Arjoon, 2005; Brown, 2004). Forming a conscious and public commitment equity begins to answer *who is responsible for enacting social justice* in higher education (Byrne-Jimenez & Orr, 2013). This first step requires reclaiming agency, self-reflection, and care for others. The managerial system aims to make people believe they have no agency and that involvement is futile. Neoliberal logics have disciplined the individual to tie self-worth to productivity and merit, which signal what one is deserving of or not, including the privilege to speak out against authority (Chen & Buell, 2018). Formal roles on campus (e.g. contingent faculty, academic advisor, etc.) do not inherently determine the worth or potential of individuals' contributions to the policymaking process. Change begins with seeing how one's own subjectivity has been colonized by neoliberalism and "remak[ing] the self" through self-care and having the "the courage to be [y]our own authority without obedience to another" in order to reconstitute one's agency (Koopman qtd. in Alakavuklar & Alamgir, 2018, p. 35). Individuals reclaim their ethical sensibilities and instead of allowing neoliberal logics to define organizational ethics and ways of operating, new values and ethical perspectives can be brought to the fore. Unionization campaigns exemplify the activation of staff to take back control of their working conditions together and work in concert across units. In collective processes, described fully in the next section, the newly conceived individual ethics are further refined in and through relationships to rearticulate shared values for governing the university.

Self-reflection is essential to self-empowerment, accountability, and promoting collective welfare. Campus stakeholders committed to restoring the university to its role as an inclusive, public sphere have to pause, question, and consider the clear evidence of decisions producing injustice and inequity within and without the campus community. According to Brown (2004), a goal of "critical reflection [is] to externalize and investigate power relationships and to uncover hegemonic assumptions" (p. 84). Hegemonic assumptions which result in inequity and injustice not only operate at the group level, but in individual attitudes and interpersonal interactions. It can be both empowering and troubling to the self-concept when examining deeply held assumptions, values, beliefs, and the moral/ethical consequences of one's actions in maintaining a culture of inequity. One level of self-reflection might appear as a male faculty member asking himself: "Why haven't I noticed I often complain about decisions made by my current department chair who is a woman?" Taking this a step further toward cultivating a socially just mindset, the reflection may be: "What larger patterns of gender dynamics at my institution mirror how I interact with women colleagues in my department, and how might this relate to how their decisions are welcomed or rejected by senior administrators?" The process may lead to realizing one's own complicity in inequity, but reflection is intended to help craft a new set of morals, intentions, and concrete actions that will move members of the campus community toward reclaiming their agency. Self-examination helps illuminate our own role in unequal campus dynamics so we can stop being part of the cycle. Rather than permitting neoliberal logics to define organizational and individual ethics, refusal to participate helps begin the process of transforming the policymaking process and generating collective resistance (Alakavuklar & Alamgir, 2018).

A public commitment to socially just shared governance anchors on care for others. Leaders and members of shared governance bodies who are committed to equity must become aware of who is not in the room and explicitly ask colleagues to correct the absence: Who is not present to vote on this policy proposal, but should be? Who is not present but may be negatively impacted by the implications of this decision? Policies are often made on behalf of those with the least decision-making power, such as students and hourly-wage staff, without consulting the intended recipients or including them with equal voting power to approve proposed changes. Leaders must shift their perspective to prioritize collective well-being over efficiency and profit. Foucault argues "care for the self is ethical in itself, but it implies complex relations with others, in the measure where this ethos of freedom is also a way of caring for others" (Fornet-Betancourt, Becker, Gomez-Müller, & Gauthier, 1987, p. 118). Self-empowerment and a deeper awareness of inequitable conditions is in service toward socially responsible action with regard for collective well-being rather than narrow self-interest. Importantly, producing equitable outcomes requires collaboration, working "with others and for others" (Alakavuklar & Alamgir, 2018, p. 35). Self-reflection can also be encouraged and role-modeled by administrators, faculty and staff, rather than being left to individuals. For instance, administrators who seek to implement diversity training for faculty and staff can generate more buy-in by also participating and sharing how they have changed their leadership as a result. Key positions, such as committee chairs, can maintain the reflective process by asking group members to review which perspectives have not been considered and what biases might be informing their decisions. Faculty professional development might also include methods for student reflection in the classroom. The public conscious commitment can be encouraged by individuals and groups. For example, the chair of a senate executive committee might ask the group to explore recent decisions that are slated for review—asking questions about whether appropriate input has been sought? Have views been widely reviewed? Biases considered?

As individuals recognize their disenfranchisement from shared governance, reclaiming their own power must extend to working with fellow community members to do the same in order to cultivate a collective shift in the operations of the campus. The remaining sections describe group-level change and actions to shift shared governance toward social justice and equity.

WIDENING THE CIRCLE

Socially just governance includes all campus stakeholders in the analysis of problems directly affecting them and in the policymaking process itself to ensure equitable outcomes. Widening the circle of shared governance involves asking *who is present* and *how are people involved* in decision-making (Byrne-Jimenez & Orr, 2013)? The most visible evidence of the decline of shared governance is the consolidation of policymaking authority to a handful of voices and perspectives, namely in terms of campus role and social identity group membership. From its origins, shared governance has mostly applied to tenured faculty. Our vision for future shared governance is one where all members of campus have a voice in policy structures: students, contingent faculty, and staff. Students are mentioned in the 1966 AGB/AAUP/ACE joint statement but then were dropped shortly after in shared governance models which formed. While many public institutions instituted having a student trustee or board member and made requirements for students on key campus committees, this practice has always been uneven and less a norm or expectation. However, higher education leaders abroad are recognizing the pedagogical role of student involvement in shared governance, which include preparation for democratic participation, personal development, and feeling part of the university community (Bergan, 2003).

Seventy percent of the faculty are off the tenure track and generally excluded from governance. Therefore, to make governance more inclusive and representative of the faculty, contingent faculty need to be included in shared governance (Kezar & Sam, 2010a). This is somewhat challenging as their appointments typically do not pay for them to participate and faculty contracts will need to be revised to achieve this goal

(Kezar & Sam, 2010b). In fact, studies have demonstrated that when contingent faculty are included in governance there are more equitable decisions made that help support them in the workplace and ensure they have adequate working conditions to conduct their role. Thus, data supports that widening the circle even within the faculty category does lead to more just and equitable decisions (Kezar and Sam, 2014).

While faculty inclusion in shared governance has declined in the last two decades, staff on many campuses have never been included in decision-making. There is precedent with campuses that have established campus or university councils that include all stakeholder groups in governance. Increasingly collective bargaining that represents workers across higher education is also serving as a voice in policymaking at least as it relates to working conditions. Unions are arguing that staff deserve input into their working conditions, grievance procedures, and protections from administrative overreach in terms of audits of employees.

Equitable representation of social groups who have been historically underrepresented and excluded in higher education must also be core to the new formation of shared governance in order to identify problems in campuses policies. Formal shared governance bylaws have never directly stated the relevance of compositional diversity within the governing body. In an analysis of senior leadership within the Ivy League institutions, Gasman, Abiola, and Travers (2015) found all-white leadership in the presidencies and provostships. Academic deanships had more diverse occupants, but were still majority white. Faculty and student compositional diversity are significant to consider and forecast the demographics of inclusive democratic policymaking bodies. In 2016, the faculty composition nation-wide was 76% white, which impacts the pool of tenured faculty who may serve on academic senates and assume senior level academic administration (US Department of Education, 2018). Student body diversity also matters and while here we have discussed racial demographics, the inclusion of historically underrepresented groups also takes into account gender, socioeconomic status, sexual orientation, religion, etc. And increasingly in a world where the sciences are beginning to dominate campus policies and priorities, there needs to be a balance among faculty that includes a strong voice for those in the humanities and social sciences. A plurality of identities—social identities and campus roles—among staff, faculty, and students is needed in order to form an equitable process inclusive of those who are systematically devalued and excluded.

Part of giving voice and creating agency for other groups, whether it be contingent faculty, staff of color, or a humanities professor, will mean relinquishing of power by those who traditionally have had authority. Giving up power is tied to its redistribution among the wider campus community. Rather than simply asking administrators to step down or re-allocate responsibilities, the relinquishment/redistribution of power is centered on creating a collective that is empowered to weigh in on critical decisions together. While the president may be the sole person legally entitled to sign off on policy changes, how everyone else, from students to staff to adjuncts, is involved in a tangible manner which affects the outcome is a process that can be more carefully attended to in future shared governance. In political science, the concept of participatory governance draws upon the plurality of its citizenry to better identify and address vexing social problems. As an alternative to traditional representative democracy, participatory governance deliberately expands the number and range of voices included in policymaking (Wampler, 2012). Listening must accompany the expansion of voices as feedback is sought after and decisions are deliberated. Participation must not only be created, but also fully incorporated, especially by those who have long held power.

Key to participatory governance is providing campus stakeholders with multiple involvement opportunities in decision-making. Wampler (2012) offers a tripartite conception of stakeholder involvement and outlines three roles: participant, representative, and the represented. For example, a proposal for mandatory diversity training for all faculty and staff may be considered by soliciting campus-wide feedback in an online survey and series of town halls. Through this opportunity all stakeholders directly *participate* and give feedback to administration. The training proposal is then discussed among various constituencies (e.g. within a staff council, student organization, etc.) and viewpoints from each stakeholder group are brought into a university committee composed of students, staff, faculty, and administration. Each constituency is *represented* in the ultimate decision-making body composed of elected *representatives*. When senior-level executives interface with representatives ultimately those discussions are reported back to those unable to attend closed meetings, which may elicit further action and public feedback from the larger campus community. By providing stakeholders with numerous involvement opportunities to participate in policymaking, power extends beyond a select few to as much of the campus as possible.

What we have described resembles already ongoing practices, however uneven, in higher education. For power to truly be redistributed, the campus community needs to be empowered and decisions must be realigned with social justice and equity intentions (Fung & Wright, 2001). Determining who to include must take into account who will be directly affected by a proposed policy, as well as who will implement new procedures. Since individual policies are unique to its scope and set of groups impacted, widening the circle does not imply a free-for-all regarding input to every major policy decision. A proposed mandate on extra security for all student events with over 200 attendees might involve student leaders from a wide array of groups, including cultural and activist organizations, facilities staff, campus security, student group advisors, and student affairs leadership. In addition to who should be involved, campus stakeholder perspectives should shift from an advisory status to one of authority. The work of a staff, faculty, and student-led university committee on racial equity must be implemented, not merely publicized or archived in meeting notes. Results from campus surveys can be publicized and leadership can demonstrate how survey findings are linked to budget reallocations and revised policies.

Widening participation in policymaking sets the stage for discussion informed by multiple viewpoints that can bring attention to and reframe campus problems. Transformative discourse *in* shared governance activities may then bring campus stakeholders together in a way that co-constructs understanding of the problem and potential solutions through equalizing dialogue.

TRANSFORMATIVE DISCOURSE

A diverse group of campus stakeholders, each with a commitment to social justice and equity, is the foundation for transformative discourse in the shared governance process. Policy proposals and troubleshooting campus issues occur in discussion and collaboration—one of the main mechanisms for *how social justice is enacted* (Byrne-Jimenez & Orr, 2013). Rather than maintaining the status quo of profit-making and market efficiency, transformative decision-making is focused on "creative analysis of difference, power, and privilege" in order to respond to oppressive conditions (Fine, Weiss, & Powell, 1997, p. 249). Brown (2004) promotes rational discourse for social justice-minded leaders, which involves extended conversation, listening, and openness to new perspectives.

It may be easy to think of examples in which administrators or faculty engage in problem-solving in order to secure or enhance their own positions. The dialogue in such cases is within a small group of high-status individuals who may be acting to preserve the institution or themselves at the cost of further excluding perspectives who seek a change in process. Hoekema (2001) suggests plurality in decision-making involves less hierarchy and a shift away from a lens of self-interest and organizational preservation. Schon and Rein's (1995) notion of frame reflection can help uplift each campus stakeholder's unique perspective on governance issues. The various identities among campus stakeholders means there are just as many frames of interpretation through which staff, faculty, and students understand institutional inequities and ethical dilemmas. The discourse needed to foster democratic participation and investment in campus policymaking begins with dialogue and group reflection on the issue at hand and defining the problem together (Hoekema, 2001; Schon & Rein, 1995). This is a very different starting point than with the neoliberal position of self-interest and it builds on the ideas of wisdom and mindfulness presented in the introductory chapter. Shared governance which begins with everyone's voice on equal standing can begin a radically new way of defining the institution's collective priorities and the steps taken to meet those needs.

In 2007, Asian American and Pacific Islander (AAPI) students at the University of California, Los Angeles sought to reform ethnic data collection in response to racial inequity in admissions at their campus. The campaign became system-wide upon reflecting upon the needs of underrepresented AAPI ethnic minorities across the University of California and through engaging in discussion with other student leaders to develop a multi-campus campaign. Scaling up the problem of underrepresentation to a system-level issue garnered the attention of executive leadership and the successful implementation of data disaggregation within one year (Poon, Dizon, & Squire, 2017). As a campaign, the work was largely educational, which resulted in multiple opportunities for dialogue among students and with administration. Rather than a campaign relying on protests, administrators and students learned more about the critical needs facing Southeast Asian and Pacific Islander populations and came to redefine underrepresentation. Co-constructing a problem with the collective effort of diverse voices can lead to a policy solution that recognizes the needs of those affected, and represents the ethics of the campus community.

We recognize frame reflection does not inherently eliminate status hierarchies or everyday political maneuvering. There are often inadequate mechanisms for individuals participating to listen, and leaders often have few skills in or processes that emphasize how to obtain and draw out viewpoints from those who are quiet and to get those who tend to dominant spaces to listen. Without this, dominant voices will continue to overshadow any other legitimate views and will likely reinforce existing power conditions rather than challenge them. One alternative mode is intergroup dialogue, a student-focused innovation in higher education intended to promote greater understanding across social identities as well as foster alliances for social change. Successful dialogue is predicated on listening, and can be equally beneficial to shared governance. Purposeful and open-minded listening to differing viewpoints enables the possibility of perspective taking, empathy, identifying commonalities and conflicts, and generating questions to further the dialogue (Zuñiga, Nagda, Chesler, & Cytron-Walker, 2007). A key purpose of listening is collaboration: we listen to others' viewpoints in order to understand, find meaning, and find agreement. We may change our point of view and/or reflect more deeply on our perspective. In earnestly listening to others, we suspend our beliefs, assumptions, and arguments so as to be enlightened by our colleagues. Listening and engaging in dialogue, versus debate, acknowledges all members of a group hold useful pieces to assemble a solution better than what any one position could put forth (United States Institute of Peace, 2015).

Listening and dialogue can help transform shared governance into a meaningful structure for social justice. Sustained listening across difference viewpoints can shift dynamics from antagonistic to cooperative, and zero-sum thinking to efforts at win-win outcomes. When administrators are difficult to access and withhold information from students, protest and demonstrations are often the response, especially regarding politically charged issues, such as tuition rises, university investments and corporate partnerships, and racial injustice. Transparent communication and a willingness to listen from both students and administration on issues of inequity may produce consensus, but more importantly, listening and reflection can lead to "deeper and richer understandings of our own biases as well as where our colleagues are coming from on particular issues and how each of us differently constructs those issues" (Brown,

2004, p. 93). The process may also reveal the limitations of the available perspectives in the group and raise the question of who is not present, who is being excluded, and who is being silenced. Transformative discourse can change not only the starting point of problem-solving but also the process of who is empowered to be part of the policymaking process. From this deep understanding, discourse within shared governance can be focused toward addressing oppression and inequity facing the university internally as well as its engagement with the broader public. In examining a policy about student evaluations, it is important to bring in the views of many individuals that may not be obvious without drawing in and listening to different and non-dominant views. Faculty of color and women are often the target of discrimination and bias by students and allowing these groups to share their experiences and to bring in research on this topic can enrich a policymaking process.

In order for democratic discourses to emerge, those leading shared governance processes (e.g. board chairs, academic senate presidents, faculty and staff council chairs, and student governments presidents) will need training in social justice-based facilitation and conflict mediation. Prejudice reduction workshops and speaker panels of people with marginalized identities are two learning opportunities to increase awareness of one's own biases, the nature and realities of discrimination, and how to listen through discomfort in order to learn (Brown, 2004). Social justice-based facilitation training, offered by organizations such as the Social Justice Training Institute (SJTI), prepare leaders to identify and interrupt exclusionary group dynamics as well as artfully raise issues of inequity that may be apparent in how people are discussing an issue in order to redirect dialogue back toward social justice and equity. Training in these areas and their execution in shared governance promotes transformative discourse, which draws its strength from the diversity of voices and the multiple avenues available toward achieving equitable outcomes.

DYNAMIC INSTITUTIONALIZATION

While shared governance has declined and become superseded by neoliberal logics, social justice is often obstructed when the institution's operations and practices are viewed as tradition and therefore unchanging or resistant to change. However, for the intended outcomes of widening the circle of participation and transformative discourse to become tangible and felt, shared governance processes must include the capacity to reflect and evaluate the impacts of policy decisions and revise accordingly, rather than keep structures in place as is often the case. We propose the notion of dynamic institutionalization as an iterative action for how social justice can occur, such as through reflexivity, policy reversal, and resistance to unjust institutional practices and processes.

Throughout this volume we are calling for critical questioning of the taken-for-granted and normative. Reflexivity within shared governance bodies can reveal when policies need to change and when structures themselves must be resisted. Shared governance processes as tending toward normative affirmation misses out on the kind of questioning needed for social justice and undoing "oppressive structures and mechanisms prevalent both in education and society" (Freire & Macedo, 1995, p. 383). Instances of alleged repression of free speech are embroiling campuses. These are opportunities to revisit the campus' community values, look to examples which prioritize the needs of marginalized identities, and implement conduct policies within legal bounds (Lawrence, 1990). Rather than only asking colleagues to brainstorm and protect the institution's legal and financial interests, collective reflection must focus on correcting disproportional and unjust impacts on marginalized groups within the campus.

The following questions offered by Smith, Yosso, and Solorzano (2007, p. 567) exemplify a way for rethinking traditional approaches to policymaking. These emphasize the ways race can be brought into policy processes but these same question areas can be used among other groups (socioeconomic status, gender) or for other issues (e.g. redistribution of opportunity, power differences, arts vs. humanities):

1) How has or can race and racism in our institution play a role in the everyday decisions we make? How about gender and gendered racism?
2) How is our institution meeting or exceeding our institutional responsibility to enroll, retain, and graduate Students of Color?
3) If we value the experiential knowledge of Faculty, Staff, and Students of Color, have we nurtured direct and consistent lines of communication with them?
4) How does our university mission reflect a genuine commitment to social justice? How can this commitment be implemented and integrated into the leadership culture as the day-to-day decisions are made?
5) What analytical tools and practical methods can we engage to better know and understand the racial and gendered histories and contemporary conditions of our institution?

The answers that may arise from these or similar questions may be uncomfortable, disconcerting, and reveal an image of the institution that is unsettling. The process of changing oneself and the culture of the institution is not overnight or simple. However, this kind of reflection on policies can shed light on disparate impacts of institutional processes and structures that harm minority members of the community.

Dynamic institutionalization is the outcome of the organizational changes which result from collective reflection among decision-makers. One way to avoid ossification of longstanding, but unjust policies is to reverse and eliminate the effects of such policies and even the policies themselves (Stewart, 2018). Reversing policies invites an opportunity to further increase campus participation in shared governance and check for consistency between institutional structures and social justice goals. Attending to the harm done on those most vulnerable benefits the campus community as a whole through cultivating a cultural shift toward collective accountability. Elimination of policies and seeking to undo harm opens the avenue for new institutional mechanisms that may lead to social justice and equity outcomes. For example, a campus may have a policy regarding plagiarism that is not attentive to how different cultures perceive the issue and may be overly punitive to students who come from other countries and not have a strong enough developmental function that would be attentive to these individuals' unique worldviews and unfairly penalize them.

It may not always be possible to engage in a formal and structured process as we have described thus far. Dynamic institutionalization recognizes that longstanding institutional norms can divert social justice goals. Reversing oppressive power dynamics may not be amenable to individuals with ultimate legal authority over the institution. Resisting institutional rules and engaging in direct refusal and action against authority may thus be essential to directing organizational change toward social justice and equity. At some point, campus stakeholders may need to utilize direct resistance strategies to garner more power such as campus sit-ins, protests, strikes, and other collective efforts aimed at challenging existing power relationships. Direct action is one of the few ways to challenge managerial control under a neoliberal regime (Alakavuklar & Alamgir, 2018). Such forms of resistance can be seen in governance today, at places that have seen the excesses of neoliberalism. For example, at USC the faculty were able to remove the president who had great favor from the board by signing a petition demanding he be fired and delivering it to the board of trustees. The letter was shared with the media and other influential groups. Then a public forum was held to air concerns (again the media were invited) and protests followed the forum. This type of direct action and resistance to those in power about wrong-headed decisions is needed on campuses and has been largely missing in recent decades in which apathy has seized shared governance processes. Resistance can also manifest through enacting one's commitment to equity throughout the "everyday struggles of the workplace" (Alakavuklar & Alamgir, 2018, p. 31). At any scale, resistance is a vehicle through which to redefine and assert a new way of governing to achieve social justice and equity.

In summary, inclusion and affirmation of diversity, redistribution of power and resources, equal participation, and systematic change constitute our definition of social justice and equity. Shared governance must be anchored in these values and outcomes. Conscious public commitment moves individual actors into the process for engaging in collective ethical leadership. Widening the circle ensures diverse voices are heard in the decision-making room. Transformative discourse allows shared governance bodies to wrestle with uncomfortable issues that are named and attend to the underlying justice issues at stake. Finally, dynamic institutionalization brings in a new model of change that is responsive and relevant to meet the university's social justice and equity goals. Each component of the model discussed is interconnected and shared governance can be moved toward social justice and equity at any point through individual and collective actions.

CONCLUSION

Shared governance can be one of the most powerful tools for redistributing power and creating more social just and equitable decisions, policies, and resultant practices in higher education. It has the possibility to reshape higher education institutions in very fundamental ways that implicate and reshape administrative processes noted throughout this book. Governance touches on planning, budgeting, policies, and parameters within which all administrative structures take place. As the chapter on culture within this book describes, revising a major process like shared governance on campus can challenge and reshape the neoliberal culture that has taken hold of campuses. Through the process described in this chapter we provide a framework for not only reclaiming shared governance but moving toward a truly democratic approach.

QUESTIONS FOR REFLECTION AND DISCUSSION

1. Choose an institution you have attended or are currently based in. What is its shared governance structure? How does the on-paper governance structure match with how campus stakeholders experience and participate in shared governance? Review the model for shared governance introduced in this chapter: How are social justice and equity reflected (or missing) in your campus' shared governance structures and decision-making outcomes?

2. Identify a campus controversy (e.g. the admissions scandal, a racial crisis, etc.), and gather details of the incident, the campus response, and the actions of various stakeholders. Imagine you are an administrator and apply the social justice and equity model for shared governance to craft an alternative response. What would be your public stance on the issue? How would you involve yourself, students, and colleagues in a response? What policies would you set in place or amend to prevent future controversies?

3. Reflect on your participation in shared governance. What committees or roles have you held, and how did your participation enhance your commitment to the campus community? What particular perspective did you contribute to the group? If you have not participated in shared governance, what obstacles have

prevented your participation? What support do you need to take this step and encourage your colleagues to do the same?

RESOURCES

We recommend the following documents as references to understand shared governance:

1966 Joint Statement on Government of Colleges and Universities by the American Council on Education (ACE), American Association of University Professors (AAUP), and the Association of Governing Boards of Universities and Colleges (AGB): www.aaup.org/report/statement-government-colleges-and-universities

2017 AGB Board of Directors Statement on Shared Governance: https://agb.org/reports-and-statements/agb-board-of-directors-statement-on-shared-governance/

2009 Study on Faculty, Governing Boards, and Institutional Governance by TIAA-CREF Institute: www.tiaainstitute.org/sites/default/files/presentations/2017-02/ahe_governance0110_03.pdf

REFERENCES

Alakavuklar, O. N., & Alamgir, F. (2018). Ethics of Resistance in Organisations: A Conceptual Proposal. *Journal of Business Ethics, 149*(1), 31–43.

American Association of University Professors, American Colleges & Universities (1944). *Statement of Principles on Academic Freedom and Tenure*. Retrieved from www.aaup.org/report/1940-statement-principles-academic-freedom-and-tenure.

Arjoon, S. (2005). Corporate governance: An ethical perspective. *Journal of Business Ethics, 61*(4), 343–352. https://doi.org/10.1007/s10551-005-7888-5

Association of Governing Boards of Colleges and Universities, American Association of University Professors, American Council on Education (1966). *Statement on Government of Colleges and Universities*. Retrieved from www.aaup.org/report/statement-government-colleges-and-universities.

Barrow, C. W. (1992). Corporate liberalism, finance hegemony, and central state intervention in the reconstruction of American higher education. *Studies in American Political Development, 6*(2), 420–444.

Bell, L. A. (2007). Theoretical Foundations for Social Justice Education. In M. Adams, L. A. Bell, & P. Griffin (Eds.), *Teaching for Diversity and Social Justice* (pp. 1–14). New York: Routledge.

Bergan, S. (2003). *Student participation in higher education governance*. Retrieved from www.coe.int/t/dg4/highereducation/Governance/SB_student_participation_FR.pdf

Brown, K. M. (2004). Leadership for Social Justice and Equity: Weaving a Transformative Framework and Pedagogy. *Educational Administration Quarterly, 40*(1), 77–108.

Byrne-Jimenez, M., & Orr, M. T. (2013). Evaluating Social Justice Leadership Preparation. In L. C., Tillman & J. J. Scheurich (Eds.), *Handbook of Research on Educational Leadership for Equity and Diversity* (pp. 670–702). New York: Routledge.

Chen, G. A., & Buell, J. Y. (2018). Of models and myths: Asian(Americans) in STEM and the neoliberal racial project. *Race Ethnicity and Education, 21*(5), 607–625.

Cummings, W. K., & Finkelstein, M. (2009). Global trends in academic governance. *Academe, 95*(6), 31–34.

Fine, M., Weiss, L., & Powell, L. (1997). Communities of difference: A critical look at desegregated spaces created for and by youth. *Harvard Educational Review, 67*(2), 247–284.

Fornet-Betancourt, R., Becker, H., Gomez-Müller, A., & Gauthier, J. D. (1987). The ethic of care for the self as a practice of freedom: An interview with Michel Foucault on January 20, 1984. *Philosophy and Social Criticism, 12*(2–3), 112–131.

Freire, P., & Macedo, D. (1995). A dialogue: Culture, language, and race. *Harvard Educational Review, 65*(3), 377–402.

Fung, A., & Wright, E. O. (2001). Deepening Democracy: Innovations in Empowered Participatory Governance. *Politics and Society, 29*(1), 5–41.

Gasman, M., Abiola, U., & Travers, C. (2015). Diversity and senior leadership at elite institutions of higher education. *Journal of Diversity in Higher Education, 8*(1), 1–14.

Giroux, H. (2002). Democratic Public Sphere. *Harvard Educational Review, 72*(4), 425–464.

Hoekema, A. J. (2001). Reflexive governance and indigenous self-rule: Lessons in associative democracy? *Critical Review of International Social and Political Philosophy, 4*(1), 157–186.

Kezar, A., & Sam, C. (2010a). *Understanding the new majority of non-tenure-track faculty in higher education: Demographics, experiences, and plans of action.* Association for the Study in Higher Education Report, 36(4). San Francisco, CA: Jossey-Bass.

Kezar, A., & Sam, C. (2010b). Beyond contracts: Non-tenure track faculty and campus governance. *The NEA 2010 almanac of higher education* (pp. 83–91). Washington, DC: National Education Association.

Kezar, A., & Sam, C. (2014). Governance as a catalyst for policy change: Creating a contingent faculty friendly academy. *Educational Policy, 28*, 425–462.

Lawrence, C. (1990). If he hollers let him go: Regulating racist speech on campus. *Duke Law Journal, 3*, 431–483.

Lucas, C. J. (1998). *Crisis in the Academy: Rethinking Higher Education in America.* New York: Palgrave Macmillan.

Poon, O.A., Dizon, J.P.M, & Squire, D. (2017). Count Me In! Ethnic Data Disaggregation Advocacy, Racial Mattering, and Lessons for Racial Justice Coalitions. *Journal Committed to Social Change on Race and Ethnicity, 3*(1), 92–124.

Pusser, B. (2006). Reconsidering Higher Education and the Public Good: The Role of Public Spheres. In W. G. Tierney (Ed.), *Governance and the Public Good* (pp. 11–28). Albany, NY: SUNY Press.

Rhoades, G. (1996). Reorganizing the faculty workforce for flexibility: Part-time professional labor. *The Journal of Higher Education, 67*(6), 626–659.

Robertson, S. L., & Dale, R. (2013). The social justice implications of privatisation in education governance frameworks: A relational account. *Oxford Review of Education, 39*(4), 426–445.

Schon, D. A., & Rein, M. (1995). *Frame Reflection: Toward the Resolution of Intractable Policy Controversies.* New York: Basic Books.

Schuster, J. H., & Finkelstein, M. J. (2006). *The American Faculty: The Restructuring of Academic Work and Careers.* Baltimore, MD: Johns Hopkins University Press.

Slaughter, S.A., & Leslie, L. L. (1997). *Academic Capitalism: Politics, Policies, and the Entrepreneurial University.* Baltimore, MD: Johns Hopkins University Press.

Slaughter, S. A., & Rhoades, G. (2004). *Academic Capitalism and the New Economy: Markets, State, and Higher Education.* Baltimore, MD: Johns Hopkins University Press.

Smith, W. A., Yosso, T. J., & Solorzano, D. G. (2007). Racial primes and black misandry on historically white campuses: Toward critical race accountability in educational administration. *Educational Administration Quarterly, 43*(5), 559–585.

Stewart, D. L. (2018). Minding the Gap Between Diversity and Institutional Transformation: Eight Proposals for Enacting Institutional Change. *Teachers College Record, 120*(14).

Talburt, S. (2005). Ideas of a University, Faculty Governance, and Governmentality. In *Higher education: Handbook of theory and research* (pp. 459–505). New York: Spring.

Tierney, W. G. (Ed.) (2006). *Governance and the Public Good.* Albany, NY: SUNY Press.

Tierney, W. G., & Minor, J. T. (2003). *Challenges for Governance: A National Report.* Los Angeles, CA: Center for Higher Education Policy Analysis.

United States Institute of Peace (2015). *Comparison of Dialogue and Debate*. Retrieved from www.usip.org/sites/default/files/2017-01/Dialogue%2Bvs%2BDebate%2B-%2BUSIP%2BGlobal%2BCampus.pdf.

US Department of Education, National Center for Education Statistics (2018). *The Condition of Education 2018 (NCES 2018–144), Characteristics of Postsecondary Faculty*.

Wampler, B. (2012). Participation, representation, and social justice: Using participatory governance to transform representative democracy. *Polity*, 44(4), 666–682.

Zuñiga, X., Nagda, B.A., Chesler, M., & Cytron-Walker, A. (2007). *Intergroup Dialogue in Higher Education: Meaningful Learning About Social Justice*. San Francisco, CA: Jossey-Bass.

3

CHOOSE WISELY

Making Decisions With and For Equity in Higher Education

JULIE POSSELT, THERESA HERNANDEZ, AND CYNTHIA D. VILLARREAL

Monica sits back, crosses her arms, and looks around the table. All eyes are on her, as the committee waits for their chair to make the next move. For the last 50 minutes, they have debated the merits of two great internal candidates to promote as Director of Advancement Initiatives. They now find themselves at an impasse with ten minutes left in the meeting. One candidate fits the job description perfectly. Timothy has credentials from elite universities, great recommendations from familiar names, and a fundraising record that a committee member described as "short, but flawless." However, several on the committee have voiced concern that the job description, which was effectively cut and pasted from the last time they hired for this role, does not reflect what the reorganized unit needs now, nor the direction this newly designated Hispanic-Serving Institution is pointed in terms of philanthropy. This contingent of the committee favors Trina, whose fit with the Director of Advancement Initiatives is not what Tim offers, but who comes with different strengths: many more years of experience at the university, strong connections to leaders in the surrounding community, and a record of innovation and successful fundraising in positions at another Minority-Serving Institution. Both are strong candidates—it's a fact that cannot be denied. "Apples or oranges," Monica thinks to herself, "Who we've been or what we want to be. The recommendation to the Vice President is basically up to me."

For higher education administrators, every day comes with decisions, and every decision comes with trade-offs. Some are consequential, like the choice between two finalists for an important position, as in the vignette above. Others, including how to write a position description, may seem more mundane in the moment, but come with ripple effects that affect later decisions. How can administrators treat everyday decision making as a lever that mitigates inequalities rather than reproducing them? In this chapter, we begin to answer that question by introducing a new framework for equitable decision making that builds on established theoretical frameworks for decision making. We then illustrate this framework's core components (i.e. criteria, process, outcomes) through empirical research in two higher education contexts important to many administrators, namely admissions and hiring. The chapter will close with recommendations for managing the opportunities and threats to equity when practitioners face decisions big and small.

FRAMEWORKS FOR MAKING DECISIONS

Ideas about how to optimally make decisions are as old as our most ancient writings about politics and power. The idea of deliberative democracy, for example, came into being in Athens in the fifth century BC. It proposes that decisions should be made by as many people as will be affected by their outcomes, through a process that forces voters to articulate reasons for their preferences. In so doing, they are forced to debate the merits and drawbacks of various options, which both results in better decisions and forces an acknowledgment of the value propositions that underlie possible actions. This political view of decision making has seen a resurgence in recent decades, including in education. Other views used to analyze and understand decision making in higher education contexts have emerged from other academic disciplines. Rational choice and bounded rationality originated in economics and organization theory, while psychology has advanced the study of cognitive and social biases, and anthropologists have provided useful insights about cultural dimensions of making decisions. We review those perspectives in the following sections.

RATIONALITY AND ITS LIMITS

Bounded rationality offered a corrective to an idealized view that decisions are made through a rational sequence of steps in which an actor articulates goals, decision criteria, and alternatives, then analyzes the situation and makes a decision that will maximize benefits and minimize costs. Through studies in mostly corporate environments, March (1994) outlined two often observed decision-making logics, noting most people's decisions are not as rational as the prevailing view suggests. Under the *logic of consequences*, actors make decisions based on analyses of the consequences likely to follow specific alternatives. They think not only about the benefits and drawbacks of possible choices, but also the expected consequences that are likely to come with those choices. The trouble is, we can never know exactly what those consequences will be in reality; therefore, we are acting on imperfect information, so the decision is never as rational as it may look. The *logic of appropriateness* offers an alternative framework. It asserts that individuals make decisions by assessing their identities, relevant rules or norms associated with their identities, and the appropriateness of various options given these identities and rules. For example, when faced with the decision of whether or not to sanction a high-performing employee for persistent tardiness, a supervisor might think about their own social identities, the norms for timeliness that accompany their identities, and whether those norms make tardiness a serious breach or no big deal. This view recognizes that real people with personal histories and cultures are involved, and that few people escape such considerations when making decisions.

Neither classic rational choice nor bounded rationality, however, offer direct ways of understanding how and why inequities so frequently arise from the decisions that individuals and organizations make. Blindspots in these theories to power and privilege—especially in the conduct and impact of decision making—may help explain why so many leaders trained in universities teaching these established models go on to make decisions that reproduce social inequities. Higher education administrators striving to enact equity in their decisions can do better than these perspectives by considering other frameworks.

COGNITIVE AND SOCIAL BIASES

Studying the forms and effects of bias (defined as systematic error), as well as strategies to mitigate it, has advanced the scholarship of decision making greatly. Scholars in behavioral economics, decision theory, and psychology alike have identified and examined the impact of bias. Recent higher education scholarship has examined cognitive biases and social biases. For example, correspondence bias (that is, attributing decisions to an individual's personality rather than the situation in which they made the decision) has been studied with respect to both college admissions and grade assignment/inflation (Bastedo & Bowman, 2017; Moore, Swift, Sharek, & Gino, 2010). A novel experiment by Bastedo and Bowman (2017) found that admissions decision-makers selected higher proportions of low SES students when provided with additional information about applicants' high school context. Lower SES students have better college opportunities when admissions takes into account that they are more likely to go to high schools with fewer resources.

The concepts of implicit and explicit bias are also important for thinking about improving decision making for equity. Both types are predicated on the concept of preferences. Explicit biases are conscious, intentional expressions of preference that communicate attitudes or stereotypes about groups or individuals. Implicit biases, on the other hand, are unconscious preferences reflecting attitudes or stereotypes that do not necessarily align to espoused values. The latter has received considerable attention in recent years by scholars looking at higher education, for we can see its effects everywhere. Higher education scholars have uncovered effects of implicit bias in faculty email responses (Milkman, Akinola, & Chugh, 2015), evaluations of résumés (Bertrand & Mullainathan, 2004; Moss-Racusin, 2012), conference reviews (Roberts & Verhoef, 2016), online course evaluations (MacNell, Driscoll, & Hunt, 2015), and more. For example, Katherine Milkman and her colleagues sent out 600 emails to faculty members that implied the sender was a prospective PhD student requesting a short conversation to discuss the possibility of research together in a PhD program. They kept the body of the message identical, varying only the name at the bottom of the email by gender and race. The results showed that faculty responded more frequently and more promptly to messages whose senders suggested they were men and who were White, relative to messages whose senders implied they were women, Black, Chinese, and/or Indian. The results were most pronounced in private universities (Milkman et al., 2015). Identifying the presence of such biases—which maintain their power largely through their invisibility—is the first step to checking and undermining them. Left unchecked, such social biases are pernicious, in that they can become embedded in the culture and therefore invisible to members. We turn to discussing the role of culture in decision making next.

DECISION MAKING AND ORGANIZATIONAL CULTURE

Organizational culture is "the system of values, symbols, and shared meanings of a group including the embodiment of these values, symbols, and meaning into material objects and ritualized practices" (Corbally & Sergiovanni, 1986, p. viii). As an ever-present facet of organizational life that shapes the interpretations—and thus actions—of its members, culture and subcultures shape decision making of all parties associated with higher education: students' choices of where to enroll, professors' syllabi and research design decisions, trustees' policy and budget votes, and more. This view regards the organization at least as much as an "interpretive undertaking than a rationalized structure with clear decision-making processes" (Tierney, 2008).

Schein (2010) persuasively argued that leaders have particular influence in transmitting and embedding culture through their decisions. Primary embedding mechanisms include role modeling; allocating resources; and selecting, recruiting, and retaining members. Secondary mechanisms follow, articulating and reinforcing the culture. They include the design of space, systems, and procedures; and formal statements, such as the mission, which concretize commitments, values, and history. Through actors' interpretations, actions, and the subsequent material consequences, individuals embed power and privilege in decision making and the organization.

A FRAMEWORK FOR EQUITABLE DECISION MAKING

Across these varied theories, several themes emerge as important factors for equity-minded practitioners to keep in mind when making decisions. Figure 3.1 represents these themes in an integrated framework. First, we observe that decision-making criteria and processes each operate as levers for enhancing or reducing the overall equity of a given decision's outcome. Whether explicit or left implicit, the criteria and process provide the basis and practice for actions that ultimately contribute to broader patterns of inequality. These are, perhaps, the core factors that practitioners should keep their eye on, and therefore we will revisit them in detail in illustrating what the literature says about decision making in admissions and hiring.

In addition—and across criteria, processes, and outcomes—decision-makers' priorities and preferences play a vital role. Holding fast to one preference—either for a particular type of criterion, a particular sort of decision-making process, or a particular outcome of decision making—means that other preferences may be downplayed in importance. Indeed there are either-or situations in which a "yes" vote to elevate some criterion, process, or outcome appears to mean a "no" vote to something else. However, wisdom can help transform apparent either-or decisions into both-and decisions. When revamping an organizational structure, the appearance of a forced choice between outcomes that prioritize representation or effective leadership may simply require time and creativity to identify an option that accommodates both priorities. Too often equity is cast as incompatible with, secondary to, or inherently divergent from efficiency or excellence. A simple reframing and return to the details of the situation can facilitate a more holistic and inclusive view of the decision at hand.

Third, decisions in higher education are almost always context-specific and, if one looks closely enough, they are therefore marked by the complexity that comes with attention to detail. As represented by the nested boxes in Figure 3.1, micro-level decision-making situations are embedded within larger contexts (see the text in the upper side of the boxes) which have associated manifestations of power (see the italicized text in the lower side of the boxes). Decisions are made by people, often nested in committees, which are nested within other socio-organizational contexts such as colleges, disciplines, and society. Each individual, committee, and broader context will hold multiple priorities and preferences of their own, not to mention power dynamics and biases that are both implicit and explicit, which rarely overlap perfectly. The process of individual and collective judgment is laden with multiple identities of varying levels of saliency that can be involved at different times in the decision-making process. Because heuristics enable individuals to make decisions based on mental shortcuts from their experiences, this approach to decision making, while automatic, is prone to errors (Tversky & Kahneman, 1974). Within the uncertainty of heuristics in the process of judgment, the ease of cognitive load for the decider

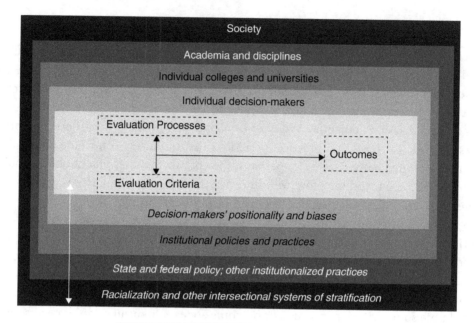

FIGURE 3.1   Framework for Equity in Decision Making

also comes with an increased ability to make judgments that are cognitively biased (Tversky & Kahneman, 1974; Bargh & Chartrand, 1999). No wonder that organizational decisions come with so much compromise!

Finally, power is a force in all decision making that affects equity, and one that practitioners and scholars alike must acknowledge and explicitly address. One simple definition of power is the ability to influence social decision making. We see it affecting decision making in two ways. On the one hand, power flows explicitly and implicitly from macro processes like racialization down to micro actions like decisions. In this way societal influences like racialization and other intersecting systems of social stratification manifest within academic environments. On the other hand, power also builds as an accumulation of micro actions through time and space, whether intentionally or not, to reinforce or transform our wider social conditions. In this instance, the individual biases and political games of academia may also come to pervade broader contexts. Figure 3.1 depicts this through the bidirectional white arrow going back and forth between micro to macro contexts. We highlight the role of power in decision making so that administrators will be more cognizant of the power relations involved and more intentional about wisely making decisions in support of equity.

Left unexamined, power has multiple channels through which it reproduces inequalities, such as societal/cultural norms, institutions, organizations, and individual decision-making situations. Inequities are thus perpetuated through the maintenance of inequality embedded in the status quo in these contexts. Other relevant considerations include racialization, intersectionality, and positionality. With the exception of scholarship on implicit bias and research on race-conscious admissions, extant perspectives rarely make explicit the roles of racialization in decision making; however, in the United States, we cannot neglect the relevance of race and yet expect equitable outcomes. Decision-makers also need to be aware of how power operates through multiple, interacting hierarchical systems that, in addition to race, include class, gender, and others. Uncovering blindspots about these matters will lead decision-makers to think more intentionally about the consequences of their decisions (i.e. will it reproduce inequities?) and/or what is appropriate for a person like them (e.g. how can I use my power/privilege as a decision-maker to create a more just organization?). Importantly for administrators' efforts toward wise decision-making, we propose the importance of attending to the ways that power dynamics are reflected in decision-making criteria, evaluation, and outcomes.

LESSONS IN DECISION MAKING FROM ADMISSIONS AND HIRING

To illustrate the relevance of this framework for common decision-making contexts in higher education, we apply it now to understanding equity threats and opportunities inherent in admissions and hiring. By applying it to these two contexts, we hope to also shed light on the kinds of considerations that need to be made in other decision-making contexts as well. The tensions and trade-offs facing admissions decision-makers are consistent with other decisions made for the purposes of enrollment management, while issues that emerge in hiring decisions will draw out common challenges of human relations decisions.[1]

For each illustration, we emphasize how equity opportunities and threats manifest in the criteria and processes that drive judgments and decisions, as well as in the outcomes themselves. In our view, we are better able to see equity manifested or under threat when we attune ourselves not only to its presence or absence in a decision generally, but rather in these three analytically important components of all decisions: criteria, processes, and outcomes. These components have a causal relationship, in that greater equity in the review criteria and processes of coming together to make choices is likely to yield outcomes that are more equitable.

ADMITTING STUDENTS

Undergraduate admissions is usually a centralized decision-making process, with applications sent to a central office, whose staff review files according to predetermined processes. In professional admissions (e.g. medical, dental, law), the process is similar, albeit with different review criteria. At the graduate level, however, students may send their applications to a common office in a graduate school, but they are sifted and reviewed at the department level by faculty. Research has highlighted equity threats and opportunities inherent in both the criteria and processes used in admissions decisions.

Admissions Criteria

In our review of the literature on admissions,[2] the most prevalent theme concerned the application criteria used in admissions decisions and how well these elements predict different definitions of success, like grades, retention, or degree completion. The major takeaway from this body of evidence for our purposes is this: No single criterion will predict all forms of success equally well for all populations. We need a comprehensive set of criteria, contextualized for individual applicants, and assessed systematically.

Quantitative Metrics in Admissions

For the ongoing questions about both equity and predicting future success, no admissions criteria type has received as much attention as standardized tests. The literature is highly varied on the question of what forms of future performance are predicted—and for whom[3]—but consistently find that the longer the time elapsed between taking the test and the measure studied, the weaker the relationship is (Kuncel & Hezlett, 2007; Mattern & Patterson, 2013). While differentially predicting GPA, graduation rates, and other performance measures (Smith & Garrison, 2005; White, Dey, & Fantone, 2009), we know that from elementary school achievement tests through to graduate and admissions entrance exam scores, standardized test scores also correlate with gender, race, and socioeconomic status (Bastedo & Jaquette, 2011; Bielby, Posselt, Jaquette, and Bastedo, 2014; Posselt, Jaquette, Bielby, & Bastedo, 2012). On average, men, high income, White, and Asian students score higher on such exams than their demographic counterparts; therefore, admissions processes that over rely on standardized test scores or use score cut-offs to make decisions disproportionately limit access to underrepresented groups (Bastedo & Jaquette, 2011; Bielby et al., 2014; Miller & Stassun, 2014; Posselt et al., 2012).

In most models, prior grade point average (GPA) emerges as the strongest single predictor of future academic performance. Yet, inconsistencies in its validity, too, have been found across institutional contexts, fields of study, and sub-populations.[4] It does not predict later performance as well for women, racially minoritized students, English learners (ELs), and students with low socioeconomic status (SES) as it does for students from more privileged backgrounds (Culpepper & Davenport, 2009; Mattern, Shaw, & Kobrin, 2011). At the graduate level, too, undergraduate GPA is the strongest predictor of graduate GPA, although results are mixed with regard to prior disciplinary specific coursework (Christensen, Nance, & White, 2012; Halberstam & Redstone, 2005; Miller, Zwickl, Posselt, & Hodapp, in press). Together, it makes clear that even the best single predictor cannot be relied upon alone—that a more comprehensive and contextualized set of criteria are needed.

Qualitative Portions of Applications

Personal statements, writing samples, letters of recommendation, and interviews are already common in many undergraduate, graduate, or professional admissions (Briihl & Wasieleski, 2004; Littleford, Buxton, Bucher, Simon-Dack, & Yang, 2018; Posselt, 2016; Potvin, Chari, & Hodapp, 2017). They add means of judging among academically qualified applicants at both the undergraduate and graduate levels (Stevens, 2007; Posselt, 2016), but with a few exceptions, have received less scholarly attention than grades and test scores (Briihl & Wasieleski, 2004; Littleford et al., 2018; Murphy, Klieger, Borneman, & Kuncel, 2009). Meta-analysis on the research about personal statements (Murphy et al., 2009), for example, concluded that while they did not offer any incremental improvement in the prediction of grades above prior GPA and test scores, they may be useful in assessing program and advisor fit. This research highlights an important point about selection and decision making: It often proceeds not only to fulfill a manifest function of identifying people who are likely to be successful, but also latent organizational functions such as creating community and reinforcing or nudging organizational culture in a new direction.

At least one study found that interviews and in-person exercises were more predictive of achievement in a doctoral program than undergraduate GPA and GRE scores (Mountford, Ehlert, Machell, and Cockrell, 2007). Medical school interviews have received the most attention, with evidence of scores related to a varying degree with non-cognitive constructs and practicum exam scores (Basco, Lancaster, Gilbert, Carey, & Blue, 2008; Ma, Harris, Cole, Jones, & Shulruf, 2016; Oliver, Hecker, Hausdorf, & Conlon, 2014). As this last point shows, qualitative aspects of admissions applications may be valued for their direct relationship to markers of future academic and professional success or for relating to non-academic qualities that people believe to be indicators of success. With respect to the latter, scholars have also explored the predictive power of non-cognitive competencies.

Non-Cognitive Competencies in Admissions

As a broad category of criteria, research on non-cognitive and socio-emotional competencies (defined broadly as self and relationship management skills used to navigate everyday life) remains inconclusive due, in part, to the inconsistent way these variables have been defined (Kyllonen, Walters, & Kaufman, 2005; Sommerfeld, 2011). William

Sedlacek (2004) articulated one set—frequently found among racially minoritized students, specifically—that includes positive self-concept, realistic self-appraisal, negotiating the system, long-range goals, strong support person, leadership, community service, and nontraditional knowledge. While some scholars determined that non-cognitive competencies are not adequate predictors of college GPA or persistence based on a meta-analysis of research using a questionnaire based on Sedlacek's work (Thomas, Kuncel, & Crede, 2007), others have found that they predict first-year GPA better than high school grades and standardized tests (Shivpuri, Schmitt, Oswald, & Kim, 2006; Sinha, Oswald, Imus, & Schmitt, 2011). What is more, these skills do not have the gender and racial disparities present in most non-cognitive measures (Shivpuri et al., 2006). Improving our assessment of non-cognitive competencies appears to be an important frontier in equitable admissions decision making.

In summary, improving decision making in admissions requires not only understanding how well different standards predict success but also scrutinizing whether these criteria do so equitably across groups and how the qualities that institutions seek in students are distributed in the population. For too long, institutions have relied narrowly on quantitative metrics that privilege students from already overrepresented populations, enabling admissions to become a mechanism for the reproduction of inequalities in higher education—and thus, the labor market. That reliance, however, is a problem not only of the criteria and their distribution, but also how those with decision-making authority put the criteria to use. To examine this, we turn to other research on the practices and policies of admissions decision making.

Admissions Processes

The backgrounds, training, and work of staff and faculty tasked with admissions decisions each impact evaluation and selection processes and, by extension, the outcome (Hodum & James, 2010; Bowman & Bastedo, 2018; Posselt, 2015). Experimental research by Bowman and Bastedo (2018) uncovered common practices and attributes of undergraduate admissions practitioners across different levels of institutional selectivity, and how these various factors are related to the admission of low SES students. They also found that admissions officers of color as well as those whose parents have less education were more likely than their counterparts to recommend admission for low SES students. Posselt's (2016) study of PhD admissions similarly found that faculty from lower SES backgrounds thought of themselves as more qualified to judge applicants from low SES backgrounds, and that they sought opportunities to "pay forward" through admissions the opportunities they knew someone at some point had extended to them. In addition, practitioners who work together for a long time in a common domain or have undergone similar training may likely develop shared sensibilities in how they evaluate potential for success in a particular field (Christensen, Lykkegaard, Lund, & O'Neill, 2018; Posselt, 2015). Together, these studies highlight that the judgment and social identities of decision-makers are intertwined;

and therefore, who is at the decision-making table matters for how information is processed and—ultimately—who is likely to be admitted.

Another dimension of decision-making processes with equity implications for admissions and many other types of selection is the evaluative work of holistic review, defined as the consideration of a wide variety of applicant characteristics, including non-cognitive or socio-emotional skills. Bastedo and colleagues (2018) identified three types of holistic review used among undergraduate admissions officers: *whole file*, which considers all aspects of the application; *whole person*, which considers many facets of the applicant's background and potential; and *whole context*, which looks at what an applicant has done in light of the opportunities they have had (Bastedo, Bowman, Glasener, & Kelly, 2018).

In practice, the work of evaluation diverges from rhetoric of holistic admissions through the way criteria are defined, applied, and contextualized. An ethnography of a liberal arts college's admissions office by Mitchell Stevens (2007) described admissions decision making as a process of evaluative storytelling, in which applicants come to be taken seriously or disregarded through the stories that admissions officers weave for one another from the details in student applications. Socioeconomic inequalities are reproduced through evaluative storytelling, Stevens argued. For example, applicants with privileged backgrounds are more likely to have had an upbringing and admissions coaching so that their record includes tone, details, and experiences through which admissions officers can craft a compelling narrative about why the student should be admitted. Narrative dynamics like these—the crafting of arguments for and against specific courses of action—are hardly limited to admissions decision making. For all the attention that evaluation criteria and processes deserve, these facets of decision making must be judged in part by the outcomes of such efforts as the research in the next section suggests.

Outcomes of Admissions Decisions: Access and Exclusion

As the previous two sections highlight, criteria, people, and processes intertwine to determine how the outcomes of admissions articulate equitable access (or not) for historically minoritized groups (Bastedo & Jaquette, 2011; Park & Liu, 2014; Redding, 2013; Smith, 2008; Sorey & Duggan, 2008).[5] There are real equity challenges for gatekeeping professionals in higher education who strive to balance limited resources and slots with the ideal of transparent evaluations of student potential that broaden access to systematically excluded groups. In many places, these practical challenges of equitable admissions decisions are framed by the overarching policy context—such as that which surrounds race-conscious admissions and affirmative action. Such policy indirectly affects the outcomes by affecting decision-making work (Caldwell, Shapiro, & Gross, 2007; Garces, 2014; Moses & Chang, 2006; Posselt, 2014). New developments in holistic review and contextualized admissions at both the undergraduate and graduate level appear to offer one strategy for managing these tensions.

HIRING FACULTY

Faculty hiring is generally decentralized, with autonomy residing at the departmental level or sometimes the school/college. A search committee holds the power to rank candidates and ultimately nominate most faculty who are eventually hired, which allows for a small group of individuals to have say over which applicants make it past each round. There is also variation in how hiring decisions are made based on institution type that will not be discussed in detail in this chapter (Lee & Chun, 2014). Rather, to illustrate the relevance of our framework in this context, we discuss how the literature on faculty hiring[6] highlights equity threats and opportunities with respect to criteria, processes, and outcomes.

Hiring Criteria

Selection and evaluation of faculty candidates often results in a debate amongst committee members based upon abstract conceptions of fit, merit, and other ideas about what a professor should do or be. The debates begin even before deliberations take place; they emerge when crafting the job announcement. This important step in the process of hiring can lead to debate because language in the posting represents the consensus view of the skills and competencies needed for the position (Smith, 2009). Insofar as there are divergent views about the role of a professor, the relevance of different types of work, and the intellectual focus that a position should fill, the job announcement becomes the place for defining criteria of who will be judged qualified or an excellent fit.

However, job announcements vary in scope and depth, and some specifically outline desired characteristics and qualifications while others may simply post a generic template about the institution and the title of the role being filled. In a study that evaluated nearly 700 job descriptions, Smith and colleagues (Smith, Turner, Osei-Kofi, & Richards, 2004; Smith, 2009) found that many job descriptions were seemingly decades out of date except for a certain few that incorporated global or technological priorities. To diversify the faculty, Smith and colleagues suggest that drafting the job description must be one of the central elements of the hiring process in which the job description is linked to institutional priorities such as diversity or equity.

Similar to the admissions process, faculty hiring criteria typically include a few standard boxes that are seen as standard to check, with some variation in expectations by hiring for junior, mid-career, and senior positions: a *curriculum vitae* should list several publications, experience teaching and designing courses, and service work to the profession and institutional community. Evaluation of service is one area in which implicit social biases are revealed: qualifications of applicants from minoritized groups are often over-scrutinized and undervalued. For example, the contributions made by racially minoritized faculty to institutional diversity initiatives are often assumed to occur at the expense of scholarly excellence (Sensoy & DiAngelo, 2017), while the same lines on a CV of a white male applicant are highly sought-after signs of engagement across diversity (Smith, Wolf, Busenberg, et al., 1996).

Research also indicates that academic elitism plays a role in the hiring of faculty. Judgments of talent and brilliance, for example, tend to inform how faculty think when looking for new colleagues, but are part of the unspoken evaluative culture rather than the structure of the job description (Lamont, 2009). And some committees use the prestige of candidates' institutional affiliations as a signal of the person's excellence (a phenomenon known as the halo effect). This practice disadvantages candidates from backgrounds that are underrepresented in the professoriate, who have been less likely to have access to elite higher education at both the undergraduate and graduate levels (Bastedo & Jaquette, 2011; Bielby et al., 2014; Posselt et al., 2012; Smith, 2009). In summary, as in admissions, traditional expectations used to judge applicant merit, excellence, and fit threaten the racial equity of hiring outcomes. Campuses can remedy these issues by focusing their efforts on aligning the job description with diversity and inclusion initiatives, defining in advance (and sticking to) criteria that will not systematically disadvantage already minoritized groups, and being explicit about prioritizing candidates with the capacity and desire to improve equity.

Processes in Faculty Hiring

The decentralized nature of the entire process and the autonomy of most search committees allows for these few faculty to have an oversized say in what qualities, skills, or competencies are deemed ideal for the position; these elements also create opacity in the process as a whole. Few topics in higher education have been more difficult to study through ethnographic or observational data collection than hiring faculty and upper-level administrators, because deliberations take place behind a veil of secrecy. Beyond the job description and setting the criteria for candidates, decisions typically come down to deliberations made by the committee after application periods have closed, additional deliberations following interviews, and finally, confirmation of recommended hires by a dean. However, the autonomy held by the committee from definition of the announcement through making a recommendation to hire suggests that the committee composition merits attention as a matter of equity. This is especially important given the evidence of homophily (i.e. preference for people like oneself) in elite hiring (Rivera, 2017). Despite the democratic process enabled by its inherent design of decision by committee, those committees will continue to reproduce the same outcomes search after search if they do not act with a willingness to advance equity and disrupt outdated notions of excellence that are predicated on unequal educational systems (Sensoy & DiAngelo, 2017).

Within faculty hiring, the process and power to make decisions may reside in the hands of many different stakeholders, not just in the hands of the committee members. Most cast the autonomous search committee as the ultimate wielder of power (Kayes, 2006; Sensoy & DiAngelo, 2017; Turner, 2002); however, administrators such as deans

(Kezar & Gehrke, 2016) and trustees (Ehrenberg, Jakubson, Martin, Main, & Eisenberg, 2012) paired with cultural and institutionalized processes (Blankenship-Knox, Platt, & Read, 2017; Freeman & DiRamio, 2016; Kezar & Gehrke, 2016; Twombly, 2005; Uzuner-Smith & Englander, 2015) also contribute to faculty hiring decisions. This lack of consensus on where decision making happens in faculty hiring is attributed to the fact that varying institutional types, with differing governing processes, are represented in the faculty hiring literature.

Biases in the Search Process

Search committee deliberations are not immune from the institutional, cultural, and discipline-specific biases that tacitly govern faculty ways of thinking. Empirical research on the search committee process highlights specific biases and threats to equity across both racialized and gendered lines. Freeman and DiRamio (2016) uncovered that PhD programs were most attracted to candidates who were graduates of other elite doctoral programs because of structural similarities across programs. Candidates that came from institutions with similar organizational cultures were sought after because expectations in networking, publishing, and mentoring students were believed to be the same. Socialization promoting the notion that top-ranked programs were the best places to recruit incoming faculty informed their decision-making process at the expense of considering candidates that went to less prestigious institutions but may have had better qualifications or different strengths overlooked by elite institutions.

The literature also shows that biases are present in committee deliberations regarding the gendered expectations of personal heterosexual relationships (Rivera, 2017) and notions of "fit" (Twombly, 2005). Committee members in one study excluded women applicants from moving on to the next round by assuming that their partners were in high-status positions that were fixed to a location. In another study, community college faculty search committees made decisions based on personal and institutional values, which are often formalized through a campus mission, but also operate as part of the unspoken rules of the organization's culture. For instance, committees placed emphasis on teaching experience and perceived notions of how candidates would "fit" with the campus culture as the qualifying factors (Twombly, 2005).

To lessen the impact of these biases and assumptions held by search committee members, some scholars argue that champions of equity are needed in search committees to serve as watchdogs and advocates for hiring diverse applicants (Smith, 2009; Smith et al., 1996). Others, however, question the wisdom of this approach, either because it appears to absolve the entire committee of attending to equity implications or because the power dynamics were more complicated than what a single advocate could handle. At one campus that was intentional about training advocates of equity to serve on search committees, the intersectional relations of power, race, gender, tenure, and discipline together shaped how these advocates were able to negotiate and resist biases in hiring (Liera, 2018). Conversations about hiring decisions were often dominated by what Liera (2018) referred to as a "bro code" that protected the status quo. Though the composition of the committee was made intentionally with regards to having trained advocates of racial equity on board, because the advocates were women or women of color, their perspectives were often dismissed when shared.

Amid ambiguity of both processes and criteria, the divergent faculty cultures valued within the academy are allowed to collide with the biases and expectations committee members hold around presupposed notions of merit (Kayes, 2006) and fit (Twombly, 2005) as well as other expectations with regards to gender and relationship status (Rivera, 2017). This ambiguity makes it challenging for hiring committee chairs to articulate their expectations, much less enact equitable processes for evaluating candidates (Blankenship-Knox et al., 2017; Cipriano & Buller, 2012) and checking colleagues on misperceptions and biases. There are opportunities to work toward equity, however, through such methods as training for *all* committee members to be advocates for racial, gender, and other forms of equity. Indeed, professional development for faculty is becoming increasingly common as an expectation of serving on faculty search committees.

Outcomes in Hiring Decisions

As indicated in the previous two sections, the combination of opaque hiring criteria along with imbalanced committee composition and bias in their deliberations combine to create conditions that may threaten the equity of outcomes. Regardless of institution type, there are many contextual factors at play when hiring decisions are ultimately made. Influences from organizational culture, prestige of graduate training, power dynamics with regards to gender, race, tenure, and department have the power to shape where and when key decisions are made. The challenges to equity may be kept in check with mindfulness and intentionality at each step of the process: actively revising job announcements to define diversity and equity-mindedness as desired qualities, ensuring that search committees represent a diverse set of voices and are adequately trained to advocate for equity, seeking both potential and achievements to date, and working to identify and disrupt biases and assumptions about minoritized candidates (Smith, 2009; Smith et al., 2004; Sensoy & DiAngelo, 2017; Kayes, 2006).

CONCLUSION: RECOMMENDATIONS FOR MANAGING OPPORTUNITIES AND THREATS TO EQUITY

1. Attend to Your Multiple Contexts

In both individual and collective types of decision making, it is important to know your organizations' (e.g. department/unit, school/college, university, discipline) histories and missions, which can shape the evaluation criteria as well as how stakeholders judge the process and outcome of a given decision. Yet, as Figure 3.1 demonstrates, institutional context is just one of the multiple contexts that matter. Equity opportunities and threats are present for individuals, committees, organizations, and institutions alike. And administrators should be mindful of the systemic nature of inequities, accounting for interactions across contexts. When engaged in leading a decision-making process or making everyday decisions, recognizing how alternatives are likely to affect specific individuals involved, specific units, and/or the institution in general can clarify how our thoughts and actions are working for or against equity.

The norms and values of a given decision-making context matter much for the potential to compromise or encourage equity. Democratic and cultural views reveal this most clearly, whereas individual-level perspectives seek commonalities across contexts. As we become more mindful of the contexts in which we are making decisions—both the political, cultural, and interpersonal dynamics as well as the formal organizational context that defines the work to be done—we can imagine ways to work with the context's dynamics and priorities to achieve more just decisions and, thus, institutions.

2. Employ Comprehensive, Contextualized, and Systematic Holistic Review

Clearly, decision making is bound up with evaluation. One cannot make decisions without making evaluations based on particular criteria (whether they are consciously chosen or left implicit); and, therefore, both evaluation processes and criteria deserve administrators' attention as they relate to the outcomes of decisions. The judgment involved in organizational decisions typically results from the application of criteria to an evaluation situation. Rather than trying to eliminate subjectivity in evaluations, research shows the greater need is for practitioners to pay greater attention to the ways that equity is impacted by both the criteria in use and the application of such criteria to come to decisions. Holistic review of the options at hand offers one such strategy.

As introduced in the discussion of admissions above, holistic review has been advanced as a means of better evaluating and selecting prospective students. However, it can also be used in a wide range of personnel decisions, including hiring, promotions, committee appointments, awards, determinations of merit pay, and more. To improve on current approaches so that they better reflect and serve equity aims, Posselt and Miller (2018) proposed a model of holistic review with three elements. Review should be *comprehensive* in the qualities of applicants that it takes into account and the types of information (e.g. parts of an application like metrics, letters of recommendation, writing samples) that it uses to infer those qualities. Decision-makers should be mindful not only of an individual's achievements to date (which can reflect unequal opportunities), but also their potential for future contributions. For hiring, this is where decision-makers' ability to approve the position description can have a transformational role.[7] To assess potential, practitioners should take into account a wide range of characteristics, including socio-emotional or non-cognitive skills (e.g. creativity, leadership, persistence, preference for long-term goals). Holistic review should also *contextualize* achievements according to student and personnel opportunities, which differ markedly by race/ethnicity, gender, and socioeconomic status, among other identities. Further, when considering metrics (e.g. impact factor and teaching evaluation scores when looking at faculty performance or test scores and grades when looking at student performance), decision-makers should recognize every metric is a statistic, that every statistic contains error, and therefore that no statistic is suitable as a sole criterion for evaluation or selection. Rather, in a holistic process, reviewers should contextualize metrics according to their statistical error, limits in predicting future success, and differential distributions in the population by race, gender, class, and the like. Finally, holistic review must be *systematic* to increase efficiency, mitigate bias, and improve consistency, transparency, and accountability. To this end, they recommend the development and use of evaluation protocols or rubrics to guide decision-makers in defining shared criteria on which everyone will be assessed (and that collectively will reflect a commitment to obtaining equitable outcomes), and then providing training and practice with the rubric before setting individuals to work reviewing files.

3. Routinize Equity Checks at Each Point of the Process

Attention to equity and justice—through mindfulness and formal equity and bias checks—is needed at all stages of the decision-making process. In enrollment management and human relations decisions such as those emphasized in this chapter, we need to take into account the ways that outreach activities shape the pool of who is available for evaluation and selection, and how the quality of our recruitment efforts enable us to attract the candidates who are selected. Equity checks at each stage of the process will render more just decisions by putting data in the hands of decision-makers.

In extended and committee-based decision-making processes, such as searches, another type of equity check may focus on the qualities of interactions among those participating in the process. A more robust, honest climate is created when leaders create occasional opportunities for individuals to share whether they feel free to express their opinion and whether the climate of the group is hospitable to discussion and respectful disagreement. This point is closely related to our next, and final, recommendation.

4. Attend to the Intersectional Positionalities of Those With Decision-Making Power

Recognizing how different decisions privilege individuals and groups is an important step for improving the practice of making decisions. Positionality, defined as one's formal position in a social system, as informed by all identities they have available to enact their agency (Battilana, 2006), shapes how individuals engage in decision making. For example, when a student serves on a committee composed of faculty and administrators, the committee chair should take steps to ensure that the student has the means to express their opinions. Otherwise, the power dynamics of this scenario may practically silence the student whose presence on the committee is to provide a voice for students. Both leaders and members of groups making decisions can act in ways that protect the voices of those who are participating in the process.

Decision-makers, too, have identities that affect the equity of outcomes. We are all likely to have subtle, implicit biases for individuals or decision alternatives, and depending upon our positionality, we may be more or less able to advocate for equity in group decision-making contexts. In situations where decisions are being made by individuals or by groups, mindfulness about one's own positionality and individual preferences is an important precursor to making decisions with wisdom—that is, with attentiveness to collective interests and multiple factors. For individuals tasked with making or facilitating decisions, it is important to check in with people from diverse backgrounds as you construct the process and weigh alternatives. In higher education, we must have the vision to see how each person's multiple identities position them in distinctive ways with respect to power, agency, and voice—and, in response, create opportunities to share decision-making power with racially minoritized and other marginalized groups.

CONCLUSION

There is no debating it: Good decision making can be difficult, even emotional for the people involved. However, literature and experience provide many lessons to improve this important facet of administrative work—to use decision making as the powerful lever it is in making our organizations more just and equitable. Some decisions, like budgeting, hiring, and admissions, take place through bureaucratic, formal processes that are frequently and widely used. Others, such as making committee assignments or deciding if and when to schedule recurring meetings, happen every day without systems yet require judgment just as much as the official processes. In both cases, we hope to have shown in this chapter that making decisions more equitable means being mindful about your own criteria for what constitutes good; managing the process with an eye to collective interests and equitable outcomes; building one's own skills as a leader in listening, evaluating, facilitating, and negotiating; supporting your colleagues' development in evaluation and selection through professional development; and demonstrating the courage to interrupt biases, both our own and those of the people around us—even when the other people are more powerful. As we attend to context, evaluate holistically, routinize equity checks, and pay attention to power and positionality, we make space for equity—both in and through our decisions.

QUESTIONS FOR REFLECTION AND DISCUSSION

1. Identify an area in which you regularly make decisions, whether it is once a day or once a year. Then identify an outcome that would contribute to equity.

2. Now, apply the framework in Figure 3.1 to that decision to identify relevant criteria, process, as well as contexts, that may affect whether the outcome of your decision contributes to equity.

3. What barriers do you face in enacting criteria and/or processes that would produce more equitable outcomes? What resources would enable you to address, and perhaps overcome, these barriers? Who can support you in obtaining these resources?

NOTES

1   In both of these contexts, importantly, decisions are made by selecting from a pool; therefore, recruitment matters much to the nature of the pool, evaluation criteria, and selection activities in which individuals and committees engage.

2   We conducted a targeted search for literature on undergraduate and graduate/professional admissions within the Proquest ERIC database, limited to English language, peer reviewed journal articles and the following search terms: "undergraduate admissions," "college admissions," "graduate admissions," "doctoral admissions," "masters admissions," "professional school admissions," "law school admissions," "medical school admissions," and "business school admissions." These searches turned up 3,387 overlapping results. Duplicates were removed. We reviewed titles and abstracts to ensure a focus on admissions in the United States, yielding 285 articles. The literature roughly fell into three areas, though not mutually exclusive: admissions criteria and efficacy for these items to predict academic performance; the ways admissions processes are carried out; and the impacts of enacting varying academic missions through criteria evaluation.

3   In a study of medical students, MCAT predicted first-year success in clerkships of White students but did not predict performance of racially minoritized students (White, Dey, & Fantone, 2009). In another professional school setting, the GMAT was found to be a good predictor of GPA in business and management programs, especially for non-US students (Koys, 2005; Sireci & Talento-Miller, 2006). Although the test also differentially and negatively predicted success for women and racially minoritized students (Hedlund, Wilt, Nebel, Ashford, & Sternberg, 2006). These results combined show that while standardized tests offer some degree of correlation with academic success for some students, they may not add much and over-reliance on them can have detrimental impact on access for marginalized groups of students (Smith & Garrison, 2005).

4   For studies of grades' differential validity in predicting future success, see Culpepper & Davenport, 2009; Halberstam & Redstone, 2005; Lanham, Schauer, & Osho, 2011; White et al., 2009. It was the best predictor of graduation at HBCUs in one study (Lanham et al., 2011), but another study found its predictive power decreases as average SAT and selectivity at an institution increases (Kobrin & Patterson, 2011; Sawyer, 2013).

5   The literature pays less attention to other marginalized populations such as undocumented, LGBTQ, and Muslim students (Gildersleeve, 2010; Marine, 2017; Stegmeir, 2017).

6   We conducted a targeted search of the literature on faculty hiring through the ProQuest ERIC database with the search terms "faculty hiring." The parameters were limited to a single search term given the dearth of literature on the topic. Limiting the results to peer reviewed journal articles yielded 58 results. Forty-four articles adequately represented our conditions; that is, they consisted of empirical evaluations of the faculty

hiring process, and represented various theoretical or conceptual approaches to diversifying faculty hiring. Though limited in number, these articles provided various access points to the study of faculty hiring decision processes from search committees, to organizational structures, to institutionalized values, to various cultures of the academy.

7 We thank Vasti Torres for this insight.

BIBLIOGRAPHY

Bargh, J. A., & Chartrand, T. L. (1999). The unbearable automaticity of being. *The American Psychologist, 54*(7), 462–479.

Basco, W. T., Lancaster, C. J., Gilbert, G. E., Carey, M. E., & Blue, A. V. (2008). Medical school application interview score has limited predictive validity for performance on a fourth year clinical practice examination. *Advances in Health Sciences Education, 13*(2), 151–162.

Bastedo, M. N., & Bowman, N. A. (2017). Improving admission of low-SES students at selective colleges: Results from an experimental simulation. *Educational Researcher, 46*(2), 67–77.

Bastedo, M., Bowman, N., Glasener, K., & Kelly, J. (2018). What are we talking about when we talk about holistic review? Selective college admissions and its effects on low-SES students. *The Journal of Higher Education, 89*(5), 782–805. https://doi.org/10.1080/00221546.2018.1442633

Bastedo, M. N., & Jaquette, O. (2011). Running in place: Low-income students and the dynamics of higher education stratification. *Educational Evaluation and Policy Analysis, 33*(3), 318–339. https://doi.org/10.3102/0162373711406718

Battilana, J. (2006). Agency and institutions: The enabling role of individuals' social position. *Organization, 13*(5), 653–676.

Bertrand, M., & Mullainathan, S. (2004). Are Emily and Greg more employable than Lakisha and Jamal? A field experiment on labor market discrimination. *American Economic Review, 94*(4), 991–1013.

Bielby, R., Posselt, J. R., Jaquette, O., & Bastedo, M. N. (2014). Why are women underrepresented in elite colleges and universities? A non-linear decomposition analysis. *Research in Higher Education, 55*(8), 735–760. https://doi.org/10.1007/s11162-014-9334-y

Blankenship-Knox, A. E., Platt, E. R., & Read, H. (2017). Rewarding collegiality: The use of collegiality as a factor in faculty evaluation and employment decisions. *Journal of Faculty Development, 31*(2), 37–42.

Bowman, N. A., & Bastedo, M. N. (2018). What role may admissions office diversity and practices play in equitable decisions? *Research in Higher Education, 59*(4), 430–447.

Briihl, D., & Wasieleski, D. (2004). A survey of Master's-level psychology programs: Admissions criteria and program policies. *Teaching of Psychology, 31*(4), 252–256. https://doi.org/10.1207/s15328023top3104_5

Caldwell, C., Shapiro, J. P., & Gross, S. J. (2007). Ethical leadership in higher education admission: Equality vs. equity. *Journal of College Admission, 195*, 14–19.

Christensen, M., Lykkegaard, E., Lund, O., & O'Neill, L. (2018). Qualitative analysis of MMI raters' scorings of medical school candidates: A matter of taste? *Advances in Health Sciences Education, 23*(2), 289–310. https://doi.org/10.1007/s10459-017-9794-x

Christensen, D., Nance, W., & White, D. (2012). Academic performance in MBA programs: Do prerequisites really matter? *Journal of Education for Business, 87*(1), 42–47. https://doi.org/10.1080/08832323.2011.555790

Cipriano, R. E., & Buller, J. L. (2012). Rating faculty collegiality. *Change: The Magazine of Higher Learning, 44*(2), 45–48.

Corbally, J. E., & Sergiovanni, T. J. (Eds.) (1986). *Leadership and Organizational Culture: New Perspectives on Administrative Theory and Practice.* Oxford, IL: University of Illinois Press.

Culpepper, S. A., & Davenport, E. C. (2009). Assessing differential prediction of college grades by race/ethnicity with a multilevel model. *Journal of Educational Measurement, 46*(2), 220–242.

Ehrenberg, R. G., Jakubson, G. H., Martin, M. L., Main, J. B., & Eisenberg, T. (2012). Diversifying the faculty across gender lines: Do trustees and administrators matter? *Economics of Education Review, 31*(1), 9–18.

Freeman, S., & DiRamio, D. (2016). Elitism or pragmatism? Faculty hiring at top graduate programs in higher education administration. *The Journal of the Professoriate* (Winter), 94–127.

Garces, L. M. (2014). Aligning diversity, quality, and equity: The implications of legal and public policy developments for promoting racial diversity in graduate studies. *American Journal of Education, 120*(4), 457–480.

Gasman, M., Kim, J., & Nguyen, T.-H. (2011). Effectively recruiting faculty of color at highly selective institutions: A school of education case study. *Journal of Diversity in Higher Education, 4*(4), 212–222.

Gildersleeve, R. E. (2010). Access between and beyond borders. *Journal of College Admission,* 206, 3–10.

Halberstam, B., & Redstone, F. (2005). The predictive value of admissions materials on objective and subjective measures of graduate school performance in speech-language pathology. *Journal of Higher Education Policy and Management, 27*(2), 261–272. https://doi.org/10.1080/13600800500120183

Hedlund, J., Wilt, J., Nebel, K., Ashford, S., & Sternberg, R. (2006). Assessing practical intelligence in business school admissions: A supplement to the Graduate Management Admissions Test. *Learning and Individual Differences, 16*(2), 101–127. https://doi.org/10.1016/j.lindif.2005.07.005

Hodum, R. L., & James, G. W. (2010). An observation of normative structure for college admission and recruitment officers. *The Journal of Higher Education, 81*(3), 317–338.

Johnston, P. C., Schimmel, T., & O'Hara, H. (2012). Revisiting the AAUP recommendation: The viability of collegiality as a fourth criterion for university faculty evaluation. *College Quarterly, 15*(1), n1.

Kahneman, D., & Egan, P. (2011). *Thinking, fast and slow* (Vol. 1). New York: Farrar, Straus and Giroux.

Kayes, P. E. (2006). New paradigms for diversifying faculty and staff in higher education: Uncovering cultural biases in the search and hiring process. *Multicultural Education, 14*(2), 65–69.

Kezar, A., & Gehrke, S. (2016). Faculty composition in four-year institutions: The role of pressures, values, and organizational processes in academic decision-making. *The Journal of Higher Education, 87*(3), 390–419.

Kobrin, J., & Patterson, B. (2011). Contextual factors associated with the validity of SAT Scores and high school GPA for predicting first-year college grades. *Educational Assessment, 16*(4), 207–226. https://doi.org/10.1080/10627197.2011.635956

Koys, D. J. (2005). The validity of the Graduate Management Admissions Test for non-US students. *Journal of Education for Business, 80*(4), 236–239. https://doi.org/10.3200/JOEB.80.4.236-239

Kuncel, N. R., & Hezlett, S. A. (2007). Standardized tests predict graduate students' success. *Science, 315*(5815), 1080–1081.

Kyllonen, P., Walters, A. M., & Kaufman, J. C. (2005). Noncognitive constructs and their assessment in graduate education: A review. *Educational Assessment, 10*(3), 153–184.

Lamont, M. (2009). *How Professors Think: Inside the Curious World of Academic Judgment.* Cambridge, MA: Harvard University Press.

Lanham, B. D., Schauer, E. J., & Osho, G. S. (2011). A comprehensive analysis of the efficacy of non-cognitive measures: Predicting academic success in a historically Black university in south Texas. *Journal of College Teaching & Learning, 8*(4), 43–51. https://doi.org/10.19030/tlc.v8i4.4193

Lee, C. D., & Chun, E. (2014). *Search Committees: A Comprehensive Guide to Successful Faculty, Staff, and Administrative Searches* (2nd edition). Sterling, VA: Stylus Publishing.

Liera, R. (2018). *Faculty learning and agency for racial equity (Doctoral dissertation).* University of Southern California.

Littleford, L., Buxton, K., Bucher, M., Simon-Dack, S., & Yang, K. (2018). Psychology doctoral program admissions: What Master's and undergraduate-level students need to know. *Teaching of Psychology, 45*(1), 75–83. https://doi.org/10.1177/0098628317745453

Ma, C., Harris, P., Cole, A., Jones, P., & Shulruf, B. (2016). Selection into medicine using interviews and other measures: Much remains to be learned. *Issues in Educational Research, 26*(4), 623.

MacNell, L., Driscoll, A., & Hunt, A. N. (2015). What's in a name: Exposing gender bias in student ratings of teaching. *Innovative Higher Education, 40*(4), 291–303.

March, J. G. (1994). *Primer on Decision Making: How Decisions Happen.* New York: Simon and Schuster.

Marine, S. B. (2017). Changing the frame: Queering access to higher education for trans* students. *International Journal of Qualitative Studies in Education, 30*(3), 217–233.

Mattern, K., & Patterson, B. (2013). Test of slope and intercept bias in college admissions: A response to Aguinis, Culpepper, and Pierce (2010). *Journal of Applied Psychology, 98*(1), 134–147. https://doi.org/10.1037/a0030610

Mattern, K., Shaw, E., & Kobrin, J. (2011). An alternative presentation of incremental validity: Discrepant SAT and HSGPA performance. *Educational and Psychological Measurement, 71*(4), 638–662. https://doi.org/10.1177/0013164410383563

McDonough, P., & Robertson, L. (2012). Gatekeepers or marketers: Reclaiming the educational role of chief admission officers. *Journal of College Admission, 214*, 92–100.

Milkman, K. L., Akinola, M., & Chugh, D. (2015). What happens before? A field experiment exploring how pay and representation differentially shape bias on the pathway into organizations. *The Journal of Applied Psychology, 100*(6), 1678–1712.

Miller, C., & Stassun, K. (2014). A test that fails. *Nature, 510*(7504), 303–304. https://doi.org/10.1038/nj7504-303a

Miller, C., Zwickl, B., Posselt, J., & Hodapp, T. (in press). Typical PhD admissions criteria exclude women and minorities but fail to predict doctoral completion. *Science Advances.*

Moore, D. A., Swift, S. A., Sharek, Z. S., & Gino, F. (2010). Correspondence bias in performance evaluation: Why grade inflation works. *Personality and Social Psychology Bulletin, 36*(6), 843–852.

Moses, M. S., & Chang, M. J. (2006). Toward a deeper understanding of the diversity rationale. *Educational Researcher, 35*(1), 6–11.

Moss-Racusin, C. (2012). Are science faculty biased against female students? Society of Personality and Social Psychology Connections. Retrieved from https://spsptalks.wordpress.com/2012/09/21/are-science-faculty-biased-against-female-students/

Mountford, M., Ehlert, M., Machell, J., & Cockrell, D. (2007). Traditional and personal admissions criteria: Predicting candidate performance in US educational leadership programmes. *International Journal of Leadership in Education, 10*(2), 191–210. https://doi.org/10.1080/13603120600935696

Murphy, S., Klieger, D., Borneman, M., & Kuncel, N. (2009). The predictive power of personal statements in admissions: A meta-analysis and cautionary tale. *College and University, 84*(4), 83–86.

Oliver, T., Hecker, K., Hausdorf, P. A., & Conlon, P. (2014). Validating MMI scores: Are we measuring multiple attributes? *Advances in Health Sciences Education, 19*(3), 379–392.

Oropeza, E., & Fujimoto, E. O. (2012). Hiring diverse faculty members in community colleges: A case study in ethical decision making. *Community College Review, 40*(3), 255–274.

Park, J. J., & Liu, A. (2014). Interest convergence or divergence? A critical race analysis of Asian Americans, meritocracy, and critical mass in the affirmative action debate. *The Journal of Higher Education, 85*(1), 36–64.

Phillips, R. (2002). Recruiting and retaining a diverse faculty. *Planning for Higher Education, 69*, 32–39.

Posselt, J. R. (2014). Toward inclusive excellence in U.S. graduate education: Constructing merit and diversity in PhD admissions. *American Journal of Education, 120*(4), 481–514.

Posselt, J. R. (2015). Disciplinary logics in doctoral admissions: Understanding patterns of faculty evaluation. *Journal of Higher Education, 86*(6), 807–833. https://doi.org/10.1353/jhe.2015.0030

Posselt, J. R. (2016). *Inside Graduate Admissions: Merit, Diversity, and Faculty Gatekeeping.* Cambridge, MA: Harvard University Press.

Posselt, J. R., Jaquette, O., Bielby, R., & Bastedo, M. N. (2012). Access without equity: Longitudinal analyses of institutional stratification by race and ethnicity, 1972–2004. *American Educational Research Journal, 49*(6), 1074–1111. https://doi.org/10.3102/0002831212439456

Posselt, J. R., & Miller, C. W. (May 2018). It's time for the talk. *Inside Higher Ed.* Retrieved from www.insidehighered.com/admissions/views/2018/05/07/doctoral-programs-need-rethink-their-use-standardized-tests-opinion

Potvin, G., Chari, D., & Hodapp, T. (2017). Investigating approaches to diversity in a national survey of physics doctoral degree programs: The graduate admissions landscape. *Physical Review Physics Education Research, 13*(2), 020142-1–020142-13. https://doi.org/10.1103/PhysRevPhysEducRes.13.020142

Redding, A. B. (2013). Supporting international applicants and promoting an ethical model of global college admission. *Journal of College Admission, 219*, 8–15.

Rivera, L. A. (2017). When two bodies are (not) a problem: Gender and relationship status discrimination in academic hiring. *American Sociological Review, 82*(6), 1111–1138.

Roberts, S. G., & Verhoef, T. (2016). Double-blind reviewing at EvoLang 11 reveals gender bias. *Journal of Language Evolution, 1*(2), 163–167.

Sawyer, R. (2013). Beyond correlations: Usefulness of high school GPA and test scores in making college admissions decisions. *Applied Measurement in Education, 26*(2), 89–112. https://doi.org/10.1080/08957347.2013.765433

Schein, E. H. (2010). *Organizational Culture and Leadership* (Vol. 2). San Francisco, CA: John Wiley & Sons.

Sedlacek, W. E. (2004). *Beyond the Big Test: Noncognitive Assessment in Higher Education*. Indianapolis, IN: Jossey-Bass.

Sensoy, O., & DiAngelo, R. (2017). "We are all for diversity, but...": How faculty hiring committees reproduce Whiteness and practical suggestions for how they can change. *Harvard Educational Review, 87*(4), 557–581.

Shivpuri, S., Schmitt, N., Oswald, F., & Kim, B. (2006). Individual differences in academic growth: Do they exist, and can we predict them? *Journal of College Student Development, 47*(1), 69–86. https://doi.org/10.1353/csd.2006.0013

Sinha, R., Oswald, F., Imus, A., & Schmitt, N. (2011). Criterion-focused approach to reducing adverse impact in college admissions. *Applied Measurement in Education, 24*(2), 137–161. https://doi.org/10.1080/08957347.2011.554605

Sireci, S., & Talento-Miller, E. (2006). Evaluating the predictive validity of Graduate Management Admission Test scores. *Educational and Psychological Measurement, 66*(2), 305–317. https://doi.org/10.1177/0013164405282455

Smith, D. G. (2009). *Diversity's Promise for Higher Education: Making It Work*. Baltimore, MD: Johns Hopkins University Press.

Smith, D. G., & Garrison, G. (2005). The impending loss of talent: An exploratory study challenging assumptions about testing and merit. *Teachers College Record, 107*(4), 629–653.

Smith, D. G., Turner, C. S. V., Osei-Kofi, N., & Richards, S. (2004). Interrupting the usual: Successful strategies for hiring diverse faculty. *The Journal of Higher Education, 75*(2), 133–160.

Smith, D. G., Wolf, L.E., Busenberg, B., & associates (1996). *Achieving Faculty Diversity: Debunking the Myths*. Washington, DC: Association of American Colleges and Universities.

Smith, M. J. (2008). Four steps to a paradigm shift: Employing critical perspectives to improve outreach to low-SES African-American and Latino students and their parents. *Journal of College Admission*, (201), 17–23. Retrieved from http://search.proquest.com/docview/219164492/

Sommerfeld, A. (2011). Recasting non-cognitive factors in college readiness as what they truly are: Non-academic factors. *Journal of College Admission, 213*, 18–22.

Sorey, K., & Duggan, M. H. (2008). Homeschoolers entering community colleges: Perceptions of admission officers. *Journal of College Admission, 200*, 22–28.

Stegmeir, M. (2017). Muslims on campus: College-bound students, schools contend with rising intolerance. *Journal of College Admission, 237*, 34–39.

Stemler, S. E. (2012). What should university admissions tests predict? *Educational Psychologist, 47*(1), 5–17.

Stevens, M. (2007). *Creating a Class College Admissions and the Education of Elites*. Cambridge, MA: Harvard University Press.

Thomas, L., Kuncel, N., & Crede, M. (2007). Noncognitive variables in college admissions: The case of the non-cognitive questionnaire. *Educational and Psychological Measurement, 67*(4), 635–657. https://doi.org/10.1177/0013164406292074

Tierney, W. G. (2008). *The Impact of Culture on Organizational Decision-Making: Theory and Practice in Higher Education*. Sterling, VA: Stylus Publishing, LLC.

Tuitt, F. A., Sagaria, M. A. D., & Turner, C. S. V. (2007). Signals and strategies in hiring faculty of color. *Higher Education: Handbook of Theory and Research, XXII*, 497–535.

Turner, C. S. V. (2002). *Diversifying the Faculty: A Guidebook for Search Committees*. Washington, DC: Association of American Colleges and Universities.

Tversky, A., & Kahneman, D. (1974). Judgment under uncertainty: Heuristics and biases. *Science, 185*, 1124–1131.

Twombly, S. B. (2005). Values, policies, and practices affecting the hiring process for full-time arts and sciences faculty in community colleges. *The Journal of Higher Education, 76*(4), 423–447.

Uzuner-Smith, S., & Englander, K. (2015). Exposing ideology within university policies: A critical discourse analysis of faculty hiring, promotion and remuneration practices. *Journal of Education Policy, 30*(1), 62–85.

White, C. B., Dey, E. L., & Fantone, J. C. (2009). Analysis of factors that predict clinical performance in medical school. *Advances in Health Sciences Education, 14*(4), 623–623. https://doi.org/10.1007/s10459-009-9189-8

4

ELEVATING EQUITY THROUGH A STRATEGIC FINANCE APPROACH

Empowerment as the Goal

CHRISTOPHER M. MULLIN

The acquisition and use of monetary resources by actors within institutions of higher education often follow an incremental path by simply continuing the arc of strategic support initially espoused; thereby reducing a sense of agency amongst institutional leaders. While this incremental approach to budgeting is critical to budgeting officers as it provides a continuity of practice that increases stability and reduces potential errors, it hinders strategic finance and reinforces existing power structures. The increasing awareness of the moral imperative to ensure institutions of higher education serve all students, not just some students, presents a paradigm shift in the historical funding frame focused on stability. Campus leadership is expected to respond to this equity-focused paradigm shift and this is requiring them to expand the knowledge, skills, and abilities of leaders throughout the institution. To that end, the purpose of this chapter is to empower mid-level administrators within an institution of higher education with the knowledge they need to inform and engage in budget development in socially conscious and just ways and more importantly in ways that lead to transformation. The chapter, written primarily for members of the campus community working in the areas of academic and student affairs, will engage readers by first reviewing what equity has traditionally meant in to budget officers and how it is conceived for this chapter, then by looking critically at institutional context, presents a framework to identify injustices and actions that can be taken to address them.

WHAT IS MEANT BY EQUITY?

In this book, and other publications like it, there are differing definitions of what "equity" means and the institutional policies and practices needed to realize it (Bensimon, 2017; Long, 2016). Ching (2017), for example, outlined nine different definitions of equity along a continuum. In higher education finance circles, the term "equity" is defined in the Integrated Postsecondary Education Data System (IPEDS) of the National Center for Education Statistics online glossary as "The excess of a private, for-profit institution's assets over its liabilities. It is the claim or stake of the owners." Other equity-based terms applied by the Office of Federal Student Aid (FSA) include "equity ratio," "equity strength factor score," "adjusted equity," "modified equity," and "equity weighted score" (FSA, 2016). For nonprofit and for-profit private institutions in particular, these uses of "equity" have bearing on their ability to participate in the federal student financial aid programs; the Pell Grant program, Direct Loan program and Campus-based Aid programs such as Work Study. While these definitions are in very tangible ways important terms of practice, they do not address injustices embedded in policy and practice.

For the purposes of this chapter, the last of nine definitions for equity provided in the online version of the Merriam-Webster dictionary is most applicable; as written equity is defined as "a body of legal doctrines and rules developed to enlarge, supplement, or override a narrow rigid system of law." I deconstruct and interpret this definition in the following manner to frame it within a higher education context. The sentence fragment "a body of legal doctrines and rules" refers to the policies and practices that govern an institution's practice. The next fragment "developed to enlarge, supplement, or override" is interpreted to mean that there are actions that can be taken within the institution to change policy and practice. And finally, the remaining fragment "a narrow rigid system of law" is understood to mean the systemic barriers in place that do not account for institutional context and population. So, the definition of equity can be reframed to apply to institutions of higher education as "the institutional policies and practices that can be changed to address systemic barriers that do not account for institutional context and population."

This chapter, therefore, focuses on actions that may be undertaken to align fiscal resources to an institutionally dependent version of equity. Institutional context is important because whether you are working at a tribal institution, a community college, a highly selective institution or a for-profit provider, the injustices will manifest themselves differently. You need to look at your institutional context critically, identify the injustices that exist, and take actions to rectify them. These three steps frame the chapter.

LOOKING CRITICALLY AT INSTITUTIONAL CONTEXT

In order to create an equity-focused budget, mid-level administrators need to be aware that their institution's budget consists of revenues and expenditures developed within a funding ecosystem and further how the strategic plan serves as a lever to drive funding decisions. This section examines both areas, providing foundational knowledge requisite to understand the funding ecosystem and how they are incorporated into an institution's strategic plan. Particularly it helps in understanding basic budget assumptions that can then be challenged.

UNDERSTANDING THE FUNDING ECOSYSTEM

Institutions of higher education, public and private, operate within a funding ecosystem (Figure 4.1) that is constantly changing. For example, in 2018 five of the top ten policy issues—sluggish state revenues, affordability, economic and workforce development, state responses to population shifts, and performance funding—were different than those of four years ago (Hurley, Harnish, & Parker, 2015; Harnish & Opalich, 2018). When policy issues shift, it signals that the level of intensity on various revenue sources and expenditures may change, and with it the focus on policies related

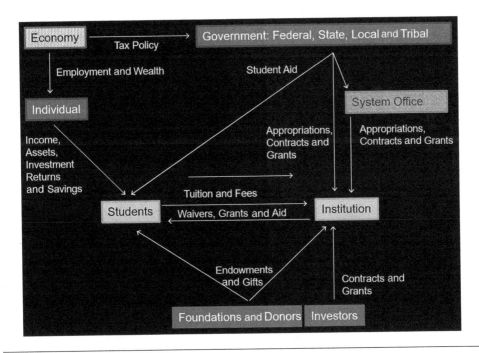

FIGURE 4.1   Funding Ecosystem
Note. For a more detailed understanding of the funding ecosystem, see McKeown-Moak & Mullin (2014).

to revenues or expenditures. So, for example, if governmental revenues decrease then there may be heightened attention to tax policy.

To justify the need for fiscal resources to state leaders, philanthropic entities, and alumni and federal agencies, institutional leadership teams—the president, boards of trustees and legislative affairs staff—must have a firm understanding not only of each source of institutional revenue within a funding ecosystem, but also the amount of money coming from each source as compared to competitors, the arguments for those investments, and the reasons why investments are not being made in an institution (Mullin, Baime, & Honeyman, 2015). And, once acquired, institutions work to allocate funding within their institutions within certain expenditure categories developed by accountants, and to withhold some amount when possible for times when revenue projections fall short of estimates. This section situates the reader within the institutional context by providing an overview of both institutional revenues and expenditures.

Revenue

Broadly speaking, the primary sources of revenue to an institution are derived from students, governments, and private sources (i.e. philanthropy/foundations and investors). The amount of money originating from each revenue source to an institution will vary, as in some cases a university may rely heavily on tuition and fee revenue whereas another university may rely more heavily on appropriations from a government. To engage in budgetary conversations, administrators must familiarize themselves with their institution's sources of revenues because it helps to identify where the power structures lie and which related institutional policies may be up for revision. In addition, an institution's mission helps to determine the revenue sources most important to them. Aside from the obvious recognition that private colleges do not receive direct appropriations from governments, mission also helps to understand why community colleges do not receive vast amounts of federal research dollars and similarly why a university does not receive a direct appropriation from local governments. To provide further clarity, Table 4.1 summarizes revenue sources for public and private four-year institutions and public community colleges. Among other facts, it shows public two-year colleges receive 66% of their revenue from governmental appropriations as compared to 0% for private universities.

Expenditures

A brief overview of expenditures is provided as background information to familiarize the reader with the types of expenditure categories common to higher education. In 2017, public institutions received $155.7 billion in support (Laderman & Carlson, 2018). These funds are expended and reported to the Integrated Postsecondary Education Data System of the United States Department of Education in ten expenditure categories—instruction, research, public service, academic support, student services, institutional support, auxiliary enterprises, net grant aid to students,

TABLE 4.1 Revenue Sources, by Sector: Fiscal Year 2015–16

Revenue Category	Sector		
	Two-year Public	Four-year Public	Four -year Private
Revenues			
Tuition and Fees	16%	22%	39%
Government Grants & Contracts	7%	14%	14%
Government Appropriations	66%	23%	0%
Private Funders	1%	3%	31%
Other Revenue*	11%	38%	31%
Total Funding	$55,526,641,091	$308,863,970,970	$181,732,428,343
Expenditures			
Instruction: Salaries & Wages	42%	28%	32%
Research	0%	12%	10%
Public Service	2%	5%	1%
Academic Support	9%	8%	8%
Student Services	11%	5%	8%
Institutional Support	17%	8%	13%
Aid to Students	10%	3%	9%
Auxiliary Enterprises	4%	10%	0%
Hospitals	0%	15%	11%
Independent Operations	0%	1%	3%
Other Expenditures	7%	5%	3%
Total Expenses	$53,491,616,000	$301,205,293,000	$187,837,897,503

Note. The "Other" category includes revenue from auxiliary enterprises such as hospitals, funding for buildings, returns from investments, and other services. Totals may not add to 100% due to rounding. (*)

Source. Author's analysis of Digest of Education Statistics webtables 333.10, 333.40, 334.10, and 334.30 available from https://nces.ed.gov/programs/digest/current_tables.asp

hospital services, and operations and maintenance of physical plant—applicable to all functions of the institution. Most notable are the expenditure categories that have a direct impact on learning. Coined "Education & Related" (E&R), these expenditure categories reflect spending on activities core to the academic function of the institution: instruction, student services, and a prorated share of expenditures on administration, operations and maintenance (Desrochers & Hurlburt, 2016). The average amount of E&R spent per full-time equivalent student varies by institution sector, from 75% at public community colleges to 43% at public research universities (due in part to research expenditures; Desrochers & Hurlburt, 2016).

Within each E&R category, a portion of funds are dedicated for salaries and fringe benefits (excluding health care, life insurance or retirement contribution) or to fulfill contracts with vendors for services. However, some percentage of funds is discretionary, meaning decisions on how to spend them are not predetermined and present an opportunity to advance and provide fiscal support of an equity agenda during the development of an institution's budget. To redirect these expenditures and realize an equity agenda, identifying the strategic direction guiding an institution must not only be understood by members of the leadership team, but by members of the campus community including professionals from academic and student affairs.

THE STRATEGIC PLAN

The next step to pursue an equity agenda is to familiarize yourself with and understand your institution's strategic plan. An institution's strategic plan serves as the decision framework against which operational decisions are rationalized and balanced. It guides monetary and non-monetary decisions made by institutional leaders. During its development, members of the Board of Regents (or Governors or Trustees) engage in focused conversations on institutional priorities. These resulting institutional priorities align with mission and vision statements, and at some point are connected to quantifiable outcomes that indicate progress toward the attainment of institutional priorities. Active engagement in this process gives you the opportunity to ensure an equity agenda is included as an institutional priority and measured accordingly.

Given the role it plays in key conversations amongst institutional leaders, gaining a firm understanding of an institution's strategic plan is *the* starting point for advocating and securing funds internally. It is this document that each argument, discussion and proposal should tie back into as it shows your support for not only the equity agenda you are advancing but how it benefits the strategic direction of the institution. Taking such an action allows you to have stronger footing for resource reallocations.

After reviewing your institution's strategic plan there are some key questions to ask to critically examine whether the institution is supporting an equity agenda. First, does the mission or vision statement use the generic term "student" or does it present an asset-based framing of students? For example, will the institution "teach students" or will it "engage and nurture the talent and abilities within each student"? Second, are there either strategic objectives or key initiatives that specifically focus on removing institutionally constructed structural barriers to best nurture the talent existing within faculty, staff and/or students?

In the event the strategic plan does not support an equity agenda, you must find a way to tie the equity agenda to the strategic plan in the short term, until it is next revised. This can be accomplished by creating key objectives to meet a strategic plan goal and proposing these key objectives at a formal meeting of the Board of Governors/Regents, by publishing your proposal in the school newspaper or other high-profile media outlets and/or by leveraging strategic allies.

A FRAMEWORK TO IDENTIFY INJUSTICES

One way to identify injustices is to reframe the concepts used to make budget decisions. This section presents a three-prong approach to examining return on investment

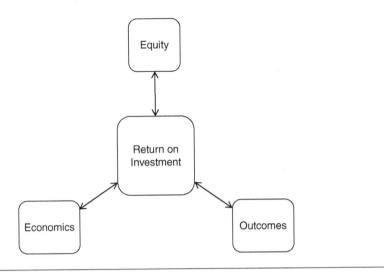

FIGURE 4.2 Equity-Infused Return on Investment Framework

(ROI) which includes equity in addition to economic and outcome measures (see Figure 4.2).

The reason why a ROI framework is proposed is that institutional Boards of Trustees/Governors/Regents who approve institutional budgets are often comprised of successful business people, who think in terms of measuring success. To them, a primary framework for understanding the impact of their own investments is through ROI. Historically, ROI is largely described and defined by economists who refer to the association between educational attainment and public and private benefits including but not limited to a higher likelihood of being employed, higher initial and lifetime earnings, having a job with fringe benefits, improved health, increased volunteering, a decreased need for public assistance, an increased likelihood of civic leadership, and an increased likelihood of contributions to charities (Association of Governing Boards, 2017; Carnevale, Jayasundera, & Gulish, 2016; Ma, Pender, & Welch, 2016). However, while these standard ROI data points focused on economics and outcomes are valuable to communicating the impact of education, when making institutional decisions the critical element of equity is often missing. This means one can have an increase in institutional economics and an increase in outcomes without acknowledging the impact on equity-focused populations of interest. For example, institutions with large endowments enroll small numbers of low-income students and in some cases, such as Harvard, make them engage in work study to earn financial aid that includes cleaning the dorms of fellow students (Bauer-Wolf, 2019). This is not acceptable.

To address this issue, Mullin (2018b) expanded the existing two-part ROI framework to include equity. The result is a three-prong approach to examining ROI that asks that economics, outcomes and equity be examined together, rather than independently.

ECONOMIC OUTCOMES

Any undertaking within an institution needs to not only be educationally justifiable, it also needs to be economically justifiable. While there are any number of measures required by accounting standards to assess the viability of an institution, there are others that are helpful. For example, the weighted average instructional cost per credit hour allows institutions to understand the costs of offering a program (Mullin, 2018c). By being transparent and illustrating to a campus community the variables that go into the measure, it also provides for participants to understand the factors driving the instructional costs. The shared and increased understanding not only allows for a shared understanding of how programs are funded, it allows for innovative new ideas that may advance equity and operational efficiencies. Other economics measures identify the costs associated to get a student to completion (cost per completer); the amount of tuition and fees a student avoids paying if course selection and success is realized (avoided costs); the marginal value of students being retained (incremental value); and the initial amount of money needed to augment and change practice (upfront costs), for example.

OUTCOMES MEASURES

The outcomes of education are likely the most well-known ROI measures. They include short-term outcomes such as course pass rates, credits attempted as compared to those earned, the percentage of students meeting a milestone event (i.e. 15, 30 or 60 credit hour), or retention rates. Then there are the long-term outcomes such as total credit hours earned as part of a degree, time to degree completion and the graduation rate.

All of these outcome data can be disaggregated by race/ethnicity, income or first-generation status. This disaggregation is necessary but not wholly sufficient to address equity. Simply showing there is a gap, what Gutiérrez (2008) frames as "gap-gazing," does not support an identification of the systemic barriers that may be exacerbating differences in success, supports a deficit-based perspective of students and promotes a narrow definition of learning and equity. For example, the Arkansas community colleges (ACC)—a membership-based association of community colleges—identified low-income students as being less successful in colleges. Through follow-up conversations with students, ACC came to realize that many students lacked reliable transportation to get to college. As part of a federal program, ACC worked to ensure funding was reallocated to offset transportation barriers for students after talking with them revealed that. Unfortunately, it was later discovered that the public bus schedule got the students to class after it had started, and additional conversations around scheduling needed to occur to ensure this barrier was removed.

EQUITY MEASURES

To better understand the implications of actions institutions are taking, a series of equity-focused measures were developed. One measure was developed to quantify the difference in access to foundational courses (access rate gap; Mullin, 2018a). By looking at which sub-populations of students were enrolling in developmental as compared to gateway courses, an institution can see if their placement policies are advancing equity or not by answering questions such as "Is a larger proportion of Hispanic students placed in developmental education than Asian students?" or "Are Alaskan Natives more likely to be enrolled in gateway courses than developmental math courses?" Another measure that looks at the long-term outcomes for students that might not be felt for a while is the percentage of students earning a grade of "D" in a foundational (ie. gateway) course such as English 101 or College Algebra. The reason this equity outcome matters is that these courses are critical to further success and a sense of success as demarcated by a "D" also falsely suggests success for students as courses with a grade of "D" rarely transfer into upper division programs.

In each of these measures the focus is on identifying structural barriers within the institution that can be remedied and not measures that place the burden on the student. The Achievement Gap, for example, is a well-known outcome that can be used for comparative purposes and is illustrative of existing inequities. It may be worth augmenting the traditional ways of examining students to include interactions of student characteristics to support equity-focused change. For example, one can perpetuate the model minority myth that all Asians are good at school by comparing course outcomes of Asians to other races or ethnicities. Alternatively, the measure can compare high-, middle- and low-income Asians to high-, middle- and low-income races to get a more nuanced look at which students are being underserved. In an unpublished study from four cohorts of nationally representative data extracted from the National Postsecondary Student Aid Study of the United States Department of Education, for example, Mullin, Whinnery, and Pompelia (2019) found that while Hispanics were most likely to enroll in developmental education, this was only true for Hispanics over the age of 24 or with a high school grade point average less than 3.0. This suggests the need for a more targeted intervention focused on adult learners (young Hispanics were doing well comparatively) and placement policies. These equity measures, in combination with economic and outcome measures, provide a more holistic and richer foundation from which an institution can make decisions about the allocation of resources through the budgeting process.

ACTIONS TO RECTIFY INJUSTICES

This section outlines three actions to rectify injustices in support of an equity agenda within an institution. One is to build allies and strategic alliances so that they can identify when and where they can question basic assumptions guiding an institution's budgetary process. Another is to take a proactive budgeting approach by advocating for the creation of a more inclusive budgeting approach. A third is a reactive budgeting approach to ensure that any budget cuts resulting from an unanticipated decrease in revenues are done strategically to support an equity agenda rather than to appease all members of the campus community.

Strategic Allies and Alliances

Pursuing an equity agenda requires one to develop key institutional allies who will also support within-institution allocations and financial policy decision making. It is all too easy to envision institutional powerbrokers as adversaries, but that is a problematic approach. More often than not, institutional leaders have aspirations to make relevant contributions during leadership conversations, want to document the impact of their work, have limited time to engage in non-administrative tasks, and value solutions over problems.

The fundamental element of any strategic alliance is for both parties to claim success through a negotiated compromise. To give you an upper hand it is worth remembering that every member of the campus community has objectives they seek to achieve and document on their annual performance reviews. Using, or advocating for, an institutional priority within the strategic plan that either already focuses on advancing equity or framing an existing priority in a way that advances an equity agenda as your rationale for action allows for a common cause.

It is important that you develop a rapport with key figures who will serve as your allies and serve in support of a common cause. They are powerfully positioned individuals that know who you are when engaging with leaders and, over time, will express confidence in your leadership, knowledge, and commitment to the institution's strategic direction during conversations that occur when you are not present. It may be advantageous to formalize a group of allies into a formal "alliance" if institutional leadership are not being responsive to, or inclusive of, voices supporting an equity agenda.

A place to start the development of allies is to identify which of the institution's strategic plan priorities supports an equity agenda. Take time to think, and research, how the priority may or may not currently inform equitable policy and practice. Ask yourself questions, including:

- Who is a champion for prioritizing equity in my department or division or college? Are they a champion for equity or do I need to cultivate them as my ally?
- What does success on an equity priority look like?
- Where can I find more information about a priority that will advance equity?
- When is progress on equity discussed?
- How can I align my approach to equity to the priority?

The answers to these questions not only describe the context in which you are working, they provide information you need to take action. Take the time to fully examine and understand them.

Create More Inclusive Budgeting Approaches

To create a more equity-focused budget, move the institution to an approach that is more likely to result in the implementation of equity-focused actions. Budget development processes that are more transparent and inclusive provide the best opportunity to identify and strategically respond to financially supporting activities that do not support—or do not include—an equity focus.

Barr and McClennan (2018) provide a useful typology to situate an institution's existing budgeting approach as they outline four budgeting approaches ranging from most inclusive to least inclusive. The four approaches are centralized, informational, consultative, and participative. In brief:

- The *centralized* approach assumes that decision-makers have requisite expertise to develop the budget. Budgeting decisions are made at the institutional level with little/no input from others (faculty, staff, etc.). The benefits of this approach are that changes can be made quickly, costs are easily controlled and redistributing funds from one area to another is achieved with relative ease. The centralized approach does not encourage sound management of funding, lowers morale as faculty and staff are less informed about the rationale for funding decisions and therefore spend more time trying to manipulate a "closed" system that supports its implementation.
- The *informational* approach to budgeting assumes that faculty and staff should be informed of major budget decisions after they are developed. In this approach budget priorities and estimated revenues are shared without soliciting feedback. It is more transparent than the centralized approach to budgeting but is still exclusionary of the campus community.
- A more inclusive budgeting approach is the *consultative* approach. This approach assumes faculty, staff, and students enhance administrative decision making. In practice, budget priorities and estimated revenues are enhanced by soliciting feedback from campus community before decisions are made. As a result, ownership of the budget by the campus community is increased. This process does require more time and can be labor intensive, however.
- The most inclusive budgeting approach is the *participative* approach. This approach to budgeting assumes that faculty and staff know best how to manage their units. Budget priorities and estimated revenues are determined largely by input from the faculty and staff. As a result, faculty and staff feel ownership over the budget. Like the consultative approach, this approach to building a budget requires time and is labor intensive.

Less inclusive budgeting practices rely on the expertise of leadership to advance an equity agenda while limiting the contributions of the campus community. Alternatively, inclusive budgeting approaches empower members of the campus community to understand and identify the rationale for expenditures while also leveraging their expertise to support an equity agenda. And while inclusive approaches may seem daunting to budget officers, inclusive approaches are being employed across the country.

For example, St. Petersburg College began in 2010 to develop its budget using a participative approach. Members of the Board of Trustees meet in workgroups with members of the campus community, in December, to identify strategic priorities. Then, in January and February members of the campus community can submit and present their proposal to the Board for consideration (www.spcollege.edu/friends-partners/about/college-budget-information).

While the approach applied at an institution is the decision of leadership, it is important to understand an institution's approach and then advocate for a more inclusive budgeting approach to ensure the diverse needs of the campus community are considered and understood as budgetary decisions are being made. Once achieved, actively participate in the process to ensure efforts to support equity are central to the decision-making process. A useful framework to apply are the three "Cs" of primacy, frequency, and recency. That is to say be engaged first (primacy), be engaged often (frequency) and be the last word before a decision is made (recency; McKeown-Moak & Mullin, 2014).

Make Strategic Budget Cuts

History is instructive to support proactive budgeting practices during economic hardships. By forming workgroups to understanding each potential action and how much is budgeted for it, institutions can prioritize actions that have the smallest impact on populations served through an equity agenda in the event of a budget shortfall.

Operationally speaking, institutional budgets are plans to expend a set amount of revenue. These plans rely on accurate projections of incoming revenue for the year. When revenue projections are incorrect, and institutional leaders have to reconsider the proposed budget, tough decisions need to be made. All too often, the easy political answer of cutting all budgets equally (i.e. across-the-board cuts) is implemented by campus leadership. While this approach is politically convenient as it allows for all institutional functions to equally "feel the pain," it may disproportionately impact an institution's equity agenda.

Mullin, Baime, and Honeyman (2015) reviewed the literature to identify and categorize the approaches institutional leaders took when expenditures have to be unexpectedly reduced. They developed six categories of actions to include: administrative control and management; instructional staffing; examine academic offerings;

enhancing revenues; institutional advancement; and strategic organizational change. Whereas the last three categories focus on increasing revenue for the institution, the first three provide insight into cost-cutting measures. In summary,

- *Administrative control and management* actions largely include deferring purchases and maintenance on buildings, reducing staffing costs (salary and benefits) by subcontracting services, consolidating offices and increasing the teaching load of administrators;
- *Instructional staffing* actions largely impact faculty by freezing salaries, hiring, professional development, and/or travel, as well as altering benefits, increasing the use of adjunct faculty, or increase class sizes; and
- *Examine academic offering* actions include a reexamination of program performance and concomitant pruning of existing programs or grafting them onto existing majors, expanding dual enrollment offerings to increase enrollments and reducing course offerings by raising class minimum enrollments.

CONCLUSION

This chapter presented how equity has traditionally been defined by budget officers and offered a new way to define it with a deliberate focus on equity. It then examined how to look at institutional context critically, presented a framework to identify injustices and then closed with actions to advance an institutionally focused equity agenda. The actions and approaches of institutions like St. Petersburg College or the colleges of Arkansas highlighted in this chapter must not be the exception to the rule. As academic and student affairs professionals you are now empowered with foundational information to engage in the development of institutional budgets and elevate equity through a strategic approach.

QUESTIONS FOR REFLECTION AND DISCUSSION

1. Locate the strategic plan for an institution you either work for or wish to work for.
   a) Does the strategic plan mission or vision statement use the generic term "student" or does it present an asset-based framing of students? If so, share the mission or vision statement and detail how it supports an asset-based framing of students. If not, rewrite the mission or vision statement to present an asset-based framing of students.
   b) Are there either strategic objectives or key initiatives that specifically focus on equity? If so, share what it is and share what makes it equity-oriented. If not, draft an equity-based strategic objective or key initiative, and articulate how it aligns it to the existing mission or vision statement.

2. For the institution examined in question 1, locate the annual report, which may track the implementation of the strategic plan; note the name of the report may vary. Once obtained, look for measurable outcomes focused on equity. If you found one or more metrics, list them and explain how they support equity. If you did not find a metric focused on equity, either create one or cite one from the literature and then articulate how it aligns to an existing strategic objective or key initiative of the existing strategic plan.

3. Contact the budget office at the institution for which you have answered questions 1 and 2 with the intent to identify which of the four budgeting approaches—centralized, informational, consultative, or participative—the institution employs. Explain the answer you received from the budget office and add citations to any documents and resources provided by the budget office to support the response.

REFERENCES

Association of Governing Boards of Universities and Colleges (2017). *Return on investment in college education* (The Guardians Initiative: Restoring the public trust). Washington, DC.

Barr, M. J., & McClennan, G. S. (2018). *Budgets and financial management in higher education, 3rd ed.* San Francisco, CA: Jossey-Bass.

Bauer-Wolf, J. (2019, April 10). Dirty Jobs. *Inside Higher Ed.* Available from www.insidehighered.com/news/2019/04/10/debate-raging-over-harvards-federal-work-study-program

Bensimon, E. (2017). *Making American higher education just.* Los Angeles, CA: University of Southern California, Center for Urban Education Rossier School of Education.

Carnevale, A. P., Jayasundera, T. & Gulish, A. (2016). *America's divided recovery: College haves and have-nots.* Washington, DC: Georgetown University Center on Education and the Workforce.

Ching, C. D. (2017). *Constructing and enacting equity at a community college.* Los Angeles, CA: University of Southern California, Rossier School of Education.

Desrochers, D., & Hurlburt, S. (2016, January). *Trends in college spending: 2003–2013 Where does the money come from? Where does it go? What does it buy?* Washington, DC: Delta Cost Project, American Institutes for Research.

Federal Student Aid (2016). *Federal student aid handbook with active index: 2016–17.* Washington, DC: U.S. Department of Education. Available from https://ifap.ed.gov/fsahandbook/attachments/1617FSAHbkActiveIndexMaster.pdf

Gutiérrez, R. (2008). A "gap-gazing" fetish in mathematics education? Problematizing research on the achievement gap. *Journal for Research in Mathematics Education,* 39(4).

Harnish, T., & Opalich, D. (2018). *Higher education state policy issues for 2018* (Policy Matters). Washington, DC: American Association of State Colleges and Universities.

Hurley, D. J., Harnish, T., L., & Parker, E. A. (2015). *Top 10 higher education state policy issues for 2015* (Policy Matters). Washington, DC: American Association of State Colleges and Universities.

Laderman, S., & Carlson, A. (2018). *SHEF: 2017: State higher education finance.* Boulder, CO: State Higher Education Executive Officers.

Long, A. (Ed.) (2016). *Overcoming educational racism in the community college: Creating pathways to success for minority and impoverished student populations.* Sterling, VA: Stylus Press.

Ma, J., Pender, M., & Welch, M. (2016). *Education pays 2016: The benefits of higher education for individuals and society.* New York City: College Board.

McKeown-Moak, M., & Mullin, C. M. (2014). *Higher education finance research: Policy, politics, and practice.* Charlotte, NC: Information Age Publishing, Inc.

Mullin, C. M. (2018a). *Access rate gaps: Calculating a return on investment outcome* (Strategic Investment Impacts). Denver, CO: Strong Start to Finish, Education Commission of the States.

Mullin, C. M. (2018b). *Understanding impact: A holistic return on investment framework for developmental education*. Denver, CO: Strong Start to Finish, Education Commission of the States.

Mullin, C. M. (2018c). *Weighted average instructional costs per credit hour: Calculating a return on investment outcome (Strategic Investment Impacts)*. Denver, CO: Strong Start to Finish, Education Commission of the States.

Mullin, C. M., Baime, D. S., & Honeyman, D. S. (2015). *Community college finance: A guide for institutional leaders*. San Francisco, CA: Jossey-Bass.

Mullin, C. M., Whinnery, E., & Pompelia, S. (2019, March 28). *National trends in developmental education enrollment and policy*. Presentation at the 2019 Strong Start to Finish Learning Network Convening, Denver, CO.

5

PRACTITIONER REFLECTION

Working in Topsy-Turvy Higher Education Environments

VASTI TORRES

Anyone who serves as an academic administrator in higher education today understands that the most important skill in the current climate is the ability to change and adapt to the environmental influences imposed on our institutions (Jones, Schuh, & Torres, 2017). External and internal influences create a constant topsy-turvy environment that can create confusion or disorder, yet most administrators adapt to this by understanding the differences between the desired and the real outcomes within the institution. This balancing act seems to promote a cycle of understanding the ideal situation—the norms—and the aspirational compromises that can emerge. This reflection will use this hypothetical cycle to describe how academic administrators approach decision making amidst a topsy-turvy environment.

The chapters in this part attempt to present the ideal philosophical and socially just approach to academic decision making within institutions. Throughout the chapters, there are acknowledgments of the institutional norms that influence these processes, but it is also important to recognize the compromises that likely emerge in day-to-day practice. This reflection will be focused on the ideal, the norms, and the compromise that typically emerges for academic administrators in higher education. In order to place the reflection within the context of my own experiences, I begin by providing some background that influences my positionality and insight as an academic administrator.

My career choices can be described as unconventional. Though I am tenured full professor, I began my career as a student affairs practitioner. After spending 15 years in practice and rising to a senior level student affairs administrator position, I chose to make the switch and begin the tenure track process as an assistant professor. After 14 years as a full-time faculty member with the rank of full professor and directing a research center for several years, personal reasons prompted me to make a geographic move and accept a position as an academic Dean of a College. This latest academic administration position truly highlighted the constant external and internal pressures that can emerge within academic units. The nature of faculty culture can prompt individuals to look out for their own interest over those of others, or community. This type of culture is difficult to balance when individuals consider themselves more important than any program or organizational goals. As a Latina I place a high value on the needs of the community as equal to my own. While I was in student affairs, I seldom experienced tension between my cultural sense of community and the inner workings of my environment. The practice of using committees to make decisions and moving forward initiatives seemed to complement my collaborative nature. When I became a faculty member I found the individualistic and competitive nature of gaining merit (or academic prestige) as creating tension between my own values and others within my environment. Though I experienced tension between my values and the competitive nature of academic prestige in faculty life, I also acknowledge that I played the game relatively well and garnered sufficient academic prestige to be able to leave highly conflictual environments. Academic administration heightens the individualistic and competitive traits so that a leader is defending their unit while competing with other units for resources. The combination of individualistic approaches of faculty members' expectation (the norms) and the demand that externally imposed metrics be met by an academic unit (the ideal), without interrogation (compromise) of the appropriateness of the metric, makes academic leadership a delicate balance of change and consistency. The contradictions and competing forces between the striving for metrics to make the institution ideal to the outside world, the individualistic driven norms, and the compromised outcomes are what creates a topsy-turvy environment for leaders.

These conflicting elements in academic administration solidified my desire to return to the faculty and to focus on research that can help underrepresented students and teaching graduate students how to make difference. Because of these experiences, I understand both the philosophical ideal that higher education institutions should have and acknowledge how the norms of being an academic administrator create compromise within higher education today. While compromise is an important administrative trait, it is important to acknowledge that while compromise around work issues is expected, it does not require you to compromise on your personal ideals.

THE IDEAL

Chapter 2 by Kezar and Dizon highlights the ideal philosophy that undergirds shared governance within higher education institutions. This ideal is based on decades of evidence that institutional checks and balances should be executed by multiple groups on campus; thus allowing for more equitable policy decisions. There is no doubt that having multiple groups on campus weigh in and examine policies would greatly improve both the policy in question and the overall transparency of decision making within an institution. This chapter also makes a case for engaging staff and students as part of that shared governance. Shared governance would not likely prevent the issues that emerged at USC, Penn State, or Michigan State, but it is a logical assumption that a clear system of checks and balances would have helped identify these issues and not perpetuate the injustice.

The ideal reasons for shared governance are also based on socially just reasons. Yet, these reasons are not clearly understood outside and in some cases within higher education. As this chapter acknowledges, shared governance has been co-opted by outside influences. The lack of understanding of the ideals of shared governance also influences how hiring and admissions committees can work toward the ideals of equity. Posselt, Hernandez, and Villarreal substantiate the tremendous power that search committees and admissions committees exert over future faculty and students within our institutions. By pointing out bias at the individual, institutional, and disciplinary levels, the Framework for Equity in Decision Making centers the decision-making process within an equity focus. While this is a difficult goal, it is an important one to constantly consider in daily practice.

The previous chapter is an example of decision making with an equity focus. Mullin attempts to share the knowledge and skills necessary for mid-level administrators to make budgetary decisions that reflect socially just experiences for all students. In order to accomplish this, administrators must promote programs that take into account the needs of underrepresented students and focus on providing services that can truly assist students in being successful. The ideal expressed in these three chapters seem to make so much common sense that it is difficult to explain why it is not the norm. In reality, the norm is much more convoluted and stained by the individual self-interest. This is why it is important to consider the pressures around existing norms when administrators attempt to guide the actions with the ideal in mind.

THE NORMS IN PRACTICE

The quote that "neoliberal logics have disciplined the institution to tie self-worth to productivity and merit ..., including the privilege to speak out against authority" (Chapter 2, p. 29) provides a concise rationale why the norms of how academic administration works today is not the same as the ideal. The accountability movement exerts pressure on public institutions to align with state priorities regardless of the mission institutions seek to fulfil (Hillman, 2016). This type of control over the definition of "success" creates metric-centric decision making that is not consistent with shared governance, but rather is directive and top-down. Because neoliberal logics are valued over other aspects, like learning, within the higher education experience, the use of metric-centric leadership is substituted for thoughtful considerations about what students need (Torres, Renn, & Rios, 2018). The proliferation of academic administrators is focused on assuring metrics are met and therefore take on the role of driving behaviors through economic incentives. This level of top-down directive leadership frustrates faculty and provides the de facto permission to not be engaged in the governance of the institution. The norms around today's shared governance is that it is rare to see senior or superstar faculty assume a role in shared governance structures.

This abdication of governance and decision making by the senior faculty further exasperates the reproduction of the majority merit-centric culture—often adding to existing toxic environments for anyone who wants to focus on socially just approaches. In my experience over the years, individuals are very good at rationalizing their choices and co-opting language that is inclusive in order to hire or admit those that will sustain the status quo. As an example, as a Dean, faculty would often twist strategic priorities to rationalize their request when the request would only serve the self-interest of the faculty member. This would include funding release time to create experimental courses without any evidence that there was student interest or expecting funding for research without any attempt to access if external funding could be available in the future. These examples illustrate why our institutions are sustained and the culture that drives innovation or change for socially just actions is drowned out by those who understand that keeping the status quo is easier and requires less energy. The only efforts that can work are those that align with the majority merit-centric cultures within the institution and provide incremental changes that provide positive optics rather than deep change to truly support student success. Though it is not unusual to hear that deep change is needed, the actual mechanism for creating deep change that seems to work finds convergence with existing institutional cultures. As a result socially just approaches to change tend to compromise on something.

Among the academic administrators most influenced by the norms of administration, the mid-level administrator is most likely to be frustrated. Though Mullen focuses on the mid-level administrator's courageous decisions, the reality of micromanaging through metric-centric leadership provides little flexibility in budgets, so the suggestion to focus on discretionary funding makes sense to create socially just change. In addition, higher education institutions tend to create multiple mid-level agents. The most often cited are the department chair or director of centers; yet, in reality many Deans or division heads feel like mid-level managers when they are attempting to cushion metric-centric decisions within their broader goals of the unit. In leadership, perception is often more valued than facts; therefore it is critical to approach every situation by thinking through the multiple perspectives (lens) used within an institution. The ability to make socially just budgetary decisions are evaluated from multiple perspectives within the institution—many of which are not based on external optics rather than internal needs. What is "just" is in the eye of the beholder and readily critiqued if your opinion differs from those working to maintain the status quo.

An example of how external optics transcends internal needs is the metric of excess credit hours and the decision to charge higher tuition to students who accumulate too many excess hours. On the surface this makes perfect sense—why would we want students to take too many credit hours? Administrators that work with first-generation college students understand the tension that arises when excess credit hours as a student success metric is not seen from multiple perspectives. On the one hand, everyone should want students to graduate in time and without additional expenses. This desire is based on all elements of an educational system working perfectly. Yet, on the other hand, charging more for excess hours requires first-generation college students to make decisions early in their journey—often without sufficient understanding of the requirements or consequences. If a student needs multiple pre-requisites prior to entering a major (e.g. advance math courses for engineering), it is unlikely they will be able to complete their degree without excess credit hours. By not interrogating this metric, institutions are not considering the ideal of participatory decision making that could influence the norms of accepting a metric only because of the external optics. Without this interrogation, excess-credit hour metric is an example of decision making that only considers one perspective without understanding the complexity found within diverse student experiences.

In providing this norm, I am attempting to acknowledge the rough spots that the literature sometimes glosses over. Though this reality seems bleak, I do believe most administrators create aspirational compromises that provide hope for the future.

THE COMPROMISE

Change must begin with exploring whether one's own behavior has likely been co-opted and having the courage to exert one's own authority (see Chapter 2). Within practice, the compromise is focused on changing the culture of a unit. I always hoped for the ideal and worked toward it, but understood that change requires a give-and-take approach. Even when change seems inevitable, few think that change is good and the status quo works for this reason—it benefits those currently with power. Complacency does not serve students and can seldom be seen as a socially just approach to administration; yet it is the easier path to take. This recognition does require courageous action that must be carried out by those that carry the most power within our campus. In some cases that can be a Dean, but at other times a senior level faculty member can use their "power for good" and advocate for socially just decisions. Courage from an entry-level person is admirable, but without collaborative grassroots efforts it is not likely to be effective. A compromise that a socially just academic leader can make is to create an environment where grassroots efforts are valued rather than punished or seen as detrimental to the career of early-career staff. This is where mid-level staff can make a tremendous difference, yet they must also manage up the line of authority to assure that grassroots efforts can be taken seriously.

One of the ways that academic administrators can create socially just compromises is by recognizing that position descriptions are critically important to changing the culture toward a more equitable focus for all involved. In this book, the chapter by Liera and Ching highlights the difference in hiring when Hispanic Serving Institutions (HSIs) prominently display this designation in position descriptions. Recently I gave a lecture at an HSI about working with Latinx students using criteria indicating "readiness" to work with these students (Torres & Zerquera, 2012) and found that the only time the HSI designation was mentioned at the institution was within the institutional description for grants. This lack of attention (not acknowledging the HSI designation) to diverse environments and the skills necessary to work with diverse students, is an example of how a position description would not reflect what the students at the institution need from faculty and staff. Position descriptions are often dusted off from the previous search rather than engaging on what is needed in this search. Paying attention to what goes into a position description is one of the roles of academic administrators and one that can promote the compromise to change the composition and practice of a unit.

Creating diverse environments requires self-reflection by individuals, institutions, and systems (see Chapter 3). Reflection is not something that academic administrators do well and is seldom used intentionally during day-to-day practice. The culture of doing, without reflection, further inculcates the status quo. Shared governance and equity in decision making would create an environment where socially just budgeting could prevail. In order to accomplish this there would need to be deliberate reflection and acknowledgment about how that is not currently happening within the institution. As an example, only elite institutions prioritize financial need in their institutional aid packages; others tend to focus on prestige-seeking behaviors by privileging merit over the access function of institutions. Recognizing that an institutional decision prioritizes certain individuals (or merit only) is the first step to creating budgetary decisions that are equitable.

The compromises academic leaders make to create more equitable organizations are typically not easily seen by those around them. As a leader I knew that if I was completely transparent I would open myself to criticism from some faction of the unit. The key to this compromise is understanding the power dynamics of the individuals within your unit. In my case, the senior faculty were strongly in favor of the status quo and the early-career faculty were the ones seeking change in processes and governance. This was not an ideal situation, but as the leader I was willing to navigate this tightrope for what I perceived as socially just change. This meant that I knew I would need to bare the criticism—a compromise I was willing to make. Administrators having to walk this tightrope must consider the personal options they have if their compromises do not work and they end up falling off the tightrope. For me this was one of the times that I was glad to have the "academic prestige" that offered me other options in my career if my navigation of creating change did not work. At times, I found my reliance on the knowledge that I could leave the institution an ironic compromise given my personal values around community.

THE "DAMNED IF YOU DO AND DAMNED IF YOU DON'T" CONUNDRUM

In many ways, the cycle of recognizing the ideal, the norms, and the compromises creates a conundrum for many administrators. In the daily work as academic administrators, each member of the unit feels that their needs are the most critical and seldom understands the bigger picture in which administration must make choices. While it may feel like you are damned if you do and damned if you don't, placing emphasis on the process and being explicit about how decisions are made and mechanisms that build transparency may help in bridging the ideal of shared governance into an institutional norm. As an academic leader I often had to remind faculty leaders and associate deans steering change that they needed to trust the process. Frankly, there were times when the process was not clear and barriers to change were very visible. Yet, as a socially just leader one can only hope that if you are clear on the reasons for change, respond to questions as honestly as possible, and create mechanisms for dissenting opinions to be heard, then you have done the best you can. I admit that in some cases there were times that it did not matter that there was a process and the self-interest of individuals drove the very loud opposition. This is not meant to create a dichotomy of win or lose when creating organizational change; rather it is about being honest about how these issues can feel personally. Though frustrating at times, considering the ideal allows for the belief that even if you are "damned" by others you "did" the best you could and maintained your own ideals—a worthy compromise.

CONCLUSION

Every institutional context is different and the norms that guide decision making are seldom clear and often create the guessing game of what might work. Yet, it is important to remember the ideal, since forgetting that will only cement the feeling of being stuck in the status quo. It is difficult to recruit good academic administrators, but perhaps if institutions considered the ideal of shared governance, strong leaders may be willing to take on the inherent conundrum that comes with today's neoliberal external pressures, because there would be an understanding that there is room to compromise to create more equitable decision making. Unless we acknowledge this constant conundrum that can emerge between the ideal and the daily norms of practice, academic administrations will continually be frustrated within the topsy-turvy environment that encompasses academic administration.

QUESTIONS FOR REFLECTION AND DISCUSSION

1. Think about your experiences in higher education, either as a student or professor. Describe a situation where you experienced tension between the external "optics" of the situation and your own convictions.

2. Torres wrote, "The contradictions and competing forces between the striving for metrics to make the institution ideal to the outside world, the individualistic driven norms, and the compromised outcomes are what creates a topsy-turvy environment for leaders." How can a system of checks and balances on power, within shared governance, combined with critical reflection on the part of decision-makers about the equity implications of their own behavior, enable administrators to negotiate this environment? Is there anything else you would wish to add to enable negotiation?

3. Torres advised her colleagues that "in steering change that they needed to trust the process." What makes "trusting the process" reasonable or difficult for you? What would enable trust?

REFERENCES

Hillman, N. W. (2016, May). Why performance-based college funding doesn't work. *The Century Foundation*. Retrieved from https://tcf.org/content/report/why-performance-based-college-funding-doesnt-work/.

Jones, S. R., Schuh, J. H., & Torres, V. (2017). Shaping the future. In J.H. Schuh, S.R. Jones, & V. Torres (Eds.), *Student Services: A Handbook for the Profession, 6th Edition* (pp. 550–566). San Francisco, CA: Jossey-Bass.

Torres, V., Renn, K., & Rios, R. (2018). *An organizational model for student success integration: Critical analysis of institutional approaches*. Paper presented at the Association for the Study of Higher Education, November 17, 2018. Tampa, FL.

Torres, V. & Zerquera, D. D. (2012). Hispanic serving institutions: Patterns, predictions, and implications for informing policy discussions. *Journal of Hispanics in Higher Education*, 11(3), 259–278.

PART II

HUMAN RESOURCES

6

RETHINKING MENTORING

*Integrating Equity-Minded Practice in Promoting Access
to and Outcomes of Developmental Relationships*

KIMBERLY A. GRIFFIN

Over the last decade, I have spent a lot of time interviewing students and faculty, leading workshops, and writing journal articles about mentoring relationships in higher education. If I reflect on what initially led me to this work, I think immediately of how these relationships translated to my own growth and development, often in unexpected and surprising ways. For example, mentors helped me discover higher education and student affairs as a potential career when I was an undergraduate; they recognized and encouraged my potential. As a doctoral student, my mentors pushed me, cultivating and critiquing my research and writing skills. And throughout my life, all of my mentors have affirmed my identity and reminded me how important it is to add my voice as a woman of color to discourses in higher education research and practice.

In many ways, mentoring research affirms my personal experiences and speaks to its importance as a strategy to promote the success of emerging scholars and leaders. Access to mentoring and developmental relationships, or associations between junior and senior individuals focused on the junior member's professional and/or personal development and growth (Kram, 1988), translate to countless positive personal and professional outcomes. Research has focused largely on outcomes for students and faculty, connecting these relationships to cognitive growth and development, career aspirations, confidence and self-efficacy, and sense of belonging (Crisp, Baker, Griffin, Lunsford, & Pifer, 2017; Mayhew et al., 2016; Olson & Jackson, 2009; Phillips, Dennison, & Davenport, 2016; Schrodt, Cawyer, & Sanders, 2003; Zellers, Howard,

& Barcic, 2008). Scholarship that focuses specifically on administrators and emerging campus leaders suggests that mentoring can be an important source of encouragement and assistance as junior and mid-career professionals navigate and ascend administrative hierarchies, providing insights into senior roles and responsibilities and helping individuals build their networks (Brown, 2005; León & Nevarez, 2007).

Mentoring relationships have also been highlighted as particularly important for individuals who have minoritized identities, or are members of groups that are more subject to oppression and marginalization based on social constructs like race, gender identity and expression, ethnicity, religion, and sexual identity. Scholarship focusing on undergraduate and graduate women (Chesler & Chesler, 2002; Ong, Wright, Espinosa, & Orfield, 2011), students of color (Cole & Griffin, 2013; Patton, 2009), members of the LGB community (Renn, 2007), and people who are trans* or gender non-conforming (Dugan, Kusel, & Simounet, 2012) notes that mentors can provide important academic and psychosocial support as students navigate challenging campus environments, particularly where they feel unwelcome or marginalized. Mentors can have a similarly powerful impact on minoritized faculty, affirming their talent and facilitating a sense of belonging and connection to the academy, fostering skills development, increasing access to academic networks, and providing insight into departmental politics (Chesler & Chesler, 2002; Gibson, 2004; Zambrana et al., 2015). Similarly, both informal relationships and formal mentoring programs have been credited with helping minoritized administrators advance as they manage racism, sexism, and homophobia, providing them access to advice and guidance, professional development opportunities, and broader networks of information and support (Brown, 2005; Jackson & Harris, 2000; Olson & Jackson, 2009).

Mentoring is often recommended as a strategy to increase diversity in higher education (e.g. Brown, 2005; Byars-Winston, Gutierrez, Topp, & Carnes, 2011; Jackson & Harris, 2000; Olson & Jackson, 2009). It is assumed that mentoring programs and policies will provide greater access to these relationships, improving the educational, professional, and social outcomes of individuals from minoritized populations. These outcomes are then anticipated to translate to higher rates of overall success and the improved representation of individuals from minoritized communities in the student, faculty, and administrative bodies on campus. While well intentioned, this line of thinking focuses solely on increasing diversity, centering numerical outcomes and increasing the representation of minoritized groups. I assert that we cannot assume that increased access to mentorship will result in improved outcomes for all. There are aspects of mentoring that can perpetuate the challenges minoritized individuals face in the academy, rather than promote equitable outcomes. For example, engagement in mentoring relationships is not equitably distributed across mentors or proteges, and developmental relationships can reinforce hierarchies already present in the academy.

Thus, to be truly successful, mentoring must go beyond being encouraged and available via policies and programs. Institutional leaders must take responsibility for not only serving as mentors, but also creating conditions that intentionally support the access to, development of, and positive outcomes resulting from developmental relationships. An equity-based perspective facilitates our ability to make this shift, refocusing attention on how institutions perpetuate inequality and sustain barriers that prevent minoritized individuals from gaining access to beneficial resources (Pena, Bensimon, & Colyar, 2006; Stewart, 2017). Importantly, equity-based perspectives also remind us to assess whether all equally benefit from institutional interventions (Malcom-Piqueux & Bensimon, 2017; Stewart, 2017), in this case developmental relationships. This chapter tackles these issues, drawing on mentoring research and theory to address four areas administrators must consider as they aim to develop mentoring strategies that promote equity. First, we must continually ask who has access to mentorship, followed by who is expected to serve as mentors and offer support. Administrators must also carefully attend to differences in the quality of mentoring relationships and interactions taking place. Finally, institutional leaders must consider the power dynamics inherent in mentoring relationships and how they can perpetuate marginalization and inequity in the academy. In addition to recommending a comprehensive reorientation in administrators' thinking about mentoring and its potential to increase diversity, this chapter closes with specific strategies institutional leaders can adopt to translate these principles into practice, reforming the ways mentoring is perceived, supported, assessed and rewarded to promote increased equity for mentees and mentors from minoritized populations.

ACCESS TO MENTORS

While there is a body of research that suggests there are few differences across identity groups in terms of who does and does not have a mentor (Johnson, 2016), there is some evidence that women, men of color, and those who are the first in their family to pursue postsecondary education have less access to mentors (Cianni & Romberger, 1995; Kim & Sax, 2009). While women of color who are faculty and administrators may develop extensive networks of support to promote their advancement, this support often comes in the forms of faith and spirituality, peers, friends, and family rather than meaningful professional mentoring relationships (Patitu & Hinton, 2003; Thomas & Hollenshead, 2011). In a study focusing on leaders of color, men appeared more assertive in developing professional mentoring relationships, whereas women were less likely to have access to support. Women of color participating in the study anticipated that someone would reach out, leaving them less likely to have a mentor within their organization (Chang, Longman, & Franco, 2014).

Challenges in locating a mentor may be exacerbated by many minoritized scholars' and administrators' desires to work with mentors who share their most salient identities (Baker, Pifer, & Griffin, 2014; Blake-Beard, Bayne, Crosby, & Muller, 2011; Chesler & Chesler, 2002; Patton, 2009). Similarity is often the foundation of strong mentoring relationships, and potentially rewarding connections can be developed based on shared work habits, areas of professional expertise, or personal interests (Baker et al., 2014). However, homophily, or attraction based on shared identity, often drives mentees' early perceptions of fit in their relationships (Baker et al., 2014; McPherson, Smith-Lovin, & Cook, 2001). Indeed, sharing a minoritized identity can be an important location from which to build trust and deep connections based on shared experiences of marginalization (Johnson, 2016), as women, men of color, LGB individuals, and trans* people seek mentors that understand what it is and means to embody their identity in the academy (Baker et al., 2014; Patton, 2009; Renn, 2010). While this may be an adaptive strategy that allows for more fulfilling relationships and comprehensive support, it also limits the number of potential mentors to which individuals have access given the small numbers of senior leaders and potential mentors with minoritized identities (Brown, Davis, & McClendon, 1999; Chesler & Chesler, 2002).

Mentors also demonstrate identity-based preferences when choosing proteges. Homophily, which Johnson (2016) refers to as "psychological cloning," can manifest as an unconscious desire to replicate oneself, driving mentors to support proteges that remind them most of themselves and with whom they share core salient identities. Looking beyond perceived similarity, mentor implicit and explicit biases also can shape their preferences and invitations to engage. Multiple studies, largely focusing on faculty behaviors, suggest potential mentors assume women and men of color are less able, driven, and likely to succeed, making them less attractive as mentees. For example, Johnson (2016) notes that many senior scholars assume women are less able scholars and researchers, more likely to leave their professions to start a family, less assertive or motivated than their male counterparts. As such, they may be less likely to seek out women as mentees. Similarly, multiple studies show that underrepresented racial and ethnic minority faculty and graduate students encounter lower expectations and stereotypes about their ability and belonging in the academy (Johnson-Bailey, Cervero, & Bowles, 2009; Kelly & McCann, 2014; Turner, 2002), which makes them less likely to be invited to form close, trusting relationships with senior scholars who could serve as mentors (Felder, 2010). In fact, research suggests faculty respond most favorably to White males and are more likely to be open to scheduling informational meetings with them or offer career support (Milkman, Akinola, & Chugh, 2012; Moss-Racusin, Dovidio, Brescoll, Graham, & Handelsman, 2012). These patterns can and often do manifest in similar ways in administration. Administrative leaders and supervisors can also miss the potential and downplay the abilities of minoritized professionals based on their own biases and beliefs (Jean-Marie, Williams, & Sherman, 2009; Patitu & Hinton, 2003), diminishing the likelihood that developmental relationships will form.

Not recognizing how the power of homophily and bias can be a barrier to equity in the academy can magnify disparities in access to mentorship. Considering that senior faculty and administrators are largely White and male, relying on identity matches means that White and male mentees will have more access and continue to be more likely to have mentors. Senior leaders also may have beliefs, conscious and unconscious, that lead them to be less interested in supporting minoritized junior colleagues because they perceive them as less able or likely to succeed. Thus, as administrators make decisions about who they would like to mentor and develop mentoring programs and policies, they must be mindful of how the drive to connect with those most like oneself and beliefs about other groups can drive decision-making about engagement in mentorship and take affirmative steps to address homophily and bias.

IMBALANCED DISTRIBUTIONS OF LABOR

Although senior leaders and administrators may tout the value of mentoring, there are few incentives built into reward systems that acknowledge a commitment to these activities (Baez, 2000; Tierney & Bensimon, 1996). Relationships that provide mentees with a balanced professional and socioemotional support, meet needs for personalized guidance, and affirm mentees' identities and experiences with marginalization, require a continuous investment of effort, often above and beyond a mentor's other professional responsibilities. Taking on additional work responsibilities, presenting at conferences, and participating in visible campus committees and task forces may be assessed and rewarded more regularly than serving as a mentor as indicators of potential and achievement. In addition to not being work that "counts," mentoring may distract from the activities most connected to advancement. Thus, time invested in these relationships may not only go unrewarded and unrecognized; it may translate to additional negative outcomes because it detracts from activities that are celebrated.

This dynamic is made more problematic and becomes relevant to conversations about equity because of the unequal distribution of the work associated with mentorship. Research and public discourse point to how women, men of color, and members of the LGB community are more frequently called upon to mentor and support students and junior colleagues (Griffin & Reddick, 2011; Johnson, 2016; Joseph & Hirshfield, 2011; O'Meara, Kuvaeva, Nyunt, Waugaman, & Jackson, 2017). As noted above, some of these disparities are rooted in whom people seek out as mentors; however, sexist and racist expectations often individually and collectively translate to differential mentoring and advising loads. Sexism and gender dynamics in the academy often require women to engage in more emotional labor and academic service, leading to women being asked to do more service than their male colleagues (O'Meara et al., 2017). This work not only translates to more mentees; expectations that women will be more caring, helpful, supportive, and invest more of themselves in their relationships translates to substantial commitments that often go unrecognized and unappreciated. Race and racism can also shape expectations, as faculty and administrators of color are expected to do more than their colleagues to support marginalized communities on campus (Baez, 2000; Padilla, 1994). These dynamics are exacerbated for women of color who experience racism and sexism simultaneously. Research suggests women of color receive more requests for mentorship and expectations that they will support students in deep, intensive ways that differ from the expectations placed on White women and men of color (Griffin & Reddick, 2011). Some refer to this phenomenon as a form of "othermothering," (Collins, 2000), highlighting how the comprehensive academic and socioemotional commitments made by mentors resemble fictive kinships and familial support. Researchers have documented how women of color, and Black women in particular, often serve as othermothers (Guiffrida, 2005; Hirt, Amelink, McFeeters, & Strayhorn, 2008; Posselt, 2018). This level of investment can be fulfilling for mentees and personally rewarding for mentors; yet, researchers also suggest that it is professionally distracting and stressful, potentially increasing the likelihood of more negative outcomes (Griffin & Reddick, 2011; Turner, González, & Wong, 2011).

Equity-minded administrators must consider not only who is being mentored, but who is expected to do the majority of the work associated with mentoring. If we continue to tap the same individuals over and over for these responsibilities, and if promotion and reward processes continue to ignore or downplay the important contributions mentors make to the development of the next generation of leaders, we concentrate the potential negative implications of mentorship among those most marginalized and vulnerable in the academy. This is certainly not meant to discourage participation in mentoring programs and developmental relationships; for many, mentoring allows for the fulfillment of commitments to community uplift and can be personally rewarding (Baez, 2000; Griffin, 2013). However, ignoring how structural barriers and environmental factors punish rather than reward mentors and disproportionately affect those from minoritized communities perpetuates inequality. Thus, equity-minded administrative leaders must take care to ensure that mentoring responsibilities are fairly shared across professionals and that engagement in mentoring is recognized in substantive ways that translate to meaningful rewards and recognition.

RELATIONSHIP QUALITY

An equity-based perspective reminds us that in addition to access to a mentor, we must be mindful of the extent to which individuals experience relationships of similar depth and quality. Scholars have found notable evidence that individuals with minoritized identities experience a different quality of interaction and support in their mentoring relationships. For example, Cianni and Romberger (1995) found that while they technically may have access to mentorship, women and people of color perceived less access to support, encouragement, professional development opportunities, resources, and information from supervisors than their White and male counterparts, limiting their career development.

In addition to different access to information, there may be distinctions in the kind of support mentees need and mentors are comfortable with providing. Relationship quality can be diminished when mentors are reluctant to recognize their mentees' identities, intentionally or unintentionally ignoring how they may impact their professional experiences (Zambrana et al., 2015). The oppression and marginalization minoritized individuals face in the academy may necessitate unique or distinct forms of support which may be missed, particularly if mentors embrace a colorblind ideology and aim to treat all mentees as the same (McCoy, Winkle-Wagner, & Luedke, 2015). When identity is minimized, it can be difficult to build the trust necessary to reap the benefits of mentoring relationships; mentees may feel like they cannot share an important aspect of themselves, and mentors may give advice that is off the mark or miss the impact and implications of marginalizing experiences (Zambrana et al., 2015).

Simply having a mentor is not enough to bring about the transformative power of mentoring relationships. These relationships are composed of a series of interactions that meet mentees' needs and ultimately promote their growth and development. Ensuring that mentors are able to engage in ways that are the most helpful is key to the success of any relationship. Yet, it appears that even when they are able to find mentors, the needs of individuals from minoritized communities often go unmet. The factors that limit access to mentoring relationships can also influence relationship quality, with social stereotypes and biases potentially leading mentors to provide different forms of support to their proteges based on perceived potential and ability, leaving women and men of color less likely to get more intensive and direct guidance. Further, in the interest of being "fair," mentors may overlook the need to recognize how their mentees' identities inform their lives, goals, and professional experiences. As is often the case, endorsement of a colorblind ideology perpetuates rather than diminishes inequality, and campus leaders must closely examine whether and how mentors and mentees discuss and honor identity in the context of their relationships.

POWER DYNAMICS AND DYSFUNCTION

Finally, traditional notions of mentoring endorse relational dynamics that can reinforce paradigms of power and privilege in the academy. Within a traditional framework, mentors are older, more senior and established in the organizational hierarchy, and take responsibility for cultivating the career of a junior colleague. Rather than engaging in a relationship based on equality and reciprocity, it is assumed that the mentor will give support and the mentee will gratefully receive it (Ensher & Murphy, 2005). There are certainly narratives that suggest that some mentors take advantage of the often unequal power dynamic in their relationships. Mentors have been accused of stealing their proteges' work, sabotaging career opportunities, engaging in abusive and manipulative behavior, or shirking their mentoring role and responsibilities (Eby & Allen, 2002; Eby, Butts, Durley, & Ragins, 2010; Johnson, 2016; Kumar & Blake-Beard, 2012).

These dynamics are further complicated when mentors have direct supervisory or evaluative roles in the mentee's workplace, muddling the extent to which the mentor has control over the kinds of decisions the mentee makes. For example, professionals may be mentoring members of their team or have a role in their mentees' selection for high-profile committees, nomination for awards, or hiring and promotion processes. When mentors have decision-making power and are more senior in established academic hierarchies, it can complicate relationships, making disagreements, decisions not to follow advice, or distance within the relationship feel dangerously significant, with the potential for long-term and wide-reaching professional implications.

Ultimately, a mentoring relationship can be defined as dysfunctional if one or both members are not having their needs met, are experiencing distress, or if the costs of the relationship are outweighing the benefits (Johnson, 2016). Dysfunctional relationships have real implications; research suggests that bad experiences in mentoring relationships can outweigh the good (Eby & Allen, 2002; Kumar & Blake-Beard, 2012), and as such, may translate to a lack of productivity, dissatisfaction, and disengagement that can perpetuate rather than close disparities in the academy. While dysfunction can potentially take place in any developmental relationship, it is important to acknowledge how mentees from minoritized backgrounds can be placed at heightened levels of risk. Many see developmental relationships as a safe and developmental space, which may be particularly important given the negative and often hostile environments many minoritized students, scholars, and emerging leaders face in the academy. Facing dysfunction, marginalization, and oppression within their mentoring relationships may take an additional toll, widening outcomes gaps rather than narrowing them. Equity-minded administrators must be more aware of how relationships can be potentially harmful, refraining from assumptions that any and all access to a mentor is good or helpful. Mentors must be assigned and monitored with care to ensure that the relationship is functioning in a healthy way for both mentees and proteges and is not a site for continued oppression and marginalization.

MOVING THE CONVERSATION FORWARD: A MODEL FOR EQUITY-MINDED MENTORING

An equity-based approach to mentoring increases the likelihood that relationships will be structured, instituted, and rewarded in ways that promote the success of all parties involved. I have developed the Equity-Minded Mentoring Model (or EM³, see Figure 6.1), which offers administrators a way to conceptualize enhancing equity in

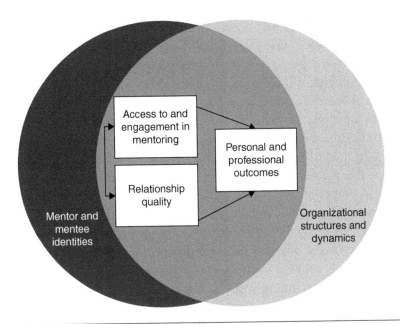

FIGURE 6.1   The Equity Minded Mentoring Model (EM³), developed based on extant research and theory on mentoring, equity, and inclusion in higher education

their own relationships, as well as a way to think about developing mentoring policies, programs, and practices that are more likely to enhance equity and ultimately lead to increases in diversity. The EM³ acknowledges the experiences and outcomes of both mentors and proteges, as well as a more nuanced understanding of mentoring that highlights the connection between engagement, relationship quality, and relationship outcomes. These components are situated within context (represented by a Venn diagram), acknowledging the larger individual and institutional factors that can influence all aspects of developmental relationships.

The three boxes at the core of the EM³ acknowledge the importance of embracing good mentoring practice and focus on the connection between access and engagement in mentoring relationships, relationship quality, and relationship outcomes. *Access and engagement* captures the "who" in mentorship: who has access to the benefits associated with mentoring and who is expected to engage and take on the majority of the intellectual and emotional labor associated with these relationships. *Relationship quality* addresses what happens within the relationship, the information shared, nature of interactions, and closeness and sense of trust between mentee and mentor. The arrows indicate that for mentees, access to a mentor is important, but not assumed to be the only factor related to positive *personal and professional outcomes*. Rather, access *and* relationship quality determine mentees' personal and professional outcomes. Thus, as we think about facilitating more equitable outcomes in higher education generally, and among administrators specifically, we must be mindful about providing individuals with access to relationships that meet their needs and are grounded in trust, respect, and care.

The model similarly postulates that mentors' engagement in and quality of developmental relationships will have implications for their own outcomes. Mentors can reap substantial benefits from engaging in and forming close relationships with their proteges, and these relationships have been linked to job satisfaction, career success, and organizational commitment (Ghosh & Reio, 2013). However, a high level of engagement in mentoring requires a great deal of time and energy, which can be distracting and detrimental to a mentor's ability to complete other tasks. Additionally, relationship dysfunction can have negative implications for mentors, leading to diminished reputation, stress, and decreased productivity (Lunsford, Baker, Griffin, & Johnson, 2013). Ensuring that mentors have an appropriate and personally manageable number of proteges, and that these relationships are psychologically healthy and generative, will likely result in more favorable outcomes for mentors.

Situating this understanding within a larger context that acknowledges *identity* and *organizational structures and dynamics* pushes us to be equity minded in our personal mentoring practice, as well as when we create policies and programs that promote developmental relationships. It is critical to be cognizant of how *mentor and mentee identities* determine the extent to which individuals have access to mentoring relationships. Given that mentors are often attracted to those who share their most salient identities (Johnson, 2016) and that individuals who have reached the top of the administrative hierarchy and are in positions to mentor are often members of the most privileged groups (e.g. White, male, cisgender, heterosexual), many administrators with minoritized identities may not find a match. Homophily can also translate to higher rates of engagement for mentors who have marginalized identities, as mentees seek them for guidance and support as they navigate identity-based challenges and hostile environments (Griffin & Reddick, 2011; O'Meara et al., 2017). Identity also has implications for relationship quality. Proteges with minoritized identities often report lower levels of relationship quality (e.g. Patton, 2009), and the hierarchical nature of traditional relationships can foster dysfunction and dissatisfaction for individuals who are already on the margins.

The importance of identity is amplified when it is considered in concert with *organizational structures and dynamics*. The intersection of these two dimensions in the EM[3] reminds us that as administrators engage in equity-minded practice, they must recognize how mentors' and proteges' identities differentially expose them to power, privilege, and oppression. Identity-based marginalization (e.g. racism, sexism, ableism) is embedded within the structures of higher education, and administrators must recognize how expectations, policies, and decisions made by institutional leaders amplify rather than mitigate the challenges associated with mentoring in the academy. For example, the psychosocial costs associated with the heavy mentoring loads that many women and men of color carry are exacerbated by institutional hiring, advancement, and reward structures that do not recognize this work as valuable service to the institution. A lack of structure, formal policy, or oversight of developmental relationships may leave those most vulnerable without recourse if their mentors are negligent or causing harm. Thus, as administrators become more equity minded, they must consider not only what structures, policies, and procedures are in place and whether they have implications for mentors and proteges; they must also attend to how these practices can have very different implications across campus communities.

STRATEGIES TO ADDRESS INEQUITIES AND PROMOTE BETTER OUTCOMES

When administrators implement this model, they may experience a shift in perspective that allows them to innovate and reconsider not only how they are engaging in their personal mentoring relationships, but also how they evaluate others and structure mentoring programs and opportunities. I have included principles to follow and specific strategies below that are consistent with the EM³, have overlapping implications, and the potential to shift who is engaging in mentoring relationships, the quality of the interactions, and access to relationship outcomes.

Formalizing Expectations

In many cases, there are implicit rather than explicit expectations around mentorship, which contributes to unequal levels of access to and engagement in mentoring. For example, mentoring junior colleagues is rarely listed as a formal professional expectation or responsibility in administrative job descriptions. If mentoring is included as a formal responsibility, there are rarely guidelines about how many mentees someone should have nor is emphasis placed on the importance of cultivating relationships with individuals who have minoritized identities.

Clearly stated expectations about engagement in mentoring provide new avenues for holding those not participating or only supporting those who are most like themselves accountable, as well as recognizing and promoting administrators who frequently mentor and have more diverse networks. For example, when expectations are formalized, engagement in developmental relationships can be considered in hiring decisions and performance reviews. This level of oversight can lead to more equitable distributions of the mentoring load, clarifying that *all* will be expected to invest time and energy, not just the women and men of color who have traditionally been relied upon. Further, setting clear expectations that administrators will support and develop a diverse group of mentees can make mentors more mindful of who they seek out as potential proteges and expands who has access to developmental relationships. Addressing how mentoring is recognized can also influence mentors' personal and professional outcomes, drawing additional attention to the unique ways in which women, men of color, and individuals embrace other marginalized identities that contribute to the academy, more adequately celebrating their work and investment in the development of the next generation of institutional leaders.

Incentivizing Participation

Providing more attractive incentives may also encourage wider engagement in mentoring and offer additional support to minoritized professionals who often participate in developmental relationships at higher rates. While many campuses offer mentoring awards or allow individuals to indicate mentoring as a form of service to the profession, these forms of recognition may not be sufficient to increase access and engagement or encourage time investments that would result in better relationship quality. Creating opportunities for mentors to apply for supplemental grants, receive time releases, or renegotiate engagement in other forms of campus service may encourage participation and interest while also increasing the likelihood that individuals with minoritized identities receive support.

Leaders should also consider how to bring more prestige and visibility to mentoring awards, perhaps connecting them to financial incentives for individuals or departments, or more widely and visibly recognizing mentors' commitments and achievements. While it is outside of a specific institution, the Spencer Foundation offers an excellent example. They have initiated a new grant, the Spencer Mentor Award, which provides selected mentors with $25,000, recognizing their extraordinary contributions to the training and professional development of graduate students and junior scholars. Such an award offered by an institution or a respected professional association can highlight the importance of mentorship and celebrate mentors' time and contributions, perhaps encouraging others to participate.

Professionalizing Mentoring

Administrators may also consider creating new professional roles charged with offering identity-aware mentorship and guidance to increase access to mentoring and improve relationship quality. Individuals on campus who have been identified as effective mentors that honor identity in their relationships could be offered supplemental salary to more broadly serve the campus community, implementing good mentoring practice with proteges that may be outside of their unit or functional area. Richard McGee at Northwestern University and Angela Byars-Winston at the University of Wisconsin have engaged in research and practice focused on the implementation of career coaching programs for graduate students and junior faculty, and found that trained coaches that honor identity are uniquely positioned to promote career outcomes for their proteges (read more at Byars-Winston et al., 2011; Williams, Thakore, & McGee, 2016). Similar principles can and should be translated to relationships within higher education administration.

There is certainly no one way to professionalize mentoring and multiple strategies could be successful; the central principle is to make offering culturally sensitive mentoring someone's job, and to ensure that potential proteges know that these resources exist. Team leaders could be hired to create communities of practice for minoritized administrators, offering information on navigating administrative systems and hierarchies, socioemotional support, and opportunities to cultivate broader networks. Administrators could also consider contracting with well-trained and experienced external consultants who can offer similar forms of support, significantly increasing the likelihood that junior and mid-career professionals are able to find the specific assistance and resources they need.

Identity Awareness in Professional Development for Mentors

Professional development may also be helpful in promoting equity in mentoring relationships by improving relationship quality. In addition to highlighting the norms and values associated with good mentoring practice overall, it is critical that these interventions emphasize unique dimensions of working with minoritized populations, helping mentors recognize the importance of their and their mentees' identities as they form relationships, how academic cloning and bias can affect both the formation and quality of relationships, and the importance of effective cross-cultural communication (Johnson & Gandhi, 2015).

Mentor training is an increasingly popular strategy. The National Research Mentoring Network (NRMN, https://nrmnet.net/) offers high-quality resources largely targeting students, faculty, and administrators implementing mentoring programs and policies. Short-term workshops and trainings can also provide guidance, helping mentors understand the scope of their responsibilities and learn about campus resources that can support their practice. It is also important to create opportunities for mentors to engage in long-term, more intensive training (Pfund et al., 2014; Pfund, Pribbenow, Branchaw, Lauffer, & Handelsman, 2006). If institutions are unable to implement training programs, curating websites or printed manuals that offer access to guidebooks and other resources highlighting promising practice in mentorship can be a good first step. The University of Michigan's Center for Research on Teaching and Learning offers comprehensive resources for faculty on their website (www.crlt.umich.edu/faculty/facment). These kinds of resources could be expanded to address the needs of administrators as well and be shared more widely with campus communities.

Assessment, Reporting, and Accountability

Some of the challenges associated with providing equitable access to high-quality mentoring relationships and addressing relationship dysfunction are rooted in our ability to assess relationship quality. Some institutions are creating ways for students to report on the quality and nature of their relationships with their professors. For example, when I was a professor at Penn State, the College of Education asked my advisees to complete a short assessment of whether and how I was meeting their needs and expectations. The Center for the Improvement of Mentored Experiences in Research (CIMER; https://cimerproject.org/) offers evaluative tools to assess mentoring relationships in the context of undergraduate research. However, there are few strategies that have been developed to assess the depth and quality of the relationships administrators form.

Developing more accurate assessment strategies and data systems are important steps to take in the process of increasing equity in access to high-quality mentoring relationships. Given inequities in relationship quality by identity, it is important to collect information that allows for deeper insight into the identities of the individuals mentors are supporting, the behaviors they are engaging in, and the time and energy being invested in their relationships. Creating, publicizing, and encouraging the use of reporting structures that allow proteges to anonymously share their concerns or incidents of marginalization and oppression will promote equity by more quickly allowing institutional leaders to identify problematic relationships.

Further, innovative methods of data collection, analysis, and disaggregation are recommended. Social network analysis, which maps how individuals are connected and resources are exchanged in relationships, has been used as a tool in mentoring research by scholars like Meghan Pifer and Vicki Baker (Pifer, 2011; Pifer & Baker, 2013). However, it is rarely leveraged by campuses to better understand the extent to which administrators are engaged in homophilous mentoring networks or the kinds of support to which they have access (if proteges) or are providing (if mentors). Examining mentors' and mentees' social networks can provide a strong foundation from which to establish professional development plans, illuminating both whether mentees have access to the support they need and whether mentors are reaching out to proteges from diverse backgrounds. Also, given the importance of understanding how intersectionality may shape who has access and is expected to engage in mentoring, our efforts must go beyond comparing measures of access and engagement, quality, and outcomes associated with mentoring by singular identities. Rather, assessing these dimensions based on race and gender, gender and administrative position, or sexual identity and gender may reveal nuances and patterns previously missed.

CONCLUSION

Given its power to serve as a social lever and provide access to support and guidance, mentoring can and should be a strategy widely supported and implemented by institutional leaders to increase access and success in higher education for the most marginalized. However, while mentoring has the potential to be helpful, and in many cases transformational, it is also important to not see the mere existence of mentoring programs or relationships as a panacea. If mentoring is seen as an activity that is "nice, but not necessary," many may not consider the time and energy worth the investment, continuing to leave the heavy lifting to those who feel special commitments to mentoring or working with marginalized communities. Institutional leaders must continually ask whether and how mentoring is available to all who seek support, meeting proteges' needs, and being shared and recognized as a valued service to the academy. Without these steps, the efficacy of mentoring programs and policies will continue to benefit some, but not all participants, and our field will miss valuable opportunities to promote and support a more diverse body of scholars and institutional leaders.

QUESTIONS FOR REFLECTION AND DISCUSSION

1. What are your most salient identities, and how have they influenced your access to mentoring and the quality of those relationships in the past? How would you like your identity to be recognized or honored in mentoring relationships in the future?
2. Given the context of your unit and/or institution, which strategies do you think should be implemented and would be the most effective for improving minoritized administrators' access to mentoring relationships, relationship quality, and the outcomes associated with mentoring?
3. Case Study: Imagine that you supervise a mid-level professional who is a woman of color. She is committed to, but overwhelmed by, her commitment to mentoring students. At the same time, she finds her relationship with her assigned mentor to be very difficult. She describes him as helpful and kind, but demanding of her time, micromanaging her professional development plans, and possessive, adamant that she does not seek advice from anyone else. How would you advise her and intervene to offer her support?

FURTHER READING

Johnson, W. B., & Smith, D. (2016). *Athena Rising: How and Why Men Should Mentor Women*. New York: Routledge.

National Academies of Sciences, Engineering, and Medicine (2017) *Effective Mentoring in STEMM: Practice, Research, and Future Directions: Proceedings of a Workshop–in Brief*. Washington, DC: The National Academies Press. https://doi.org/10.17226/24815.

REFERENCES

Baez, B. (2000). Race-related service and faculty of color: Conceptualizing critical agency in academe. *Higher Education*, 39(3), 363–391. https://doi.org/10.1023/A:1003972214943

Baker, V. L., Pifer, M. J., & Griffin, K. A. (2014). Mentor-protégé fit. *International Journal for Researcher Development*, 5(2), 83–98. https://doi.org/10.1108/IJRD-04-2014-0003

Blake-Beard, S., Bayne, M. L., Crosby, F. J., & Muller, C. B. (2011). Matching by race and gender in mentoring relationships: Keeping our eyes on the prize. *Journal of Social Issues*, 67(3), 622–643. https://doi.org/10.1111/j.1540-4560.2011.01717.x

Brown II, M. C., Davis, G. L., & McClendon, S. A. (1999). Mentoring graduate students of color: Myths, models, and modes. *Peabody Journal of Education, 74*(2), 105–118. https://doi.org/10.1207/s15327930pje7402_9

Brown, T. M. (2005). Mentorship and the female college president. *Sex Roles, 52*(9–10), 659–666. https://doi.org/10.1007/s11199-005-3733-7

Byars-Winston, A., Gutierrez, B., Topp, S., & Carnes, M. (2011). Integrating theory and practice to increase scientific workforce diversity: A framework for career development in graduate research training. *CBE—Life Sciences Education, 10*(4), 357–367. https://doi.org/10.1187/cbe.10-12-0145

Chang, H., Longman, K. A., & Franco, M. A. (2014). Leadership development through mentoring in higher education: A collaborative autoethnography of leaders of color. *Mentoring & Tutoring: Partnership in Learning, 22*(4), 373–389. https://doi.org/10.1080/13611267.2014.945734

Chesler, N. C., & Chesler, M. A. (2002). Gender-informed mentoring strategies for women engineering scholars: On establishing a caring community. *Journal of Engineering Education, 91*(1), 49–55. https://doi.org/10.1002/j.2168-9830.2002.tb00672.x

Cianni, M., & Romberger, B. (1995). Perceived racial, ethnic, and gender differences in access to developmental experiences. *Group & Organization Management, 20*(4), 440–459. https://doi.org/10.1177/1059601195204004

Cole, D., & Griffin, K. A. (2013). Advancing the study of student–faculty interaction: A focus on diverse students and faculty. In M. B. Paulsen (Ed.), *Higher Education: Handbook of Theory and Research* (pp. 561–611). New York: Springer.

Collins, P. H. (2000). *Black Feminist Thought: Knowledge, Consciousness, and the Politics of Empowerment.* New York: Routledge.

Crisp, G., Baker, V.L., Griffin, K.A., Lunsford, L.G., & Pifer, M.J. (2017). *Mentoring undergraduate students.* ASHE Higher Education Report (vol. 43, no. 1). San Francisco, CA: Jossey-Bass.

Dugan, J. P., Kusel, M. L., & Simounet, D. M. (2012). Transgender college students: An exploratory study of perceptions, engagement, and educational outcomes. *Journal of College Student Development, 53*(5), 719–736. https://doi.org/10.1353/csd.2012.0067

Eby, L. T., & Allen, T. D. (2002). Further investigation of protégés' negative mentoring experiences. *Group & Organization Management, 27*(4), 456–479. https://doi.org/10.1177/1059601102238357

Eby, L. T., Butts, M. M., Durley, J., & Ragins, B. R. (2010). Are bad experiences stronger than good ones in mentoring relationships? Evidence from the protégé and mentor perspective. *Journal of Vocational Behavior, 77*(1), 81–92. https://doi.org/10.1016/j.jvb.2010.02.010

Ensher, E., & Murphy, S. (2005). *Power Mentoring: How Successful Mentors and Proteges Get the Most out of Their Relationships.* San Francisco, CA: Jossey-Bass.

Felder, P. (2010). On doctoral student development: Exploring faculty mentoring in the shaping of African American doctoral student success. *The Qualitative Report, 15*(2), 455–474.

Ghosh, R., & Reio Jr, T. G. (2013). Career benefits associated with mentoring for mentors: A meta-analysis. *Journal of Vocational Behavior, 83*(1), 106–116.

Gibson, S. K. (2004). Being mentored: The experience of women faculty. *Journal of Career Development, 30*(3), 173–188. https://doi.org/10.1177/089484530403000301

Griffin, K. A. (2013). Voices of the "othermothers": Reconsidering Black Professors' relationships with Black students as a form of social exchange. *The Journal of Negro Education, 82*(2), 169. https://doi.org/10.7709/jnegroeducation.82.2.0169

Griffin, K. A., & Reddick, R. J. (2011). Surveillance and sacrifice: Gender differences in mentoring patterns of Black professors at predominantly White research universities. *American Educational Research Journal, 48*(5), 1032–1057. https://doi.org/10.3102/0002831211405025

Guiffrida, D. (2005). Othermothering as a framework for understanding African American students' definitions of student-centered faculty. *The Journal of Higher Education, 76*(6), 701–723. https://doi.org/10.1080/00221546.2005.11772305

Hirt, J. B., Amelink, C. T., McFeeters, B. B., & Strayhorn, T. L. (2008). A system of othermothering: Student affairs administrators' perceptions of relationships with students at Historically Black Colleges. *NASPA Journal, 45*(2), 210–236. https://doi.org/10.2202/1949-6605.1948

Jackson, S., & Harris, S. (2000). African American female college and university presidents: Experiences and perceptions of barriers to the presidency. *Journal of Women in Educational Leadership, 5*(2), 119–137.

Jean-Marie, G., Williams, V. A., & Sherman, S. L. (2009). Black women's leadership experiences: Examining the intersectionality of race and gender. *Advances in Developing Human Resources, 11*(5), 562–581. https://doi.org/10.1177/1523422309351836

Johnson-Bailey, J., Cervero, R. M., & Bowles, T. A. (2009). Rooted in the soil: The social experiences of Black graduate students at a southern research university, *Journal of Higher Education, 80*(2), 178–203. https://doi.org/10.1353/jhe.0.0040

Johnson, M. O., & Gandhi, M. (2015). A mentor training program improves mentoring competency for researchers working with early-career investigators from underrepresented backgrounds. *Advances in Health Sciences Education, 20*(3), 683–689. https://doi.org/10.1007/s10459-014-9555-z

Johnson, W. B. (2016). *On Being a Mentor: A Guide for Higher Education Faculty* (2nd ed.). New York: Routledge.

Joseph, T. D., & Hirshfield, L. E. (2011). "Why don't you get somebody new to do it?" Race and cultural taxation in the academy. *Ethnic and Racial Studies, 34*(1), 121–141. https://doi.org/10.1080/01419870.2010.496489

Kelly, B. T., & McCann, K. I. (2014). Women faculty of color: Stories behind the statistics. *Urban Review, 46*(4), 681–702. https://doi.org/10.1007/s11256-014-0275-8

Kim, Y. K., & Sax, L. J. (2009). Student–faculty interaction in research universities: Differences by student gender, race, social class, and first-generation status. *Research in Higher Education, 50*(5), 437–459. https://doi.org/10.1007/s11162-009-9127-x

Kram, K. E. (1988). *Mentoring at Work: Developmental Relationships in Organizational Life.* New York: University Press of America.

Kumar, P., & Blake-Beard, S. (2012). What good is bad mentorship? Protégé's perception of negative mentoring experiences. *Indian Journal of Industrial Relations, 48*(1), 79–93.

León, D. J., & Nevarez, C. (2007). Models of leadership institutes for increasing the number of top Latino administrators in higher education. *Journal of Hispanic Higher Education, 6*(4), 356–377. https://doi.org/10.1177/1538192707305344

Lunsford, L. G., Baker, V., Griffin, K. A., & Johnson, W. B. (2013). Mentoring: A typology of costs for higher education faculty. *Mentoring & Tutoring: Partnership in Learning, 21*(2), 126–149.

Malcom-Piqueux, L., & Bensimon, E. M. (2017). Taking equity-minded action to close equity gaps. *Peer Review, 19*(2), 5.

Mayhew, M. J., Rockenbach, A. J., Bowman, N. A., Seifert, T. A., Wolniak, G. C., Pascarella, E. T., & Terenzini, P. T. (2016). *How College Affects Students: 21st Century Evidence that Higher Education Works* (3rd ed.). San Francisco, CA: Jossey-Bass.

McCoy, D. L., Winkle-Wagner, R., & Luedke, C. L. (2015). Colorblind mentoring? Exploring White faculty mentoring of students of color. *Journal of Diversity in Higher Education, 8*(4), 225–242. https://doi.org/10.1037/a0038676

McPherson, M., Smith-Lovin, L., & Cook, J. M. (2001). Birds of a feather: Homophily in social networks. *Annual Review of Sociology, 27*(1), 415–444. https://doi.org/10.1146/annurev.soc.27.1.415

Milkman, K. L., Akinola, M., & Chugh, D. (2012). Temporal distance and discrimination: An audit study in academia. *Psychological Science, 23*(7), 710–717. https://doi.org/10.1177/0956797611434539

Moss-Racusin, C. A., Dovidio, J. F., Brescoll, V. L., Graham, M. J., & Handelsman, J. (2012). Science faculty's subtle gender biases favor male students. *Proceedings of the National Academy of Sciences, 109*(41), 16474–16479. https://doi.org/10.1073/pnas.211286109

O'Meara, K., Kuvaeva, A., Nyunt, G., Waugaman, C., & Jackson, R. (2017). Asked more often: Gender differences in faculty workload in research universities and the work interactions that shape them. *American Educational Research Journal, 54*(6), 1154–1186. https://doi.org/10.3102/0002831217716767

Olson, D. A., & Jackson, D. (2009). Expanding leadership diversity through formal mentoring programs. *Journal of Leadership Studies, 3*(1), 47–60. https://doi.org/10.1002/jls.20095

Ong, M., Wright, C., Espinosa, L., & Orfield, G. (2011). Inside the double bind: A synthesis of empirical research on undergraduate and graduate women of color in science, technology, engineering, and mathematics. *Harvard Educational Review, 81*(2), 172–209. https://doi.org/10.17763/haer.81.2.t022245n7x4752v2

Padilla, A. M. (1994). Ethnic minority scholars, research, and mentoring: Current and future issues. *Educational Researcher*, *23*(4), 24–27. https://doi.org/10.3102/0013189X023004024

Patitu, C. L., & Hinton, K. G. (2003). The experiences of African American women faculty and administrators in higher education: Has anything changed? *New Directions for Student Services*, *104*(104), 79–93. https://doi.org/10.1002/ss.109

Patton, L. D. (2009). My sister's keeper: A qualitative examination of mentoring experiences among African American women in graduate and professional schools. *The Journal of Higher Education*, *80*(5), 510–537. https://doi.org/10.1080/00221546.2009.11779030

Pena, E. V., Bensimon, E. M., & Colyar, J. (2006). Contextual problem defining: Learning to think and act. *Liberal Education, Spring*, 48–55.

Pfund, C., House, S. C., Asquith, P., Fleming, M. F., Buhr, K. A., & Burnham, E. L. (2014). Training mentors of clinical and translational research scholars: A randomized controlled trial. *Academic Medicine*, *89*(5), 774–782. https://doi.org/10.1097/ACM.0000000000000218.Training

Pfund, C., Pribbenow, C. M., Branchaw, J., Lauffer, S. M., & Handelsman, J. (2006). The merits of training mentors. *Science*, *311*(5760), 473–474. https://doi.org/10.1126/science.1123806

Phillips, S. L., Dennison, S. T., & Davenport, M. A. (2016). High retention of minority and international faculty through a formal mentoring program. *To Improve the Academy*, *35*(1), 153–179. https://doi.org/10.1002/tia2.20034

Pifer, M. J. (2011). Intersectionality in context: A mixed-methods approach to researching the faculty experience. *New Directions for Institutional Research*, *2011*(151), 27–44.

Pifer, M. J., & Baker, V. L. (2013). Managing the process: The intradepartmental networks of early-career academics. *Innovative Higher Education*, *38*(4), 323–337.

Posselt, J. (2018). Normalizing struggle: Dimensions of faculty support for doctoral students and implications for persistence and well-being. *Journal of Higher Education*, *89*(6), 988–1013. https://doi.org/10.1080/00221546.2018.1449080

Renn, K. A. (2007). LGBT Student leaders and Queer activists: Identities of Lesbian, Gay, Bisexual, Transgender, and Queer identified college student leaders and activists. *Journal of College Student Development*, *48*(3), 311–330. https://doi.org/10.1353/csd.2007.0029

Renn, K. A. (2010). LGBT and Queer research in higher education. *Educational Researcher*, *39*(2), 132–141. https://doi.org/10.3102/0013189X10362579

Schrodt, P., Cawyer, C. S., & Sanders, R. (2003). An examination of academic mentoring behaviors and new faculty members' satisfaction with socialization and tenure and promotion processes. *Communication Education*, *52*(1), 17–29. https://doi.org/10.1080/03634520302461

Stewart, D-L. (2017). Colleges need a language shift, but not the one you think (essay). Retrieved August 27, 2018, from www.insidehighered.com/views/2017/03/30/colleges-need-language-shift-not-one-you-think-essay.

Thomas, G. D., & Hollenshead, C. (2011). Resisting from the margins: The coping strategies of Black women and other women of color faculty members at a research university. *The Journal of Negro Education*, *70*(3), 166–175.

Tierney, W. G., & Bensimon, E. M. (1996). *Promotion and tenure: Community and socialization in academe*. Albany, NY: State University of New York Press.

Turner, C. S. V. (2002). Women of color in academe: Living with multiple marginality. *The Journal of Higher Education*, *73*(1), 74–93. https://doi.org/10.1353/jhe.2002.0013

Turner, C. S. V., González, J. C., & Wong, K. (2011). Faculty women of color: The critical nexus of race and gender. *Journal of Diversity in Higher Education*, *4*(4), 199–211. https://doi.org/10.1037/a0024630

Williams, S. N., Thakore, B. K., & McGee, R. (2016). Career coaches as a source of vicarious learning for racial and ethnic minority PhD students in the biomedical sciences: A qualitative study. *PloS one*, *11*(7), e0160038.

Zambrana, R. E., Ray, R., Espino, M. M., Castro, C., Douthirt Cohen, B., & Eliason, J. (2015). "Don't leave us behind": The importance of mentoring for underrepresented minority faculty. *American Educational Research Journal*, *52*(1), 40–72. https://doi.org/10.3102/0002831214563063

Zellers, D. F., Howard, V. M., & Barcic, M. A. (2008). Faculty mentoring programs: Reenvisioning rather than reinventing the wheel. *Review of Educational Research*, *78*(3), 552–588. https://doi.org/10.3102/0034654308320966

7

RECONCEPTUALIZING "MERIT" AND "FIT"

An Equity-Minded Approach to Hiring

ROMAN LIERA AND CHERYL CHING

INTRODUCTION

In the 1960s, multiracial coalitions of college students "espous[ing] the rhetoric and tactics of Third World revolutionaries" (Ryan, 2015, p. 413) called for radical changes to institutions of higher education.[1] Among their demands was the hiring of leaders and faculties who reflect the background, knowledge, and experiences of racially minoritized communities (e.g. Asian, Blacks, Latinx, Native Americans) (Ngyuen & Gasman, 2015; Ryan, 2015). Sixty years into this project, administrative and faculty bodies remain racially homogenous (Eddy, 2018; Sensoy & DiAngelo, 2017). Across two- and four-year public and private not-for-profit colleges, 79% of executive, administrative, and managerial positions, and 76% of full-time faculty positions, are occupied by whites (Almanac, 2017; U.S. Department of Education, 2018). In 2015, as students across the nation publicly demanded the end of systemic and structural racism in higher education, they again called for the hiring of more administrators and faculty from racially minoritized backgrounds who can address issues of racial injustice (We the Protestors, 2015).

In this chapter, we join scholars and practitioners[2] who approach the limited racial diversity of college administrators and faculty as an equity and social justice issue (e.g. Eddy, 2018; Sensoy & DiAngelo, 2017). We focus on race in particular, not to diminish other equity and social justice claims, but because racial equity and justice remain elusive in higher education despite over a century of policies and reform efforts (Harper, Patton, & Wooden, 2009). The need for racial equity in academic hiring is increasingly urgent as the numbers of Asian, Black, Latinx, and Pacific Islander college students continue to grow (Kena et al., 2016). The demographic mismatch between racially diverse student populations and racially homogenous administrator and faculty bodies is an injustice to the former, who research shows are better served by racially minoritized practitioners who are more likely to foster their achievements (Fairlie, Hoffmann, & Oreopoulos, 2014); use culturally relevant and affirming pedagogies (antonio, 1999; Milem, 2001); curb stereotype threat (Steele, 1997); develop personal relationships with them (Levin, Walker, Jackson-Boothby, & Haberler, 2013); enhance their sense of belonging (Benitez, James, Joshua, Perfetti, & Vick, 2017; Chapa, 2006; Harris & Wood, 2013; Hurtado & Carter, 1997); advocate on their behalf (Allen, Epps, Guillory, Suh, & Bonous-Hammarth, 2000; Guiffrida, 2005); and be someone with whom they can identify and more easily approach (Cole & Griffin, 2013).

Equally important, the slow progress toward racially diversifying administrator and faculty populations suggests that what has been done so far is not enough; continued effort is needed to unsettle, even unseat, how academic hiring is done. Following earlier scholarship on administrator and faculty hiring, we argue that meeting the demands for racial diversity and equity in academic hiring is challenged by criteria of "merit" and "fit" that are normed to white, male, and Western European epistemological ideals (e.g. Busenberg & Smith, 1997; Danowitz Sagaria, 2002; Eddy, 2018; Sensoy & DiAngelo, 2017). "Merit" includes criteria used to determine whether applicants have the requisite experience and competence to meet position requirements and responsibilities (Posselt, 2016; Rivera, 2015), while "fit" encompasses criteria used to evaluate whether applicants are appropriate for an organization's culture, values, and environment (Danowitz Sagaria, 2002; Rivera, 2015; Twombly, 2005). As non-neutral, institutionalized ideals that have been constructed according to dominant perspectives on race and other social categories, interrogating conceptions of merit and fit is needed to surface these perspectives, consider their effects, and make the changes needed to realize racial equity in academic hiring processes and outcomes. To do so, we draw on the principles of "equity-mindedness," which (a) foregrounds race in analyses of how colleges operate; (b) recognizes that institutional racism is an entrenched characteristic of higher education institutions; (c) assumes that racial inequities (e.g. in academic hiring) stem from practices that are undergirded by racialized norms, beliefs, and values; and (d) places responsibility on practitioners to change those practices (Bensimon, 2007, 2012; Dowd & Bensimon, 2015).

This chapter begins with a review of key factors that contribute to persistent racial inequities in academic hiring: limited racial diversity among administrators and faculty on campus; myths and misperceptions about racially minoritized candidates; and the impact of implicit bias on decision-making. We then focus on how traditional conceptions of merit and fit shape the hiring chances of racially minoritized administrators and faculty, and suggest that reframing these conceptions in an equity-minded way is in order. In the second half of the chapter, we present a suite of "critical inquiry" tools that practitioners can use to examine how hiring is conducted on their campus, how merit and fit are currently conceived, and how equity-minded conceptions of merit and fit can be centered. The use of these tools, along with other strategies discussed throughout the chapter, can help practitioners embed racial equity in academic hiring on their campuses in deep ways.

HIRING IN HIGHER EDUCATION

Scholarly and practitioner publications have long examined academic hiring, describing administrators and faculty recruitment processes (e.g. Kaplowitz, 1986); analyzing factors that shape employer preferences and candidate choices (e.g. Taylor & Bergman, 1987); demonstrating the limited rationality and interpretive nature of academic searches (e.g. Twombly, 1992); and arguing for good "social matches" between positions and applicants (e.g. Birnbaum, 1988). Within this literature is a body of work that examines how and why racial diversity in academe remains limited, despite affirmative action and equal employment opportunity programs, institutional espousals of diversity's importance, calls from students for more representative leadership and faculty bodies, and consistent evidence demonstrating the tangible value of racially minoritized administrators and professors on student outcomes and campus experiences (Konrad & Pfeffer, 1991; Ngyuen & Gasman, 2015; Tuitt, Danowitz Sagaria, & Turner, 2007; Turner, Myers, & Creswell, 1999).

LIMITED DIVERSITY

Some studies suggest that the problem of racial inequity in academic hiring stems in part from the limited diversity of administrators and faculty already at an institution. For example, Konrad and Pfeffer's (1991) analysis of national college personnel compensation data suggests that racially minoritized (and women) candidates are more likely to be hired for senior administrative positions if individuals with similar racial (and gender) backgrounds previously held those posts, or if a campus employs a significant proportion of racially minoritized (and women) practitioners. Limited diversity also presents issues for recruitment through professional networks, which may be "segregated," thus making it difficult for news of a position to reach racially minoritized candidates (Turner, 2002, p. 17). Finally, limited diversity may mean that search committees will lack members from racially minoritized backgrounds who could offer needed perspectives to make sense of the qualifications and experiences of racially minoritized candidates, particularly those who focus on issues of race. As Turner, Myers, and Creswell (1999) note, "research interests of faculty of color are denigrated, either because the research area is not 'traditional' or because the faculty themselves are seen as inferior due to race or ethnicity" (p. 31).

Addressing the limited diversity among administrators and faculty at an institution requires long-term planning and multiple strategies, a number of which are offered in this chapter. Turner (2002) suggests that campuses with few administrators and faculty of color invite graduate students from racially minoritized backgrounds or colleagues of color from nearby institutions to serve on search committees. If this strategy is pursued, the committee chair should take care in monitoring meeting dynamics, specifically with respect to how junior and outside members are engaged and how their contributions are considered by senior peers. To counter the potential issue of segregated professional networks, Turner (2002) proposes that practitioners in departments that seek to hire take proactive steps to expand the people with whom they share job announcements. This could mean reaching out: to colleagues at institutions that are known for producing high numbers of graduates from racially minoritized backgrounds (including minority-serving institutions such as Tribal Colleges and Historically Black Colleges and Universities); to organizations devoted to advancing the success of racially minoritized groups (e.g. Society for Advancement of Chicanos/Hispanics and Native Americans in Science [SACNAS]); to diversity and equity offices of national consortia (e.g. Office of Diversity, Equity, and Student Success at the Association of American Colleges & Universities [AAC&U]); and to diversity-related publications (e.g. *Diverse Issues in Higher Education*).

MYTHS ABOUT RACIALLY MINORITIZED CANDIDATES

Other studies have linked racial inequity in academic hiring to misperceptions about racially minoritized candidates on the job market. For example, interviews with an elite cohort of 299 doctoral degree holders—all of whom received prestigious research fellowships—about their academic labor market experiences surfaced "myths" that shaped their search processes (Smith, Wolf-Wendel, & Busenberg, 1996; Smith, 2000). One such myth is they were the "beneficiaries of bidding wars" given their scarce number (Smith, 2000, p. 48). In reality, only 11 percent of those interviewed were sought out by search committees for faculty positions. Another myth is that PhDs of color are always being recruited by institutions with more prestige and resources, leading to a "revolving door that limits progress for any single institution in diversifying its faculty" (p. 50). Participant interviews suggested that the allure of financial incentives is not on its own enough to motivate a move to another institution and that the "revolving door" is more likely to occur because of hostile racial climates on campus. Turner and Myers (2000) add that there is no difference in the rate at which racially minoritized and white faculty change jobs—contrary to popular opinion.

"Debunking" these myths and others may not be easy, however as Turner (2002) advises, they "must be addressed consistently" (p. 17). Based on research indicating that personal relationships across racial lines can help mitigate the effects of racial myths and stereotypes, she suggests that institutions create structured opportunities for inter- and intra-racial interactions around the goal of enhancing understanding and inclusion. Other myth-debunking strategies center on data collection and use. For example, Moreno, Smith, Clayton-Pedersen, Parker, & Teraguchi (2006) propose that search committees review data on candidate pools disaggregated by race and ethnicity as a way of challenging the myth that there is a "limited pipeline" of qualified Asian, Black, Latinx, Native American, and Pacific Islander candidates for a position. Given that some departments may have a stronger track record of recruiting racially diverse practitioners than others (Smith, Turner, Osei-Kofi, & Richards, 2004), their hiring practices and strategies could be shared and used as the basis for campus-wide conversation and professional development (Moreno et al., 2006).

IMPLICIT BIAS

A third area of study attends to how implicit bias affects decision making during the academic hiring process. Implicit bias operates below consciousness and strikes when individuals such as search committee members have access to limited information, are under time pressure, and have to juggle multiple commitments (Staats, Capatosto, Wright, & Contractor, 2015). It is especially likely to show up under conditions of uncertainty such as with searches for campus leaders who have responsibility for complex tasks (Konrad & Pfeffer, 1991). Uncertainty heightens perceived risk, which motivates preference for what is known, or cognizable to search committees, whether it is the type of person who typically fills a role, the qualifications often associated with a position, or candidate references (Danowitz Sagaria, 2002; Konrad & Pfeffer, 1991; Kanter, 1977). This not only bounds who a search committee is willing to consider for a post but also limits who they imagine could fulfill position responsibilities. For instance, Konrad and Pfeffer's (1991) findings, which we describe above, can be read as an effect of implicit bias: the increased likelihood that a racially minoritized candidate was hired for a job previously held by a racially minoritized person could be due to that position being "typified" for a particular racial group. In field and experimental settings, scholars have shown that the *curricula vitae* (CV) of white candidates are preferred over those of racially minoritized applicants (Beattie, Cohen, & McGuire, 2013; Bertrand & Mullainathan, 2004; Gaddis, 2014). The qualifications of racially minoritized applicants are further diminished if they did not earn their degrees at prestigious research universities, if their research or academic trajectory strays from field conventions, or if their appearance, presentation, interactive style, language, and other such characteristics are not deemed a good "fit" for the organization (Tuitt et al., 2007). Such findings highlight how bias is reflected in interpretations of common qualifications—how what counts as "merit" in practice cannot be separated from the racialized schemas that decision-makers hold as they assess merit.

Those who study implicit bias note that mitigating its effects is challenging (Staats et al., 2015). While researchers agree that everyone is prone to implicit bias, which implicit biases a person holds, and the intensity of those biases, can vary. As a first step, search committee members can take steps to measure their implicit biases through tests such as the Implicit Association Test (IAT) (Project Implicit, 2011). Awareness will not inoculate a search committee member from implicit bias, however it can raise important questions about their presumed objectivity in evaluating candidates for a position, as well as identify the bias(es) to which they should attend. Fortunately, research suggests that implicit biases are malleable and hence can be modified or unlearned over time, through repeated "debiasing" practice (Staats et al., 2015, p. 65). Debiasing strategies that can be used in academic hiring processes include: (a) introducing counter-stereotypic examples of racially minoritized administrators and scholars whose race-focused work has made discipline- and/or field-changing contributions; (b) implementing a process of systematic review in which sufficient time is provided to go over candidate materials and a rubric with well-defined criteria (e.g. the criterion "excellence in research" should include multiple measures of "excellence") is used to guide evaluation; and (c) establishing an accountability system within search committees in which members are expected to defend their decision to accept or reject a candidate (Center for Urban Education, 2017; Staats et al., 2015).

MERIT AND FIT IN HIRING DECISIONS

As our discussion suggests, assessments of candidates' merit and fit for a position could be mediated by who sits on search committees and the implicit biases committee members hold; whereas the former establishes the body of knowledge and experience that can be brought to bear on evaluations of merit and fit, the latter anchor evaluations to particular standards, norms, and taken-for-granted notions of who is deemed worthy and suitable for a role.

Evidence of merit is usually discerned from a candidate's CV, cover letter, and references. It is from these materials that search committees make their first cut of the applicant pool, separating those who will receive an interview from those who will not be considered further. As "standard" application materials, they are treated as ostensibly "objective" sources of information about applicant quality and qualification (Uhlmann & Cohen, 2005). In the case of faculty searches, merit is often pegged to candidates' areas of research, epistemological and theoretical orientations, and methodological approaches. While perhaps a reasonable basis on which to judge an applicant's qualifications, as noted earlier, the qualifications of racially minoritized candidates who conduct research on "minority issues" using non-traditional methods and whose work appears in "non-mainstream journals" could be "devalu[ed]" (Turner et al., 1999, p. 31). Their scholarship could be judged as less "rigorous" relative to that of white candidates who use rational, scientific, positivist approaches (Gasman, Abiola, & Travers, 2015). With a race focus in their work, they could be seen as "diversity or ethnic specialists" rather than credible scholars who are poised to make significant contributions to the discipline or field (Sensoy & DiAngelo, 2017; Tuitt et al., 2007, pp. 516–517). These findings suggest that without search committee members who can speak to the potential of this kind of research and question traditional notions of what constitutes "good" scholarship, racially minoritized candidates' CV, cover letter, and recommendations may not be given serious review. Further complicating the evaluation of merit in academic hiring is evidence indicating that employers define merit self-servingly and assert the value of criteria that put their own credentials in a positive light—another manifestation of implicit bias (Uhlmann & Cohen, 2005). The assumption of objectivity in merit criteria can also open the door to stereotypes. Rivera (2015) found that after an initial screening of applicants' cognitive abilities, employers relied on stereotypical perceptions of interview performance—Black and Latinx men being subjected to greater scrutiny because of racial stereotypes portraying them as lacking social skills—disproportionately resulting in the elimination from the pool.

While merit is about qualification, fit is about matching the "right" applicant to the job (Tsai, Chi, Huang, & Hsu, 2011), organization (Chen, Lee, & Yeh, 2008; Higgins & Judge, 2004), or culture (Rivera, 2012). As with evaluations of merit, unstructured subjective assessments increase risks that implicit bias will enter into the hiring process and allow search committee members to draw on their emotional reactions, gut instincts, and feelings of chemistry to judge whether applicants are a good fit (Rivera, 2015). With fit, search committees are assessing qualities such as applicants' values, behaviors, tastes, identities, leisure pursuits, and self-presentation styles (Rivera, 2012). A subjective process, evaluations of fit are guided by what an organization desires *and* practitioners' personal beliefs (Rivera, 2015). For example, Danowitz Sagaria (2002) found that search chairs were more likely to express reservations about personality characteristics, behaviors, and dress only when the administrative candidate's race, gender, or both differed from their own. Search chairs believed that minoritized applicants who most closely emulated their culture, values, and behaviors had the competency to maintain the institutional culture. Perceived (in)congruence between applicants on the one hand, and the organization and its practitioners on the other hand, are associated with receiving or not receiving a job offer (Cable & Judge, 1997; Chen et al., 2008; Higgins & Judge, 2004; Kristof-Brown, 2000; Kristof-Brown, Barrick, & Franke, 2002; Tsai et al., 2011). Ultimately, search committees are not only drawn to hiring individuals with whom they share similarities, but who they find competent and whose perspectives and practices align with their intellectual and cultural ways of knowing (Gasman et al., 2015; Rivera, 2012, 2015).

The literature on critical race feminism provides a lens to understand merit and fit as racialized and gendered. According to critical race feminist scholars, US higher education is founded on a white, male, and Eurocentric epistemological perspective (Delgado-Bernal & Villalpando, 2002; Gonzales, 2018; Patton, 2016). Epistemology, understood in its simplest form as how people know what they know, shapes how individuals make sense of the world; it depends on structural positions, histories, and cultures; and informs what (and whose) knowledge and experience are valued (Gonzales, 2018; Patton, 2016; Scheurich & Young, 1997; Zuberi & Bonilla-Silva, 2008). A white, male, and Eurocentric epistemological perspective presumes that there is only one way of knowing and understanding the world (Delgado-Bernal & Villalpando, 2002). In higher education, this epistemology values an elite educational background, perspectives and methods that reflect linearity and objectivity, and practices and knowledge informed by the work of white men. In search committees, merit and fit can work together to disadvantage minoritized applicants and devalue epistemologies different from Eurocentric epistemologies. For example, during a first-round interview for a dean of equity position at a community college, one applicant, a white man, advocates for programs and services that extant research shows, on average, to close outcome gaps and that can be offered to all students. The research he is citing for this work, however, has predominantly white samples. Another applicant, an Asian woman, proposes race-conscious, culturally relevant programming for racially minoritized students only, based on an ethic of authentic care. The search committee, which is populated by members who subscribe to the belief that community college is for all students, balk at the idea of the ethnic of care, whom they judge as holding values that are antithetical to the aims of their college. In this example, the search committee's deference to research using statistics generated on mostly white samples reflects a certain Eurocentric epistemology that views statistics as a proxy to measure a job applicant's qualifications while assessing the applicant's values. In doing so, search committees ignore and exclude epistemologies that centralize a culturally relevant programming that is motivated by an ethic of care because of a misalignment in ways of knowing.

Without questioning how merit and fit are conceptualized, and how decision-makers interpret evidence of each, candidates whose knowledge and experience do not align with conventional notions will continue to be disadvantaged; in American higher education, these candidates are more likely to be from minoritized backgrounds (Eddy, 2018; Sensoy & DiAngelo, 2017). When search committee members fail to realize that their merit criteria are socially constructed and subjectively assessed rather than objective and rationally evaluated, they are likely to select candidates who reflect their disciplinary and personal identities, a phenomenon that social scientists call homophily (Lamont, 2009; Posselt, 2016). They are also more likely to label applicants who share their backgrounds (e.g. race, gender, epistemologies) as "collegial," relatable, and exciting (Posselt, 2016; Rivera, 2015; Sensoy & DiAngelo, 2017), and to judge them competent contributors to the organizational mission (Twombly, 2005). In this way, search committees that do not recognize—much less challenge—how their social and professional backgrounds ground prevailing definitions of merit and fit are more likely to value candidates who are white and/or who use approaches that are deemed rationale, linear, and scientific when evaluating administrator and faculty candidates.

AN EQUITY-MINDED RECONCEPTUALIZATION OF MERIT AND FIT

Given the centrality of merit and fit criteria in hiring and given that their taken-for-granted conceptions reinforce dominant norms, we argue that they must be reconceptualized in ways that further racial equity. As noted earlier, equity mindedness offers one possible reframing (Bensimon, 2007, 2012; Dowd & Bensimon, 2015). Equity-minded conceptions of merit and fit do not reinforce search committees' social and professional preferences; instead, they focus on what and how administrator and faculty candidates can do to advance racial equity for students and their campus. An equity-minded reconceptualization of merit expands the discussion and evidence of qualification from traditional markers to those that foreground candidates' experience with race and equity work (Table 7.1). For example, key criteria of equity-minded merit are experience teaching and mentoring racially minoritized students, and the ability to critically reflect on how college practices produce racialized outcomes. In addition to evaluating administrative candidates' leadership experience and technical expertise, an equity-minded framework looks for evidence of creating and leading initiatives designed to improve the environmental conditions for minoritized groups. An equity-minded framework values administrator and faculty candidates who not only have experience and expertise with racial equity and justice, but who recognize that college students have multiple identities that inform their engagement on campus (Bensimon, 2012; Dowd & Bensimon, 2015). For example, the experiences of a first-generation college student who identifies as a Latinx cisgender woman are different from a first-generation college student who identifies as indigenous non-binary.

Danowitz Sagaria (2002) observes that fit is not a replacement for competence or academic and professional experience; rather, fit is an "additional filter" that search committees used to judge candidates. Informing this filter is search committee members' comfort with the candidate and whether they believed others in the university would accept the candidate. As part of their evaluation of fit, search committees evaluate, often uncritically, candidates' body language and social interactions in order to identify and distinguish those whose behaviors aligned with unspoken workplace norms. When search committees do not question whether and how their expectations for fit align with their intellectual and cultural ways of knowing, they risk eliminating qualified minoritized candidates based on these criteria. With equity-minded fit, the focus is on hiring administrator and faculty candidates who reflect the racial diversity of the student body, and importantly, students' experiences, epistemologies, and social interests (Table 7.2). Search committee members who assess for fit from an equity-minded perspective look for evidence of understanding the experiences of minoritized groups, as well as how their colleagues and students from minoritized backgrounds interact with and respond to candidates during campus visits. Equity-minded conceptions of merit and fit mean that search committees will recruit and

TABLE 7.1 Traditional vs. Equity-Minded Conceptions of Merit

	Traditional Merit	**Equity-Minded Merit**
Training	Degrees earned from elite institutions Experience working with well-known advisors or programs	Training in racial equity and social justice work Experience with self-reflection and willingness to reflect on racialized outcomes of practice
Experience	Number of years working in leadership positions Technical and functional expertise Experience working in similar or higher ranked colleges and universities	Experience creating, organizing, and/or leading programs for minoritized groups Experience working with minoritized groups including students, administrative staff, and/or faculty
Research	Number of publications in top-tier, peer-reviewed journals Grants awarded	Publications that examine issues of race and racial equity Grants that support research, policy, and practice-based work focused on racial equity
Teaching	Number of years teaching Variety of courses taught	Experience teaching and mentoring racially minoritized students Experience using culturally relevant pedagogies Incorporates authors from minoritized groups in course syllabi
Service	Program, department, professional association leadership Committee work Journal and conference reviewing	Experience working as an equity advocate for students from minoritized backgrounds

Note. Adapted with permission from the Center for Urban Education (2017, p. 32).

TABLE 7.2 Traditional vs. Equity-Minded Conceptions of Fit

	Traditional Fit	**Equity-Minded Fit**
Values	Approaches to learning as an individual enterprise in which students are responsible for their success or failure	Holds high expectations of racially minoritized students Prioritizes the knowledges and needs of racially minoritized students Approaches learning as a collaborative enterprise
Identities	Reflects search committee's identities	Reflects students' racial/ethnic identities Can connect with students through multiple identities
Leisure pursuits	Values and pursues social activities that are Western European in origin	Values and pursues social activities that are not only Western European in origin
Self-presentation	Speaks, acts, and dresses like most administrators and faculty Leadership or decision-making style	Speaks, acts, and dresses in ways that authentically resonate with racially minoritized students

Note. Adapted with permission from the Center for Urban Education (2017, p. 32).

hire administrator and faculty candidates who are race conscious, understand that racial inequity is an outcome of institutional racism, and acknowledge their responsibility for achieving racial equity, which yields a higher number of racially minoritized people in hiring pools.

CRITICAL INQUIRY INTO MERIT, FIT, AND THE ACADEMIC SEARCH PROCESS

Having laid out the characteristics of equity-minded merit and fit, what's next? How do practitioners, particularly those involved in academic hiring, reconceptualize taken-for-granted understandings of merit and fit, and reconfigure search processes with an eye toward racial equity? According to Smith and colleagues (2004), while efforts such as "special hire" interventions have helped diversify the faculty, without "interrupting the usual," the number of racially minoritized faculty hires will remain low (p. 133). As noted, the strategy we propose for interrupting the usual is critical inquiry. Following the work of Bensimon and colleagues, we define critical inquiry as a process of examining and reflecting on a practice (e.g. hiring) and the artifacts (e.g. hiring interview protocols) used to enact that practice in order to "deconstruct and reconstruct knowledge about racial equity" (Bensimon, Polkinghorne, Bauman, & Vallejo, 2004; Dowd & Bensimon, 2015, p. 40). Through critical inquiry, practitioners can develop awareness of practices that foster racial inequities *on their campus* and cultivate *local, context-specific* approaches to remediating those practices. For hiring practices in particular, critical inquiry is: (a) essential to re-conceptualizing merit and fit in equity-minded ways; (b) aided by tools that help practitioners question the racial consequences of the usual, design more equitable processes and practices, and develop their equity-minded competence; and (c) needed to assess whether academic hiring is and can be a consistently equitable project.

Here, we present a series of tools that combine previously developed insights and strategies for diversifying the faculty (e.g. Sensoy & DiAngelo, 2017; Smith, 2000; Tuitt et al., 2007; Turner, 2002) with critical inquiry. Doing so recognizes the good advice that scholars of academic hiring have created while showing how practitioners can implement their guidance in ways that are equity-minded, that interrupt existing conceptions of merit and fit, and that increase the likelihood that racially minoritized, equity-minded administrators and faculty are recruited. By "tools," we refer to practical devices—instruments, protocols, guides—that can help structure the critical inquiry process, point to areas that practitioners should include in their analysis of a practice, and offer ideas about how to reconfigure the practice to promote racial equity (Bensimon & Hanson, 2012). Important to note is that the tools presented here do not cover the entire hiring process. We focus on four key aspects of the process, describing tools that advance critical inquiry into: (1) hiring process and outcomes;

(2) job announcements; (3) conceptions of merit and fit; and (4) interview protocols. It is also important to say that our intent is *not* to present an exhaustive inventory of critical inquiry tools; rather, our aim is for the tools provided here to serve as a blueprint for developing additional tools that suit a campus' hiring process.

HOW ARE YOUR ADMINISTRATORS AND FACULTY HIRED? INTERROGATING PROCESS AND OUTCOMES

Interrogating how search processes typically unfold and what hiring outcomes are typically produced are key to understanding the scope of racial inequity in hiring on a campus. This critical inquiry is about getting the "lay of the land" *and* about increasing awareness of how aspects of the hiring process may contribute to the limited recruitment of racially minoritized administrators and faculty. Strategies include commissioning "racial audits" of administrator and faculty recruitment and hiring before searches commence (Moreno et al., 2006; Turner, 2002). In a racial audit, data on hiring patterns and outcomes for specific positions by race/ethnicity over a specified period of time are collected, analyzed, and reviewed, ideally on an annual basis. Audit findings can serve as the basis for broader discussion, as at one institution where they were presented to the president and board of trustees (Fraser & Hunt, 2011). In addition to a racial audit of hiring outcomes, we recommend that practitioners conduct racial audits of the steps leading to the final hire to see where racially minoritized candidates exit or are selected out of the process. These steps include but are not limited to: applicant pool, human resources review, initial committee review, screening interviews, finalist interviews/campus visits, and offers issued. This finer-grained analysis would reveal who, by race, "make it" from one step to the next and could help identify aspects of the search process that require further inquiry (Baldwin, Bensimon, Dowd, & Kleiman, 2011). For example, an audit showing that Black applicants comprise 25 percent of the pool for an assistant professor of higher education position, but only 3 percent of candidates who made it past the initial committee review suggests that evaluations and decisions made during the human resources and committee reviews have a negative impact on their likelihood of being hired.

Understanding what contributes to these outcomes needs to be tackled next. For this example, a deep dive into how human resources processes applications and how committees make decisions are needed: Are applications eliminated during human resources review because of factors such as missing materials? Are committees provided with racial audits of the applicant pool for the current position and past searches for similar positions? What has been the racial composition of search committees for positions such as the one currently under consideration? Are applicants' racial background a discussion point during committee review? How about the need to increase faculty diversity? Such questions can uncover plausible explanations for why, in the example mentioned above, few Black hires are made for assistant professor of higher education positions. From here, practitioners can decide whether human resource policy or practice changes are needed and put in place a routine review process for search committee composition and training.

JOB ANNOUNCEMENTS: FIRST IMPRESSIONS, INSTRUMENTS OF DOMINANCE?

Job announcements are typically thought of as functional documents that describe the position to be filled, list required and desirable qualifications, and provide instructions for submitting an application. However, job announcements can also be thought of as cultural artifacts that signal a college or university's values, identity, norms, and perceptions of students (Dowd & Bensimon, 2015; Tuitt et al., 2007). In so doing, job announcements give prospective applicants their first glimpse into an impression of the institution. For example, a job announcement that includes the sentence, "In 2001, the university was designated a Hispanic-serving institution (HSI)," suggests that being an HSI is a salient identity characteristic for this institution and that the Latinx student population is valued. Sensoy and DiAngelo (2017) importantly note that job announcements do not only communicate through direct and explicit statements but also through what is not stated. It is in the ambiguity and silences that taken-for-granted norms are reinforced, and job announcements can work as instruments of dominance generally and Whiteness specifically (Allan, Iverson, & Ropers-Huilman, 2010). For instance, a call for a "generalist" conveys that certain knowledge and expertise are core to a discipline or field without explicitly identifying that knowledge and expertise (Sensoy & DiAngelo, 2017). According to Sensoy and DiAngelo (2017), "*mark[ing]* the invisible aspects of dominance that are embedded yet go unnamed in the position description" is "one of the most powerful actions" that can be undertaken at the beginning of the hiring process (p. 562; italics in original).

From these insights, critical inquiry into job announcements investigates the language used, focusing specifically on the presence or absence of equity-minded and deficit-minded terms, the location of these terms in the announcement, and the frequency with which they appear (Table 7.3). Equity-minded terms are specific and race-conscious while deficit-minded terms obscure and emphasize what students lack, relative to white, middle-class, "college ready" students. Identifying, counting, and locating equity-minded and deficit-minded terms give practitioners a systematic way of analyzing whether job announcements convey a priority for hiring racially minoritized, equity-minded faculty, or whether they signal a desire for candidates whose backgrounds align with traditional notions of merit and fit. This analysis can serve as the basis for deeper discussion about the alignment of job announcements with racial equity goals.

TABLE 7.3 Worksheet 1 Inquiry into Job Announcements

	Term	No. of references	Term location (i.e. Introduction, Required qualifications, Desired qualifications)
Equity-minded language	Racial / ethnic equity		
	Race / racial		
	Ethnicity		
	Racially minoritized students		
	African American / Black		
	Asian		
	Latinx / Latino / Latina		
	Native American		
	Pacific Islander		
	Culture / Cultural		
	Culturally relevant/responsive pedagogy and/or leadership		
	Social justice		
	Asian American and Native American Pacific Islander-Serving Institutions		
	Hispanic-Serving Institutions		
	Predominantly Black Institutions		
	Racial equity gap		
Deficit language	Underrepresented minority (URM)		
	At-risk / high need		
	Underprepared		
	Disadvantaged		
	Non-traditional		
	Underprivileged		
	Achievement Gap		

Note. Adapted with permission from the Center for Urban Education (2017, p. 11).

WHAT ARE SEARCH COMMITTEES LOOKING FOR? UNPACKING "MERIT" AND "FIT"

As Turner (2002) and others have noted, the composition of the search committee shapes how the hiring process proceeds, as well as who among applicants emerge as viable candidates for a position. Best practice advice tends to focus on *who* should sit on the search committee in order to achieve administrator and faculty diversity: practitioners with different viewpoints, those who have *not* repeatedly served on past searches, and racially minoritized practitioners of senior standing on campus. The assumption that a search committee with diversity in thought and racial identities is a condition for recruiting racially minoritized administrators and faculty is sound. However, given our discussion above on how merit and fit are social constructions grounded in white, male, and Eurocentric understandings of which professional qualifications are deemed worthy and which personal attributes and styles are deemed suitable for a position, we add that search committee members, regardless of their identities, should surface how they define merit and fit. Here, critical inquiry aims to make explicit the oft-embedded assumptions about members' normative understandings of merit and fit, as well as the qualities and skills they typically associate with these concepts. It can also help interrogate whether conceptions of merit and fit are more traditional or equity-minded, and if the former, then whether they potentially undermine the hiring of racially minoritized, equity-minded candidates.

Critical inquiry into merit and fit should be conducted *before* a hiring process commences. It proceeds in three steps and first asks search committee members to consider their understanding before engaging in collective sensemaking. First, each search committee member should complete the following sentences on separate sheets of paper: (a) "When considering a candidate's 'merit' for this position, I think about these qualities ..."; (b) "When considering a candidate's 'fit' for this position, I think about these qualities ...." Next, group together the responses for merit and the responses for fit and discuss what search committee members have shared. We recommend that search committees conduct separate discussions for merit and fit. The following questions can help structure the discussions: (a) What do our responses suggest about the criteria for merit/fit that we associate with this position? (b) In what ways do these criteria for merit/fit align with traditional/equity-minded conceptions? (c) Based on these criteria for merit/fit, who will likely surface as strong candidates for the position? (d) How would these criteria for merit/fit impact candidates from racially minoritized groups? Based on the discussions, participants in the exercise can construct merit and fit criteria for the position that incorporate the equity-minded conceptions described above and that search committee members agree to use in their evaluation of candidates.

WHO IS ALLOWED TO SHINE? THE ROLE OF INTERVIEW PROTOCOLS

The screening interview is arguably one of the most important aspects of the hiring process and serves as an opportunity for candidates and search committee members to meet, interact, and get to know each other. It is during the interview that candidates can speak to the qualifications that they believe make them worthy for the position and demonstrate qualities they feel make them suitable for the job specifically and institution more generally. *What* candidates are able to share during the interview, however, depends on the questions they are asked. For example, faculty candidates can talk about their scholarship, its significance, and methodological robustness only if the interview includes questions about research. If the interview does *not* include questions about their experience teaching and supporting racially minoritized students, then candidates do not have an opening—unless they create one themselves—to speak about their use of culturally relevant pedagogy. Likewise, candidates for an administrative role such as dean of students can only talk about initiatives that are specifically geared to supporting Black, Latinx, Native American, and Pacific Islander students if they are asked about how they have fostered racial equity at their current or previous institutions.

Also, *how* candidates' responses to interview questions are assessed depends on committee members' interpretation. As discussed, although candidates may think their skills and accomplishments qualify them for the position, committee members may not if they associate other kinds of accomplishments and skills as evidence of merit. Fit is similarly subjected to interpretation. Interviews are thus spaces of intuitive judgment, and generally, human intuition is flawed when it comes to evaluating future success in an organization. Kahneman (2011) found that the use of structured interview protocols with questions that elicit facts about an applicant's life, coupled with a standard formula to assess applicant responses, were crucial for combatting bias in the intuitive judgments that emerge through interviews. Although structured interview protocols and standard evaluation formulas can curb implicit bias, there remains the issue of disciplinary, methodological, and epistemological bias, which we noted earlier are racialized. Even as a standard interview question invites faculty applicants to speak about their research, if a racially minoritized candidate presents a focus primarily on race issues, committee members with little to no equity-minded competence could read and rate that response as too "narrow" or "specialized." Or, if in response to a question about experience with "diversity" initiatives, a Latinx vice president for student services candidate shares how they have developed programs for low-income, first-generation college students rather than for Latinx students specifically, then committee members who are *not* equity-minded could interpret and judge that response as "unbiased" and as evidence of a practitioner who can support and relate to all students.

Critical inquiry into screening interviews first examines whether search committees are required to use structured protocols and standard evaluation rubrics at all, and if so, how search committees actually utilize these protocols and rubrics. A review of human resource policies around hiring, followed by a survey of past search committee chairs and members, could surface the evidence needed to answer these questions. The survey could ask questions such as: (a) Before serving on a search committee, did you receive training in how to conduct a screening interview and how to evaluate candidate responses? (b) During screening interviews, did the committee follow the protocol as designed? (c) Following a screening interview, did the committee use an evaluation rubric to rate a candidate's responses? (d) When deciding who to move to the finalist stage, how were the evaluation rubric ratings used, if at all? If structured protocols and standard evaluation rubrics are *not* used, a campus should make the needed changes in hiring policies and ensure fidelity in their implementation.

The second critical inquiry into screening interviews asks for a review of the interview protocol and a search committee discussion of how potential responses to each question are associated with particular assumptions about merit and fit, and whether certain responses are likely to be read in racialized ways. Search committee discussion can be structured around questions such as: (a) Based on past searches, what responses will each interview question likely elicit and are those responses indicative of traditional or equity-minded merit or fit? (b) How would we rate these responses based on our evaluation rubric? (c) Do we find that our evaluation rubric favors responses that demonstrate traditional or equity-minded merit or fit? (d) Based on past searches, how likely is it that racially minoritized candidates who focus on race—and for faculty positions, those who use race-focused epistemologies or methodologies—will make it to the finalist stage? (e) What changes—if any—do we need to make to our interview protocol and evaluation rubric so that racially minoritized candidates who demonstrate equity-minded merit and fit can shine? We recommend that detailed notes be taken of this discussion and that responses to (a) (b) (c) and (d) be reviewed before evaluating a candidate's interview in order to calibrate committee members' interpretation.

CONCLUSION

In this chapter, we engaged the question of how traditional conceptions of merit and fit reinforce investments in white, male, and Eurocentric norms, and in so doing, (a) stymie efforts to diversify administrative and faculty bodies and (b) recruit those who possess the experience, skill, and equity-minded competence to support racially minoritized students. In addition to proposing (re)conceptualized notions of merit and fit, we describe the role of critical inquiry as a way of developing the knowledge and know-how to begin reshaping the academic hiring process in racial equity and social justice terms.

QUESTIONS FOR REFLECTION AND DISCUSSION

1. At your campus, what conceptualizations of merit and fit create and maintain barriers to hire racially minoritized administrators and faculty?
2. How can an equity-minded framework help your campus surface and change conceptualizations of merit and fit that impede the hiring of racially minoritized administrators and faculty?
3. Case study: Imagine that you are the search chair for a hiring committee at your campus. You make it clear to other search committee members that you plan on unpacking merit and fit and the ways they bias hiring decisions. Two search committee members, both senior white men, vocalize their disapproval of changing the way the campus has historically done the hiring. How do you approach

such resistance from search committee members? What challenges do you anticipate encountering when addressing resistance to changing hiring procedures that perpetuate biased understandings of merit and fit?

NOTES

1   We thank Estela Mara Bensimon, Lindsey Malcom-Piqueux, and the staff of the Center for Urban Education whose work served as the basis for our discussion of equity-minded conceptions and inquiry into academic hiring.
2   We use "practitioners" to refer to faculty, staff, and administrators who bear responsibility for supporting students.

REFERENCES

Allan, E. J., Iverson, S. V., Ropers-Huilman, R. (Ed.) (2010). *Reconstructing Policy in Higher Education: Feminist Poststructural Perspectives*. New York: Routledge.

Allen, W. R., Epps, E. G., Guillory, E. A., Suh, S. A., & Bonous-Hammarth, M. (2000). The Black academic: Faculty status among African Americans in U.S. higher education. *Journal of Negro Education, 69*(1/2), 112–127.

Almanac (2017). *Gender, Race, and Ethnicity of College Administrators, Faculty, and Staff, Fall 2015*. Retrieved from www.chronicle.com/article/Gender-RaceEthnicity-of/240488.

antonio, a. i. (1999). Faculty of color and scholarship transformed: New arguments for diversifying faculty. *Diversity Digest, 3*(2), 6–7.

Baldwin, C., Bensimon, E. M., Dowd, A. C., & Kleiman, L. (2011). Measuring Student Success. *New Directions for Community Colleges, 153*. doi:10.1002/cc.438

Beattie, G., Cohen, D., & McGuire, L. (2013). An exploration of possible unconscious ethnic biases in higher education: The role of implicit attitudes on selection for university posts. *Semiotica, 197*, 171–201. doi:10.1515/sem-2013-0087

Benitez, M., James, M., Joshua, K., Perfetti, L., & Vick, B. S. (2017). "Someone who looks like me": Promoting the success of students of color by promoting the success of faculty of color. *Liberal Education, 103*(2), 50–55.

Bensimon, E. M. (2007). The underestimated significance of practitioner knowledge in the scholarship on student success. *The Review of Higher Education, 30*(4), 441–469.

Bensimon, E. M. (2012). The Equity Scorecard: Theory of change. In E. M. Bensimon, & L. Malcom (Ed.), *Confronting Equity Issues on Campus: Implementing the Equity Scorecard in Theory and Practice* (pp. 17–44). Sterling, VA: Stylus.

Bensimon, E. M., & Hanson, D. (2012). The Equity Scorecard process: Tools, practices, methods. In E. M. Bensimon, & Malcom, L. (Ed.), *Confronting Equity Issues on Campus: Implementing the Equity Scorecard in Theory and Practice* (pp. 64–72). Sterling, VA: Stylus.

Bensimon, E. M., Polkinghorne, D., Bauman, G., & Vallejo, E. (2004). Doing research that makes a difference. *The Journal of Higher Education, 75*(1), 104–126. doi:10.1353/jhe.2003.0048

Bertrand, M., & Mullainathan, S. (2004). Are Emily and Greg more employable than Lakisha and Jamal? A field experiment on labor market discrimination. *The American Economic Review, 94*(4), 991–1013.

Birnbaum, R. (1988). Presidential searches and the discovery of organizational goals. *The Journal of Higher Education, 59*(5), 489–509.

Busenberg, B. E., & Smith. D. G. (1997). Affirmative action and beyond: The woman's perspective. In M. Garcia (Ed.), *Affirmative Action's Testament of Hope: Strategies for a New Era in Higher Education* (pp. 149–180). Albany, NY: SUNY Press.

Cable, D. M., & Judge, T. A. (1997). Interviewers' perceptions of person-organization fit and organizational selection decisions. *Journal of Applied Psychology, 82*(4), 546–561.

Center for Urban Education (2017). *Institute on Equity in Faculty Hiring at Community Colleges Toolkit.* Los Angeles, CA: Rossier School of Education, University of Southern California.

Chapa, J. (2006). The educational pipeline and the future professoriate: Who will teach California's and the nation's Latino and African American college students? In G. Orfield, & C. L. Horn (Ed.), *Expanding Opportunity in Higher Education: Leveraging Promise* (pp. 243–259). Albany, NY: SUNY Press.

Chen, C-H. V., Lee, H-M., & Yeh, Y-J. Y. (2008). The antecedent and consequence of person-organization fit: Ingratiation, similarity, hiring recommendations and job offer. *International Journal of Selection and Assessment, 16*(3), 210–219.

Cole, D., & Griffin, K. A. (2013). Advancing the study of student–faculty interaction: A focus on diverse students and faculty. In M. B. Paulsen (Ed.), *Higher Education: Handbook of Theory and Research* (Vol. 28). Dordrecht, The Netherlands: Springer.

Danowitz Sagaria, M. A. (2002). An exploratory model of filtering in administrative searches. *The Journal of Higher Education, 73*(6), 677–710. doi:10.1080/00221546.2002.11777177

Delgado-Bernal, D., & Villalpando, O. (2002). An apartheid of knowledge in academia: The struggle over the "legitimate" knowledge of faculty of color. *Equity & Excellence in Education, 35*(2), 169–180.

Dowd, A. C., & Bensimon, E. M. (2015). *Engaging the "Race Question": Accountability and Equity in U.S. Higher Education.* New York: Teachers College Press.

Eddy, P. L. (2018). Expanding the leadership pipeline in community colleges: Fostering racial equity. *Teachers College Record, 120*, 1–18.

Fairlie, R. W., Hoffmann, F., & Oreopoulos, P. (2014). A community college instructor like me: Race and ethnicity interactions in the classroom. *The American Economic Review, 104*(8), 2567–2591.

Fraser, G. J., & Hunt, D. E. (2011). Faculty diversity and search committee training: Learning from a critical incident. *Journal of Diversity in Higher Education, 4*(3), 185–198. doi:10.1037/a0022248

Gaddis, S. M. (2014). Discrimination in the credential society: An audit study of race and college selectivity in the labor market. *Social Forces, 93*(4), 1451–1479.

Gasman, M., Abiola, U., & Travers, C. (2015). Diversity and senior leadership at elite institutions of higher education. *Journal of Diversity in Higher Education, 8*(1), 1–14.

Gonzales, L. D. (2018). Subverting and minding boundaries: The intellectual work of women. *The Journal of Higher Education, 89*(5), 677–701.

Guiffrida, D. (2005). Othermothering as a framework for understanding African American students' definitions of student-centered faculty. *The Journal of Higher Education, 76*(6), 701–723.

Harper, S. R., Patton, L. D., & Wooden, O. S. (2009). Access and equity for African American students in higher education: A critical race historical analysis of policy efforts. *The Journal of Higher Education, 80*(4), 389–414.

Harris III, F., & Wood, J. L. (2013). Student success for men of color in community colleges: A review of published literature and research, 1998–2012. *Journal of Diversity in Higher Education, 6*(3), 174–185.

Higgins, C. A., & Judge, T. A. (2004). The effect of applicant influence tactics on recruiter perceptions of fit and hiring recommendations: A field study. *Journal of Applied Psychology, 89*(4), 622–632.

Hurtado, S., & Carter, D. F. (1997). Effects of college transition and perceptions of the campus racial climate on Latino college students' sense of belonging. *Sociology of Education, 70*(4), 324–345.

Kahneman, D. (2011). *Thinking Fast and Slow.* New York: Farrar, Strauss and Giroux.

Kanter, R. M. (1977). *Men and Women in the Corporation.* New York: Basic Books.

Kaplowitz, R. M. (1986). *Selecting College and University Personnel.* Washington, DC: Association for the Study of Higher Education.

Kena, G., Hussar, W., McFarland, J., de Brey C., Musu-Gilette, L., Wang,… Dunlop Velez, E. (2016). *The Condition of Education 2016.* Washington, DC: US Department of Education, National Center for Education Statistics.

Konrad, A. M., & Pfeffer, J. (1991). Understanding the hiring of women and minorities in educational institutions. *Sociology of Education, 64*, 141–157.

Kristof-Brown, A. L. (2000). Perceived applicant fit: Distinguishing between recreuiters' perceptions of person-job and person-organization fit. *Personnel Psychology, 53*, 643–671.

Kristof-Brown, A. L., Barrick, M. R., & Franke, M. (2002). Applicant impression management: Dispositional influences and consequences for recruiter perceptions of fit and similarity. *Journal of Management, 28*, 27–46.

Lamont, M. (2009). *How Professors Think: Inside the Curious World of Academic Judgment.* Cambridge, MA: Harvard University Press.

Levin, J. S., Walker, L., Jackson-Boothby, A., & Haberler, Z. (2013). *Community Colleges and their Faculty Of Color: Matching Teachers and Students.* Retrieved from http://c4.ucr.edu/documents/GSP2report_ C4finalJuly152013.pdf

Milem, J. F. (2001). Increasing the diversity benefits: How campus climate and teaching methods affect student outcomes. In G. M. Orfield (Ed.), *Diversity Challenged: Evidence on the Impact of Affirmative Action* (pp. 233–249). Cambridge, MA: Harvard Education Publishing Group.

Moreno, J. F., Smith, D. G., Clayton-Pedersen, A. R., Parker, S., & Teraguchi, D. H. (2006). *The Revolving Door for Underrepresented Minority Faculty in Higher Education: An Analysis from the Campus Diversity Initiative.* Washington, DC: Association of American Colleges & Universities.

Ngyuen, T.-H., & Gasman, M. (2015). Activism, identity and service: The influence of the Asian American movement on the educational experiences of college students. *History of Education, 44*(3), 339–354. doi:10.1080/0046760X.2014.1003338

Patton, L. D. (2016). Disrupting postsecondary prose: Toward a critical race theory of higher education. *Urban Education, 51*(3), 315–342.

Posselt, J. R. (2016). *Inside Graduate Admissions: Merit, Diversity, and Faculty Gatekeeping.* Cambridge, MA: Harvard University Press.

Project Implicit. (2011). *Take a test.* Retrieved from https://implicit.harvard.edu/implicit/

Rivera, L. A. (2012). Hiring as cultural matching: The case of elite professional service firms. *American Sociological Review, 77*(6), 999–1022.

Rivera, L. A. (2015). *Pedigree: How Elite Students Get Elite Jobs.* Princeton, NJ: Princeton University Press.

Ryan, A. (2015). Counter college: Third world students reimagine public higher education. *History of Education Quarterly, 55*(4), 413–440. doi:10.1111/hoeq.12134

Scheurich, J. J., & Young, M. D. (1997). Coloring epistemologies: Are our research epistemologies racially biased? *Educational Researcher, 26*(4), 4–16.

Sensoy, Ö., & DiAngelo, R. (2017). "We are all for diversity, but …": How faculty hiring committees reproduce whiteness and practical suggestions for how they can change. *Harvard Educational Review, 87*(4), 557–580.

Smith, D. G. (2000). How to diversify the faculty. *Academe, 86*(5), 48–52.

Smith, D. G., Turner, C. S., Osei-Kofi, N., & Richards, S. (2004). Interrupting the usual: Successful strategies for hiring diverse faculty. *The Journal of Higher Education, 75*(2), 133–160.

Smith, D. G., Wolf-Wendel, L. E., & Busenberg, B. E. (1996). *The pipeline for achieving faculty diversity: Debunking the myths.* Paper presented at the Annual Meeting of the Association for the Study of Higher Education, Memphis, TN.

Staats, C., Capatosto, K., Wright, R. A., & Contractor, D. (2015). *State of the Science: Implicit Bias Review 2015.* Retrieved from http://kirwaninstitute.osu.edu/wp-content/uploads/2015/05/2015-kirwan-implicit-bias.pdf

Steele, C. M. (1997). A threat in the air: How stereotypes shape intellectual identity and performance. *American Psychologist, 52*(6), 613–629.

Taylor, M. S., & Bergman, T. J. (1987). Organizational recruitment activities and applicants' reactions at different stages of the recruitment process. *Personnel Psychology, 40*, 261–285.

Tsai, W-C., Chi, N-W., Huang, T-C., & Hsu, A-J. (2011). The effects of applicant résumé contents on recruiters hiring recommendations: The mediating roles of recruiter fit perceptions. *Applied Psychology: An International Review, 60*(2), 231–254.

Tuitt, F. A., Danowitz Sagaria, M. A., & Turner, C. S. V. (2007). Signals and strategies in hiring faculty of color. In J. C. Smart (Ed.), *Higher Education: Handbook of Theory and Research* (Vol. 22, pp. 497–535). Dordrecht, The Netherlands: Springer.

Turner, C. S. V. (2002). *Diversifying the Faculty: A Guidebook for Search Committees.* Washington, DC: Association of American Colleges and Universities.

Turner, C. S. V., & Myers, S. L. (2000). *Faculty of Color in Academe: Bittersweet Success.* Needham Heights, MA: Allyn and Bacon.

Turner, C. S. V., Myers Jr., S. L., & Creswell, J. W. (1999). Exploring underrepresentation: The case of faculty of color in the midwest. *The Journal of Higher Education, 70*(1), 27–59.

Twombly, S. B. (1992). The process of choosing a dean. *The Journal of Higher Education, 63*(6), 653–683.

Twombly, S. B. (2005). Values, policies, and practices affecting the hiring process for full-time arts and sciences faculty in community colleges. *The Journal of Higher Education, 76*(4), 423–447. doi:10.1080/00221546.2005.11772291

Uhlmann, E. L., & Cohen, G. L. (2005). Constructed criteria: Redefining merit to justify discrimination. *Psychological Science, 16*(6), 474–480.

Umbach, P. D., & Wawrzynski, M. R. (2005). Faculty do matter: The role of college faculty in student learning and engagement. *Research in Higher Education, 46*(2), 153–184. doi:10.1007/s11162-004-1598-1

U.S. Department of Education, National Center for Education Statistics (2018). *The Condition of Education 2018* (NCES 2018–144). Characteristics of postsecondary faculty.

We the Protestors. (2015). *The demands.* Retrieved from www.thedemands.org/.

Zuberi, T., & Bonilla-Silva, E. (Eds.). (2008). White Logic, White Methods: Racism and Methodology. Lanham, MA: Rowman & Littlefield.

8

SOCIAL JUSTICE AND COLLECTIVE BARGAINING IN HIGHER EDUCATION

Untangling the Issues

DANIEL J. JULIUS

A COMPLEX CONTEXT

The relationship between "social justice" and "collective bargaining" is interwoven, complicated, and longstanding.[1] Making sense out of what is transpiring on campus today vis-à-vis these two concepts requires an understanding of the definitions used to characterize these terms, the interpretation of definitions over time, the arc of social movements in the United States, and the nuts and bolts of collective negotiations (which involve table dynamics and the legal and legislative parameters framing labor-management relationships).

Whether social justice informs collective bargaining processes at all also reveals a cacophony of ideas, values, opinions and views, some of which are connected to what actually occurs in collective bargaining negotiations, others not. Social justice, when applied to labor management relationships, revolves around the correction of injustice to various social groups.[2] Labor management relations revolve around power and influence shaped by legal precedent, legislation and the "hammer and anvil" of the bargaining process itself.

Contemporary points of view on the efficacy of these concepts reflect differences in opinion over the meaning of social justice, and how it impacts collective bargaining, the role of unions, universities and their obligations to society, the rights of those attempting to unionize, the ethics or lack of them inherent in capitalism, Catholic and Protestant social teachings, community organizing, institutionalized racism, diversity, inclusion, and salary equity. All these concepts are echoed in the current debate and sometimes find their way into negotiations involving particular employee groups.

The relationship between these issues is further complicated because "social justice" concerns are often raised on campus through student boycotts, legislative lobbying or other forms of advocacy simultaneously with or away from the bargaining process. "Social justice" has also been used in the context of other major initiatives in higher education unrelated to collective bargaining, for example, student success, enhancing graduation retention rates and the like. Here again, definitions and intent are important. If for example by social justice we mean protecting employees from arbitrary decision making, unfair terminations or fair and equitable grievance and arbitration provisions, such matters are often central to labor management relationships. If, however, by social justice we are referring to more expansive anti-discrimination protections, fair trade policies, anti-poverty initiatives, anti-globalization campaigns, race, gender and human rights issues, these concerns, however important, may not easily be accommodated in bargaining. Generally, the further away "social justice" is from the heart of the labor–management relationship, the more likely that union demands will be found not to be mandatorily negotiable and dropped at the bargaining table, particularly if compensation packages are improved.

There is an old adage in labor relations among practitioners that suggests one's point of view is determined by what side of the table one sits. There is another quip about tables and universities applicable here which posits, if we constructed a table with enough sides for all constituencies with a rightful claim to the university, it should be a round table. With these two "table" caveats in mind, this chapter will endeavor to untangle the issues followed by recommendations on how the parties could approach collective bargaining from a social justice perspective.

LABOR HISTORY AND SOCIAL JUSTICE CONCERNS

Many would agree labor unions have historically advanced social justice. From their inception, the earliest attempts in the United States to merge social justice and assertion of worker rights dates back to eighteenth-century New England and the mid-Atlantic region. Industries devoted to rope and barrel making, the construction of canvass sales for ocean-going sailing vessels, and a new textile industry, provide early examples of how these concepts shaped conflicts over the rights of respective parties and the boundaries of jurisdictional territories between communities, laborers, and owners. Well into the twentieth century, powerful elites, the courts and federal legislation defended owners in these conflicts, not workers.[3]

Early in the American labor movement we find a growing divide between those who advocated social reform and workplace democracy versus "business unionism," or what many ninenteenth- and twentieth-century labor leaders referred to as "bread and butter" unionism. These differences in orientations and approaches are evident today, as we shall see.

A practical form of collective bargaining has transcended (with a few exceptions) more ideological approaches. This has not been the case in Europe, Latin America or South Africa. In the United States, "ideology" has been less a factor and, in most jurisdictions, securing higher wages and better working conditions continues to drive bargaining. The old collective bargaining quip, "let's rise above principle and settle this contract," infuses labor management dynamics to this day. However, through the years labor unions have successfully addressed important societal issues such as child labor, the length of a working day, living wages, health and welfare, the environmental safety of workers, medical and related benefits, and other concerns (economic prosperity, upward mobility of workers, workplace democracy) that many Americans take for granted. Gains at the bargaining table came at great personal costs to individuals and communities.

Of course, labor history is never neat and tidy. Organized crime infiltrated some unions. Nor is the record clear whether unions have advanced the rights of marginalized populations. Well into the 1950s many industrial and craft locals were forced to desegregate. Police and firefighter units in numerous cities are presently under consent decrees to hire and promote minority candidates. Over time the entrenched power of union leaders and union bureaucracies have served to protect the status quo. A number of union leaders today are sometimes perceived to exhibit lifestyles more in common with some company CEOs than with their rank and file. Social justice proponents, often using the term "Bargaining for the Common Good," a new label for social unionism, represent a very vigorous faction within the labor movement. They are focused on how to win organizing campaigns, transform union campaigns into broader human rights and community action, help dues-paying members connect to their union, and advance union membership for broader societal gains; these goals can, and do, conflict with the practical business unionism approach, perceived by many to support the status quo.

The push for social justice in higher education is more readily seen in negotiations involving employees new (and with less power) to collective bargaining; graduate assistants; part-time employees, adjuncts, and clerical employees. The impact of social justice concerns are far more difficult to discern in negotiations involving full-time faculty, laborers, or craft locals, and the like, where contracts have been in existence more than 40 or 50 years. Social justice concerns may be on the minds of faculty or craft employees, but contract clauses covering, for example, discrimination, salary distribution or "recognition" are immeasurably harder to amend once in existence for many contracts. Particularly in the give and take of "trade-offs" involved in negotiations, the notion of "if it ain't broke don't fix it," (which often refers to contract clauses which have not been the subject of grievances or arbitrations), serves as a powerful protector of the contractual status quo.

COLLECTIVE BARGAINING IN HIGHER EDUCATION

The union movement in higher education stretches back nearly 100 years, although actual negotiations with legally "recognized" unions did not occur until the legal and legislative environments became more supportive to organizing activities. Following more favorable federal legislative and judicial treatment of unions in the 1930s and 1940s, the first craft unions appeared in the Ivy League (for example, painters at Columbia in 1938) and the first faculty-only union at the New School for Social Research in the late 1940s. However it was not until the mid to late 1960s, after public sector labor legislation was passed, that unions gained a real foothold in academia commencing in New York and Michigan. Bargaining for full-time faculty was curtailed in the private sector following a Supreme Court decision in 1980 involving Yeshiva University in New York. The court found that full-time faculty in private institutions (but not graduate assistants/students, adjuncts or clerical groups) were generally excluded from coverage of the National Labor Relations Act and hence unable to claim employee status required to bargain collectively. The public sector remains as the most robust for faculty where it is estimated over a third of all faculty are represented, primarily in states (approximately 15) that are, or were, favorably disposed to public sector labor unions. Moreover, in these locales, unions have access to state legislators who not infrequently succumb to public sector union demands. There has been a great deal written about unions in academe, the reasons for their existence, the causes and consequences, which can be found in the Bibliography. For the purposes of this chapter, the following information about collective bargaining in higher education is pertinent.

Institutional and demographic factors shape the process. For example, bargaining with academic-related personnel and faculty is associated with larger institutions and public systems in the east and mid-west and several union-friendly states in the far west and Florida. For full-time faculty, institutional status tends to be inversely related to the presence of unions (this is not the case for graduate students or assistants or adjunct/part-time faculty, where the elite private sector is fertile ground for organizing campaigns). With respect to full-time faculty units, for example, only five AAU schools are organized, two of which (SUNY Buffalo and Stony Brook) are in a system. The University of Oregon and University of Florida also organized, and are no longer in state systems. Rutgers University is located in a union-friendly state where all public sector colleges and universities (and most public sector employees) are unionized. The overwhelming majority of organized public sector faculty can be found in comprehensive state college systems in locales where favorable legislation exists or existed.

Faculty unionization reflected, from its earliest inception, the desire to safeguard the academic status quo (maintain jurisdictional territory over decision making in the areas of reappointment, promotion, and tenure) and preserve hard-won gains in governance and professional autonomy. This was a reaction to what was perceived as arbitrary decision making and heavy-handed management of teaching schedules and workload on the part of the administration, which emanated, in the eyes of organized labor, from the corporatization of academe, a decline in state and federal support leading to searches for alternative revenue sources, downsizing and the like, in response to fiscal and enrollment related factors. The desire to preserve professional autonomy and safeguard the status quo, were, in my opinion, more salient than economic concerns for faculty who sought to unionize. After all, in comparison to many, full-time faculty have exceptional working conditions, salaries, and benefit packages. For this group, the union movement commencing in the 1960s was largely non-ideological and focused on "boiler plate" contract matters. These included: recognition of bargaining agents, preservation of craft-like or professional authority over entrance into and promotion through academic ranks, workload, grievance and arbitration provisions. What occurred in academe from a labor relations perspective did not entirely mirror collective bargaining in industry. There are a few unique aspects of labor agreements; for example, the preservation of academic freedom and "academic judgment" which is normally withheld from arbitral review.[4]

Unions representing faculty have partnered and in some cases merged with other unions regardless of organizational differences or ideology. For example, more full-time faculty are represented by joint affiliations of the AFT, NEA or AAUP than are represented by a single non-aligned bargaining agent. This has not been the case with graduate students, clerical or adjunct/part-time employees. Here the more established academic unions initially found it awkward, for a variety of reasons, to represent units comprised solely of graduate students or assistants, particularly at elite private schools or in larger state systems.[5] More often than not, bargaining representative for these groups, where their status as employees is often contested, tend to be unions known as industrial unions (UAW, CWU, UE, SEIU) in search of new dues-paying members. Moreover, despite a great deal of rhetoric to the contrary, claims by one bargaining agent to be more effective in advancing the rights and benefits of particular employee groups are suspect and few, if any, scholarly or objective studies demonstrate this to be the case.

It is in the organizing and negotiations of "first-time" contracts covering graduate students, part-time, adjunct faculty, clerical employees where the emergence of social justice concerns are most salient. Why is this the case? To begin with, collective bargaining relationships are new or emerging. Once contracts have been ratified and the parties are living with them, it is much harder to change existing language and, in bargaining "trade-offs," more established unions have dropped "common good" proposals in favor of economic gains. Secondly, social justice has been a potent force for organizing the more marginalized and non-represented employees. It is less surprising that contract proposals from newly organized groups reflect social justice precepts.

NEGOTIATING FROM A SOCIAL JUSTICE PERSPECTIVE

In response to the question, how can parties effectively negotiate based on principles inherent in social justice, the following recommendations may be of value. Although this question may seem superfluous to some union advocates with social justice agendas, it is germane to employer representatives who may interpret social justice proposals as a needless and perhaps harmful expansion in the scope of bargaining, or demands they have little, if any, power to effectuate, or as arguments for higher compensation based on abstract principles. Consequently, the parties would be well served to try to do the following;

1. Agree upon shared definitions of social justice and how these definitions apply in the collective bargaining setting.

    Proposals that seem straightforward to union negotiators may be interpreted as so far out of scope to employers they may be reluctant, for a variety of reasons, to discuss them. Universities are not social service agencies nor can institutions, on their own, in my opinion, alter structural inequalities in society. Putting aside the question of whether the latter is possible or desirable, proposals which may seem morally or ethically sound to one party may be viewed with extreme skepticism by the other, or thought to be beyond the control of either party to address regardless of what is negotiated. Expansion of the scope of arbitral review for non-mandatory subjects of bargaining may dissuade conversation on matters that appear basic and directly relevant to those with a social justice perspective. Shared definitions enable the parties to identify concrete proposals that will satisfy constituencies who shape bargaining from afar and, more importantly, whose support is necessary to ratify agreements.

2. Agree on accurate costs of proposals and a shared methodology to "cost out" proposals.

    This is important for several reasons; first, what might seem like a negligible cost to the union may in fact seem overwhelmingly costly to the institution. For example, take the matter of benefit coverage for transgender operations. While this may be a negligible expense for employees in one bargaining unit, institutions, should they agree to provide coverage, may be legally obligated to provide these benefits to all employee groups. In such cases costs assume a very different proportion.

    In this context "fair and equitable" to one party may simply be unaffordable to the other. Further, changing institutional budget and resource priorities may require agreement of important external constituencies and reconsideration of tuition (not always under the control of university officials), revenue streams, deferred maintenance, operating expenditures, and the like. If agreement can be reached beforehand on meaningful institutional "comparators" and costing methodologies, arguments can be ameliorated to the benefit of the parties. Take the seemingly straightforward issue of a "living wage" which is often predicated on factors associated with the cost of living (COL) in a particular locale. Agreement on a COL cost methodology could advance negotiations and arguments on whether the COL is similar or different in Berkeley, New Haven, Cambridge or Ann Arbor. In fact, such arguments have delayed negotiations for months to the detriment of all concerned.

3. Educate all parties about the fundamentals of collective bargaining and possibilities inherent in established processes to address challenging social justice issues. Unions representing graduate students in particular often appear not to have a firm grasp on the essential basics of negotiations in place for nearly a century. For example, appointing "team coordinators" or "revolving negotiators" as chief spokespersons may seem reasonable to some union advocates and ridiculous and non-productive to experienced employer representatives.

CONCLUSION

Not understanding what constitutes an "unfair labor practice" or an "end run" can derail negotiations and destroy trust between the parties; the latter an essential ingredient for success in negotiations. The value of arriving at a "tentative agreement" (and knowing what that means in the bargaining context) is essential if negotiations are to be productive. The importance of establishing and adhering to "ground rules," the purpose of tweeting or taping bargaining sessions, or viewing compromise as capitulation (the above lead to non-productive outcomes) should be understood.

In the long run, bargaining will not conclude effectively if viewed as political theater, but operates well when longstanding best practices, procedures, and guidelines are employed. For example, employing "side bar" discussions or union-management committees (which are given a defined scope, timelines, and meet away from the table, making recommendations to the parties) constitutes an effective approach, one used successfully for the last 75 years to resolve contract disputes. This strategy, recently used by the University of California in negotiations with the UAW, proved effective in addressing social justice issues.[6]

Bargaining processes are cyclical. They reflect the needs, interests, and influence of various employee groups and employers at particular historical times. Newer bargaining relationships are often focused on concerns, many of which were settled long ago in contracts for other employee groups. Once matters are negotiated and codified into collective bargaining agreements, they become, over time, the "status quo", and, as such, are more challenging to change. Tom Mannix, now long retired and one of the early pioneers of labor relations in higher education in New York, Michigan and California in the 1960s and 1970s, once observed in regard to this matter that codification or maintenance of the status quo represents real advances to some, or a detriment to others, depending on the rights and privileges, or lack of them, the respective parties had prior to bargaining. Over time if social justice proposals are embraced by the individuals and constituencies (labor or management) who determine bargaining outcomes, such concepts will inevitably be codified into labor agreements and become the "status quo" which will be as they are now, the subject of debate for a future generation.

QUESTIONS FOR REFLECTION AND DISCUSSION

The following variables list conditions under which social justice precepts are introduced during negotiations, possibly shape negotiation discussions, and result in contract clauses which reflect social justice concerns.

- The age of the bargaining relationship and whether the contract represents a successor agreement or first-time contract.
- The definition of the scope of bargaining in federal, state labor statutes, or scope as determined through past practice.
- The type of employee group represented and the extent to which social justice issues were utilized to initially organize them.
- The extent to which a particular faction of employees in a bargaining unit have embraced social justice and have the organizational power to ensure such concerns are acted upon.
- The views, skills, sympathies, and levels of trust between the chief negotiators. Experienced negotiators on both sides of the table find ways to introduce such precepts or, conversely, ensure they will not be advanced during negotiations.
- The primary issues framing bargaining and the extent to which leaders at (or away) from the table are in a position to exercise power or absorb organizational conflict that is invariably needed to obtain bargaining objectives.
- The extent to which important constituencies who impact negotiations support social justice concerns/issues during negotiations.
- The agenda of a bargaining agent representing employees and whether that agent also represents (and has negotiated contracts with) other employees in the same institution or system.
  1. Are there items in this list that, though relatively invisible to the public eye, seem especially important? Which ones, and why?
  2. To what extent do these conditions depend on people and their actions vs. conditions that may seem outside the control of actors in the immediate situation?
  3. Imagine that you are facilitating a bargaining process. Identify three of these factors that you would strive to leverage as a leader. Consider two or three specific actions you could take to facilitate that, individually or with others, to enhance social justice in the bargaining process.

NOTES

1 I would like to thank the following people for their helpful suggestions on this chapter: Leigh Settlemoir Dzwik, Oakland University; Theodore H. Curry III, Michigan State University; Nick DiGiovanni, The Law Firm of Morgan, Brown and Joy in Boston; Nadine Fishel, University of California; William Wesley Connellan, University of Florida; William Herbert, National Center for the Study of Collective Bargaining in Higher Education and the Professions, CUNY; Matthew Kinservik, University of Delaware; John D. Vander Weg, Wayne State University; Asmara Tekle, Texas Southern University.

2 More recently this has been referred to as Social Movement Unionism (SMU), or Social Unionism, a trend of theory and practice in contemporary trade unionism. SMU is distinct from many other models of trade unionism because it concerns itself with more than organizing workers around workplace issues, pay and terms and conditions. It engages in wider political struggles for human rights, social justice, and democracy. SMU grew out of political struggles in developing countries and was theorized as a distinct industrial relations model in the late 1980s and early 1990s. In this model, trade unions are not distinct from social movements and form part of a wider ecosystem of political activism that includes faith groups, civic and residents' organizations and student groups, organized into democratic umbrella organizations and with a manifesto to which affiliates are committed. SMU attempts to integrate workers, trade unions and the labor movement into broader coalitions for social and economic justice. Thus, in theory, unions and other organizations support each other in what are seen as mutually beneficial goals.

3 The influence of the Catholic and Protestant churches can be found on both sides of conflicts involving workers and owners.

4 It might be of interest to note that arbitrators who work in industry, those who adjudicate disputes in the NFL or NBA, or for unions representing city or state workers, teachers, firefighters, police, ballet dancers, journalists or airline pilots, serve as arbitrators for colleges and universities. Collective bargaining has proved itself to be very elastic and flexible. The industrial labor relations environment has accommodated unionized colleges and universities regardless of how unique faculty or administrators believe their working arrangements and institutional cultures are. Arguments around "professionalism versus unionism" were brought forward by those scholars who wrote in the 1970s about the emergence of collective bargaining for faculty. These concerns were eventually muted due to a lack of evidence to substantiate such claims and as industrial labor relations processes, precedents and procedures from industry and other public sector jurisdictions, were adopted and adapted in academic organizations. By the early 1990s, none other than Clark Kerr, former President of the University of California, and an industrial labor relations scholar, identified faculty unionization as an extension of shared governance and a formalized assertion of professional rights. A very cogent argument can be made which suggests collective bargaining has preserved professional or craft-like prerogatives and rights. Information on the numbers of faculty unionized, their bargaining agents and the like, can be found at the National Center for the Study of Collective Bargaining in Higher Education and the Professions, www.hunter.cuny.edu/ncscbhep

5 In recent years the AFT has been active organizing graduate students at elite institutions (Cornell, Brown, University of Chicago, Georgetown, and Pennsylvania among others). It would also appear that social unionism is stronger in graduate student union campaigns.

6 At the University of California the UAW (a union with a social justice agenda) clearly articulated concerns for human rights and discrimination issues and proposed the following: divestment of retirement funds in fossil fuels; demilitarization of the campus police; all gender restrooms including signage and conversion of single stalls; sanctuary campus; and no cooperation with DHS on immigration issues.

    The parties recently settled a four-year contract and agreed to a one-time committee to discuss campus policing, an immigration side letter outlining procedures, and language for all gender restrooms. The above notwithstanding, which social justice precepts are introduced, or the proclivity to drop social justice language in favor of more acceptable "boiler plate" clauses, is not always clear cut. During negotiations between Tufts University and graduate students represented by SEIU, the union argued to expand the definition of discrimination based on "socioeconomic status." However, the final clause agreed upon by the parties is a standard anti-discrimination clause. Social justice concerns were introduced but for whatever reasons were dropped. Other issues, on many campuses, where social justice issues are raised, include gender equity in pay, Title IX, with respect to sexual assault on campus, and paid family leave. At the University of Vermont, Plymouth State University, Wayne State University, Michigan State University, and the University of Florida, unions representing graduate assistants or students proposed lesser overall salary increases in favor of larger increases for lower-paid members. Examples of a complex relationship between social justice and business union interests can also be discerned in negotiations over concepts such as "seniority" and "across-the-board" salary increases. Using seniority, for layoffs, economic benefits or other actions (seniority being a very hard-won concept for unions), often favors those who have been in the organization the longest and if used to determine benefits or layoff status, employees newly hired (who may be women or those from marginalized groups) can be disadvantaged. Across the board salary percent increases, very common in many negotiations, provide for higher raises to longer-serving employees; those who have reached top-step salaries (after all, 3% of $70,000 represents a higher amount than 3% of $35,000). Here too, union proposals may conflict with the values of individuals who are more concerned with pay equity or the rights of recently hired employees. The situation becomes more complex when lower-paid part-timers and tenured faculty are in the same bargaining unit. Tension also arises when, for example, unions have the right not to represent those who refuse (or cannot afford to pay) union dues.

BIBLIOGRAPHY

Alliance of Progressive Labor (n.d.) *Fighting Back with Social Movement Unionism: A Handbook for APL Activists. Part 4: Social Movement Unionism.* https://drive.google.com/file/d/0B-jQ_KiGYi-LOTFSanBrU2cwWFU/view

American Association of University Professors. (2005, May 24). *Contingent Appointments and the Academic Profession.* Policy Statement. www.aaup.org/statements

American Association of University Professors (2005, September 23). *Statement on Collective Bargaining.* www.aaup.org/statements/Redbook/Rbcb.htm

Arnold, G. B. (2000). *The Politics of Faculty Unionization: The Experiences of Three New England Universities.* Westport, CT: Bergin & Harvey.

Aronowitz, S. (1998). Are unions good for professors? *Academe, 84,* 12–17.

Ashraf, J. & Williams, M. F. (2008). The effect of faculty unions on salaries: Some recent evidence. *Journal of Collective Negotiations 32*(2), 141–150.

Bacon, D. (2014). Community college and the fight for social justice. *Perspective, 45*(2), 3–7.

Baldridge, J. V. & Kemerer, F.R., and associates (1981). *Assessing the Impact of Faculty Collective Bargaining.* Washington, DC: American Association for Higher Education.

Bargaining for the Common Good in Higher Education Convening. (n.d.) *Rutgers School of Management and Labor Relations.* https://smlr.rutgers.edu/news/bargaining-common-good-higher-education-convening

Bargaining for the Common Good (2018, March 1). *Activists Strategize to Bring Common Good to Higher Ed.* www.bargainingforthecommongood.org/labor-strategize-to-bring-common-good-to-higher-ed/

Barriage, S. (2016, February 26). The Role of the Union in Promoting Social Justice. *Perspectives on Libraries As Institutions of Human Rights and Social Justice* (1-78635-058-0, 978-1-78635-058-9)

Begin, J. P. (1973, April). Collective Bargaining and Collegiality. *Proceedings, First Annual Conference.* National Center for the Study of Collective Bargaining in Higher Education and the Professions. Ed. Maurice C. Benewitz. New York: Bernard M. Baruch College, City University of New York, pp. 109–116.

Benjamin, E. (1994) Patterns of professional evaluation and assigned duties in faculty collective bargaining agreements. *Higher Education Collective Bargaining during a Period of Change. Proceedings, Twenty-Second Annual Conference.* National Center for the Study of Collective Bargaining in Higher Education and the Professions. New York: Bernard M. Baruch College, City University of New York.

Benjamin, E., & Mauer, M. (Eds.) (2006). *Academic Collective Bargaining.* New York: American Association of University Professors and Modern Language Association of American.

Bernhardt, A., & Osterman P. (2017). Organizing for good jobs: recent developments and new challenges. *Work and Occupations* (0730-8884), *44*(1). https://doi.org/10.1177/0730888415625096

Berry J. (2005). *Reclaiming the Ivory Tower: Organizing Adjuncts to Change Higher Education*. New York: Monthly Press Review

Berry, J. & Savaris, M. (2012). *Bargaining Agents in Institutions of Higher Education*. R. Boris (Ed.). New York: National Center for the Study of Collective Bargaining in Higher Education and the Professions, Hunter College, City University of New York.

Beyer, G. J. (2017). Advocating Worker Justice. *Journal of Religious Ethics*, 45(2), 230–254. https://doi.org/10.1111/jore.12175.

Brill, E. A. & Levy, T. I. (2002). Are you prepared for student unionization? *Business Officer*, 41–44.

Cain, T. (2013). *The research on faculty unions*. Retrieved from: http://iprh.wordpress.com

Cain, T. R. (2017). Campus Unions: Organized Faculty and Graduate Students in U.S. Higher Education. *ASHE Higher Education Report*, 43(3), 7–163. https://doi.org/10.1002/aehe.20119

Carnegie Council on Policy Studies in Higher Education (1977). *Faculty bargaining in Public Higher Education: A Report and Two Essays*. San Francisco, CA: Jossey-Bass.

Carr, R. K., & Van Eyck, D. K. (1973). *Collective Bargaining Comes to the Campus*. Washington, DC: American Council.

Chandler, M. K. (1967). Craft bargaining. In J. Dunlop & N. Chamberlain (Eds.), *Frontiers of Collective Bargaining* (pp. 50–74). New York: Harper and Row.

Chandler, M. K., & Julius, D. J. (1979). *Faculty vs. Administration: Rights Issues in Academic Collective Bargaining*. New York: National Center for the Study of Collective Bargaining in Higher Education and the Professions, Bernard M. Baruch College, City University of New York.

Chandler, M. K. & Julius, D. J. (1986), By whose right? Management rights and governance in the unionized institutions. *Unionization and Academic Excellence: Proceedings, Thirteenth Annual Conference*. National Center for the Study of Collective Bargaining in Higher Education and the Professions. J. M. Douglas (Ed.) New York: Bernard M. Baruch College, City University of New York.

Chandler, M. K., & Julius, D. J. (1987). Determining outcomes of collective bargaining in two-year institutions. *Community Junior College Quarterly of Research and Practice*. Part I, 1(4), 203–226, and Part II, 12(1), 1–20.

Chandler, M. K., Julius, D. J., & Mannix, T. M. (1977) Is institutional prestige, affiliation, and region as determinants of collective bargaining. *Higher Education Review*, 1(1), 13–27.

Common Good on Campus. (n.d.) #CommonGoodOnCampus. [Twitter]. https://twitter.com/search?q= %23 CommonGoodOnCampus&src=tyah

Davis, D. (2017). *Contingent Academic Labor: Evaluating Conditions to Improve Student Outcomes*. Sterling, VA: Stylus.

DeCew, J. W. (2003). *Unionization in the Academy: Visions and Realities*. Lanham, MD: Rowman & Littlefield.

DiGiovanni, N. (2011) This much I know is true: The five intangible influences on collective bargaining. *Journal of Collective Bargaining in the Academy*, 3, http://thekeep.eiu.edu/jcba/vol3/iss1/5/

Ehrenberg, R. (Ed.) (2004) *Governing Academia*. Ithaca, NY: Cornell University Press.

Ehrenberg, R., Klaff, D., Kezsbom, T., & Nagowski, M. (2004) Collective Bargaining in American Higher Education. In R. G. Ehrenberg (Ed.), *Governing Academia* (pp. 209–232). Ithaca, NY: Cornell University Press.

Elam, S., & Moskow, M. H. (1969). *Employment Relations in Higher Education*. Bloomington, IN: Phi Beta Kappa.

Etzioni, A. (1959). Authority structure and organization effectiveness. *Administrative Science Quarterly*, 4, 43–67.

Flannery, M. E. (2018, April 18). Bargaining for the Common Good in Higher Education. *Nea Today*. http://neatoday.org/2018/04/18/bargaining-for-the-common-good-higher-education/

Freeman, R. B., & Medoff, J. L. (1984). *What do Unions Do?* New York: Basic Books.

Fuller, R., Brown, M. K., & Smith, K. (Ed.) (2017) Adjunct Faculty Voice: Cultivating Professional Development and Community at the Front Lines of Higher Education. *The New Faculty Majority*. Sterling, VA: Stylus.

Furdeck, C. (n.d.) Conference Workshop on Social Movement Unionism. https://web.archive.org/web/20050830120503/www1.minn.net/~nup/workshop.htm

Garbarino, J. W. (1975). *Faculty Bargaining: Change and Conflict*. New York: McGraw-Hill.

Garbarino, J. W. (1980). Faculty unionism: The first ten years. *Annals of the American Academy of Political and Social Science*, 448, 74–84.

Garbarino, J. W. (1986) Faculty collective bargaining: A status report. In S. M. Lipset (Ed.), *Unions in Transition*. San Francisco, CA: Institute of Contemporary Studies.

George, C. E., Ingle W. K., & Pogodzinski, B. (2018) Exploring the Politics of Collective Bargaining and Unions in Education. *Educational Policy, 32*(2), 143–151.

Gumport, P. J. (2000). Learning academic labor. *Comparative Social Research* (Vol. 19, pp. 1–23). Stamford, CT: JAI Press.

Gumport, P. J., & Jennings, J. (1998). Graduate student employees: Unresolved challenges. *Journal of the College and University Personnel Association, 48*(3–4), 35–37.

Gumport, P. J., & Puser, B. (1997). Restructuring the academic environment. In M. Peterson, D. Dill, & L. Mets (Eds.), *Planning and Management for a Changing Environment: A Handbook on Redesigning Postsecondary Institutions*. San Francisco, CA: Jossey-Bass.

Hedrick, D. W., Henson, S. E., Krieg, J. M., & Wassell, Jr., C. S. (2011). Is there really a faculty union salary premium? *Industrial and Labor Relations Review, 64*(3), 558–575.

Herbert, W. A. (2017). The History Books Tell It? Collective Bargaining in the 1940s, *Journal of Collective Bargaining in the Academy, 9*.

Hodgkinson, H. L. (1971). *Institutions in Transition: A Profile of Change in Higher Education*. New York: McGraw-Hill.

Hoffman, E., & Hess, J. (2004). *Contingent and Faculty Organizing in CFA: 1975–2005*. www.chicagocal.org/downloads/conference=papers/Hoffman=Hess.pdf

Hollinger, D. (2001). Faculty governance, the University of California, and the future of academe. *Academe, 87*.

Houh, E. S. (2016). Campus Activism, Academic Freedom, and the AAUP. *Academe, 102*(6), 17–21.

Huber, S., & Luce, S. (2001, October 18). Building Social Movement Unionism. www.labornotes.org/2001/10/building-social-movement-unionism

Hurd, R. W., & Woodhead, G. (1987). The Unionization of clerical workers at universities and colleges. *Newsletter, 15*(3). National Center for the Study of Collective Bargaining in Higher Education and the Professions. Bernard M. Baruch College, City University of New York.

Hutcheson, P. A. (2000) *A Professional Professoriate: Unionization, Bureaucratization, and the AAUP*. Nashville, TN: Vanderbilt University Press.

ILO. ILO Highlights Global Challenge to Trade Unions. *International Labour Organization*. www.ilo.org/global/about-the-ilo/press-and-media-centre/news/WCMS_008032/lang--en/index.htm

Jacoby, D. (2005) *Is Washington state an unlikely leader? Progress on addressing contingent work issues in academia*. http://depts.washington.edu/uwaaup.parttimejac.htm

Jakopovich, D (2009, June). *Uniting to Win: Labor-Environmental Alliances*. www.informaworld.com/smpp/content~db=all~content=a912901178

Jencks, C., & Riesman, D. (1975). *The Academic Revolution*. Garden City, NJ: Doubleday.

Johnson, B., Cavanaugh, P., & Mattson, K. (Eds.) (2003). *Steal This University: The Rise of the Corporate University and the Academic Labor Movement*. New York: Routledge.

Julius, D. J. (1977). Collective bargaining in higher education: The first decade. *Research Currents*, ERIC Clearinghouse on Higher Education, November.

Julius, D. J. (1985). *Collective Bargaining in Higher Education*. Washington, DC: College and University Personnel Association.

Julius, D. J. (1993). The Status of Faculty and Staff Unions in Colleges and Universities: 1930s–1990s. In D.J. Julius (Ed.), *Managing the Industrial Labor Relations Process in Higher Education*. Washington, DC: College and University Personnel Association.

Julius, D. J. (1999). The current status of graduate student unions: An employer's perspective. In C.J. Naples (Ed.), *Collective Bargaining and Accountability in Higher Education: A Report Card, Proceedings, Twenty-eighth Annual Conference*. New York: National Center for the Study of Collective Bargaining in Higher Education and the Professions, Bernard M. Baruch, City University of New York.

Julius, D. J. (2003). Unionization in higher education: The case of academic employees in large public systems. *California Public Employee Relations, 161*.

Julius, D. J. (2004). Effective management of collective bargaining in higher education. In E. Benjamin and M. Mauer (Eds.), *Academic Collective Bargaining: An AAUP Introduction for Faculty and Graduate Students*. Washington, DC: Modern Language Association and American Association of University Professors.

Julius, D.J. & Chandler, M.K. (1989). Academic bargaining agents in higher education: Do their achievements differ? *Journal of Collective Negotiations*, 18(1), 9–58.

Julius, D. & DiGiovanni, N. (2013, April). *Academic Collective Bargaining: On Campus Fifty Years*. Center for Studies in Higher Education, Research and Occasional Paper Series. Berkeley, CA: University of California.

Julius, D., & DiGiovanni, N. (2016, December). What factors affect the time it takes to negotiate faculty collective bargaining agreements? *Journal of Collective Bargaining in the Academy*.

Julius, D. J., & Gumport, P. J. (2002). Graduate student unionization: Catalysts and consequences. *The Review of Higher Education*, 26(2), 187–217.

Kemerer, F. R., & Baldridge, J. V. (1976). *Unions on Campus*. San Francisco, CA: Jossey-Bass.

Kerr, C. (1969). Industrial relations and university relations. *Proceedings, Twenty-First Annual Meeting*. Madison, WI: Industrial Relations Research Association.

Kerr, C. (1992). Patterns of faculty unionization in higher education. In J. M. Douglas (Ed.), *Proceedings, Twentieth Annual Conference*. New York: National Center for the Study of Collective Bargaining in Higher Education and the Professions. Bernard M. Baruch College, City University of New York.

Kezar, A. (Ed.) (2012). *Embracing Non-Tenure Track Faculty: Changing Campuses for the New Faculty Majority*. New York: Routledge.

Kezar, A. (2013). Departmental cultures and non-tenure-track faculty: Willingness, capacity, and opportunity to perform at four-year institutions. *Journal of Higher Education*, 84, 153–188.

Kezar, A., & Sam, C. (2013). Institutionalizing equitable policies and practices for contingent faculty. *The Journal of Higher Education*, 84(1), 56–87.

Klein, M. W. (2012). Ten years after Managed Professionals: Who owns intellectual property now? *Journal of Collective Bargaining in the Academy*, 2(2). http://thekeep.eiu.edu/jcba/vol2/iss1/2

Kochan, T. A, Katz, H. C., & McKersie, R. B. (1986). *The Transformation of American Industrial Relations*. New York: Basic Books.

Labor Notes Magazine. www.labornotes.org/

Ladd, E. C., & Lipset, S. M. (1973). *Professors, Unions and American Higher Education*. Berkeley, CA: The Carnegie Commission on Higher Education.

Lee, B. A. (1978). *Collective Bargaining in Four-Year College: Impact on Institutional Practice*. AAHE-ERIC Higher Education Research Report 5. Washington, DC: American Association of Higher Education.

Lee, B. A. (1981, April). Contractually Protected Senates at Four-Year Colleges. *The Legal and Economic Status of Collective Bargaining in Higher Education*. Proceedings, Ninth Annual Conference. National Center for the Study of Collective Bargaining in Higher Education and the Professions. Ed. Joel M. Douglas. New York: Bernard M. Baruch College, City University of New York.

Leslie, D. W. (1998). The Growing Use of Part-Time Faculty: Understanding Causes and Effects. *New Directions for Higher Education, Number 104*. San Francisco, CA: Jossey-Bass.

May, A. M., Moorhouse, E. A., & Bossard, J. A. (2010). Representation of women faculty at public research universities: Do unions matter? *Industrial and Labor Relations Review* 63(4), 699–718.

McCartin, J. A. (2016). Bargaining for the Common Good. *Dissent (00123846)*, 63(2), 128–135.

Mortimer, K. P. (1993). The context of collective bargaining in American colleges and universities. In D. Julius (Ed.), *Managing the Industrial Labor Relations Process in Higher Education*. Washington, DC: College and University Personnel Association.

Mortimer, K. P., & McConnell, T. R. (1979). *Sharing Authority Effectively*. San Francisco, CA: Jossey-Bass.

Moser, R. (2001). *The new academic labor system, corporatization, and the renewal of academic citizenship*. www.aaup.org/Issues/part-time/cewmose.htm

Myers, V. (2017, March 17). Bargaining for social justice. *American Federation of Teachers, AFL-CIO*. www.aft.org/news/bargaining-social-justice

Myers. V. (2018, February 26). *Unions and allies work together for the common good on campus*. American Federation of Teachers, AFL-CIO. www.aft.org/news/unions-and-allies-work-together-common-good-campus

Nelson, C. (2011). *What faculty unions do.* Retrieved from: www.popecenter.org/commentaries/article .html?id=2489

Ormsby, J. G., & Ormsby, S. Y. (1988). The effect of unionization on faculty job satisfaction: A longitudinal study of university faculty. *Journal of Collective Negotiations in the Public Sector, 18,* 327–336.

Osborne-Lampkin, L., Cohen-Vogel, L., Feng, L., & Wilson, J. J. (2017, December 6). Researching Collective Bargaining Agreements: Building Conceptual Understanding in an Era of Declining Union Power. *Educational Policy, 32* (2), 152–188.

Pfeffer, J. (1992). *Managing with Power.* Boston, MA: Harvard Business School Press.

Rabban, D., & Euben, D. (2000). *Brief of amicus curiae American Association of University Professors in support of petitioner united automobile workers, AFL-CIO. NYU v. UAW.* New York University 332 NLRB 1205.

Reiss, J. (2005). Social Movement Unionism and Progressive Public Policy in New York City. *Just Labour, 5* (Winter 2005). www.justlabour.yorku.ca/Reiss.pdf

Rhoades, G. (1998). *Managed Professionals: Unionized Faculty and Restructuring Academic Labor.* Albany, NY: SUNY Press.

Rhoades, G. (2017). Negotiating Whose Property It Is, for the Public Good. *New Directions For Higher Education,* doi:10.1002/he.20226.

Rhoads, R., & Rhoades, G. (2002). The public discourse of U.S. Graduate Employee Unions: Social Movement Identities, Ideologies, and Strategies. *The Review of Higher Education: The Journal of the Association for the Study of Higher Education, 26*(2), 163–186.

Riley, K. (2015). Reading for Change: Social Justice Unionism Book Groups as an Organizing Tool. *Perspectives On Urban Education, 12*(1), 70–75.

Salancik, G. R., & Pfeffer, J. (1974). The Bases and uses of power in organizational decision making: The case of the university. *Administrative Science Quarterly, 19,* 453–473.

Schell, E. E. (2001). Toward a new labor movement in higher education: Contingent labor and organizing for change, *Workplace,* 4(1). www.louisville.edu/journal/workplace

Scipes, Kim. Understanding the New Labor Movements in the "Third World": The Emergence of Social Movement Unionism, a New Type of Trade Unionism. *Critical Sociology.* www.labournet.de/diskussion/ gewerkschaft/smu/The_New_Unions_Crit_Soc.htm

Sheed, W. (1973). Whatever happened to the labor movement: A report on the state of the unions, *The Atlantic, 232,* Summer.

Sneiderman, M., & Fascione, S. (2018, January). Going on Offense During Challenging Times. *New Labor Forum.* http://newlaborforum.cuny.edu/2018/01/18/going-on-offense-during-challenging-times/

Tullock, G. (1994). The effect of unionization on faculty salaries and compensation. *Journal of Labor Research, 15*(2), 199–200.

Voos, P. (1997). Economic and social justice through collective bargaining: The USA in the coming century. *Industrial Relations Journal, 28*(4), 292–298.

Waterman, Peter. (1993). *Social-Movement Unionism: A New Union Model for a New World Order.* Fernand Braudel Center. JSTOR 40241259. www.jstor.org/stable/40241259

Wells, P., & Ingley, C. (2017). Unions in higher education – leadership in the era of automation. Retrieved from http://draweb.njcu.edu:2048/login?url=https://search.proquest.com/docview/1980087 857?accountid=12793

Wickens, C. M. (2008). The organizational impact of university labor unions. *Higher Education 56*(5), 545–564.

9

PRACTITIONER REFLECTION

Leading for Social Justice in Enrollment Management and Policy

JEROME A. LUCIDO

This is a reflection on leadership for social justice in the context of a career in admissions and enrollment management. It is written during a time of widespread public outrage in America about the results and fairness of the college admission process following an historic scandal, one that includes bribery and fraudulent credentials used to gain entry at a number of the nation's most prestigious universities ("College admissions scandal," 2019). At the same time that the scandal has rendered the public indignant about the inequities in college admission, the institutions themselves claim victimhood rather than responsibility (Brennan & Magness, 2019; Cranley, 2019; Jones, 2019; "UT issues statement," 2019; Wermund, 2019). It is an excellent atmosphere for examining leadership for social justice. Indeed, the antecedents for scandal have been set for decades, even centuries, as have been the inequities. This chapter will touch on some of them, with a focus on leading toward change and advancing equity in the face of competing demands.

SLOW PROGRESS

American higher education institutions are intensely proud of their efforts at diversity and equity. Just ask them. You will receive lists of activities, partnerships, commitments and some actual evidence of progress (Ellis, 2019). In the face of this, they remain a principal force in the reproduction of a heavily stratified society (Karabel, 2006; Waller, Ingram, & Ward, 2017). Indeed, it is true that gains have been made in the context of a colonial history that began with higher education only for male elites and the clergy and has—over four centuries—gradually become democratized. Key points in the broadening of institutional purposes and of those served included the Morrill Act, which is credited with the founding of the Land Grant colleges and universities; the GI Bill, which provided for the education of military veterans returning from the Second World War; and the growth of colleges, universities, and community colleges in response to the population spurt of the Baby Boom generation. The Higher Education Act of 1974 largely stimulated the growth noted in the latter (Thelin, 2011).

During all but the most recent decades, however, the primary beneficiaries of this growth have been white and male (Thelin, 1982). One might wonder save for the stimulus of the US government if would there have been much progress at all. Only in the most recent decades, for example, have women begun to outnumber men in higher education (Conger & Dickson, 2017). Also, in recent decades, and as demographic changes have taken place, low-income students and individuals from historically excluded or underrepresented populations have become a greater focal point for recruitment (Grawe, 2018). This more recent trend includes fervent defense of affirmative action when race-conscious admission policies have been challenged in the courts (*Fisher v. University of Texas at Austin*, 2013; *Gratz v. Bollinger*, 2003; *Grutter v. Bollinger*, 2003; Totenberg, 2014). Diversifying a class, therefore, has become a recent and important agenda.

TUITION DEPENDENCE AND THE PRESTIGE HIERARCHY

Inequities remain, however, that range from the scandalous to the structural, and they impede substantial progress at every level of higher education. It is as a system in which gains have been made and not yet enough. Of course, there is much more to this history, including how institutions are financed and how they sustain themselves. Indeed, due to government disinvestment and other forces, colleges and universities are increasingly dependent upon tuition revenues to pay faculty, retire facilities debt, and deliver student services (Zumeta, Breneman, Callan, & Finney, 2012). With tuition revenue as a driving motivation, equity often takes a back seat as full-paying students become prized targets for recruitment.

Moreover, colleges and universities care deeply about how they compare to their peer and competitor institutions. Whether at the highest level of selectivity at the national level or within the many tiers of the educational hierarchy, a close eye is kept on rankings, research productivity, graduation rates, student retention rates, and measures of faculty and student quality. Prestige is the coin of the realm and competition is intense. Similar to the dynamic of tuition generation, the drive for prestige and status leaves little place for students whose backgrounds cannot enhance the institutional profile. Sadly, among those excluded are students who attend schools without strong academic offerings, little to no college counseling, and whose families are without college experience (and whom they often help to support financially and with other family responsibilities).

A TROUBLESOME TRIANGLE

So we see that institutions have compelling internal drivers that establish their priorities for students and for resources. In short, these drivers can be depicted as a triangle of dueling priorities with the vertices labeled prestige, institutional revenue, and diversity (Hossler & Bontrager, 2014). Student recruitment, financial aid, student transition services, and student retention services are pursued toward these ends. This means that students are sought and served based upon their academic capabilities, their ability to pay or not to pay, and their personal and cultural backgrounds. The vertices may be pictured as equal, but in operation they are not. The drive for academic and reputational prestige and the necessity of institutional revenues render the push for diversity, no matter how well intended, a lesser priority. In reality, it is most often done at the margins. This is a high-stakes game, and a new class of leaders—known as enrollment managers—is charged with resolving the often-conflicting institutional goals of prestige, net revenue, and diversity.

Leading for social justice, in the world of college admissions and enrollment management, largely means ensuring educational opportunity and progress for the full spectrum of American society through equitable means and measures. But the tripartite goals just discussed put social justice efforts at a disadvantage. It is time to address how to widen the doors of opportunity and for institutions to more fully fulfill their obligation, often noted in their mission statements, to serve the public interest.

THE SPACE FOR MORAL ACTION

Educational philosopher Harry Brighouse urges leaders to find their "moral space for action" (Brighouse, 2011). He means that we as leaders should find ways that we can forward social justice and educational equity within the context of our work. Going further, once we identify those ways, he urges us to "then expand them" (Brighouse, 2011). How can we follow this sage advice in the face of conflicting priorities that militate against the change we would like to see? In the world of enrollment management, we can begin by placing a mirror up to our practices and then honestly examining whether they contribute to or detract from the goal of educational equity. Moreover, we can hold that mirror up to our own efforts as leaders, ask ourselves if we have advocated effectively for change, and determine how we might better do so in the future. Let us begin that examination here.

STRUCTURAL BARRIERS

Claims on Admission Spaces

There are multiple claims on admission spaces. These include alumni, donors and influencers, talent-based programs such as student-athletes and musicians, student diversity, and, of course, the academic programs to be filled. Each spot in the class represents an institutional resource to be expended on educational excellence, student diversity, alumni and donor relations, and campus life. Of course, each of these claims is not available to all who apply. To what extent, if any, should children of alumni, donors and other powerful individuals be advantaged in the process? To what extent should talent-based programs, and those who run them, have an influence in the admission decision? The answers provide places to look for Brighouse's space for moral action. Certainly, families without wealth have little ability to access donor spaces just as families without college backgrounds have no access to alumni spaces. Can such activity be reduced or eliminated? Are there other ways to serve these powerful constituents without reducing opportunity for all?

Definitions of Merit

Academic achievement, ability, and promise are fundamental criteria for college enrollment (Lucido, 2014). Too often, however, rote and narrow uses of simple metrics replace thoroughgoing evaluation. Higher test scores, test preparation, grade point averages and grade inflation are well correlated with greater income (Hurwitz & Lee, 2018). In an equitable process, such measures must be understood and utilized only within the context of a student's educational background and opportunity.

Admission Plans

Early Decision admission plans permit students who have a clear first-choice college to apply early and get an early answer from their selected school. However, these plans also stipulate that any student admitted under such a program is required to attend. Thus, students are not afforded the length of their senior year to make their final college choice and they may have to do so before knowing how much financial aid they will receive, if any at all. Only students with sophisticated college knowledge and resources can take advantage of these plans. Still, they persist because they secure with great certainty the presence on campus of students with the ability to pay. At the very least, colleges should make public the number of students who apply for and who are admitted, and the percentage of the class filled, within these programs. A better solution is to eliminate such programs. This would allow every student a fair chance to explore and make application to college under a reasonable time schedule, and it would allow every admitted student the majority of their senior year and full knowledge of their financial aid package before making their final commitment to a given institution.

Merit Aid and Discounting

At the heart of intense competition and inequity in student enrollment are non-need based aid programs including merit scholarships and outright tuition discounts. While some of these funds are awarded to students with financial need, the real purposes of such programs are twofold: the enhancement of the academic profile and the financial bottom line of the institution (Martin & Eddy, 2012). Space limitations prevent a thoroughgoing discussion, but these practices have multiple deleterious impacts on equity. They are inflationary to the cost of education due to institutions trying to outdo one another in the merit aid battle, and they award institutional resources to those who do not need the funding (Heller, 2008). Moreover, merit aid is awarded disproportionately to those students who have many viable college choices. The logic for the latter is straightforward. Students who are least likely to attend a given college are awarded more funds to encourage them to forego their choice of another institution. Advantage again goes to the advantaged.

Recruitment Decisions and Demonstration of Interest

The issues noted above are often in plain sight, but some remain hidden. Call them micro-inequities, though their impact is not small (Hossler & Lucido, 2019). Recruiters target their efforts at the schools and students who will meet institutional goals. This means that those with the ability to maintain and increase the institutional profile and the tuition pool receive an abundance of visits while low-income schools and students receive far less attention. This practice, while rational in its attention to institutional priorities, reinforces the inequities inherent throughout the system. Moreover, since institutions seek to predict who is most likely to attend, many provide an admission advantage to students who have demonstrated the greatest interest. Of course, those with the resources to visit campus, attend college fairs and events, and make the most contact are the students with the greatest available resources.

A BRIEF DISCUSSION ON REMEDIES

Any plan for introducing equity and social justice into the admissions and enrollment environment must address two fundamental matters: rebalancing the prestige, net revenue, and diversity triumvirate and effectively changing the admission and student aid practices noted here (among others that space limitations disallow). An observation is appropriate at this point in this reflection. I have known precious few leaders in the field who did not understand and internalize the transformative power of education for all. With such understanding comes commitment to equity and diversity. As noted at the very start, however, institutional goals permit these leaders to pursue these ends primarily at the margins. In actual practice, application numbers and test scores cannot go down; admission rates cannot go up; and net revenue projections must be met. Once those matters are assured, diversity can be pursued. Further, failure to enhance the student profile and meet net revenue goals has job security consequences. This means that an equity-minded leader must have institutional savvy, compelling data, communication skill, persuasiveness, and good ideas. It is a tall order but it is also a worthy, fulfilling and important challenge.

ACCEPTING RESPONSIBILITY TO LEAD CHANGE

Some years ago, I had the privilege to chair the Task Force on Admissions in the 21st Century, a remarkable group of over 40 influential admission leaders and college counselors that was convened by the College Board (College Board Task Force, 2008). In doing so, I became convinced that our system must change to meet the needs of a changing country. I wrote then, and will repeat now a few calls to action.

One very important answer—perhaps the only good answer—to this difficult set of questions is to accept the mantle of leadership. Indeed, admission and enrollment leaders are in the very best position to hold up a mirror to what we see, to ask our leaders to look at their reflection, and then to ask if what they see is healthy for students and for the nation. But in doing so, we must know how to influence institutional leadership. Here are a few bulleted guidelines to move the needle on change:

- Understand how the agenda of your leaders is set, and know what matters to them and to others like them. In what forums do social justice matters get addressed? How might an emphasis on social justice further their objectives? Who indicates receptivity to social justice issues and why?
- Find legitimate and persuasive ways to be on the agenda. What are the right forums for your expertise, research, ideas, and initiatives? In what forums would they be best received? Who would be best to present them?
- Teach your leaders about the imperatives and benefits of diversity through presentations, publications, and the values you exhibit in your programs (and use the great body of research that exists).
- Use the power of stories and examples; they are memorable, and they can be influential in getting social justice items on the agenda.
- Involve them in your programs and professional activities; have them begin to teach and tell the stories of equity and diversity.
- Frame your messages to them wisely; know when political, economic, or social frames work best. Will your initiatives aid in bringing more resources to the campus? Would they aid in relieving political pressure? Would they resolve issues of public trust and visibility? Understand how your proposals further institutional objectives.
- Use visible authorities, experts, or thought leaders within the field; you need not make every point yourself. Occasionally, an outside expert can drive home an agenda.

- Remind leaders of their own strongly held educational values and remind them of the public service obligations outlined in your institutional mission and purpose.

As my career has progressed, it is the employment of the above methods, usually in some combination with the last item, that have resonated the best. This is particularly true when proposing new initiatives and building a case and coalition for change. In a sentence, well-timed, well-crafted, and well-delivered change proposals have greater salience, and a greater chance of acceptance, when tied to institutional mission.

Two Examples Are Illustrative

The University of North Carolina at Chapel Hill is the nation's first public university and has long served as one of its finest. The primary competitors of UNC are Duke University, Wake Forest University, Davidson University, and the University of Virginia. Each of these competitors offers an early decision plan that requires students to commit to the institution at the time of the application. This placed great pressure upon UNC to create its own early decision program to effectively compete in its own market, which it did for several years. However, research on whom the program served demonstrated that low-income and ethnic minority students were poorly served by the program. Moreover, research also demonstrated that a strong cadre of highly competitive students existed who believed that early programs were unfair and who wanted their full senior year to make their college decision. These data were presented to trustees, alumni leaders, and administration with a recommendation to drop early decision. The initiative met with approval, and as a result the university was hailed by the *New York Times* and the collegiate press as a leader in equitable admission policy (Flores, 2002; Lippert, 2002; Schemo, 2002).

Similarly, the Carolina Covenant, UNC's loan-free financial aid program, was introduced to the chancellor, provost, and trustees, at a time when student loan volume had increased and highly able low-income students and their families were reluctant to incur debt. With research that demonstrated that the cost of providing additional need-based grant would justify the additional enrollment of low-income students, and more effectively meet UNC's public mission, the program was approved and continues to be in effect (UNC, 2019).

ADDRESSING SALIENT ISSUES

Accepting the mantle of leadership means more, of course, than gaining approval and resources from leadership. This reflection started there because successful enrollment leaders have a rare opportunity to influence institutional change given the importance of student enrollments to mission attainment, institutional stature, and the bottom line. However, addressing the admission and student aid issues noted earlier is critical to achieving more equitable results and to the demonstration of a commitment to equity to the members of the enrollment team and to institutional partners and observers. It is not an easy set of tasks. Staff members must be trained to widen the definitions of merit used in selection. Recruitment plans must include concentrated and consistent presence in under-served schools and communities. Student aid must be directed to the institutional objective of diversity, which includes students of ethnic and socioeconomic difference. External and internal communications must include the demonstrated value of a diverse learning environment. Staff selection and development must be consistent with the values of equity and inclusion. In short, leading an enrollment organization toward social justice means that one must lead both up and down the organization.

IN IT TO WIN IT

When one has reached the point in a career when a reflection like this can be written, many ups, downs, and disappointments have occurred. One persistent disappointment, and where this chapter began, is the snail's pace of change, despite the energy, commitment, and skill applied by so many dedicated leaders and practitioners. Structural barriers and societal inequities are difficult to undo as bureaucracies are designed and built to withstand change. This means that one must be in it for the long haul. With that in mind, and once again drawing from prior work and commentary, here are additional guidelines for effectiveness over time and to stay resilient in the face of resistance and incremental change.

- Know that change comes in both small increments and big waves
- Celebrate your wins
- Reframe and be persistent with your losses
- Choose your battles wisely
- Know that your timing matters
- Live to fight again

A DEMOGRAPHIC DIVIDEND

Marta Tienda, a sociologist at Princeton, spoke recently at a conference held at the USC Center for Enrollment Research, Policy and Practice. During her talk, she outlined the major thrusts in American history that propelled higher education to greater purpose and to greater service (Tienda, 2015). Those included the landmark pieces of legislation like the Morrill Act, GI Bill and Higher Education Act outlined early in this chapter. She then wondered aloud, why it was that similar investments are not being made today when the demographics of the country demonstrate that enormous educational gains must be made with populations who have been historically underserved and excluded? Why is it, she wondered, that when once we sought to yield economic and social dividends from population shifts, today we see changing demographics through a deficit lens (Tienda, 2015)?

This chapter has been about doing better and about changing from within through the wise and relentless push for social justice through organizational change. Tienda reminds us that social justice is good for our nation and our institutions. Let us join with her to seek the demographic dividend of a more diverse, inclusive, and stronger society through the power of higher education.

QUESTIONS FOR REFLECTION AND DISCUSSION

1. Describe three institutional priorities served by the admissions function and discuss the impact of these forces on equity and diversity.
2. Outline the structural barriers to equity and diversity that are at play in admission programs, and identify how these practices create disadvantages for students from low-income and first-generation college-going families.
3. Consider remedies that address the structural barriers identified in Question 2, and suggest the methods by which these remedies can be presented to and adopted by campus leadership.

ADDITIONAL RESOURCES

Lucido, J. (2014). How college admission decisions are made. In D. Hossler & B. Bontrager (Eds.), *The Handbook of Strategic Enrollment Management*. San Francisco, CA: Jossey-Bass.

REFERENCES

Brennan, J., & Magness, P. (2019, March 14). Universities play the victim in admissions scandal, but they're far from blameless. *Reason*. Retrieved from https://reason.com/2019/03/14/universities-play-the-victim-in-admissio/

Brighouse, H. (2011, January). Ethical exigencies and opportunities: The space for moral action. Presented at annual 2011 CERPP Conference, Los Angeles, California. https://cerpp.usc.edu/2011/10/05/2011-case-for-change-in-college-admissions/

College admissions scandal: Your questions answered. (2019, March 23). *New York Times*. Retrieved from www.nytimes.com/2019/03/14/us/college-admissions-scandal-questions.html

College Board Task Force on Admissions in the 21st Century. (2008, November). *Preserving the Dream of America*. Retrieved from https://secure-media.collegeboard.org/digitalServices/pdf/advocacy/admissions21century/preserving-the-dream-of-america-college-board-letter-to-the-profession.pdf

Conger, D., & Dickson, L. (2017). Gender imbalance in higher education: Insights for college administrators and researchers. *Research in Higher Education*, 58(2), 214–230. https://doi.org/10.1007/s11162-016-9421-3

Cranley, E. (2019, March 12). 8 colleges were named in the massive college-admissions scandal. Here's how they're responding. *Insider*. Retrieved from www.insider.com/college-admissions-scandal-school-responses-2019-3#university-of-san-diego-8

Ellis, L. (2019, March 18). We asked 20 elite-college admissions deans about the bribery scandal. Here's what they said. *The Chronicle of Higher Education*. Retrieved from www.chronicle.com/article/We-Asked-20-Elite-College/245920

Fisher v. University of Texas at Austin, 570 U.S. __ (2013).

Flores, C. (2002, May 3). U. of North Carolina at Chapel Hill drops early-decision admissions. *The Chronicle of Higher Education*. Retrieved from http://libproxy.usc.edu/login?url=https://search-proquest-com.libproxy1.usc.edu/docview/214685283?accountid=14749

Gratz v. Bollinger, 539 U.S. 244 (2003).

Grawe, N. (2018). *Demographics and the demand for higher education*. Baltimore, MD: Johns Hopkins University Press.

Grutter v. Bollinger, 539 U.S. 306 (2003).

Heller, D. E. (2008). *Financial aid and admission: Tuition discounting, merit aid and need-aware admission* (Discussion Paper). Arlington, VA: National Association for College Admission Counseling.

Hossler, D., & Bontrager, B. (Eds.). (2014). *Handbook of strategic enrollment management*. San Francisco, CA: Jossey-Bass.

Hossler, D., & Lucido, J. (2019, April 22). College admissions side doors. *Inside Higher Ed*. Retrieved from www.insidehighered.com/admissions/views/2019/04/22/if-colleges-dont-act-deal-inequities-college-admissions-government-will?utm_source=Inside+Higher+Ed&utm_campaign=686a7840fb-AdmissionsInsider_COPY_01&utm_medium=email&utm_term=0_1fcbc04421-686a7840fb-197699165&mc_cid=686a7840fb&mc_eid=19862ed532

Hurwitz, M., & Lee, J. (2018). Grade inflation and the role of standardized testing. In J. Buckley, L. Letukas, & B. Wildavsky (Eds.), *Measuring Success: Testing, Grades, and The Future of College Admissions* (pp. 64–93). Baltimore, MD: Johns Hopkins University Press.

Jones, S. (2019, March 14). Colleges can't fix their unfair admissions process on their own. *New York Magazine*. Retrieved from http://nymag.com/intelligencer/2019/03/college-admissions-scandal-inequality.html

Karabel, J. (2006). *The Chosen: The Hidden History of Admission and Exclusion at Harvard, Yale, and Princeton*. Boston, MA: Houghton Mifflin Company.

Lippert, J. (2002, April 26). UNC drops early admissions. Retrieved from https://yaledailynews.com/blog/2002/04/26/unc-drops-early-decision-admissions/

Lucido, J. (2014). How college admission decisions are made. In D. Hossler & B. Bontrager (Eds.), *The Handbook of Strategic Enrollment Management*. San Francisco, CA: Jossey-Bass.

Martin, J., & Eddy, P. (2012). *Tuition Discounting through Unfunded Institutional Aid at Private Baccalaureate Colleges*. ProQuest Dissertations Publishing. Retrieved from http://search.proquest.com/docview/1034372186/

Schemo, D. (2002, April 26). A key university abolishes early decision admissions. *New York Times*. Retrieved from http://search.proquest.com/docview/92194617/

Thelin, J. R. (1982). *Higher Education and its Useful Past: Applied History in Research and Planning*. Cambridge, MA: Schenkman Publishing.

Thelin, J. R. (2011). *A History of American Higher Education*. Baltimore, MD: Johns Hopkins University Press.

Tienda, M. (2015, January). Diversity as a strategic advantage. Presented at annual 2015 CERPP Conference, Los Angeles, California. Retrieved from https://cerpp.usc.edu/2015/10/03/college-admission-2025-embracing-the-future/

Totenberg, N. (2014, April 22). High court upholds Michigan's affirmative action ban. *NPR*. Retrieved from www.npr.org/2014/04/22/305960143/high-court-upholds-michigans-affirmative-action-ban

University of North Carolina at Chapel Hill. (2019). *The Carolina Covenant*. Retrieved May 6, 2019, from https://carolinacovenant.unc.edu/

UT issues statement on college bribery lawsuit. (March 14, 2019). *FOX 7*. Retrieved from www.fox7austin.com/news/local-news/ut-issues-statement-on-college-bribery-lawsuit

Waller, R., Ingram, N., & Ward, M. R. (Eds.). (2017). *Higher Education and Social Inequalities: University Admissions, Experiences, and Outcomes*. London: Routledge.

Wermund, B. (2019, March 12). Admissions scandal reveals why America's elite colleges are under fire. *Politico*. Retrieved from www.politico.com/story/2019/03/12/college-admission-scandal-1265869

Zumeta, W., Breneman, D. W., Callan, P. M., & Finney, J. E. (2012). *Financing American Higher Education in the Era of Globalization*. Cambridge, MA: Harvard Education Press.

PART III
ACCOUNTABILITY AND DATA

10

LEADERSHIP FOR EQUITY-MINDED DATA USE TOWARD RACIAL EQUITY IN HIGHER EDUCATION

ALICIA C. DOWD AND BRANDEN D. ELMORE

Colleges and universities have a great deal of data representing the academic experiences and progress of their students.[1] Numerous administrative offices such as institutional research, planning and assessment, enrollment management, and admissions compile a wide variety of data-saturated reports on a regular basis. Staff, faculty, and administrators at some institutions have endeavored to use their data to understand the ways that their policies and practices function as barriers or enablers of college access, retention, and degree completion among different racial and ethnic groups. When these forms of data use are motivated by the desire to address racial discrimination and systemic injustices that marginalize members of racially and ethnically minoritized groups in postsecondary education, they are characterized as "equity-minded" (Bensimon, 2007; Bensimon & Malcom, 2012; Felix & Fernandez Castro, 2018; Witham & Bensimon, 2012).

Equity-mindedness is an ethical framework for problem framing and decision making. With respect to racial disparities and stratification in higher education, being equity-minded means taking institutional responsibility to close racial equity gaps in college access, experiences, and completion. Many scholars, organizations, and institutions are calling on higher education leaders to make an institutional commitment to racial equity. This chapter shows how data use can be part of equity-minded leadership in colleges and universities, highlighting effective strategies, challenges, and pitfalls. Equity-minded data use, as characterized in this chapter, is conscious of both race and racism, with an affirmative commitment to anti-racist policies and practices (Bensimon, 2018). Broadly speaking, leadership for equity-minded data use requires dual competencies. On the one hand it requires knowledge of the craft (i.e., the technical dimensions) of using data disaggregated by race and ethnicity in a transparent, iterative, and sustained way. On the other, it requires a critically informed, anti-racist approach to the interpretation of racial disparities revealed in institutional data.

In regard to craft, equity-minded data use is enhanced by use of fine-grained measures of student progress and success. Examples of fine-grained measures include course-to-course retention and credit accumulation rates defined for specific cohorts of students (e.g. first-time students whose initial course enrollment indicates an interest in pursuing a science major). The use of such fine-grained, "close-to-practice" data makes data "actionable" because data users can then pinpoint specific educational policies and practices that are having a negative disparate impact on students who are members of racially minoritized groups (Dowd et al., 2018). However, data use and leadership decision making do not occur in a vacuum, and this is where it is essential for leaders to cultivate racial literacy (Guinier, 2004) and critical frames of reference for race-conscious dialogues surrounding data use.

ORGANIZATION OF THE CHAPTER

In this chapter, we begin by describing the Equity Scorecard, an approach to data use developed by Professor Estela Mara Bensimon and colleagues at the University of Southern California Center for Urban Education (CUE) (Bensimon & Malcom, 2012; Bustillos, Rueda, & Bensimon, 2011; Dowd & Bensimon, 2015; Harris & Bensimon, 2008). The Equity Scorecard presents a model for equity-minded data use that has been widely implemented across the United States and focuses specifically on addressing racial equity issues (see e.g. Bensimon, Dowd, Longanecker, & Witham, 2012; Bensimon, Polkinghorne, Bauman, & Vallejo, 2004; Bustillos et al., 2012; Witham, Chase, Bensimon, Hanson, & Longanecker, 2015). This is especially relevant because we draw insights in this chapter about equity-minded data use from a case study we conducted of administrators, faculty, and staff who were involved in the Equity Scorecard.

Next, we present examples of equity-minded data use using findings from two universities in our case study, which we refer to as Hillside University and Old Main University (pseudonyms). We provide positive examples of data use that is principled, transparent, iterative, and connected to core areas of institutional functioning (e.g. advising, curriculum, budgeting). We also acknowledge challenges, especially the difficulty of involving faculty in equity-minded changes to these practices.

Gaining expertise with the technical and organizational aspects of data use is a necessary but insufficient step. White administrators who engage in racial equity work, like those we feature in the examples in this chapter, must also bring a critical awareness to data discussions of the ways racism manifests in words, omissions, and deeds. Otherwise, they risk breaking down the trust and buy-in to participation, collaboration, and decision making that is necessary for meaningful data use toward organizational change in educational settings (Datnow, Greene, & Gannon-Slater, 2017; Datnow & Park, 2018; Hallett, 2010; Kezar, 2011; Lester & Kezar, 2012; Marsh, 2012; Marsh & Farrell, 2015; Schmidt & Datnow, 2005). To highlight these risks, in the third section, we describe various forms of harmful discourse, the "words that wound" (Matsuda, Lawrence, Delgado, & Crenshaw, 1993; Staples, 2010, p. 54) that emerge during conversations about data disaggregated by race and ethnicity. Examples taken from interviews with Black administrators in our case study illustrate these concepts.[2] The concluding section provides recommendations for leaders to develop awareness of racist discourse and the capacities for an anti-racist response.

THE EQUITY SCORECARD: A PRACTITIONER INQUIRY MODEL OF DATA USE

The Equity Scorecard involves faculty, staff, and administrators in practitioner inquiry, the systematic use of data to improve one's own practices. CUE's Equity Scorecard involves practitioners in discussion of a variety of data—about students, about institutional performance, and more—in group settings where faculty, administrators, and staff have a chance to make sense of the data together. The data discussed include numerical data called "vital signs" that are grouped into indicators of access, retention, and graduation. These numerical data are derived from institutional databases and are disaggregated by race and ethnicity (and sometimes by other indicators such as gender, Pell Grant eligibility as a proxy for income status, or the student's secondary school district). Discussions are also informed by qualitative data, which is collected by participating practitioners, for example through observations and document analyses.

During Equity Scorecard implementation, inquiry protocols, guided discussions of data, and case studies give practitioners a chance to become aware of and unlearn racist assumptions about differences in cultural practices and values. These discussions provide team members with critically informed descriptions and examples of "equity-mindedness" to serve as a cognitive frame for race-conscious data interpretation. These frames call for practitioners to act as institutional change agents (Bensimon, 2007; Bensimon, Dowd, Stanton-Salazar, & Dávila, in press), to use their power, authority, and networks to reform policies and practices in more just ways. In the setting of our case study, Equity Scorecard professional development institutes and "evidence team" meetings were opportunities for evidence team members to receive coaching from CUE action reserchers not only on technical aspects of displaying and interpreting data, but also on the language of equity-minded data interpretation.

Prior case studies provide examples of practitioners who, after bringing equity-minded frames of analysis to bear on their own policies and practices, made

consequential changes to promote racial equity goals. For example, through participation in the Equity Scorecard, a mathematics department chair revamped his leadership and hiring practices (Felix, Bensimon, Hanson, Gray, & Klingsmith, 2015); an
institutional researcher took a more active role as a teacher and data coach to involve
colleagues in equity-minded inquiry (Dowd, Malcom, Nakamoto, & Bensimon,
2012); a faculty member who came to see that White privilege had allowed her to view
a complete lack of Black students in her classroom as normal took a role as a faculty
leader (Dowd, Bishop, & Bensimon, 2015); and another faculty member changed her
advising practices and institutionalized mentoring in her department to stem the loss
of Black and Latinx students from campus (Liera & Dowd, 2018). In all of these cases,
the particular changes mentioned occurred as the practitioner adopted a stronger,
critically conscious stance as an equity-minded agent of change.

THE CRAFT OF EQUITY-MINDED DATA USE

In this section, we demonstrate the craft of equity-minded data use. To animate our
discussion, the section begins with a vignette depicting (with the use of pseudonyms)
the leadership for equity-minded data use of two White male administrators, Provost
Michael Daniels and Associate Provost Robert Turner of Hillside University, who
were participants in a case study we conducted. After pointing out the positive aspects
of equity-minded data use depicted in the vignette, we note the challenges Michael
Daniels and Robert Turner experienced at Hillside University when they attempted
to engage faculty in this work. To inform strategic responses to these challenges,
which were experienced by others in our study, we highlight lessons learned at Old
Main University, where faculty played an active role as equity change agents (Dowd
& Liera, 2018).

EQUITY-MINDED DATA USE: A VIGNETTE

Provost Michael Daniels was quite satisfied with his decision to reduce class sizes at
his university. Under a previous administration, his university had pushed student-
to-faculty ratios higher to get a top ranking on a teaching efficiency metric that was
part of the state university system's performance-based funding (PBF) plan. With a
new president and executive team now in place, new priorities were emerging. Not
only had Dr. Daniels' class size reduction decision garnered him faculty support, but
with the university's equity goals in mind, it was the right thing to do. With a declining
population of high school graduates and state funding on the wane, the university
could ill afford to lose any more students. It was imperative to get more students
through the door, to improve access for students of color, and to keep students enrolled
through effective instruction and advising. Given that Black and Latinx students left
the university at higher rates than White students, directing resources to reduce class

sizes and focusing on student success rates promised to advance the university's racial equity goals. These commitments motivated Provost Daniels to play an active role in creating and supporting the work of the Equity Scorecard evidence team.

At the same time that he was allowing student/faculty ratios to decrease, Daniels and his administrative colleague Dr. Robert Turner, who was the leader of the Equity Scorecard evidence team, were working to improve institutional performance on other metrics that revealed racial disparities, especially student retention rates. By conducting cohort analyses of new full-time students through credit accumulation and re-enrollment milestones semester-to-semester, Turner realized that two-thirds of the students who started out as undeclared majors left the university without degrees, a substantially larger proportion than those who started out as declared majors. Referring to the retention metrics, Turner exclaimed, "This is the one that shocks me... If you're undecided [not in a major], one out of every three of you is not in good academic standing... If you start undecided, term one to term three—one year—you don't stay!"

Rather than interpreting these data as a problem with the students who started out undecided about their major, Daniels and Turner interpreted them as a problem of institutional performance. As a result, a number of changes were made at Hillside University to better support students at multiple points of their academic journey. University communications were revamped to send clearer messages much earlier to applicants, emphasizing "We're here to help you" choose a major and a career. A student success center was created where student advisors who were trained in different areas of specialization could work together to counsel students. In addition, career choice self-assessment inventories, meetings with faculty who could advise students on choice of major, and career counselors were among the resources marshalled to provide this help.

In comparison to previous practice, Daniels and Turner also adopted a much more transparent approach to data use. Under the old leadership, access to institutional data was tightly controlled. Reports provided by the institutional research office completely lacked credibility. This lack of transparency led faculty to request their own university's data from the state university's system office so they could use it when negotiating issues such as teaching load. Daniels understood data as a resource for problem framing and negotiations with faculty to communicate his decisions. The metrics at his disposal were useful cudgels in his sparring with faculty governance leaders to take steps to improve student success.

However, as Turner related, it was difficult to get faculty to take steps to change their mindset about the underlying causes of student success—to shift from a deficit- to an equity-minded point of view—and to get involved in changing the curriculum, pedagogy, and advising practices. Referring to a discussion he had with department chairs, Turner recalled showing them Hillside's retention data and receiving pushback against the idea that the data showed the need for institutional change. "I said 'Look, [these are] our students, this is who we have. We need to work together to help these students.'" In the face of faculty resistance, he challenged them. "Are you saying that you can't teach them or that you won't teach them?" Clearly, it was going to take more effort to effectively engage the department chairs and faculty as collaborators in racial equity work.

THE VALUE OF FINE-GRAINED COHORT ANALYSES TO MAKE DATA ACTIONABLE

Michael Daniels' and Robert Turner's transparent use of data in this situation illustrates positive aspects of data-informed decision making to improve institutional accountability for equity (Dowd & Liera, 2018). Their work demonstrated several features of equity-minded data use. They demonstrated (1) an affirmative, race-conscious use of data disaggregated by race and ethnicity; (2) iterative and sustained cycles of data use with attention to semester-to-semester and year-to year enrollment, retention, and graduation rates; and (3) a focus on making changes in institutional practices that are implicated in racially disparate negative student outcomes.

As highlighted when Turner exclaims that a retention statistic "shocks" him, they used data "close to practice" (Dowd et al., 2018), meaning that the numbers were motivating reflection and action about how their own decisions and practices were producing racial inequities. The university may have been able to earn more points in the PBF system if class sizes were not reduced, but Daniels decided that approach was not ethical, given the university's student retention issues. Turner's ability to reference the one of three students who were not being retained from among a well-defined cohort of students (undeclared majors) made information held in institutional data bases actionable (Marsh, 2012). Using such fine-grained analyses, Daniels and Turner took action to revise class sizes, student support and matriculation services, and institutional research and assessment practices. Utilizing strong conceptions of equity, they directed resources, such as counselors and career inventories toward students at transitions and milestones in the curriculum (e.g. declaring a major) that were disproportionately posing barriers to the success of Black and Latinx students.

The craft of equity-minded data use is not merely technical. Daniels' and Turner's decision making was systematic and principled, drawing on the data to inform institutional priorities and a specific policy agenda (i.e. student retention) in ways they were prepared to defend. They used the data in interaction with others, as tools for communication. The data, which included PBF and Equity Scorecard indicators, informed these leaders' decision making and they pointed to specific metrics to communicate their decisions. Their decision making was situated in their knowledge of the institution, the local context, and their students. They used the data to attempt to open a dialogue about institutional responsibility and professional values. The evident conflict with the faculty was necessary and potentially productive because it involved a negotiation of values, a call to move from deficit- to equity-minded perspectives.

Challenges remained at Hillside University, most notably the challenge of institutional transformation at the core of the educational enterprise: curriculum and instruction. Although they were both faculty members themselves prior to assuming administrative positions, Daniels and Turner were missing a close ally among the current faculty leadership. Insights from related analyses highlight the importance of faculty involvement alongside administrators (Dowd & Liera, 2018; Liera & Dowd, 2018). At Old Main University (OMU), the Equity Scorecard evidence team was jointly and collaboratively led by a Latina senior administrator and a White faculty member who both had extensive prior experience serving on equity and diversity committees and in shared governance. The OMU evidence team included a Black department chair and other active faculty participants who were directly responsible for student advising, strategic planning, governance, and curriculum policy (Dowd & Liera, 2018). In comparison, the evidence team at Hillside University included a less senior Black professor and other faculty members who did not have as much experience in shared governance.

As we show next through discussion of data use by the Equity Scorecard evidence team at OMU, these differences in team composition mattered when it came to carrying out curricular policy change.

ADDRESSING THE CHALLENGE OF FACULTY ENGAGEMENT

Numerous majors at OMU required higher SAT scores to enter the major than were required for admission to the university. The Equity Scorecard process at OMU led faculty and administrative leaders to realize that the admissions policies for these "restrictive" majors were having a disproportionate impact on Black and Latinx students. As at Hillside, cohort analyses reviewed by the evidence team at OMU showed that undeclared students had lower rates of course completion, were more likely to be placed on academic warning, and were much more likely to leave the university. Among those who did persist to graduation, fine-grained data analyses showed, undeclared majors were accumulating more credits and putting in more effort to find the right courses to fulfill their program of study. The longer time-to-degree posed the risk of loss of financial aid as students exhausted their eligibility.

To address this problem, OMU began using its data systems more effectively to track the progress of students who started out in pre-major status. New data use practices enabled a stronger focus on equity and institutional responsibility. To broaden involvement in equity-minded inquiry, evidence team members held professional development workshops for department chairs to heighten attention to the negative, disproportionate impact of "restrictive" majors on Black and Latinx students. The OMU provost created an incentive program that encouraged department chairs to apply for funds to involve faculty in cohort analyses, with the goal of closing racial equity gaps.

Viewing the data from an equity-minded perspective, faculty and administrators on the OMU evidence team questioned whether the departmental-level SAT score requirements were really warranted. While some coursework might have been necessary prerequisites, evidence team members questioned and used a variety of means to involve their faculty colleagues in questioning whether the criteria for admissions to each major were valid. They believed that other indicators of academic readiness could be adopted without resulting in lower student success in the majors.

Evidence team members also used academic program governance policies to call the attention of their faculty colleagues to inequities embedded in their curricular policy. If departments were retaining SAT scores as a metric for admitting students to their majors, they would be required to present analyses to the curriculum committee demonstrating that they had considered the equity impacts and ways to mitigate them. A structural change was also made at the university level. The bureaucratic status of undeclared major was reorganized so that students who did not know how to or were not ready to select a major would be enrolled in a department of exploratory studies, a new name and discourse that reflected the shift from a deficit to an asset-based framing, from the negative of indecision to an equity-minded appreciation of discovery and exploration.

The key factors enabling these curricular changes at OMU included faculty peer-to-peer communication, collaboration between faculty and administrators, strong institutional research support and the data quality necessary for conducting fine-grained cohort analyses, and administrative leaders willing to frame and name problems of institutional functioning from an equity perspective. With such broad engagement, faculty and leaders at OMU were able to question fundamental academic assumptions about what college students should already know about their future careers when they begin college (i.e. what to major in) and examine the validity of the use of SAT scores as a criterion for entry into a variety of major fields of study.

THE IMPORTANCE OF RACIAL LITERACY FOR DISAGGREGATED DATA USE

The interpretation of disaggregated data that reveals disparities in student access, retention, and degree completion among racial and ethnic groups is confounded by cultural deficit perspectives (Nasir & Hand, 2006) and "marjoritarian" stories that are ahistorical (Yosso, Parker, Solórzano, & Lynn, 2004). Majoritarian discourse makes claims to race-neutrality and objectivity by treating the experiences of dominant groups as natural and normative and disregarding the voices and experiences of oppressed groups. These narratives are so predominant in US society (Kendi, 2016) that Lani Guinier has highlighted "racial literacy" as an essential capability for racial justice advocates, urging them to develop "the capacity to decipher the durable racial grammar that structures racialized hierarchies and frames the narrative of our republic" (Guinier, 2004, p. 100).

Like the administrators depicted in the vignette above (who were White), Black administrators in our case study also used and led others in the use of racially disaggregated data and decision making to address racial inequities at their institutions. They communicated similar expertise with data-informed decision making and had similar degrees of success in carrying out equity-minded changes in student advising and academic support structures. However, unlike their White peers, Black leaders experienced harmful statements that weighed negatively on their exercise of leadership. They faced racism and linguistic violence expressed by colleagues and students on their campuses. Racism manifested overtly and covertly in "words that wound" (Matsuda et al., 1993). Words that wound are assaultive speech. They constitute linguistic violence, acting overtly and covertly as weapons to ambush, terrorize, wound, humiliate, and degrade an individual or group identity.

Data talk and race talk (Pollock, 2001) are inseparable in racial equity work involving data use. The task of interpreting racial equity gaps evokes cultural assumptions that vary by race. Historical and experiential memories also vary and inform data interpretations in differential ways when racially diverse groups of practitioners have conversations about racially disaggregated data.

The ability to demonstrate critical consciousness of harmful racialized discourses is an important leadership capacity for those who want to promote racial equity. Staples emphasizes that silence is a form of "collusion" that is in itself oppressive (2010, p. 55). The work of breaking that silence involves listening for, questioning, and interrupting the use of seemingly rational, civil, and race-neutral words that are racially discriminatory and racist statements. The ability to counter racist language is part and parcel of leadership for equity-minded data use, because the data are a vehicle for discussion about racial disparities.

Leaders who promote equity-minded data use will experience greater success in their efforts if they develop their racial literacy. Such preparation includes developing the capacity to name and counter harmful words, assumptions, and patterns of social interaction that stereotype, demean, and harm members of racially and ethnically minoritized groups. Table 10.1 highlights four of these forms of discourse. The examples noted emerged through discussion of racially disaggregated data use at the historically and predominantly white institutions in our case study and were related to us by Black case study participants. Racial tokenization (Kanter, 1977; Kelly, 2007; Wingfield & Wingfield, 2014), cultural taxation (Ahmed, 2012; Padilla, 1994), microaggressions (Solorzano, Ceja, & Yosso, 2000), and historical amnesia (DiAngelo, 2018; Sue et al., 2007; Yosso, Smith, Ceja, & Solórzano, 2009) were forms of discrimination encountered by Black leaders in our study.

These social phenomena erode trust, which is essential to productive conversations about racially disaggregated data among members of racially diverse groups. Leaders

TABLE 10.1 Key Concepts Necessary for Racial Literacy to Lead Equity-Minded Data Use

Harmful Form of Racialized Discourse	Quotation from Case Study Data	Interpretation of Quotation
Racial Tokenism places members of racially minoritized groups in positions of high visibility and calls on them to be experts in race relations. This creates role entrapment for professionals with multifaceted expertise (Kelly, 2007; Wingfield & Wingfield, 2014).	"I was a little uncomfortable at one point with [our team leader], because every time we would end something, he'd be like, and what do you think about that? And I felt like that Black student in the classroom, that you're the only one."	This Black administrator joined the evidence team because she appreciated "practical processes" such as evidence-based action planning. She felt called on to speak as a representative of her race, and thereby tokenized, when the team leader singled her out during data discussions.
Microaggressions are commonplace verbal, behavioral, and environmental indignities, whether intentional or unintentional, that communicate hostile, derogatory, or negative racial insults to the target person or group. The term micro does not imply a minor offense. It contrasts daily, interpersonal interactions (micro), with larger (macro) structural and sociological inequities (Solorzano et al., 2000; Sue et al., 2007).	"One might assume if we are losing African American students disproportionately, it's because they are coming to this place [that is] small town and rural.... The preliminary research of the team [showed the] prevailing reason for African-American students leaving...was their not having made the transition academically. It was never because, when I drive off campus with my friends, we are looking at cows or whatever the case may be."	This Black administrator used her racial literacy to counter microaggressions that situated African American students as "alien in their own land," a type of microaggression that treats those who are not White as foreign. White colleagues stereotyped African Americans as "urban," using this explanation instead of one supported by available data showing the poor quality of faculty advising to dismiss institutional responsibility for Black students' high departure rates. This neglect of responsibility is another form of microaggression called "denial of individual racism" (Sue et al., 2007).
Cultural Taxation places an extra burden of service on racially minoritized faculty members due to their racial or ethnic background. Padilla (1994) defines it as the "obligation to show good citizenship toward the institution by serving its needs for ethnic representation on committees, or to demonstrate knowledge and commitment to a cultural group, which may even bring accolades to the institution, but which is not usually rewarded by the institution on	"People think that Black students [and] Latino students leave because they can't make it here. Well, yeah they can't make it here but it's not necessarily because of academics. It's because of all the other issues that interfere with their progress. And so once we can get the institution to understand that and then perhaps we are set up to move to the next level, where, you know, if we are talking to these students and we can find out a lot about them if we can get them to open up. And so	This Black administrator felt that his White colleagues expected him to take on a disproportionate workload because he was Black. He reminded his colleagues they were members of a committee and should do their part to understand "all the other issues" (besides students' academic preparedness) that were driving Black and Latinx students from the campus. As he resisted cultural taxation, he felt attacked, which demonstrates the inter-relationship between cultural taxation and linguistic violence.

TABLE 10.1 (Cont.)

Harmful Form of Racialized Discourse	Quotation from Case Study Data	Interpretation of Quotation
whose behalf the service was performed" (p. 26).	much of my work, again, I get attacked sometimes because they want me to do it and I'm like, 'No, I am not doing it… you are here as part of a committee.'"	The administrator demonstrates equity-minded racial literacy by emphasizing the need to fix "the institution," not the students.
Words that Wound are messages that communicate "racial inferiority," are "directed against a historically oppressed group," and are "persecutory, hateful, and degrading" (Matsuda et al., 1993, p. 36). Words that wound are used to subjugate and characterize individuals as inadequate or less favorable. They constitute linguistic violence, which occurs in covert (coded) or overt ways. Silence is a form of "collusion" with linguistic violence that is in itself oppressive (Staples, 2002, p. 55).	"I remember one of our Deans [asking], 'Is this going to be a quota system approach to things?' 'No, it's not. We are going to be looking at particular groups of students. We fully expect to learn things that we will be able to use with other students.' An example, because then it would quickly move us away from quotas, 'What about how well women students are doing in STEM in terms of access and success? We are likely to learn some things about how to look at data and how to determine what to do about that,' because I had also been looking at data about… women in STEM."	The history of "racist ideas" (Kendi, 2016) demonstrates that the word "quota" is designed to impose fear on and to discourage access to colleges and universities by individuals who are deemed unworthy by the speaker. The accusation of a "quota" implies that members of racially minoritized groups are unjustly taking away some privilege or position that belongs to White people. The terms "quota queen" and "welfare queen" have been used as racial slurs against Black women. Confronted with the word "quota," this Black administrator defused the challenge by changing the conversation. Subsequently, she sought external resources to maintain decision-making autonomy during Equity Scorecard implementation.

should realize that the concept of trust is multifaceted. It does not rely merely on whether one person trusts another to be truthful and well intentioned in what they say or reliable in carrying out promised actions. Trust depends too on perceptions of harmful and beneficial consequences of joint action (Johnson, Johnson, & Smith, 2007, pp. 24–25). One person may trust another to interact reliably in one setting, yet fear that the consequences of their colleagues' actions will be more harmful to them than any potential beneficial consequences. Through exposure to the words, silences, and lack of action of White colleagues, Black participants in our study came to distrust that the collaborative data use and inquiry process would produce consequences beneficial enough to outweigh harmful interactions.

RECOMMENDATIONS FOR EQUITY-MINDED LEADERSHIP

Though social change is a complex undertaking, higher education leaders do indeed hold power to redesign their institutions in a more socially just manner. The presence or absence of trust in leadership decisions can have positive or negative impacts on a leader's potential for carrying out or sustaining change (Datnow & Castellano, 2000; Kezar, 2011; Marsh, 2012; Marsh & Farrell, 2015). Therefore, our recommendations emphasize strategies leaders can employ to build trust among practitioners who produce and interpret data disaggregated by race and ethnicity with the goal of improving racial equity.

Engage in Trust-Building Behavior

We offer the terms "trust builder" and "trust buster" as cognitive tools for leaders to prioritize their attention to racialized discourses (Dowd & Bensimon, 2015, p. 56, citing Tenny Mickey). The strategies of data use we described as the craft of data use—transparency, dialogue, iterative use, sustained problem framing and problem solving, resource allocation, and collaborative sensemaking—are trust builders. Failure to address linguistic violence is a trust buster. To lead effective implementation of equity-minded data use, leaders must act as a trust builder. Trust must be established and maintained through institutional discourse and interpersonal relationships to enhance the success of collective efforts (Marsh, 2012; Marsh & Farrell, 2015).

Develop a Capacity for Racism-Conscious Interpretations of Inequities

To counter these phenomena, leaders who promote equity-minded use of data should take steps to deepen their knowledge of the "history of racist ideas" (Kendi, 2016) and the cultural scripts of White amnesia (Cabrera, 2012; DiAngelo, 2018; Iverson, 2007). Leaders should seek to develop the capacity for racism-conscious interpretations of coded, seemingly race-neutral statements about racial disparities in college access, retention, and completion. The cultural scripts of White supremacy are so prevalent, dominant, and ingrained in typical patterns of White socialization that White leaders should plan to engage explicitly in unlearning and learning to develop the ability to interpret text and subtext (i.e. what is said and what goes unsaid) in racialized discourses. Only after developing this racism-conscious interpretive capacity will they be able to call out seemingly race-neutral statements that surface during the discussion of racial equity gaps and goals.

Articulate an Anti-Racist Stance

To exercise leadership for equity-minded data use, leaders must articulate an anti-racist, anti-discrimination, and anti-oppression stance. To do so effectively requires a commitment to learning about different forms of racism and the ways that colleges and universities can counter the silencing of diverse voices, thereby deconstructing Whiteness as the norm. Many institutional actors discount racial equity as a goal because they have historical amnesia and are informed by racist ideas about the motivations, intelligence, and capabilities of Black and brown people (Haney-López, 2010; Harper, 2012; Kendi, 2016; Taylor, Gillborn, & Ladson-Billings, 2009). Developing the capacity to effectively articulate an anti-racist stance requires experience and practice. Leaders should participate in professional development for this purpose. The adage that actions speak louder than words is one to keep in mind. In order to maintain credibility, words must be followed by deeds. Leadership for equity-minded data use must involve changes in policies and practices adopted to create racial equity and ongoing institutional self-assessments to gauge progress.

Develop a Multifocal Lens for Leadership

Finally, and in support of all of the recommendations above, White leaders should develop what Hodges and Welch (2018) have termed a "multifocal lens" for leadership (p. 111). A multifocal lens provided them the "ability to embrace the margin and shuttle between margin and center," which was, they found, "a source of enormous strength," enabling them to systematically gather varied perspectives of faculty, staff, and administrative colleagues (p. 111). White leaders should similarly develop the capacity for multifocal perception. Leaders at Predominantly White Institutions may not encounter many such opportunities on their campuses, given limited diversity in executive leadership roles and power dynamics that deter frank discussion. However, there are numerous ways to learn independently through various professional conferences, audio and print books, podcasts, YouTube videos, TEDtalks, and social media authored by those who are often silenced in White dominant settings. And indeed, the more that each administrator develops their knowledge, skills, and vision for equity-minded leadership, the more likely they are to influence colleagues and, collectively, begin enacting meaningful changes.

CONCLUSION

This chapter has highlighted how becoming an equity-minded leader necessitates leadership for equity-minded data use in colleges and universities. Equity-minded leadership requires dual competencies, the craft of data use and the racial literacy to name and call out racist discourse. The most effective leaders in our case study used data disaggregated by race and ethnicity in a transparent, iterative, and sustained way to identify and change policies and practices that were reproducing racial disparities. They made organizational changes intended to promote their racial equity goals (Dowd et al., 2018), which illustrates the value of adopting equity as a standard of practice for data use. The changes took place in a variety of areas, including curriculum, admissions, and assessment policies and student support programs such as orientation and advising.

As scholars engaging practitioners in this process we have learned that an inquiry process alone will not ensure equity and social justice. We have underscored attention to racism and taking an anti-racist stance is necessary to meet these goals. The case study examples of leadership for equity-minded data use and the recommendations derived from them provided in this chapter offer guidance for leaders who would like to enhance racial equity at their own institutions.

QUESTIONS FOR REFLECTION AND DISCUSSION

1. According to the authors, what does equity mean? Why is it important to engage in race- and racism-conscious, equity-minded data use?
2. How were data used in the examples provided in this chapter? How do these data use practices compare with data use at your own institution? In your own experience? What steps have you taken or could you take to provide leadership for equity-minded data use?
3. What is racial literacy and why is it important to effective leadership for equity-minded data use? What steps, if any, have leaders taken at your institution to support professional development for racial literacy?

RESOURCES

- *Podcast:* Biewen, J. (Producer/Host). (2017, August 24). *Seeing White: Transformations* [Audio podcast]. Duke University, Center for Documentary Studies. Retrieved from www.sceneonradio.org/episode-45-transformation-seeing-white-part-14/
- Ibram X. Kendi's website: www.ibramxkendi.com/
- Robin DiAngelo's website: https://robindiangelo.com/
- University of Southern California Center for Urban Education website: https://cue.usc.edu/

NOTES

1 This work was funded through the Study of Data Use and Organizational Learning under Conditions of Accountability by the Spencer Foundation. The authors wish to thank Estela Mara Bensimon for her contributions to the research design; Marlon Fernandez Castro, Cheryl Ching, Joanna Drivalas, Román Liera, and Keith Witham for collaboration in related analyses of our case study data; CSHE-affiliated faculty and doctoral students; and the editors for comments on earlier drafts of this chapter.

2 In total, our 95 case study interviews involved 64 administrators, faculty, and staff at five universities in the same public university system that had implemented the Equity Scorecard as part of a system-wide initiative. Of these participants, 13 identified as Black or African American, 47 as white, and 5 as Latinx or of Asian ancestry. These numbers reflect the racial composition of students and practitioners at the universities in our study. We reference White and Black administrators in our study because of 24 administrators who were interviewed none identified as Asian and only 2 identified as Latinx, with one of

those participants declining the option to audiotape the interview. The patterns in our data are clearer from the audiotaped interviews involving 7 Black and 15 White administrators; therefore we base our interpretations on that data.

REFERENCES

Ahmed, S. (2012). *On Being Included: Racism and Diversity in Institutional Life.* Durham, NC: Duke University Press.

Bensimon, E. M. (2007). The underestimated significance of practitioner knowledge in the scholarship of student success. Review of Higher Education, *30*(4), 441–469.

Bensimon, E. M. (2018). Reclaiming racial justice in equity. Change: The Magazine of Higher Learning, May–August, 95–98.

Bensimon, E. M., Dowd, A. C., Longanecker, D., & Witham, K. (2012). We have goals: Now what? Change: The Magazine of Higher Learning, *44*, 14–25.

Bensimon, E. M., Dowd, A. C., Stanton-Salazar, R., & Dávila, B. (in press). The role of institutional agents in providing institutional support to Latino students in STEM. Review of Higher Education.

Bensimon, E. M., & Malcom, L. E. (2012). *Confronting equity issues on campus: Implementing the Equity Scorecard in theory and practice.* Sterling, VA: Stylus Publishing.

Bensimon, E. M., Polkinghorne, D. E., Bauman, G. L., & Vallejo, E. (2004). Doing research that makes a difference. Journal of Higher Education, *75*(1), 104–126. doi:10.1080/00221546.2004.11778898

Bustillos, L. T., Rueda, R., & Bensimon, E. M. (2011). Faculty views of underrepresented students in community college settings. In P. R. Portes & S. Salas (Eds.), *Vygotsky in 21st century society: Advances in cultural historical theory and praxis with non-dominant communities* (pp. 199–213). New York: Peter Lang.

Bustillos, L. T., Rueda, R., Hentschel, D., Kinney, D., Love, J., Magee, I., … Wolf, R. (2012). The math project at Los Angeles City College. In E. M. Bensimon & L. Malcom (Eds.), *Confronting equity issues on campus: Implementing the Equity Scorecard in theory and practice* (pp. 117–137). Sterling, VA: Stylus Publishing.

Cabrera, N. L. (2012). Working through whiteness: White, male college students challenging racism. Review of Higher Education, *35*(3), 375–401.

Datnow, A., & Castellano, M. (2000). Teachers' response to Success for All: How beliefs, experiences, and adaptations shape implementation. American Educational Research Journal, *37*(3), 775–799. doi:10.3102/00028312037003775

Datnow, A., Greene, J. C., & Gannon-Slater, N. (2017). Data use for equity: Implications for teaching, leadership, and policy. Journal of Educational Administration, *55*(4), 354–360.

Datnow, A., & Park, V. (2018). Opening or closing doors for students? Equity and data use in schools. Journal of Educational Change, *19*, 131–152. doi:10.1007/s10833-018-9323-6

DiAngelo, R. (2018). *White fragility: Why it's so hard for people to talk about racism.* Boston, MA: Beacon Press.

Dowd, A. C., & Bensimon, E. M. (2015). *Engaging the "race question": Accountability and equity in higher education.* New York: Teachers College Press.

Dowd, A. C., Bishop, R. M., & Bensimon, E. M. (2015). Critical action research on race and equity in higher education. In A. M. Martínez-Alemán, B. Pusser, & E. M. Bensimon (Eds.), *Critical approaches to the study of higher education* (pp. 174–192). Baltimore, MD: Johns Hopkins University Press.

Dowd, A. C., & Liera, R. (2018). Sustaining organizational change towards racial equity through cycles of inquiry. Education Policy Analysis Archives, *26*(65), 1–46.

Dowd, A. C., Malcom, L. E., Nakamoto, J., & Bensimon, E. M. (2012). Institutional researchers as teachers and equity advocates: Facilitating organizational learning and change. In E. M. Bensimon & L. E. Malcom (Eds.), *Confronting equity issues on campus: Implementing the Equity Scorecard in theory and practice* (pp. 191–215). Sterling, VA: Stylus.

Dowd, A. C., Witham, K., Hanson, D., Ching, C., Liera, R., Drivalas, J., & Castro, M. F. (2018). Bringing data to life: How savvy college leaders find the "actionable N" to improve equity and effectiveness in higher education. Retrieved from www.acenet.edu/news-room/Pages/Bringing-Accountability-to-Life.aspx

Felix, E. R., Bensimon, E. M., Hanson, D., Gray, J., & Klingsmith, L. (2015). Developing agency for equity minded change. In E. Castro (Ed.), *Understanding equity in community college practice* (Vol. 172, pp. 25–42). San Francisco, CA: Jossey Bass.

Felix, E. R., & Fernandez Castro, M. (2018). Planning as strategy for improving Black and Latins student equity: Lessons from nine California community colleges. Educational Policy Analysis Archives, *26*(56). doi:10.14507/epaa.26.3223

Guinier, L. (2004). From racial liberalism to racial literacy: Brown v. Board of Education and the Interest-Divergence Dilemma. Journal of American History, June, 92–118.

Hallett, T. (2010). The myth incarnate: Recoupling processes, turmoil, and inhabited institutions in an urban elementary school. American Sociological Review, *75*(1), 52–74.

Haney-López, I. F. (2010). Is the "post" in post-racial the "blind" in colorblind? Cardozo Law Review, *32*, 807–831.

Harper, S. R. (2012). Race without racism: How higher education researchers minimize racist institutional norms. Review of Higher Education, *36*(1), 9–29. doi:10.1353/rhe.2012.0047

Harris III, F., & Bensimon, E. M. (2008). The Equity Scorecard: A collaborative approach to assessing and responding to racial/ethnic disparities in student outcomes. In S. R. Harper & L. D. Patton (Eds.), *New directions for student services: Responding to the realities of race*. San Francisco, CA: Jossey-Bass.

Hodges, C. R., & Welch, O. M. (2018). Truth without Tears: African American Women Deans Share Lessons in Leadership. Harvard Education Press. 8 Story Street First Floor, Cambridge, MA 02138.

Iverson, S. V. (2007). Camouflaging power and privilege: A critical race analysis of university diversity policies. Educational Administration Quarterly, *43*, 586–611. doi:10.1177/0013161X07307794

Johnson, D. W., Johnson, R. T., & Smith, K. (2007). The state of cooperative learning in postsecondary and professional settings. Educational Psychology Review, *19*, 15–29. doi:10.1007/s10648-006-9038-8

Kanter, R. M. (1977). *Men and women of the corporation*. New York: Basic Books.

Kelly, H. (2007). Racial tokenism in the school workplace: An exploratory study of black teachers in overwhelmingly white schools. Educational Studies, *41*(3), 230–254.

Kendi, I. X. (2016). *Stamped from the beginning: The definitive history of racist ideas in America*. New York: NationBooks.

Kezar, A. (2011). What is the best way to achieve broader reach of improved practices in higher education. Innovative Higher Education, *36*, 235–247. doi:10.1007/s10755-011-9174-z

Lester, J., & Kezar, A. (2012). Understanding the formation, functions, and challenges of grassroots leadership teams. Innovative Higher Education, *37*, 105–124.

Liera, R., & Dowd, A. C. (2018). Faculty learning at boundaries to broker racial equity. Journal of Higher Education. doi:https://doi.org/10.1080/00221546.2018.1512805

Marsh, J. A. (2012). Interventions promoting educators' use of data: Research insights and gaps. Teachers College Record, *114*(1), 1–15. doi:www.tcrecord.org ID Number: 16805

Marsh, J. A., & Farrell, C. C. (2015). How leaders can support teachers with data-driven decision making: A framework for understanding capacity building. Educational Management Administration Leadership, *43*(2), 269–289. doi:10.1177/1741143214537229

Matsuda, M. J., Lawrence III, C. R., Delgado, R., & Crenshaw, K. W. (1993). *Words that wound: Critical race theory, assaultive speech, and the first amendment*. Boulder, CO: Westview Press.

Nasir, N. S., & Hand, V. M. (2006). Exploring sociocultural perspectives on race, culture, and learning. Review of Educational Research, *76*(4), 449–475.

Padilla, A. M. (1994). Ethnic minority scholars, research, and mentoring: Current and future issues. Educational Researcher, *23*(4), 24–27.

Pollock, M. (2001). How the question we ask most about race in education is the very question we most suppress. Educational Researcher, *30*(9), 2–11.

Schmidt, M., & Datnow, A. (2005). Teachers' sensemaking about comprehensive school reform: The influence of emotions. Teaching and Teacher Education, *21*, 949–965.

Solorzano, D. G., Ceja, M., & Yosso, T. J. (2000). Critical race theory, racial microaggressions, and campus racial climate: The experiences of African American college students. Journal of Negro Education, 60–73.

Staples, J. (2010). Encouraging agitation: Teaching teacher candidates to confront words that wound. Teacher Education Quarterly, 37(1), Progressive Teacher Education: Honoring the Work of Alan H. Jones, Winter), 53–72.

Sue, D. W., Capodilupo, C. M., Torino, G. C., Bucceri, J. M., Holder, A. M. B., Nadal, K. L., & Esquilin, M. (2007). Racial microaggressions in everyday life: Implications for clinical practice. American Psychologist, 62(4), 271–286. doi:10.1037/0003-066x.62.4.271

Taylor, E., Gillborn, D., & Ladson-Billings, G. (Eds.). (2009). *Foundations of critical race theory in education.* New York: Routledge.

Wingfield, A. H., & Wingfield, J. H. (2014). When visibility hurts and helps: How intersections of race and gender shape Black professional men's experiences with tokenization. Cultural Diversity and Ethnic Minority Psychology, 20(4), 483–490. doi:10.1037/a0035761

Witham, K., & Bensimon, E. M. (2012). Creating a culture of inquiry around equity and student success. In S. D. Museus & U. M. Jayakumar (Eds.), *Creating campus cultures: Fostering success among racially diverse student populations* (pp. 46–67). New York: Routledge.

Witham, K., Chase, M., Bensimon, E. M., Hanson, D., & Longanecker, D. (2015). Moving the attainment agenda from policy to action. Change: The Magazine of Higher Learning, 47(4), 6–15. doi:10.1080/00091383.2015.1053779

Yosso, T. J., Parker, L., Solórzano, D. G., & Lynn, M. (2004). From Jim Crow to affirmative action and back again: A critical race discussion of racialized rationales and access to higher education. Review of Research in Education, 28, 1–25.

Yosso, T. J., Smith, W. A., Ceja, M., & Solórzano, D. G. (2009). Critical race theory, racial microaggressions, and campus racial climate for Latina/o undergraduates. Harvard Educational Review, 79(4), 659–691.

11

AN EXAMINATION OF ANTI-SEXUAL HARASSMENT POLICIES AND PRACTICES

Legal Administration for Socially Conscious Campuses

JEFFREY SUN

The legal administration of higher education involves addressing competing interests, which arise from disputes or violations onto another or society (Daniel, Gee, Sun, & Pauken, 2012). For instance, in one case, parents of a deaf student, who committed suicide following an altercation, alleged a wrongful death claim against the university based on allegations that the university acted too aggressively and falsely arrested the student, who suffered from mental health challenges, rather than providing the student reasonable accommodations (*Sacchetti v. Gallaudet Univ.*, 2018). The university countered, claiming that the student's behaviors were the basis for the arrest, and it acted reasonably under the circumstances. In another case, a group of students sued a public university for its failure to respond when other students acted relentlessly in harassing and threatening a group of women through social media (*Feminist Majority Found. v. Hurley*, 2018). The university argued that the First Amendment restrained its ability to respond to the harassing and threatening posts, so the matter was beyond its control.

These brief case statements illustrate how competing perspectives about legal matters may shift the responsibility for the harm or loss. That responsibility is critically important to consider in many legal cases because often only one party prevails. While seemingly obvious, the competing interests are not simply matters of the law, and the legal administration of higher education also encounters policies that are neither clear nor consistent, which generate administrative confusion and policy adoption errors (Cantalupo, 2011). For instance, the laws and policies governing Title

IX of the Education Amendments of 1972 are undergoing significant changes. Title IX of the Education Amendments of 1972 prohibits colleges that receive federal financial assistance from discriminating based on sex in educational programs or activities (e.g. academic and co-curricular settings) (Sun, Scott, Sponsler, & Hutchens, 2014a, 2014b). Under this law, colleges must protect students from peer sexual harassment, which includes sexual violence through actions such as rape, sexual assault, and sexual coercion.

Although the policies for Title IX are changing, with a shifting focus from an overly prescriptive set of guidelines starting in 2011 to a criminal-like hearing with adversarial proceedings, which are expected to be promulgated into regulation in 2019, colleges are responsible, as part of their obligations as federal funding recipients, for complying with the new policies. A compliance oriented approach has unintended consequences. In situations of sexual misconduct, campus compliance has the inadvertent effect of overshadowing the needs of the parties, especially the victims (Sun et al., 2014a, 2014b). Yet, campus leaders have agency to make more trauma-informed approaches that are socially just and equity-minded to care for the victim and other parties in the matter. Re-engaging campus leaders in the legal administration over sexual misconduct matters with a social justice and equity-minded approach involves protecting our campus community and presenting fair and just policies and practices that redirect a mindset toward improving the campus environment rather than advancing an adversarial approach to disputes or an agnostic view to the social-emotional effects on to persons. In short, federal policies present a set of parameters for campuses to follow, but campuses, which may be overly constrained in their approaches to follow a compliance-oriented approach and protect their public image, have greater opportunities than currently exercised.

To explore the capacity of the federal policy and campus policy connection toward a more social justice and equity-minded approach, this chapter presents the federal policy context of Title IX and key policy changes between two US Presidential administrations. It also reports on the evolutionary approaches of campus legal administration to nest the reader's understanding of college policy implementation, which today largely adopts a compliance-oriented approach. In addition, the chapter dissects the assets and drawbacks to a compliance-oriented approach. Following that section, this chapter also illustrates the imbalance of power emergent from regulatory and campus policies, the advantage of social privilege in terms of scope of protections and understandings of due process, and the misguided effects of administrators' assumptions in omitting considerations of victimization and trauma. Given these legal and policy considerations that overshadow the care and concern for victims, the chapter proposes a set of actions for campus leaders to take as an effort to advance a more social justice and equity-minded approach to legal administration on college campuses.

CAMPUS SAFETY AND SEXUAL MISCONDUCT

Legal administration of higher education is particularly vulnerable to criticisms and liability around matters involving campus safety because of potential for negative publicity (Sun, 2014). For instance, in 2007 the media reported that leaders at Eastern Michigan University had been accused of covering up information involving the rape and murder of a female student at the school. According to reports of the incident, the school sought to avoid bad publicity (Bunkley, 2007; Lipka, 2007). Similarly, the US Department of Education's Office of Civil Rights also received a complaint about how the University of Notre Dame poorly handled the investigation of an alleged rape (St. Clair & Lighty, 2011). According to the complaint, Notre Dame took weeks before it conducted the investigation. In the meantime, the victim, a student at Notre Dame's sister school, St. Mary's College, committed suicide. The complaint indicated that Notre Dame had failed to conduct a thorough investigation in this case and other complaints of sexual misconduct. Also, the complaint stated that the school delayed and left some grievances unresolved. Adding to this list of campus sexual assault mishandlings, a watchdog group, the Center for Public Integrity revealed numerous instances in which colleges failed to take appropriate actions to stop alleged perpetrators—often by ignoring the grievance or delaying responses (Peebles & Lombardi, 2010).

When college policies and procedures demonstrate compliance concerns, federal policies often intervene to redirect educational institutions. In this situation, the US Assistant Secretary of Education for the Office of Civil Rights (often referred to as OCR) recognized a pattern of problems that campuses faced in administering Title IX, so she issued a Dear Colleague Letter in April 2011 calling for greater oversight and action over peer sexual harassment, especially sexual violence,[1] and outlining the requirements under the applicable laws. Contextualizing the problem, the letter highlighted the National Institute of Justice finding that approximately "1 in 5 women are victims of completed or attempted sexual assault while in college" (Ali, 2011, p. 2). Further, it noted that "approximately 6.1 percent of males were victims of completed or attempted sexual assault during college" (Ali, 2011, p. 2). Federal reports from colleges also indicated "nearly 3,300 forcible sex offenses as defined by the Clery Act" (p. Ali, 2011, p. 2). Taken together, she concluded that the "Department [of Education] is deeply concerned about this problem and is committed to ensuring that all students feel safe in their school, so that they have the opportunity to benefit fully from the school's programs and activities" (Ali, 2011, p. 2). The letter directed colleges with great detail about regulatory interpretation of standards and processes to inform students of their rights, establish reporting and review systems, investigate complaints, construct thorough and equitable panels when deliberating over sexual violence cases, implement certain evidentiary and decision-making standards, and establish disclosure and appeal protocols (Sun et al., 2014a). Among the very specific details and through additional guidance, which was issued in 2014, the general message to campus leaders was to take immediate and effective steps to eliminate the harassing conduct, prevent its recurrence, and address its effects (Ali, 2011, 2014). While the federal government made efforts to steer campuses toward complying with the administration's interpretation of Title IX, the documents presented procedural complicated steps and posed a very prescriptive approach. Consequently, there was a great deal of debate among campus leaders, the legal community, and other interested parties on how to properly implement the policy guidance—if at all (Baker, 2016, 2017; Cantalupo, 2011; Sun et al., 2014a).

In an effort to address constitutional rights of due process of alleged perpetrators and redirect attention to the new administration's interpretation of Title IX, the new administration in the US Department of Education withdrew the standards and processes outlined in April 2011, a companion administrative guidance from April 2014, and protections for gender identity discrimination. Specifically, on September 22, 2017, OCR issued a new Dear Colleague Letter suggesting that the former administration's 2011 and 2014 documents may have violated legal standards of fairness and due process (Jackson, 2017), and it ignored any discussion about the 2016 Dear Colleague Letter recognizing gender identity discrimination as encapsulated under Title IX.

In late 2018, the US Department of Education posted a Notice of Proposed Rulemaking, which is a formal proposal that announces to the nation the agency's intent to make changes to the rules and solicit public feedback for consideration. This process presents a legal avenue to provide stronger legal force of the new rules and makes efforts to overturn the rules procedurally more difficult than the Dear Colleague Letters or a guidance document as presented in 2011 and 2014. The new rules, which are likely to be promulgated in 2019, extend the administrative interpretation of how campuses must address sexual harassment complaints by adopting required procedures that somewhat resemble criminal proceedings, including live hearings similar to a court trial and a right to cross-examine through a third party (e.g. a lawyer or adviser). Further, the proposed rules limit the application of Title IX only to situations in which a college official has actual knowledge of one violating sexual harassment in an education program or activity, and the college official acted with deliberate indifference, which, in these cases, is evidenced by a college official's conscious or reckless disregard of the student's safety leading to the sexual violence. This new rule significantly loosens a college's responsibility over sexual harassment claims. Also, it limits the application of the law largely to campus-based activities and specifically excludes any activity outside of the United States (e.g. sexual violence in a study abroad program).

In short, both the newly proposed policy and the documents from 2011 and 2014 present challenges for the campus legal administration over cases of sexual misconduct. The 2011 Dear Colleague Letter and the 2014 guidance documents under the Obama Administration created procedural complicated steps and posed a very prescriptive approach. The newly proposed policy under the Trump Administration establishes a criminal-like proceeding with structured adversarial proceedings masked as due process. Thus, while institutions desire to address legal compliance and consider its public image, not all legal requirements have been sufficiently clear or stable for campus leaders, and these shifts in policies raise questions as to whose interests are these policies intended to serve.

EVOLUTIONARY VOLUNTARY APPROACHES TO LEGAL ADMINISTRATION

Legal administration of higher education has evolved over the past half-century. In the 1960s and 1970s, higher education operated with an *in loco parentis* mindset, in which the college acted in the place of a parent. Societal expectations of colleges changed during the 1980s. Judges and legislators, via court cases and legislation, started to relieve universities in many instances from liability of student injuries, particularly from accidents outside of the classroom. Notably, a federal appellate court case, *Bradshaw v. Rawlings* (1979), started this trend by declaring that universities are not an insurer of student safety, and unlike many past cases, this case ruled that the university did not owe a duty to protect students from harm emerging from a drink-driving accident following a university function because the university's scope of responsibility could not continue to extend beyond its campus and other aspects which it could control (see, e.g., Bickel & Lake, 1999). The focus shifted toward colleges as educational institutions responsible for the educational mission. However, the number of cases did not subside, in large part because policymakers increased legislation and new applications of laws and policies. For instance, in 1986 the US Supreme Court expanded the scope of Title VII of the Civil Rights Act of 1964 as a viable legal source to address sexual harassment claims as a form of sex discrimination. The civil rights law prohibited employment discrimination based on race, color, religion, sex, or national origin. Expanding the purview of sex discrimination, the Supreme Court defined sex discrimination as inclusive of sexual harassment.

About a decade later, courts recognized similar legislation such as Title IX of the Educational Amendments as a legal source to combat sexual harassment on college campuses. Title IX of the Education Amendments of 1972 prohibits colleges that receive federal financial assistance from discriminating based on sex in educational programs or activities (e.g. academic and co-curricular settings). That law, like Title VII of the Civil Rights Act of 1964, was expanded to include sexual harassment that blocked access to individuals from participating in educational programs or activities at college receiving any federal funding. In short, as Bickel and Lake (1999) described, colleges were bystanders in the legal environment. They protected their assets and carried out a minimalist approach to defending students' interests.

By the 1990s, the interest on students and other stakeholders began to shift, and campus legal administration adopted a facilitator approach. Bickel and Lake (1999) observed college leaders facilitating legal processes and policies so as to balance the rights and responsibilities of students and colleges. Legal administration in higher education considered multiple interests and recognized greater inclusion, students' rights, and educational access as priorities to the education mission. As Bickel and Lake (1999) describe, this approach was "neither extremely authoritarian nor overly solicitous of student freedom" (p. 105). Instead, campus leaders perceived their roles as partners in the learning process and collaborated with students within the boundaries of the law and institutional policy to facilitate the development of students into adulthood and independent thinking and choices. At the time, the goal for campus leaders still involved managing risks, but Bickel and Lake (1999) observed that the campus was also willing to accept "an appropriate and reasonable degree of risk" in order to facilitate students' development (p. 168). Simply put, the concern over risk levels started to subside and there was a moderate, but hedging levels of care and developmental principles involved in the decision-making processes for campus legal administration.

Starting around 2010, administrative practice in higher education started to shift to a compliance-responsive approach and has likely rested on this approach (see, e.g., Adams, 2015; Dunham, 2010). Lake (2013) points to examples, starting around 2010, when campus leaders started to move toward a compliance approach, especially with greater federal regulatory emphasis with potential punitive outcomes for failing to comply.[2] This change signaled a movement toward risk avoidance over the previous interest in balancing the rights and responsibilities of students and colleges. Portending to this shift, Bickel and Lake (1999) wrote: "College administrators and campus law enforcement officers" have been demonstrating fear of legal liability, which set off a chain reaction in which they have been "encouraged to pursue strategies in their jobs that would minimize the risk of lawsuits but not necessarily reduce risk or injury." Indeed, the literature is consistent that legislative mandates, court cases, and accountability features, including reporting and penalties, have moved the focus on balancing interests to generating a protective response over institutional interests. Lake (2013) posits that the legal and regulatory pressures have positioned administrative responses to protecting a college's administrative interests so legal risks are calculated for the university and the administrators with the goal of protecting the organization's reputation and financial liability.

This perspective is not surprising when examining risk factors and penalties associated with non-compliance of governmental mandates. For instance, Heckman (2018) draws attention to how the Clery Act mandates reporting of certain crimes within the campus vicinity and warning notifications to the campus community of actively dangerous activities in rather specific and comprehensive ways. Cantalupo (2012) also highlights that the US Department of Education has exercised this authority by fining Eastern Michigan University $350,000 and Salem International University $200,000 for failing to warn their campuses and report the data. Adding to those reporting particulars, Heckman notes that congressional changes in 2013 increased the penalties for noncompliance from "fines of $35,000 for every 'substantial' violation of the law" to $54,789 per violation after April 20, 2017 (p. 338). These increases heighten the pressures for a compliance-centered mindset. Nonetheless, the dialogue could have easily introduced the benefits and value of staffing diversification or the equity-minded approaches along with the associated opportunities including reshaping the organizational environment as the drivers, rather than a sense of legal mandates and fear of penalties.

ASSETS AND DRAWBACKS OF COMPLIANCE APPROACH

The literature highlights three advantages to the compliance approach for campus legal administration. One of these advantages to the compliance approach is its ability to generate greater organizational control over legal administration. As Adams (2015) suggests, college compliance leads to greater organizational control over the outcomes, and a compliance lens places structural elements such as enterprise systems that map employment, financial, safety, and environmental regulations. Illustrating the organizational control advantage, Lake (2013) posits that campus leaders weigh risk factors and examine options such as the degree to place physical safety measures and policies that encourage reporting to determine the level of risk exposure as a means to maintain organizational control. Consistent with that behavior, James and Wooten (2006) highlight that organizations often seek control of unknowns by adopting a response that protects the organizational image and attempts to neutralize the allegations of potential litigation. In short, campus leaders adhere to the legal, regulatory, or policy-based rules, yet they have relative discretion to the organizational priorities.

Another advantage of the compliance approach is the risk reduction associated with such an operational mindset to legal matters. A compliance approach tends to circumscribe choice and focus on protecting the organization through a set of reliable and goal-centered objectives. Rege (2006) observes that asserting federal restrictions and other similar compliance measures advance risk mitigation interests for a university because this approach reduces possibilities of inadvertent errors. For instance, in the research enterprise, the compliance approach mitigates encounters such as compromising intellectual property of industry partners, unintentionally leaking protected information that may appear to sit on the fringes of national security yet present greater vulnerability to a university, and avoiding financial and other penalties associated with regulatory violations. Similarly, in discrimination and harassment cases, the compliance approach draws heavily on formal policies and structures to guide investigations, communication, resources, and support mechanisms for complainants (James & Wooten, 2006)

The literature addressing the compliance approach to legal administration in higher education also cites psychological safety to administrators as a third advantage. Dejean (2015) observes that the compliance approach offers higher education leaders psychological safety, which her data suggest was a critical aspect to successful implementation of "both institutional and regulatory changes" (p. 49). A compliance approach tends to adopt a team-centered focus, so the adherence to the policies are centered into the group's actions of advancing the organization's interest. Thus, the work environment is welcoming of ideas and procedures that contribute to the organizational solution or support such as recommended strategies to combat unjust biases in the workplace, safety measures that curb probability of accidents, and additional reporting requirements to increase organizational awareness of evidentiary sources or potential harms (Dejean, 2015; James & Wooten, 2006; Lake 2013). Thus, while the compliance approach may be perceived as bureaucratic and cumbersome, it brings psychological safety to campus leaders and other administrative staff that the campus operations have cautionary measures that contribute to work effectiveness and team support in their legal administration practices.

While beneficial, the compliance approach presents multiple drawbacks. The literature on legal administration of higher education often references two of them. One significant drawback to the compliance approach is that it oversimplifies the legal issue and related matters failing to fully address the complex nature of a higher education operation. By focusing on a single or narrowly focused legal issue, the compliance approach does not recognize the potential for the solution to one matter colliding with rights for another matter. In Title IX cases, numerous scholars argue that the compliance approach focused too much on the complainant (Baker, B. A., 2017; Henrick, 2013) while others argued that the approach created criminalized processes focusing too much on the perpetrator (Baker, K. K., 2017; Brodsky, 2018; Cantalupo, 2012; Lave, 2017). The effect of the oversimplification is alienating stakeholders and creating environments that further conflict views on how best to resolve the issue.

Another significant drawback to the compliance approach is its rigidity to problem solving. Although a compliance approach offers opportunities for organizational control over the situation, research suggests that an overly compliant lens may stifle innovation to solve problems (Edelman & Suchman, 1997). The focus tends to be on limits and rules, particularly when fear of litigation or regulatory violations are at stake. Consequently, compliance may lead to threat rigidity effects in which campus leaders respond to fears or unknowns through freezing innovation and limiting options in favor of a narrowed set of actions and ignore other exogenous conditions. In terms of sexual misconduct hearings, the compliance approach has escalated the practice of these proceedings to appear like college courtrooms, yet an underlying problem, which is stated repeatedly in the literature, is that campuses are not meant to be adversarial mimicking courtrooms and other legal characteristics (e.g. cross examination).

POWER, PRIVILEGE, AND ADMINISTRATORS' ASSUMPTIONS

The legal administration of Title IX and related legal policies has, in some cases, exacerbated the imbalance of power and privilege exercised by campus leaders and over victims of sexual misconduct and alleged perpetrators. Indeed, the extensive legal prescription and criminal-like processes, which are applied to campus sexual misconduct cases, present serious harms to victims, especially when college proceedings are only deciding whether a student (i.e. the alleged perpetrator) violated a student conduct policy, not a criminal code. Illustrating inadvertent harm onto victims, this section presents how policies, practices, and procedures present power and privilege imbalances and harm from administrators' assumptions.

Unclear Scope of Protections and Support

Campus leaders structure the policies governing the legal administration of sexual misconduct, but the definitions of key terms and the provisions within the student conduct policy position how campuses characterize and legitimize behaviors, violations, and penalties present unclear scope of protections and understanding of terms, which lead to questions and fears as to whether the policy protects victims or furthers their vulnerability (Cantalupo, 2011, 2014). Even the prevalence of rape and sexual misconduct is highly debated in the literature and in legal practice (see, e.g., Brenner & Darcy, 2017; Cantalupo, 2009; Coker, 2016; Johnson & Taylor, 2017; Kirkpatrick & Kanin, 1957; Lave, 2016). The primary issue resides with the definitions of consent, rape, sexual assault, and other forms of sexual violence in accountability surveys, criminal statutes, and university policies. Compounding the variability in terms as recognized for data transparency, criminal action, and university disciplinary proceedings, there is a psychological dimension that these surveys, statutes, and policies overlook. For instance, empirical research on the discounting or disbelief that a sexual assault such as rape occurred is well documented in the literature (Grubb & Turner, 2012; van der Bruggen & Grubb, 2014; Weiss, 2011). Rape myths reflect the attitudes and beliefs, which are typically false yet widely held, to deny or rationalize the sexual assault actions (Grubb & Turner, 2012). The research demonstrates a presence of rape myths in society in which victims and observers "blame the victim for [the] rape, express a disbelief in claims of rape, exonerate the perpetrator and allude that only certain types of women are raped" (Grubb & Turner, 2012, p. 445). Given these variances in definition and policy and the possibility of social disbelief, victims often express great vulnerability to campus policies and practices that are unclear because they escalate the possibility of victim fear, confusion, and distrust.

Negative Effects from Reporting or Referral Policies

Legal administration of sexual misconduct cases often operate off the assumption that reporting or referral practices lead to positive effects for victims because they will receive proper treatment and other assistance. Campus leaders and even policy-makers rationalize how these reporting and referral policies advance a positive public goal, which is in the best interest of the parties, especially the victim. Yet, research and policy reports find contrary findings. Instead, mandatory reporting and referral policies generate victim fears in campus leaders and they increase the likelihood for victim harm (Brodsky, 2017, 2018; Weiss & Lasky, 2017).

Mandatory reporting and referral laws are common among state statutes when protecting children and vulnerable adults. These laws require victim voice through reporting protocols to appropriate authorities such as the police and social service agencies. Modeling those protective features since 2016, several states (e.g. Delaware, Georgia, Rhode Island, Tennessee, and Virginia) have entertained mandatory referral policies that require colleges to report sexual assault cases to the police, regardless of the victim's expressions (Brodsky, 2018). Already, Title IX requires a series of actions when individuals at a campus would be classified as "responsible persons," who are required to report sexual misconduct so that notification reaches the college Title IX coordinator. However, colleges are not required to report personally identifiable information of reluctant victims to the police, yet some do. The effect of the disclosure and law enforcement interview could lead to revictimization, which may include the victim reliving the trauma or establishing new forms of trauma along with potentially other negative effects such as lower self-worth, depression, and isolation. Brodsky (2018) also observes that campus leaders have, at times, taken the mandatory reporting or referral concept too far by "block[ing] survivors' access to essential services and accommodations, like mental health support and dorm changes, and frustrate administrators' attempts to discipline wrongdoers" when reporting or disclosure is not forthcoming (p. 132). While seemingly appropriate from a lens of compliance, this approach alienates victims and may lead to significant adverse effects, rather than a survivorship mindset.

Lack of Understanding about Victimization and Trauma

Legal administration of campus sexual misconduct cases impute meaning around victim actions that may be reasonable in other student behavior settings, but they fail to account for behaviors in situations of sexual victimization and trauma (Ellman-Golan, 2017). A line of research in psychology, counseling, sociology, and criminal justice consistently reports that a prevalent barrier to victim reporting or hesitation to reporting illustrates the presence of perceived power dimensions between the victim and authorities such as campus leaders (Aronowitz, Lambert, & Davidoff, 2012). Yet, some in the legal community have raised the counter-argument. That is, practitioners and scholars have asserted the lack of victim reporting, hesitation to report, and reluctant victims are matters beyond the scope of legal administration, especially for university administrators, but instead, campus leaders should place efforts on the due process rights of alleged perpetrators (Brenner & Darcy, 2017; Cantalupo, 2009; Curtis, 2017).

While the due process rights of alleged perpetrators are important in campus disciplinary proceedings, the data are clear about victim non-reporting rationalizations. For instance, Sable, Danis, Mauzy, and Gallagher (2006) found that college students reported personal shame and fear of not being believed as within the primary barriers for both women and men to reporting sexual assault. Additionally, Weiss (2011) examined 276 National Crime Victimization Survey narratives to investigate reasons behind victims' non-reporting of sexual assaults. Her research found that these victims neutralize sexual victimization in four ways. One way is denying criminal intent to create a positive image of the offender and rationalize that the offender has positive attributes. Another way is denying the effects of serious injury. This justification reframes the situation to appear less deviant or threatening and minimizes the harm. A third rationalization is denying the victim's own innocence to cope with the offender's actions and presents a sense of agency for the victim. A fourth rationalization is rejecting the victim label to draw greater control of the situation and develop expressions of empowerment such as instances of victim fighting off an offender. In short, these rationalizations suggest that non-reporting does not summarily represent a false characterization of the events or a minimizing effect of the harm onto the victim because the victim behaviors in a sexual assault situation do not necessarily reflect responses of parties harmed in other situations such as acts of negligence.

Social Biases on Roles and Perspectives

The law and legal administration within higher education do account for varying perspectives from among complainant/victim, alleged perpetrator, and witnesses. For instance, the law and policies consider evidentiary weight (e.g. veracity checking) and training of investigators and hearing panels. Despite these considerations, legal administration of sexual misconduct cases struggle to address social biases, which interfere with objectivity and one's ability for positional understanding of the situation. Aronowitz, Lambert, and Davidoff (2012) examine these biases in sexual assault scenarios and find that gender-based social norms within college students perpetuate the power differential and perceptual privilege. Illustrating this point, women's choice of clothing, but not men's clothing choices, influence campus perceptions and even hearing panels' rationalizations around sexual aggression and other sexual misconduct. At the same time, selected evidence suggests that social biases lead to hearing panels and juries possibly placing alleged male offenders as presumed violators or perpetrators (Aronowitz et al., 2012).

Similarly, sex roles and biases have been shown to exist in reports of sexual assaults in homosexual, bisexual, and transgender encounters. Coker (2016) argues that there is a dominant narrative that college administrators and the public have about incidents of campus sexual assault. "The paradigm victim of campus sexual assault that emerges from media stories is a white, heterosexual female who experiences nonconsensual penetration, often when she was incapacitated due to intoxication" (Coker, 2016, p. 162). Yet, data from the Centers for Disease Control and Prevention report that bisexual women had a higher lifetime prevalence of rape by any gendered perpetrator (i.e. heterosexual 17.4%, lesbian 13.1%, and bisexual 46.1%) (Walters, Chen, & Breiding, 2013). Coker (2016) also demonstrates similar patterns from the Department of Justice's 2016 Campus Climate Survey Validation Study. Further, a recent report by the Centers for Disease Control and Prevention report that "[n]early a quarter of men (24.8% or 27.6 million) in the U.S. experienced some form of contact sexual violence in their lifetime" (Smith et al., 2018, p. 3). These data support a re-examination of social heuristics around misperceptions among campus leaders who are responsible for the legal administration of sexual misconduct cases.

Criminal-Like Proceedings

Campus policies vary in terms of the extent to which the investigations and review panel hearings reflect criminal proceedings (Wilgus & Lowery, 2018). Yet, more recent analyses suggest a greater mimicking of criminal procedures. For instance, in 2002 only 22% of campus policies governing sexual misconduct at sampled institutions outlined the standard of proof for case reviews (Karjane, Fisher, & Cullen, 2002). By 2017, the percentage of colleges outlining their standard of review rose to 97% (Lave, 2017). Further, policies outlined detailed rights and proceedings for alleged perpetrators including notification, hearings, and other due process rights (Baker, K. K., 2015, 2017; Cantalupo, 2012; Lave, 2017). Yet, legal and social science scholars have argued that the criminal proceedings, which align with the compliance approach, present greater injustices than intended. In their assessment of the legal administration of sexual misconduct, these proceedings illustrate the mistreatment of the victim and the imbalance of procedural protections and unequal rights. Presenting the imbalance, Baker, K. K. (2017) argues that colleges place so much effort on creating fairness to protect the alleged perpetrator, which has a real harm to the alleged victim. Baker presents the irony of how instances of campus racial discrimination, academic cheating, or drunk driving leading to harm are cases with obvious injuries, including quite severe physical injury; however, legal administration on college campuses do not place the same level of concern and protections for violators as colleges have in sexual misconduct cases, which also present allegations of severe physical harm. Baker, K. K. (2017) also warns that "[e]ffective adversarial hearings are designed to make witnesses uncomfortable, uncertain, and, often ashamed. Shouldering that discomfort is one thing when the subject matter is a contract or a car crash; it is altogether different, and inevitably worse, when the subject is one's own sexual behavior." Accordingly, social researchers, legal scholars, counselors, and psychologists have questioned higher education practices that create a criminal-like process to addressing violations of campus policies, which are not criminal proceedings (Baker, K. K., 2015, 2017; Brodsky, 2017; Cantalupo, 2009, 2012; Curtis, 2017).

SOCIAL JUSTICE AND EQUITY-MINDED LEGAL ADMINISTRATION

Although the literature reports the compliance approach as the dominant focus for campus legal administration, not all empirical and legal policy analyses observed compliance-dominated behaviors or advocated for compliance-responsive approaches (Banyard, Plante, & Moynihan, 2004; Fortney, 2015; Jessup-Anger & Edwards, 2018). For instance, Fortney (2015) argues for a different approach to move away from the compliance mindset to an ethical infrastructure drawing on partners such as legal scholars and practitioners to evaluate and improve formal and informal policies and procedures pertaining to sexual harassment on campus. Fortney acknowledges the prevailing actions of campus leaders have directed attention to the organizational interests rather than facilitating a balanced examination of the rights and responsibilities of students and the college. Yet, the literature also suggests successful practices. This section presents four action items in order to establish a legal-administrative consciousness that challenges campus leaders to overcome or minimize the imbalance of power emergent from regulatory and campus policies; the advantage of social privilege in terms of scope of protections and understandings of due process; and the misguided effects of administrators' assumptions in omitting considerations of victimization and trauma. In doing so, this section challenges campus leaders to renegotiate the power and privilege through new policies and practices; establish new values that bring back the focus on the victim; and restore leadership priorities through an ethical infrastructure that draws on partners to collectively reconsider policies, procedures, and practices with goals of advancing a more social justice and equity-minded approach to legal administration on college campuses.

Restore Values and Demonstrate Consistency Through Policies and Procedures

In cases of sexual misconduct on college campuses, a socially just and equity-minded legal administration restores values and demonstrates consistency through policies and procedures. Campus leaders may adopt this action by articulating more fully the values of the campus and the definitions and expectations of student behavior through its policies and procedures (Koss, Wilgus, & Williamsen, 2014; Landreman & Williamsen, 2018). For instance, at the University of Illinois the campus policies and procedures assert value statements about the University's commitment to create "a safe and welcoming campus environment free from discrimination based on sex, which includes sexual assault, sexual exploitation, stalking, sexual harassment, dating violence, and domestic violence..." (University of Illinois, 2019). It adds that "[t]he University prohibits and will not tolerate sexual misconduct because such behavior violates the University's institutional values, adversely impacts the University's community interest, and interferes with the University's mission" (University of Illinois, 2019). Affirming its values, it labels the page "At Illinois... WE CARE..." (University of Illinois, 2019). Consistent with those values, the resource page presents the code of conduct, and it outlines the rights of students who have experienced sexual misconduct. Within the references of its policies, it further reinforces the value of caring and supporting students with a medical amnesty and good samaritan policy, which places safety over fear of legal or disciplinary proceedings. Typically, these policies place medical attention, often for alcohol and drug violations arising to emergencies, without leading to a disciplinary proceeding. Through this approach, "the major benefit [for survivors] may be increased opportunity to receive the medical and psychological first aid to assist in recovering from an event with significant psychological and physical trauma" (Sable et al., 2006, p. 160).

Reconsider Paradigmatic Lens

A socially just and equity-minded legal administration reconsiders models and approaches that include more than the paradigmatic lens—such as a white, heterosexual, and female victim (Coker, 2016) or the heuristic that perpetrators are often unknown to the victims and are not the first or second year students in college. A power-conscious perspective overcomes inadequacies generated from biased mindsets, uninformed policies, and misaligned practices. Instead, the dialogue among college leaders and other community members should consider data, the campus student population, and the various sub-populations to advance socially just and equity-minded legal administration when addressing campus sexual misconduct. To that end, socially just and equity-minded legal administration of campus sexual misconduct often presents three central questions: (1) Who has been harmed? (2) What are their needs? and (3) Whose obligation is it to meet those needs? (Coker, 2016). These questions interrogate how campus leaders act in the best interest of persons, develop an assessment of the intersection between the situation and persons, and create an accountability loop to ensure proper services and actions are taken (Coker, 2016; Lawton, 1999; MacKinnon, 2016).

Adopt a Trauma-Informed Care Approach with a Survivor Goal

The advocacy and practices have led to fears about due process violations to the detriment of the others who are involved in the situation. Accordingly, legal administration in higher education should construct processes in which "*student victims are just as important as the student who allegedly misbehaved*" (Stoner, 2000, p. 7). A socially just and equity-minded legal administration of campus sexual misconduct moves beyond the law and focuses on the persons by removing an overly criminalized approach with dispassionate responses. While the legal standard for a student to prevail for monetary damages in a Title IX case inquires as to whether the campus leaders demonstrated "deliberate indifference" (see, e.g., *Ross v. University of Tulsa*, 2017; *Simpson v. University of Colorado Boulder*, 2007). In other words, the law serves as the minimum support for the parties.

Traumatic experiences from sexual assault present different expressions and behaviors than what campus leaders might anticipate. Research and case law suggest that campus leaders, who have adopted effective trauma-informed care, demonstrate greater understanding of behaviors, adopt communication techniques that demonstrate care, and tend to take other steps that minimize retraumatization and revictimization of the victim (Shalka, 2015; Webb & Wyandt-Hiebert, 2018). Further, victims tend to demonstrate greater likelihood of survivor growth, disclosure, and mental health treatment when presented with trauma-informed practices (Hassijaa & Turchik, 2016). Similarly, anonymous or non-compelled, but trauma-informed practices, often encourage participation in referral services. Equally important, research suggests the value of characteristics of personnel who support victims through trauma-informed practices. For instance, the availability of sexual assault nurse examiners (Carney, 2018) and female law enforcement officers (Oehmea, Stern, & Mennicke, 2015) offer higher likelihood of effective support and proper protocols with a trauma-informed care approach. Put simply, this approach along with proper personnel impacts "how trauma influences a person's response to an incident and shapes their negotiation of its aftermath."

Although the focus in this chapter and other research has been on the victim, a socially just and equity-minded legal administration should also consider the effects of the investigations and proceedings on investigators, hearing boards, and others involved in the process. While training is already a significant component to serving in these capacities, individuals who participate in these processes are not required and often do not have services to seek treatment such as counseling or cognitive behavioral supports as counselors and social workers have available, yet treatment offers significant support in terms of processing the experiences of the student trauma.

Establish Community Intervention Program Strategies

Socially just and equity-minded legal administration of campus sexual misconduct involves a partnership with other units to present meaningful strategies that address sexual misconduct on college campuses. Programmed activities represent an effective intervention to change behavior (Banyard et al., 2004; Jessup-Anger & Edwards, 2018). These programmed activities are geared at bringing awareness of problems and agency that individuals have authority and capacity to influence or enact change. While multiple effective strategies of socially just and equity-minded legal administration are available, the most significant, tested technique is bystander intervention.

While the compliance approach for universities presents a viable approach to addressing sexual misconduct, many campuses have appreciated the effects of community participation for the care of others (Banyard et al., 2004; Coker et al., 2011). Bystander intervention illustrates such an approach by drawing on social and community influences to resolving a situation in which a potentially vulnerable student is not in a position to fully process all the conditions others have observed or make an independent decision. Accordingly, bystander intervention training—which may take place through presentations, theatrical demonstrations, role-playing, or guided learning sessions—educates peers to assess a potentially harmful event or interaction, take responsibility, and respond by intervening in the situation.

Bystander intervention contributes to the campus community in multiple ways. It changes social expectations by renorming behaviors of peers as instrumental to one's safety and well-being (Banyard et al., 2004; Witte, Casper, Hackman, & Mulla, 2017). It trains observers on techniques in order to avoid serious harm (Banyard et al., 2004; Witte et al., 2017). It also generates positive feelings, and in some cases, empowers the bystander to take action (Witte et al., 2017).

Evidence from numerous studies demonstrate the efficacy of this intervention (Banyard, 2014). A line of research concludes that bystander intervention training led to respondents or individuals whom respondents observed to take action at a significantly higher rate than students who had not participated in bystander intervention training (Banyard et al., 2004; Coker et al., 2011; Witte et al., 2017). Studies also find that the students who participated in training experiences were more likely to dispel the rape myth and identify more trauma-informed care practices (Coker et al., 2011; Witte et al., 2017). Further, bystander intervention behaviors present an effective modeling effect by inspiring others to take action in appropriate situations (Banyard, 2014). In short, intervention strategies such as bystander intervention often address social biases and engage the greater community with shared responsibility for the safety and well-being of others as well as meet the compliance requirements of the law.

CONCLUSION

Sexual misconduct represents a violation of personhood, yet campus policies and practices, as challenged by court cases and media criticism, suggest that the legal administration of sexual misconduct cases have been inequitably applied or present confusion about the degree to which campus leaders have discretionary authority to execute policies that are socially just, equitable, and compliant. This chapter hopefully dispels those myths and redirects attention to the role of campus leaders. Thus, while the legal administration of Title IX and related legal policies has, in some cases, exacerbated the imbalance of power and privilege exercised by campus leaders and over victims of sexual misconduct and alleged perpetrators, for the most part the laws and policies governing sexual misconduct in education leave the responsibility to the colleges, as policy implementers, over the decision making of aligning organizational mission and values (e.g. social justice and equity-mind practices). In light of this campus leader agency, the changes in Title IX regulation, while presenting an overly criminal-like proceeding and affording much more intrusive practices that may present challenges for victimization and trauma effects, may be adopted into college policy, procedures, and practice in a manner that counter-balances these effects with a social justice and equity-minded approach.

QUESTIONS FOR REFLECTION AND DISCUSSION

1. What are the main drawbacks of a compliance approach that impact goals of equity and social justice?
2. How might I or my team implement a trauma-informed care approach to legal decisions or procedural issues?
3. Do we engage any community intervention strategies and how might we build on these programs in order to better support our efforts at greater justice for campus stakeholders?

NOTES

1 Sexual violence is a severe form of sexual harassment, which includes rape, sexual assault, sexual battery, and sexual coercion.
2 For instance, penalties associated with a series of federal statutes and regulations—such as the Drug-Free Schools and Communities Act Amendments of 1989, 20 U.S.C. § 1011i (2019), Jeanne Clery Disclosure of Campus Security Policy and Campus Crime Statistics Act, 20 U.S.C. § 1092(f), et seq. (2019), Family Educational Rights and Privacy Act of 1974, 20 U.S.C. § 1232g (2019), Title IV of the Higher Education Act of 1965, and its amendments, 20 U.S.C. § 1001, et seq. (2019), Title IX of the Education Amendments of 1972, 20 U.S.C. §1681 et seq. (2019), and Title VII of the Civil Rights Act of 1964, 42 U.S.C. § 2000d et seq. (2019)—had the effect of placing fear in campus administrators of personal liability, employment termination, and public ridicule.

REFERENCES

Literature

Adams, N. A. (2015) Academic compliance programs: A federal model with separation of powers. *Journal of College and University Law, 41*(1), 1–24.

Ali, R. (2011). *Dear Colleague Letter: Sexual Violence (Apr. 4, 2011)*. Washington, DC: US Department of Education, Office for Civil Rights.

Ali, R. (2014). *Questions and Answers on Title IX and Sexual Violence (Apr. 29, 2014)*. Washington, DC: US Department of Education, Office for Civil Rights.

Aronowitz, T., Lambert, C. A., & Davidoff, S. (2012). The role of rape myth acceptance in the social norms regarding sexual behavior among college students. *Journal of Community Health Nursing, 29*(3), 173–182. doi:10.1080/07370016.2012.697852

Baker, B. A. (2017). When campus sexual misconduct policies violate due process rights. *Cornell Journal of Law and Public Policy, 26*(3), 533–563.

Baker, K. K. (2015). Why rape should not (always) be a crime. *Minnesota Law Review, 100*(1), 221–280.

Baker, K. K. (2016). Campus sexual misconduct as sexual harassment: A defense of the DOE. *University of Kansas Law Review, 64*(4), 777–803.

Baker, K. K. (2017). Campus misconduct, sexual harm and appropriate process: The essential sexuality of it all. *Journal of Legal Education, 66*(4), 777–803.

Banyard, V. L. (2014). Improving college campus-based prevention of violence against women: A strategic plan for research built on multipronged practices and policies. *Trauma, Violence, and Abuse, 15*(4), 339–351. doi:10.1177/1524838014521027

Banyard, V. L., Plante, E. G., & Moynihan, M. M. (2004). Bystander education: Bringing a broader community perspective to sexual violence prevention. *Journal of Community Psychology, 32*(1), 61–79. doi:10.1002/jcop.10078

Bickel, R. D., & Lake, P. F. (1999). *The Rights and Responsibilities of the Modern University: Who Assumes the Risks of College Life?* Durham, NC: Carolina Academic Press.

Brenner, H., & Darcy, K. (2017). Toward a civilized system of justice: Re-conceptualizing the response to sexual violence in higher education. *Cornell Law Review, 102*(2), 127–159.

Brodsky, A. (2017). A rising tide: Learning about fair disciplinary process from Title IX. *Journal of Legal Education, 66*(4), 822–849.

Brodsky, A. (2018). Against taking rape seriously: The case against mandatory referral laws for campus gender violence. *Harvard Civil Rights and Civil Liberties Law Review, 53*(1), 131–166.

Bunkley, N. (2007, Jul. 17). University fires officials for concealing killing. *New York Times*, p. A17.

Cantalupo, N. C. (2009). Campus violence: Understanding the extraordinary through the ordinary. *Journal of College and University Law, 35*(3), 613–690.

Cantalupo, N. C. (2011). Burying our heads in the sand: Lack of knowledge, knowledge avoidance, and the persistent problem of campus peer sexual violence. *Loyola University Chicago Law Journal, 43*(1), 205–266.

Cantalupo, N. C. (2012). Decriminalizing campus institutional responses to peer sexual violence. *Journal of College and University Law, 38*(3), 481–524.

Cantalupo, N. C. (2014). Institution-specific victimization surveys: Addressing legal and practical disincentives to gender-based violence reporting on college campuses. *Trauma, Violence, and Abuse, 15*(3), 242–257. doi: 0.1177/1524838014521500

Carney, A. Y. (2018). Public health nursing and the issue of trust in campus sexual assault. *Public Health Nursing, 35*(4), 327–336. doi:10.1111/phn.12400

Coker, A. L., Cook-Craig, P. G., Williams, C. M., Fisher, B. S., Clear, E. R., Garcia, L. S., & Hegge, L. M. (2011). Evaluation of Green Dot: An active bystander intervention to reduce sexual violence on college campuses. *Violence Against Women, 17*(6), 777–796. doi:10.1177/1077801211410264

Coker, D. (2016). Crime logic, campus sexual assault, and restorative justice. *Texas Tech Law Review, 49*(1), 147–210.

Curtis, A. E. (2017). Due process demands as propaganda: The rhetoric of Title IX opposition. *Yale Journal of Law and the Humanities, 29*(2), 273.

Daniel, P. T. K., Gee, E. G., Sun, J. C., & Pauken, P. D. (2012). *Law, Policy, and Higher Education: Cases and Materials*. New Providence, NJ: LexisNexis.

Dejean, J. S. (2015). Synching the law to resolve the disconnection between awareness and action in legally mandated diversity hiring practices in higher education institutions. *Journal of Research Administration, 46*(2), 34–54.

Dunham, S. S. (2010). Government regulation of higher education: The elephant in the middle of the room. *Journal of College and University Law, 36*(2), 749–790.

Edelman, L. B., & Suchman M. C. (1997). The legal environments of organizations. *Annual Review of Sociology, 23*(1), 479–515. doi: 10.1146/annurev.soc.23.1.479

Ellman-Golan, E. (2017). Saving Title IX: Designing more equitable and efficient investigation procedures. *Michigan Law Review, 116*(1), 155–186.

Fortney, S. S. (2015). Preventing sexual harassment and misconduct in higher education: How lawyers should assist universities in fortifying ethical infrastructure. *Minnesota Law Review Headnotes, 103*, 101–113.

Grubb, A., & Turner, E. (2012). Attribution of blame in rape cases: A review of the impact of rape myth acceptance, gender role conformity and substance use on victim blaming. *Aggression and Violent Behavior, 17*(5), 443–452. doi:10.1016/j.avb.2012.06.002

Hassijaa, C. M., & Turchik, J. A. (2016). An examination of disclosure, mental health treatment use, and posttraumatic growth among college women who experienced sexual victimization. *Journal of Loss and Trauma, 21*(2), 124–136. doi:10.1080/15325024.2015.1011976

Heckman, D. (2018). The role of the Clery Act and the campus security against violence act in combatting sexual violence on college campuses. *West Education Law Reporter, 349,* 331–366.

Henrick, S. (2013). A hostile environment for student defendants: Title IX and sexual assault on college campuses. *Northern Kentucky Law Review, 40,* 49–92

Jackson, C. (2017). *Dear colleague letter: Withdrawing the statements of policy and guidance (Sept. 22, 2017).* Washington, DC: U.S. Department of Education, Office for Civil Rights.

James, E. H., & Wooten, L. P. (2006). Diversity crises: How firms manage discrimination lawsuits. *Academy of Management Journal, 49*(6), 1103–1118. doi: 10.2307/20159822

Jessup-Anger, J., & Edwards, K. E. (Eds.) (2018). *Addressing Sexual Violence in Higher Education. New Directions for Student Services, 2018* (pp. 1–105). San Francisco, CA: Jossey-Bass.

Johnson, K. C., & Taylor, Jr., S. (2017). *The Campus Rape Frenzy: The Attack on Due Process at America's Universities.* New York: Encounter Books.

Karjane, H. M., Fisher, B. S., & Cullen, F. T. (2002). *Campus Sexual Assault: How America's Institutions of Higher Education Respond* (NCJRS Doc #196676). Washington, DC: National Criminal Justice Reference Service, U.S. Department of Justice. Retrieved from www.ncjrs.gov/pdffiles1/nij/grants/196676.pdf

Kirkpatrick, C., & Kanin, E. (1957). Male sex aggression on a university campus. *American Sociological Review, 22*(1), 52. doi:10.2307/2088765

Koss, M. P., Wilgus, J. K., & Williamsen, K. M. (2014). Campus sexual misconduct: Restorative justice approaches to enhance compliance with Title IX guidance. *Trauma, Violence, and Abuse, 15*(3), 242–257. doi: 0.1177/1524838014521500

Lake, P. F. (2013). *The Rights and Responsibilities of the Modern University: The Rise of the Facilitator University.* Durham, NC: Carolina Academic Press.

Landreman, L. M., & Williamsen, K. N. (2018). Addressing sexual violence as student affairs work. *New Directions for Student Services, 2018*(161), 35–45. doi: 10.1002/ss.20251

Lave, T. R. (2016). Ready, fire, aim: How universities are failing the constitution in sexual assault cases. *Arizona State Law Journal, 48*(3), 637–702.

Lave, T. R. (2017). A critical look at how top colleges and universities are adjudicating sexual assault. *University of Miami Law Review, 71*(2), 377–427.

Lawton, J. H. (1999). Are there general laws in ecology? *Oikos, 84*(2), 177–192.

Lipka, S. (2007). Eastern Michigan U. official says he is a scapegoat in murder inquiry. *The Chronicle of Higher Education, 53*(42), 35.

MacKinnon, C. A. (2016). Rape redefined. *Harvard Law & Policy Review, 10,* 431.

Oehmea, K., Stern, N., & Mennicke, A. (2015). A deficiency in addressing campus sexual assault: The lack of women law enforcement officers. *Harvard Journal of Law and Gender, 38*(2), 337–372.

Peebles, J., & Lombardi, K. (2010). Undetected rapists on campus: A troubling plague of repeat offenders. *iWatch News.* Retrieved from www.publicintegrity.org/investigations/campus_assault/articles/entry/1948

Rege, R. (2006). Universities should implement internal control programs to monitor compliance with export control laws. *Journal of Law and Education, 35*(2), 199–223.

Sable, M. R., Danis, F., Mauzy, D. L., & Gallagher, S. K. (2006). Barriers to reporting sexual assault for women and men: perspectives of college students. *Journal of American College Health, 55*(3), 157–162.

Shalka, T. R. (2015). Toward a trauma-informed practice: What educators need to know. *About Campus, 20*(5), 21–27. https://doi.org/10.1002/abc.21217

Smith, S. G., Zhang, X., Basile, K. C., Merrick, M. T., Wang, J., Kresnow, M. J., & Chen, J. (2018). *National Intimate Partner and Sexual Violence Survey: 2015 Data Brief.* Atlanta, GA: National Center for Injury Prevention Control, Centers for Disease Control and Prevention.

St. Clair, S., & Lighty, T. (2011, Feb. 27). Family criticizes Notre Dame in 2nd sex attack case. *Chicago Tribune,* p. 1.

Stoner II, E. N. (2000). *Reviewing Your Student Discipline Policy: A Project Worth the Investment.* Chevy Chase, MD: United Educators Insurance Risk Retention Group, Inc.

Sun, J. C. (2014). Student-to-student sexual harassment update. *NASPA Leadership Exchange, 2014* (Winter), 26–27.

Sun, J. C., Scott, L. R., Sponsler, B., & Hutchens, N. H. (2014a). *Understanding campus obligations for student-to-student sexual harassment: Guidance for student affairs professionals.* Washington, DC: NASPA-Student Affairs Administrators in Higher Education.

Sun, J. C., Scott, L. R., Sponsler, B., & Hutchens, N. H. (2014b). *Understanding campus obligations for student-to-student sexual harassment: Guidance for student affairs professionals – Addendum.* Washington, DC: NASPA-Student Affairs Administrators in Higher Education.

University of Illinois (2019). *Sexual misconduct support, response, and prevention: Campus policies and procedures.* Urbana-Champaign, IL: Author. Retrieved from https://wecare.illinois.edu/policies/campus/

van der Bruggen, M., & Grubb, A. (2014). A review of the literature relating to rape victim blaming: An analysis of the impact of observer and victim characteristics on attribution of blame in rape cases. *Aggression and Violent Behavior, 19*(5), 523–531. doi:10.1016/j.avb.2014.07.008

Walters, M.L., Chen J., & Breiding, M.J. (2013). *The National Intimate Partner and Sexual Violence Survey (NISVS): 2010 findings on victimization by sexual orientation.* Atlanta, GA: National Center for Injury Prevention and Control, Centers for Disease Control and Prevention.

Webb, K., & Wyandt-Hiebert, M. A. (2018). *Addressing sexual and relationship violence: A trauma-informed approach.* Silver Springs, MD: American College Health Association.

Weiss, K. G. (2011). Neutralizing sexual victimization: A typology of victims' non-reporting accounts. *Theoretical Criminology, 15*(4), 445–467. doi:10.1177/1362480610391527

Weiss, K. G., & Lasky, N. V. (2017). Mandatory reporting of sexual misconduct at college: A critical perspective. *Journal of School Violence, 16*(3), 259–270. doi: 10.1080/15388220.2017.1318575

Wilgus, J. K., & Lowery, J. W. (2018). Adjudicating student sexual misconduct: Parameters, pitfalls, and promising practices. *New Directions for Student Services, 2018*(161), 83–94. doi: 10.1002/ss.20255

Witte, T. H., Casper, D. M., Hackman, C. L., & Mulla, M. M. (2017). Bystander interventions for sexual assault and dating violence on college campuses: Are we putting bystanders in harm's way? *Journal of American College Health, 65*(3), 149–157. doi:10.1080/07448481.2016.1264407

Cases and Other Legal Documents

Bradshaw v. Rawlings, 612 F.2d 135 (3d Cir. 1979).

Brown v. Board of Education, 347 U.S. 483 (1954).

Feminist Majority Found. v. Hurley, 911 F.3d 674 (4th Cir. 2018)

Ross v. University of Tulsa, 859 F.3d 1280 (10th Cir. 2017).

Sacchetti v. Gallaudet Univ., 344 F. Supp.3d 233 (D.D.C., 2018).

Simpson v. University of Colorado Boulder, 500 F.3d 1170 (10th Cir. 2007).

U.S. v. Fordice, 505 U.S. 717 (1992).

Other Legal Documents

Nondiscrimination on the Basis of Sex in Education Programs or Activities Receiving Federal Financial Assistance, 83 Fed. Reg. 61462 (2018).

12

PRACTITIONER REFLECTION: FEEDING THE DATA HUNGRY

The Role of the IR Professional in Ensuring Social Justice and Equity in Higher Education

JENNIFER L. IVIE

We live in a data-hungry era. With the push for accountability to taxpayers, more and more people want to see data that confirms the efficacy of a particular good or service. With the increased expectation for data-informed decision making, it is essential for administrators to have access to the data that is needed to make those decisions. This data hunger is felt especially strongly in higher education. With the ever-present public opinion that a college degree is a waste of time and money (e.g. Newton, 2018), we in higher education feel more pressure to provide evidence to the contrary. Enter the role of the institutional research (IR) professional.

Like many IR professionals, I came to this work through experience and interest, rather than graduate training and preparation. I never aspired to working in IR. I worked as an instructor and researcher while a graduate student at a large research university. I began my professional career as a tenure-track faculty member in the department of psychology at a large, Hispanic-serving institution. I transitioned into leading faculty development at a small, regional university with a large indigenous population. Now, I serve as the director of IR and assessment at a large, urban community college—one that awards more associates degrees to indigenous students than other institutions in the nation and whose student body is more diverse than the population of the surrounding community. As a person with indigenous heritage, serving this population is very important to me. Moreover, the job aligns perfectly with my experience and affords me the opportunity to do applied work related to my doctoral degree.

I began my postsecondary studies in math education. All my life I had wanted to teach, particularly in a subject in which most people struggled. As a female who always enjoyed and succeeded in mathematics, I stood out. Girls were not supposed to be good at math. At least that is what the boys always told me. But, I was lucky. My parents never doubted my abilities, and neither did my teachers. They pushed me. They challenged me. I participated in extra programs in math, as often the only girl in the room. Unlike the many girls throughout history who have been deterred from the subject, I stuck with it. Until my junior year of college, when I found that my interest in the topic was limited to the practical and applied math. I was never able to embrace theoretical math, so I had to change majors. Like many, when I discovered what I did not want to do, I had no idea what I did want to do. Therefore, like many college students, I defaulted to psychology. I enjoyed learning about learning. I enjoyed understanding why some people were good at things when others were not. And, I found that I could apply my love of math to a field of study in which I was interested.

I earned my graduate degrees in quantitative psychology with an emphasis in educational measurement and psychometrics. A fancy way of saying I can analyze data related to people—what they know, how they think, how they feel—and I can create and evaluate surveys, tests, and other measures of what people know, think, feel, etc. I had an amazing female graduate advisor, and supportive female senior graduate students, who all served as mentors to me in a field primarily dominated by white men—the development and study of cognitive ability and other standardized tests.

As a nation, we have adopted the idea that standardized test scores will give us most of the information we need. Whether the score is being used for admissions, placement, graduation, licensure, or some other reason, we place too much faith in these tests' ability to narrow a student's chance of success down to a single number. One of the reasons I chose a field focused on educational measurement was because of the reliance we place on these measurement tools. My little sister and I grew up in the same household. We both went to the same large, urban, public high school. We had many of the same teachers. Yet, I excelled at taking tests, and she did not. I never understood how our scores could be so disparate given our similar abilities, knowledge base, and upbringing. She excelled in the languages and humanities, while I excelled in the STEM fields. However, I still outscored her on standardized tests in English. This never seemed right, or fair. If I could see these incongruities in my own home, how could these tests truly be the right way to identify if a student should be admitted to this or that university, or if he should have to take a developmental course, or if she should receive this scholarship over someone else?

The biases inherent in standardized test results are not unrecognized by the general public, let alone the field of psychometricians who work to improve these tests. Yet, institutions of higher education use them to make high-stakes decisions about students' futures, and state and federal entities use them to make funding and other high-stakes decisions about educational institutions. It is easy to defend a decision made based on a standard number by which everyone is being measured. That seems fair, right? If everyone is measured the same way, how can it be unfair? The problem is these tests do not take into account other factors outside of the moment the student took the test. They do not distinguish a low score based on lack of knowledge from a low score due to a bad day, high test anxiety, test biases, or some other external factor. Standardized tests do not allow students to truly demonstrate what they have learned through a method aligned with how they learned the material or how they will apply the material in an authentic setting. And, yet, as a data-hungry society, we cling to these scores as the end-all-be-all metrics from which we make many high-stakes decisions.

Despite decades of research that demonstrates discrimination experienced by certain racial and ethnic groups, primarily African Americans, Latinx, and Indigenous students, we continue to rely on measures such as the SAT, ACT, ACCUPLACER, and more, in higher education to make decisions that affect where the student will attend college, which courses the student will be able to take, and for which funding sources the student might be eligible (Rosales, 2018). However, the use of standardized testing has been defended in political arenas as a means by which to achieve racial equality in our educational institutions (Au, 2016). Fortunately, in the work we do as IR professionals, we are not limited to test scores to measure the effectiveness of the educational opportunities our institutions are providing for our students. We examine other outcomes measures of how well our students are learning and reaching their goals at our institution. We regularly examine equity gaps in course success, graduation, transfer, and retention rates. We collect data on student satisfaction and engagement. We examine variables such as race and ethnicity, gender, age, high school GPA, developmental placement, and credit hours attempted and earned. The data we have available to analyze is limited only by the information we enter into our student information system.

As a researcher, I focus my talents on examining factors affecting test scores and factors affected by test scores. As an educator, I focus my talents on helping students achieve learning and success in courses they dread—developmental math and statistics in psychology. As an IR professional, I focus my talents on helping constituents identify the data they need to answer the question they have and to understand the results that come from that data. As an IR professional it is important that I am able to assist developmental education faculty at my institution in making decisions about how useful placement tests are in predicting student success in courses, or help administrators recognize when there are equity gaps in performance and success of our students. And, until I served in this role, I was not fully aware of the benefit of having a strong institutional research department to help find those answers.

INSTITUTIONAL RESEARCH DEFINED

Most people stare blankly or look confused when I tell them my job title. I often try to simplify it by reducing it to: I run the office that provides data to the state and federal governments about my institution. However, in 2017, the Association for Institutional Research (AIR) published a list of functions for institutional research offices that goes well beyond this simplified definition. These functions are: identifying information needs; collecting, analyzing, interpreting, and reporting data and information; collaborating in strategic planning and evaluation; serving as stewards of data and information; and educating information producers, users, and consumers. More succinctly, Swing and Ross (2016) described the aspiration of IR "as decision support that focuses on student success" (p. 3). While much of what we have always done in IR fulfills compliance reporting needs, more and more of what we now do is evaluating which student success initiatives are improving the student experience, discovering which student or institutional characteristics are contributing to or hindering success, and exploring where and why there are discrepancies between different groups of students in their experience and levels of success.

THE FUNCTIONS OF IR FROM AN EQUITY PERSPECTIVE: IDENTIFYING INFORMATION NEEDS

If we revisit the functions of IR according to AIR, we can begin to see the role we play in ensuring a focus not only on student success overall, but student success *for all*. When helping data users and consumers identify the information they need, we must help them develop and refine their questions. Through this process, we can show the importance of disaggregating the data by different student groups (e.g. race/ethnicity, gender, SES) to identify possible representation and performance gaps. And, we can shape the question such that it is asked through an equity mindset, rather than a deficit mindset.

On any given day, our IR office receives multiple requests for analyses to answer questions like: "Is this service working?" "Is this new policy resulting in better outcomes for our students?" "Why are students not returning?" "Are students performing better in online versus face-to-face courses?" It is our duty in IR to help reframe those questions to go beyond the service, and ask questions like "For whom is this service working? And, for whom is it not?" "Is this new policy resulting in better outcomes for all students, or only for certain groups?" To revisit the example above, "if we continue to use standardized placement tests, what groups of students are being placed disproportionately more into developmental education courses? What other measures would provide more equitable results?"

Oftentimes the question or purpose of the request is lost in translation between the committee meeting where the original question was posed and the time the request is submitted to IR. In my role as the director, I serve on many committees and task forces that make recommendations to senior administrators based on data. I find this involvement helps me better understand the context from which stakeholders are asking for data and information. It allows me to ensure that consumers are asking the right questions and that we are providing the right data and information to answer those questions. It also allows me to dive deeper into the questions to examine the data from an equity perspective. You can disaggregate almost any data by categories of student demographics, thus providing a much broader perspective on the initial question.

THE FUNCTIONS OF IR FROM AN EQUITY PERSPECTIVE: WORKING WITH DATA

The next function of IR is collecting, analyzing, interpreting, and reporting data and information. This four-step process can take on many forms depending on the nature of the question asked, and the role of the person or entity requesting the information.

Data Collection and Reporting

Oftentimes official reporting is constrained by the expectations and definitions of the receiving entity. A primary function of most IR offices is to report institutional data to the Integrated Postsecondary Education Data System (IPEDS). We report data on enrollment, retention, success (graduation and/or transfer), demographics, cost to students, finances, personnel, and more. We report these data following standardized definitions of what can and cannot be included in the data. Moreover, often we are forced into categorizing data such that it does not truly represent our student demographics or our mission metrics for success.

For example, the Aspen Institute College Excellence Program uses IPEDS data to examine the impact institutions have on outcomes for "underrepresented minorities." However, this limits who is being measured to those students who classified themselves specifically as Hispanic, African American, or Native American. It does not include those students who identify as both African American and Native American. Such students are classified in IPEDS data as "two or more races." And, it does not include students who, like myself, would identify as both Native American and White. This standardization often limits our ability to make useful inferences. However, it gives us the ability to compare ourselves to peer or aspirational institutions on these limited metrics.

In addition to defining how we categorize our students and employees, compliance reporting narrowly defines metrics of success as well. As part of the Student-Right-to-Know Act, graduation rates are calculated as the total number of first-time, full-time, degree-seeking students who earned a credential within 150% of "normal time." Normal time is two years for an associate's degree. A full-time student is someone who attended full-time in her first fall semester. A first-time student is someone who has never attended college or university before except as a high school student. While IPEDS has expanded these metrics to include 200%, and now with the Outcome Measure report, six- and eight-year rates, the three-year rate is the standard stick by which we are measured in compliance reporting. However, the majority of community college students attend part-time and are referred to developmental coursework extending the time to graduation or transfer (Bailey, Jeong, & Cho, 2010). As such, the population of completers by which community colleges are measured can be quite small and not fully representative of how well we are serving our students.

As demonstrated above, compliance reporting can be quite constrained. Beyond possibly misrepresenting students demographically, the data reported for compliance purposes rarely focus on disaggregation to examine possible equity gaps. However, when we are conducting studies not for compliance, we are able to explore our data for insight into performance gaps and possible opportunities for initiatives and services that the institution could engage in to close those equity gaps. We can evaluate current programs, policies, and procedures for their effect on performance gaps in order to support decisions made about budgets, resource allocation, strategic planning, and more. The most important job we have in IR is helping end users of the data and information to ask the right questions and interpret the findings so the information is not misused or abused to fulfill a particular agenda or confirm a particular bias.

Data Analysis and Interpretation

As it states in the IR Code of Ethics and Professional Practice (AIR, 2017), data and results should be approached with objectivity and unbiased attitudes, and free from conflicts of interest. For example, I clearly have a bias against standardized testing. While my bias is supported by research, I must remain objective when serving on our developmental education committee and examining what measures should be used to best place our students. If the data show that a standardized test score is the best predictor of student success in a particular course, it is my obligation to report those results as matter of fact without trying to explain away why those results were found.

It is recognized in the field of quantitative research methods that how data are analyzed and presented can influence how the results are interpreted. In 1954, Darrell Huff first published a book titled *How to Lie with Statistics* (Huff, 1954). This book became a standard textbook in introductory statistics courses and has sold more than one and a half million copies (Steele, 2005). The book demonstrates how easily one can manipulate the presentation of data and results to give the illusion that a difference exists when it does not or vice versa. Such manipulation can vary from changing the range on the y-axis in a graph so that it appears there is a large difference between men and women on a standardized test of math ability to taking a correlation between gender and math ability and declaring causality. Not only must we IR professionals remain unbiased in our design, analysis, and interpretation, we must help our data consumers recognize when their own biases may be coloring their interpretations or planned use of the results.

THE FUNCTIONS OF IR FROM AN EQUITY PERSPECTIVE: COLLABORATING IN STRATEGIC PLANNING AND EVALUATION

As mentioned above, the work we do in IR can greatly influence the work of strategic planning and evaluation for an individual service or class, a department or school, or the entire institution. At many institutions, the work of IR is housed in an office or area called Institutional Effectiveness. On their website, the Association for Higher Education Effectiveness (AHEE) defines institutional effectiveness as "integrated functions that support institutional performance, quality, and efficiency." The data and analyses we provide in IR should be ultimately used to help improve performance, quality, and efficiency. As such, IR professionals often play a large role in strategic planning and evaluation at their institution.

The power of data is that we can identify sub-groups of students or employees who are struggling, figure out why, and create initiatives and resources to intervene and increase their chances of success. But, we have to be willing to ask the right questions and accept responsibility for the answers. As IR professionals, we need to help our consumers and users of information understand that the data should be used to expose inequities in order to influence positive change within our institutions.

THE FUNCTIONS OF IR FROM AN EQUITY PERSPECTIVE: SERVING AS STEWARDS OF DATA

The Merriam-Webster dictionary defines stewardship as "the conducting, supervising, or managing of something, especially the careful and responsible management of something entrusted to one's care." Blair et al. (2015) define data stewards as "individuals who are responsible for promoting appropriate data use through planning, policy, and protocols at your institution… Data stewards are responsible for data quality and integrity" (p. 2).While this definition does not limit data stewardship to the institutional research office, it is apparent that we serve as data stewards for our institutions. From an equity perspective, this means we must ensure that the data we pull from our information systems and the information we provide to our consumers is accurate and up to date. We must provide definitions that help ensure data users are not misrepresenting information. For example, it is important, as outlined above, that data users understand that our percentage of Native American students as defined by IPEDS is not equal to our percentage of students with indigenous heritage. Thus, when examining equity gaps based on race/ethnicity, we must recognize the limitations of the data if we use one data source (IPEDS race/ethnicity classification) versus another (actual student identified racial/ethnic categories).

THE FUNCTIONS OF IR FROM AN EQUITY PERSPECTIVE: EDUCATING DATA PRODUCERS, USERS, AND CONSUMERS

One of the pitfalls of leading a very active IR office at an institution hungry for data to support decision making, is working with constituents who are not data literate. Often we must help a consumer change her question from "I want to show that" to "I want to know if." The former clearly demonstrates a bias toward a particular outcome. Also, as IR professionals we have to ensure that our consumers are prepared to receive the answer to their question. For example, if we want to work to improve course performance, we need to examine gaps in course performance by different student groups. If we find that one particular group is not performing well in a course, we must make sure that the recipients of that information are prepared to ask, "what could we be doing to marginalize this group of students? How could we better serve these students?", rather than respond with confirmation of deeply held prejudices or a loss of self-efficacy as an educator. To ensure that the data we have been entrusted with is being used appropriately, we must educate our consumers in this manner.

This education can come in the form of formal professional development opportunities or simple one-on-one conversations. These conversations might include defining the different data points to ensure we are providing the correct list of students or correct aggregated dataset. Or helping consumers understand why anecdotal evidence might not converge with large generalizable data findings. Or, even more importantly, how the results can be used to make decisions to decrease equity gaps and provide for a more socially just educational environment.

SOCIAL JUSTICE IN HIGHER EDUCATION

The term social justice has its origins in mid-nineteenth-century Catholicism, meaning the "uniform state distribution of society's advantages and disadvantages" (Novak, 2009, p. 1).Today, there are many definitions of the term. In their chapter in this book on organizational culture, Museus and LePeau define social justice in terms of resistance to systemic oppression so that "everyone has equal opportunity to thrive regardless of their backgrounds and situation." They acknowledge the role of higher education in this resistance. Kezar and Dizon's chapter on shared governance embraces Bell's definition of social justice, as "full and equitable participation of people from all social identity groups in a society that is mutually shaped to meet their needs... respectful of human diversity and group differences, and inclusive and affirming of human agency and capacity for working collaboratively with others to create change" (Bell, 2007, p. 1).

The focus of this book is on the roles of various educational administrators in the pursuit of social justice and equity in higher education, from the chief financial officer, to legal counsel, to human resources. Much of the work they must do to ensure socially just decision making and resource allocation relies on data provided by offices of institutional research or their equivalent. Because of this, it is essential that IR professionals are versed in the concepts and practices to ensure social justice and equity in higher education. In institutional research, if we are to help reduce effects of social injustice, we must do so with regular care given to examining data from an equity-minded orientation. We must regularly delve deeper into questions about performance and outcomes, satisfaction and engagement, to explore possible gaps between different student groups. We must be willing to ask hard questions and provide results that might not reflect well upon the institution or people within.

We often fail to realize the impact of the work we do in IR, because we do not directly work with students. However, the data collection and analysis that we perform impacts decisions made by senior administrators, policymakers, and funders, as well as by faculty and frontline staff that touch students' lives every single day. We must honor that role by ensuring involvement in the question design, integrity in our analyses, objectivity in our interpretations, and never-ending curiosity in our quest for answers.

QUESTIONS FOR REFLECTION AND DISCUSSION

1. Do campus stakeholders believe data speaks for itself? How might I (we) change that mindset? What is the problem of this belief (i.e. that data speaks for itself)?
2. Is our institutional research office at the table to inform key policies and decisions that shape equitable outcomes on campus? How might we map key areas to become more involved? How can we build effective partnerships and relationships to extend our ability to bring data to decision making?
3. As an administrator, how do I decide when to use data, what data I will use, and how it will be interpreted? And are these decisions informed with an equity lens?
4. What partners do I have that maintain an equity lens toward data and can help groups and units on campus in their work to use data?

REFERENCES

Association for Institutional Research (AIR) (2017). *Duties and functions of institutional research.* Retrieved October 12, 2018 from www.airweb.org/Duties-Functions-IR

Au, W. (2016). Meritocracy 2.0: High-stakes, standardized testing as a racial project of neoliberal multiculturalism. *Educational Policy, 30*(1), 39–62. SAGE Journals.

Bailey, T., Jeong, D. W., & Cho, S-W. (2010). Referral, enrollment, and completion in developmental education sequences in community colleges. *Economics of Education Review, 29*(2), 255–270.

Bell, L. A. (2007). Theoretical foundations for social justice in education. In M. Adams, L. A. Bell, & P. Griffin (Eds.), *Teaching for Diversity and Social Justice.* New York: Routledge.

Blair, D., Briner, K., Dani, V., Fary, M., Fishbain, J., Kelly,… Owen, K. (2015). Establishing data stewardship models. EDUCAUSE Center for Analysis and Research Working Group Paper collection.

Huff, D. (1954). *How to Lie with Statistics*. New York: W. W. Norton & Company.

Newton, D. (December, 2018). Please stop asking whether college is worth it. *Forbes*. Retrieved from www.forbes.com/sites/dereknewton/2018/12/16/please-stop-asking-whether-college-is-worth-it/#487e205d30d2

Novak, M. (December 29, 2009). Social justice: Not what you think it is. *Heritage Lectures* (delivered June 10, 2009). The Heritage Foundation.

Rosales, J. (Spring 2018). The racist beginnings of standardized testing: From grade school to college, students of color have suffered the effects of biased testing. *NEA Today Magazine*. National Education Association. Retrieved October 13, 2018 from www.nea.org/home/73288.htm.

Steele, J. M. (2005). Darrell Huff and fifty years of How to Lie with Statistics. *Statistical Science, 20*(3), 205–209.

Swing, R. L., & Ross, L. E. (2016). *Statement of aspirational practice for institutional research*. Association for Institutional Research: Tallahassee, Florida. Retrieved October 12, 2018 from www.airweb.org/aspirationalstatement.

PART IV

CULTURE AND STRUCTURE

13

NAVIGATING NEOLIBERAL ORGANIZATIONAL CULTURES

Implications for Higher Education Leaders Advancing Social Justice Agendas

SAMUEL D. MUSEUS AND LUCY A. LEPEAU

In the spring of 2017, the National Institute for Transformation and Equity organized a panel of national leaders in education to discuss how educators could advance social justice within the context of existing social and political turbulence that characterized the national climate. During this discussion, the facilitator posed the following question: Why do we avoid conversations about the need for some people to make sacrifices in order to advance equity? The panelists reacted with comments that we should not view equity as a zero-sum game, and they argued that sacrifices do not necessarily need to be made because equity is good for everyone. The facilitator agreed that people should not espouse the perspective that we are in a zero-sum game and the panel moved on to the next topic of discussion.

While it is true that equity should not be viewed as a zero-sum game and a more equitable world is a positive thing for all who exist within it, such arguments are rarely effective when engaging people who must give up the power and resources that they have gained through existing systems of oppression in order to make society more equitable. Most people often or always see such redistribution of resources as a sacrifice. Thus, the argument that equity is "good for all," has limited utility in a neoliberal world at best.

Equally important is the reality that our tendency to avoid conversations about sacrifice can perpetuate misperceptions that power can shift from those in positions of privilege to oppressed communities without the former relinquishing some control and resources that they have disproportionately accessed and now hold. In reality, such surrendering is necessary for a redistribution of resources to be feasible. As the editors of this volume suggest in the Introduction, to better understand these realities and have more fruitful conversations about advancing equity, those of us who advocate for social justice *must* consider how neoliberalism buttresses systemic oppression and our own psyche, as well as how these processes diminish the efficacy of social justice efforts. The current chapter aims to contribute to this more thorough engagement of neoliberalism in discussions about equity.

Given that social justice is sometimes interpreted and applied in varied ways, it is important to define it before moving forward. Throughout this chapter, we use the term *social justice* to refer to efforts to resist systemic forms of oppression and cultivate a more equitable world—one that centers democracy as a primary core value and in which everyone has equal opportunity to thrive regardless of their backgrounds and situations. In the last decade, college and university leaders[1] have increasingly found themselves at the center of heated debates about social justice. Some of these leaders developed their careers through advocating for justice, and many did not. Regardless of their backgrounds, these leaders are facing progressively turbulent times as they remain embedded in structures of systemic oppression and are confronting increased pressures to resist those systems from the diverse communities that they serve.

There is a long history of social movements challenging the role of institutions of higher education in reinforcing systemic oppression and demanding that these organizations adapt to better serve diverse communities and advance democratic ideals. In the 1960s and 1970s, for example, the Third World Liberation Front and other college student coalitions organized movements to advocate for college environments and curricula that did not simply reinforce the status quo but responded to the challenges face by oppressed communities (Gosse, 2005; Umemoto, 1989). The fact that those advocating for social justice today are voicing these same—or at least very similar—concerns highlights the durability of systemic oppression and how it shapes institutions of higher education. These realities also underscore the weight of the challenges faced by those advocating for social justice within the academy.

What is not the same as the 1960s and 1970s, however, is the political economy that provides the context for current student movements. Specifically, over the last 50 years, society's elite has effectively advanced a neoliberal agenda and system within which we are currently embedded (Giroux, 2007, 2008, 2011). While capitalism is an ideology that prioritizes free markets and consumer choice over state regulation, neoliberalism can be described as a paradigm that permeates every aspect of society at the expense of moral imperatives. Neoliberal ideologies shape political economies that permit few private interests to maximize control over power, resources, social life, and political processes through the exploitation of the vast majority of society (McChesney, 1998). In turn, the concentration of power among the elite allows them to further maximize their own economic profits and other resources. This vicious cycle of exploitation is at the core of the neoliberalism regime.

The limited understanding of the role of neoliberalism in shaping systemic oppression and constraining efforts to advance justice within higher education is significant for multiple reasons. First, neoliberalism is inextricably intertwined with and reinforces other forms of systemic oppression, such as white supremacy and heteropatriarchy (Goldberg, 2009; Inwood, 2015). Second, neoliberalism has permeated just about everything that happens on college campuses and heavily determines what is (il)legitimate knowledge and action within institutions of higher education, valorizing investment of energy and resources in efforts that reinforce this system and diminishing the desire to make investments in agendas of advanced social justice (Darder, 2005). Moreover, the neoliberal regime creates institutions that reward agendas and efforts that conform to core tenants of neoliberal logics, ensuring that even work that is designed to advance equity often simultaneously reinforces neoliberal rationalities, thereby reifying the very systems that they are designed to disrupt, deconstruct, and combat. The question then becomes, how do leaders advance social justice if they are embedded in a system that prioritizes, legitimizes, and sometimes only permits behaviors that reinforce neoliberal ideologies? Put another way, how do higher education leaders advocate for social justice in a time of growing corporatization and a declining value of education for democracy?

In this chapter, we seek to stimulate discussion aimed at answering the aforementioned question. In the next section, we briefly discuss the historical origins and core tenants of neoliberalism. Then, we provide an overview of some key ways in which neoliberalism has shaped the culture of institutions of higher education and the cultural barriers that leaders must face as they advocate for social justice. Finally, we provide some recommendations for leaders who view social justice as a top priority.

THE ORIGINS AND CORE TENETS OF NEOLIBERALISM

The historical emergence of neoliberalism highlights the ways in which it is inextricably bound with other systems of oppression (Goldberg, 2015; Inwood, 2015). As discussed in the introduction of this volume, the neoliberal regime arose as a consequence of economic crises and social movements calling for justice in the 1960s and 1970s. Keynesian economic theory, which promotes embedding government and corporate activities in social and political networks to limit economic exploitation of working classes, dominated the mid-twentieth century. In the 1970s, however, Keynesian policies were increasingly perceived to be failing. In addition, the civil rights movements were challenging white supremacy and heteropatriarchy. The economic crisis provided an opportunity for the conservative machine to promote alternative strategies that emphasized the deregulation of markets and mass privatization, which gained increased public support in the 1980s during the era of Reaganomics and provided the foundation for the emergence of neoliberal values and policies. These efforts silenced liberal calls to hold both public and private institutions responsible for contributing to the strengthening of democracy and displacing them with expanding free-market mentalities and consumerism discourses (Giroux, 2007). In this way, at its roots, neoliberal ideology was a response to, and suppression of, the increased democratization happening during the civil rights movement.

Neoliberalism has been described as sophisticated, evolving, and adapting to various contexts, but there are some key elements of the neoliberal apparatus (Adsit, Doe, Allison, Maggio, & Maisto, 2015; Burford, 2017; Darder, 2005; Darder, 2005; Davies, 2005; Giroux, 2008, 2011; McChesney, 1998; Morrisson, 1993; Muehlebach, 2013). They include the following:

- *Consumerism*: Neoliberalism is founded on ideals of consumer choice, contributing to a culture in which the value of people, actions, and priorities are determined by how much revenue they might generate. Those who engage in behaviors that reinforce neoliberal systems through such revenue generation are valorized.
- *Competitive individualism*: Neoliberal ideologies prioritize free-market *individualism and competition*, which reinforce false beliefs in meritocracy, and create a culture in which every person prioritizes their own self-interest.
- *Surveillance*: While neoliberalism promotes free markets and individualism, perceived individual autonomy is fabricated, as the neoliberal regime constructs dehumanizing systems of surveillance (e.g. monitoring and reporting) to ensure that members of the system comply with neoliberal ideals, and trust is eradicated.
- *Precarity*: As neoliberal forces economically starve and place responsibility of fiscal sustainability on individuals, the latter find themselves in a precarious existence and feel an increased need to fight for their own survival.
- *Declining morality*: The aforementioned neoliberal structures converge to reinforce an increased focus on fiscal exigency and profit-making, while eradicating beliefs that government and social institutions have any responsibility for the public good.

While neoliberalism is certainly an ideology that permeates larger society, it is clear that neoliberal philosophies have been both forced upon institutions of higher education by external pressures and fully uncritically embraced by many within higher education. In the following section, we discuss some of the ways in which neoliberalism has contaminated higher education and permeates the cultures that exist within US colleges and universities.

NEOLIBERALISM AND THE CULTURE OF HIGHER EDUCATION

Neoliberalism has shaped the US system of higher education in myriad ways. While a comprehensive analysis of these effects is beyond the scope of the current chapter, we briefly discuss those that are most relevant to the experiences of leaders advocating for social justice within institutions of higher education. Specifically, we discuss how neoliberal ideologies have shaped the *cultures* that exist on college and university campuses. This discussion is informed both by existing literature and our observations working with over 100 institutions across the nation to advance the diversity and equity efforts on their campuses.

Culture has long been recognized as a force that significantly shapes behavior within organizations and a worthy focus of analysis (Geertz, 1973; Tierney, 1988). Culture is developed and transmitted throughout history and has been described as an invisible tapestry that holds an organization together (Kuh & Whitt, 1988). It is grounded in shared assumptions held by members of an organization, and reinforced by the values, traditions, and artifacts that serve as markers of institutional identity (Schein, 2010). However, culture is also comprised of ceremonies, rituals, symbols, heroes, and stories that facilitate the entry into, and continued membership of people who belong to, a given culture. Geertz (1973) described culture by asserting that people are "suspended in webs of significance" that they themselves have spun.

While organizational theorists have identified culture as a major domain of scholarly analysis over three decades ago, the study of culture was not central to higher education research at that time (Tierney, 1988). It could be hypothesized that the decline of cultural analyses is itself an effect of neoliberalism on higher education scholarly agendas and research activity. After all, culture is a complex concept that is difficult to understand (Kuh & Whitt, 1988), and investing the intellectual energy required to analyze complex community and organizational cultures can be (mis)perceived as a liability within the context of neoliberal systems of surveillance and expectations that reward large numbers of easily quantifiable and monitored outputs regardless of their depth and impact on society (Giroux, 2007, 2008). Thus, it could be argued that engaging in an analysis of culture is an act of anti-neoliberal resistance in and of itself.

Most higher education leaders understand that culture is important (Bolman & Deal, 2008; Kuh & Whitt, 1988; Tierney, 1988). This is because culture drives the behavior and decision making of members of organizations, even in ways that they do not fully understand. Therefore, in the current discussion, we unpack how neoliberal forces shape institutional culture, in order to better understand how these influences might consciously or subconsciously influence leaders' reinforcement of, or resistance to, systemic oppression.

Given the complexity inherent in analyzing the concept of culture, identifying clearly defined elements that help make sense of organizational cultures can aid in understanding them. To designate such concepts for this discussion, we draw on Tierney's (1988) framework of organizational culture, which delineates six foci of cultural analysis within higher education organizations: the institution's environment, mission, information (or knowledge), socialization, strategy, and leadership. The following sections focus on five of these six concepts, given that *leadership* is the overarching focus that permeates the entire discussion.

Neoliberal Environments: External Economic and Political Pressures

Institutions of higher education and their leaders are constantly bombarded by neoliberal pressures. After the acceleration and growth of neoliberalism in the 1980s, state governments divested from systems of higher education (Bonds, 2006). Neoliberal ideologies promoted perspectives that college education is a private good, leading to declining beliefs and the role of higher education serving the public. In line with these perspectives, conservative and some liberal politicians advocated for the de-funding of higher education.

While most states continue to diminish the proportion of the budget that is allocated to their higher education systems, one of the most extreme recent examples of state fiscal starvation of higher education systems comes out of Wisconsin. Between 2015 and 2017, the Republican-controlled government slashed the University of Wisconsin budget by $250 million and instituted a performance funding plan that increases competition among campuses, even though there is little evidence that such programs have any positive impact on educational outcomes (Hillman, Tandberg, & Fryar, 2015; Tandberg & Hillman, 2014). These actions contributed to an institutional precarity, and system campuses developed proposals to cope with the budget cuts. Not surprisingly, several institutions began constructing plans to eliminate academic programs within the humanities and social sciences that were less revenue-generating and have historically been charged with preparing college graduates to live and lead in a diverse democracy (Conde, 2018; Kaeding, 2017). Under neoliberal regimes, academic programs that are designed to advocate for democracy and social justice are often the first entities that are downsized or eliminated in times of perceived economic hardship, because they typically generate less revenue and are devalued by neoliberal agendas and those who adopt them (Darder, 2005).

Just as neoliberalism and precarity create conditions where individuals feel forced to fight for their own survival, neoliberal forces have led to a climate of institutional precarity in which administrators are pressured to invest energy and resources in activities that will generate revenue and (they hope) will bolster their reputation and prestige. In addition, national systems and structures, such as institutional rankings, have emerged to reify and fuel such organizational behavior. In a never-ending quest to rise in the rankings and boost prestige, higher education institutions funnel increasing amounts of resources away from education processes that strengthen democracy, diverting them to activities that will generate more money.

Such efforts are often viewed as benign, but a deeper analysis of examples in which communities have fought back tells a different story. Take, for example, the case of San Francisco State University, where the current president decided to funnel resources toward creating science and technology departments and athletic programs at the expense of ethnic studies. When the university's administration announced significant budget cuts to the school of ethnic studies in 2016, hundreds of community members, faculty members, and students waged protests that lasted weeks to voice their discontent, and a handful of students went on a hunger strike that lasted until one of them was sent to the emergency room. When a life could have been lost and the potential damages outweighed the benefits of prioritizing neoliberal agendas over community needs in the eyes of university leaders, the latter acquiesced to protester demands to replenish the budget of the school of ethnic studies. This example also demonstrates how democratic processes, such as protest, can pressure administrators to advocate for social justice despite constant and pervasive neoliberal influences.

Institutional precarity also makes organizational leaders more susceptible to external pressures from direct sources of revenue, such as the web of donors that influence institutional behavior (e.g. corporations and alumni). Indeed, researchers have found that diversity agendas can be met with resistance from members of the institution, as well as sources of power and influence that are external to the institution (Kezar, 2010), and our ongoing work with campuses across the nation confirms that leaders seeking to advance justice continually face such resistance. Thus, when collective resistance to institutional oppression emerges on college campuses, external demands to maintain the status quo are likely to surface as well.

Neoliberal Missions: Espoused, But Not Enacted, Justice Values

While institutions are driven by their mission to varying degrees, few would argue with the notion that these missions have some influence on culture and behavior on these campuses. Mission statements are perceived to be important enough that institutions spend significant amounts of time revisiting and revising them to ensure that they guide campus communities in the right direction (Association of American Colleges, 1994). Specifically, institutional missions help organizational members decipher campus priorities from secondary or peripheral interests and cultivate a shared sense of purpose grounded in the former (Hartley, 2002; Keller, 1983). Thus, college and university missions provide a guide that informs notions about what is valued and where energy should be invested within an organization.

So, what do institutional missions tell us about neoliberalism, campus culture, and social justice? Evidence suggests that institutional leaders routinely espouse missions and strategic plans that tout values of diversity and creating welcoming environments for students, but these espoused commitments are often not coupled with adequate distribution of resources to combat oppression and create a more equitable world (Ahmed, 2012; Iverson, 2006, 2010; LePeau, Hurtado, & Davis, 2018; Wilson,

Meyer, & McNeal, 2012). One does not need to look far to identify the ways in which mission statements reinforce neoliberal rationalities at the expense of social justice agendas. Case in point: Princeton University, currently ranked #1 among research universities according to US News and World Report, has a mission that emphasizes how it "advances learning through scholarship, research, and teaching of unsurpassed quality, with an emphasis on undergraduate and doctoral education that is distinctive among the world's great universities, and with a pervasive commitment to serve the nation and the world." Explicit in the statement is Princeton's position that it is "among the world's great universities" and does work "with unsurpassed quality," thereby clearly and explicitly centering the capital and prestige that accompany the Princeton name and affiliation. While the mission statement does mention "a pervasive commitment to serve the nation," there is no clarity regarding what this phrase means. Such a statement could just as easily mean serving society's elite by advancing neoliberal rationalities, as it could signify advocating a social justice agenda.

The intent here is not to suggest that Princeton University is more responsible for perpetuating neoliberal systems than other institutions, especially given the reality that this type of rhetoric is reflected in mission statements among prestigious campuses across the United States and world. Nor is our goal to perpetuate perspectives that prestigious universities are more worthy of analysis and attention. Our aim is to show that universities perceived to be society's *model* educational institutions often espouse missions that reinforce neoliberal logics and lack clear focus on equity, providing little direction and leverage for leaders who seek to advance social justice. Moreover, because so many institutions seek to emulate these campuses so that they too can garner more prestige and resources, the prestigious university's neoliberal foci symbolize the belief that other institutions should strive in ways that advance neoliberal logics.

Neoliberal Knowledge Economy: Equating Quality with Revenue

Scholars have noted that different forms of knowledge are valued to varying degrees within higher education (Museus, Ledesma, & Parker, 2015; Patton, 2016). For example, research documents the ways in which faculty from historically marginalized backgrounds regularly experience the devaluation of their equity-oriented research agendas. However, research and discourse on (in)equity in higher education often clarifies that knowledge from marginalized communities is devalued, without engaging in deeper discussions to unpack the underlying mechanisms through which such devaluation is justified within institutions.

Critical theorists highlight how neoliberal foundations inform the ways in which different types of information are valued, with knowledge that conforms to neoliberal agendas being more appreciated because of their capacity to generate revenue and prestige (Davies, 2005; Slaughter & Rhoades, 2004). As mentioned, neoliberal assaults in Wisconsin provide a stark example of how institutional precarity and the prioritization of neoliberal forms of knowledge converge to create a perilous situation for academic programs and scholars who do not conform to neoliberal ideologies. Typically, it is those programs that operate in the academic borderlands and directly challenge the status quo on a regular basis that are most vulnerable in such times (Darder, 2005). Indeed, in the 1980s and 1990s, when scholarly alliances designed to generate liberatory knowledge and support anti-imperialist struggles began to flourish in the academic borderlands, neoliberal forces equipped institutions of higher education with tools to weaken this expansion and suppress voices from the margins. Specifically, arguments to protect financial exigency and the need to cut budgets were increasingly used to justify eliminating programs, instituting hiring freezes, and rejecting tenure cases of radically progressive faculty.

Neoliberal forces have made their way into the academic borderlands as well (Darder, 2005; Davies, 2005). In some cases, academic programs and scholars in fields that emerged from the community, such as ethnic studies, have adopted more traditional research agendas and methods to earn legitimacy within the neoliberal system. It is also worth noting that such conformity sometimes happens subconsciously. This is not surprising, given that one of the ways in which pervasive systems operate is that they inculcate into us worldviews that solidify and normalize assumptions about what is (not) legitimate behavior. We begin to internalize such worldviews as early as undergraduate education, as we begin consuming scholarly research through college courses, but this indoctrination often accelerates in graduate education as future professionals in the academy become socialized to conform to neoliberal expectations. In turn, as the editors discuss in the introduction of this volume, the permeation of neoliberal logics in the professional psyche constrain and eliminate possibilities to advance social justice.

Neoliberal Socialization: Planting Seeds of Oppression in Future Professionals

While some of the ways in which the neoliberal regime has infiltrated higher education are more difficult to identify, it could easily be argued that graduate student socialization is one area in which the effects of neoliberalism are clearly evident. Scholars have written about ways in which higher education reproduces itself through the socialization of those coming into the system (Bauder, 2006; Becher, 1989; Said, 1994). Given the pervasiveness of neoliberalism in higher education, these forces have begun to significantly drive socialization processes.

As future higher education administrators and faculty members are socialized into the academy, the systems and structures in place inculcate corporatized perspectives and behaviors into them (Darder, 2005; Mitchell, 1999; Smith, 2000). These perspectives reinforce neoliberal ideologies, and therefore carry the seeds of oppression. Future professionals who will eventually hold significant power within colleges and universities are pressured to eradicate their humanized connections with their communities and critical epistemological foundations that provide the potential to challenge neoliberal systems that serve the elite. Instead, they are initiated into a system that encourages or forces them to focus on careerist goals and priorities.

As a result, those who enter academia in order to advance social justice find it exponentially difficult to do so. Increasing intellectual energy gets invested in figuring out how to populate CVs with quantifiable evidence that one has met neoliberal expectations, students are taught to out-present and out-publish each other, and they face increasing pressures to learn how to secure money in addition to carrying out the democratic goals that drove them to academia. The outcomes of these processes are that young professionals experience heightened anxieties, as well as increased challenges pursuing collective agendas that have the power to advance social justice and help universities reclaim their commitment to democratic education (Mitchell, 2002; Smith, 2000; Solem & Foote, 2004; Willis, 1996).

Neoliberal Strategy: The Normalized Prioritization of Neoliberal Agendas Over Justice

Organizational leaders in higher education employ different strategies to advance social justice agendas. Some leaders recognize that they must make compromises in other areas in order to invest more resources in equity goals and initiatives, while others seek to invest the minimum amount of energy and time needed to pacify those who express discontent with the current neoliberal cultures that permeate their campuses. In many of these cases, however, strategies for enhancing social justice are first assessed for the degree to which they are feasible—or desirable—within existing neoliberal contexts and through a neoliberal sensemaking framework. That is, institutional leaders often assess whether alternatives for advancing social justice might lead to compromising other priorities and initiatives that reinforce neoliberal structures. If the strategies are determined to compromise neoliberal agendas, they are deemed impossible or undesirable. We believe that this could be the greatest barrier to leaders meaningfully advancing social justice within institutions of higher education.

Of course, the idea that social justice conflicts with academic excellence is not new. In fact, we were writing about this assumption being a significant barrier to advancing equity many years ago (e.g. Jayakumar & Museus, 2012). However, the many ways in which such assumptions shape institutions of higher education are not well understood. We have observed that institutional leaders make strategic assessments about the various ways in which institutional changes to advance equity might hinder neoliberal agendas. For example, organizational leaders will often focus on whether expanding access to their institutions will lower standardized test scores and compromise their standings in national rankings; administrators who are pressured to sever ties with donors publicly committing racist acts focus on the resources that will be compromised; institutional leaders who field calls to replace dehumanizing mascots or remove statues that valorize persons who committed heinous acts toward communities of color weigh the consequences of morality against the loss of donations from alumni; and recommendations to create new systems and structures that are more equitable are (more often than not) dismissed because they would require redirecting resources away from more revenue-generating arenas within the institution (e.g. science and technology fields). These are just a few of the many ways in which existing neoliberal structures disincentivize leaders' advancement of justice.

STRATEGIES TO ADVANCE SOCIAL JUSTICE IN A NEOLIBERAL ERA

If leaders aim to seriously advance social justice agendas, they must figure out ways to navigate and circumvent the omnipresent barriers engendered by the neoliberal regime. In this final section, we offer a handful of recommendations that are grounded in the proceeding analysis and intended to start a conversation about how leaders can create space and opportunities for their constituents to engage in acts of resistance to neoliberal agendas.

Minimize the Power and Influence of Oppressive External Forces

As mentioned above, leaders are heavily influenced by external forces, and conversations about social justice rarely reveal how to minimize the impact of these external influences. While institutional leaders cannot control state government funding decisions, they can strategically make efforts to shape some external environments. For example, institutional leaders can promote the inclusion of social justice advocates on the Board of Regents or Trustees of their campuses. Leaders also have the capacity to determine how much they allow these external forces to influence their behavior. Campuses that truly value social justice must be willing to forgo contributions from donors who actively seek to uphold the status quo in order to prioritize equity over fiscal growth. Of course, we realize that compromising fiscal growth in a neoliberal society means risking one's own reputation and revenue, but we also know that such risks are necessary to advance justice. We return to this point later in the section.

(Re)Focus the Mission and Resources on Advancing Democracy and Justice

The growth of neoliberalism within US society has contributed to what we understand as an urgency for civic (re)awakening, which can be facilitated by institutions refocusing their missions on democratic education. Institutional leaders can engage campuses across the community in the process of (re)envisioning their mission to be more socially just, in order to maximize buy-in and investment in the mission across their campuses.

Leaders who live out such missions on their campuses must support faculty and staff in embedding social justice throughout the curricula, programs, and activities at their institutions. This can be done by supporting efforts to create support and reward systems that prioritize advancing social justice. Such systems might include research and teaching innovation grants, annual review processes, and promotion and tenure reviews that center the degree to which activities advance a social justice agenda as a core evaluation criterion. In addition, rather than investing their institution's resources in programs and activities primarily based on how much revenue they might generate, leaders can allocate funding based on whether these programs and activities help achieve a mission to advance social justice. This would mean rewarding academic programs that center these values in their mission.

Embrace and Support Resistance from the Ground

Institutional leaders who experience campus unrest often focus their reaction and energies on how to regulate, temper, or suppress faculty and student activism before it "goes viral." This reaction might be considered an effect of the neoliberal regime as well, as it is driven by the desire to limit damage to the institution's prestige and market value. Alternatively, however, some leaders view such resistance as a fundamental democratic process and interpret protestors' actions as applying the pressure that can creates opportunities for change and allow leaders to more effectively enact a social justice agenda. Leaders who welcome resistance from the ground can inform alumni and other stakeholders of these pressures and explain how the changes they are making align with the mission for democratic education and a better world. The can also maximize the likelihood that social justice goals of leadership within the institution converge with those of those on the ground, which can function to increase the effectiveness of such efforts (Kezar, 2012; Pearce & Conger, 2003).

To proactively support resistance movements, educational leaders can teach students, faculty, and staff about how organizational decisions are made. If leaders create a culture of supporting resistance movements, everyone at the institution might better understand how discussing divergent perspectives and questioning decision making can be a productive part of the cultural fabric of the campus, and those advocating for change might better understand the things for which they can and should advocate. Leaders can create educational opportunities to proactively teach about mechanisms available to enable people to bring campus community perspectives to administrators, strategies for creating forums to discuss contentious issues, and skills for approaching social change in culturally relevant and responsive ways.

Create Subversive Structures of Support, Rewards, and Socialization

Leaders can create subversive structures of socialization and support. For example, institutional leaders can construct committees charged with examining how to embed social justice into annual and promotion review processes. Leaders can also allocate resources to give faculty members course releases and release staff members from work time so that they can deeply study critical forms of pedagogy, re-examine and deconstruct their courses and programs, and construct new ways of teaching for a diverse democracy. Institutional leaders can commit to being heavily involved in faculty and staff searches and ensure that equity is integrated throughout the entire process, including the construction of the qualifications and position announcement, selection of candidates, and interview processes.

Institutional leaders can also create socialization processes that deviate from neoliberal norms. For example, institutional leaders can support the creation of spaces of resistance where campus community members can critically examine existing problems that emanate from the neoliberal regime (e.g. publish-or-perish mentalities, the never-ending quest for external funding, mental health challenges that might result from never-ending neoliberal pressures), and explore questions regarding how they can cultivate more humanized educational environments that are relevant to the communities they serve (Museus, 2014). These types of processes could include spending significant time storytelling, critiquing the current support and reward structures on campus, and strategizing how to cultivate communities that can resist neoliberal pressures and advance social justice.

It is important for institutional leaders to counter the constant messages that socialize graduate students into the neoliberal culture that permeates academia. Institutional leaders should include graduate students—many of whom will become leaders within academic institutions—in the conversations and efforts outlined above. Moreover, we have observed the ways in which neoliberal forces, and the resulting constant pressures to produce greater numbers emanating, create unrealistic and unhealthy expectations among graduate students, and institutions can ensure students receive information about realistic expectations of early career professionals.

CONCLUSION

We recognize that, in order for leaders to adopt some of the aforementioned recommendations, they must make sacrifices. Some of their constituents will not like such decisions. Leaders may be critiqued for propagating liberal agendas. Leaders may also fail to challenge neoliberal forces because it could jeopardize the immediate rewards that accompany conformity to the system. In this chapter, we discussed some ways in which tenets of neoliberalism shape institutional cultures so that leaders can be more cognizant when they may be lured into making decisions that reinforce these systems. To advance social justice agendas, however, leaders must adopt and implement strategies that require immediate risk to achieve long-term equity goals.

QUESTIONS FOR REFLECTION AND DISCUSSION

- Of the neoliberalism tenets, which one causes tensions for you in your current work as a leader? Discuss these tensions with your peers or colleagues.

- What sacrifices have you made, if any, to advance equity efforts? What sacrifices do you think need to be made in your own context (e.g. organization, academic program, leadership) to advance social justice?
- Think about your own institutional context. Given the recommendations offered, what specific steps would be necessary to enact one or more of the recommendations?

NOTE

1 Throughout this chapter, we use "leader" broadly to refer to those who assume positions of power and authority within institutions of higher education, including (but not necessarily limited to) executive administrators and members of executive leadership teams and committees.

BIBLIOGRAPHY

Adsit, J., Doe, S., Allison, M., Maggio, P., & Maisto, M. (2015). Affective activism: Answering institutional productions of precarity in the corporate university. *Feminist Formations, 27*(3), 21–48.

Ahmed, S. (2012). *On Being Included: Racism and Diversity in Institutional Life.* Durham, NC: Duke University Press.

Association of American Colleges (1994). *Strong Foundations: Twelve Principles for Effective General Education Programs.* Washington, DC: Association of American Colleges.

Bauder, H. (2006). Learning to become a geographer: Reproduction and transformation in academia. *Antipode, 38*(4), 671–679.

Becher T. (1989). *Academic Tribes and Territories: Intellectual Enquiry and the Culture of Disciplines.* Columbus, OH: Open University Press.

Bolman, L. G., & Deal, T. E. (1984). *Modern Approaches to Understanding and Managing Organizations.* San Francisco, CA: Jossey-Bass.

Bolman, L. G., & Deal, T. E. (2008). *Reframing Organizations: Artistry, Choice, and Leadership.* San Francisco, CA: John Wiley & Sons.

Bonds, A. (2006). Profit from punishment? The politics of prisons, poverty and neoliberal restructuring in the rural American Northwest. *Antipode, 38*(1), 174–177.

Burford, J. (2017). What might "bad feelings" be good for? Some queer-feminist thoughts on academic activism. *Australian Universities' Review, 59*(2), 70–78.

Conde, X. (2018). UW-Stevens Point considering eliminating up to 70 positions to balance budget. *Wisconsin Public Radio.* Retrieved from www.wpr.org/uw-stevens-point-considering-eliminating-70-positions-balance-budget.

Darder, A. (2005). Schooling and the culture of dominion: Unmasking the ideology of standardized testing. In G. F. Fischman, P. McLaren, H. Sünker, & C. Lankshear (Eds.), *Critical Theories, Radical Pedagogies, and Global Conflicts* (pp. 207–222). New York: Rowman & Littlefield.

Davies, B. (2005). The (im)possibility of intellectual work in neoliberal regimes. *Discourse: Studies in the Cultural Politics of Education, 26*(1), 1–14.

Geertz, C. (1973). *The Interpretation of Cultures.* New York: Basic books.

Giroux, H. (2007). *The University in Chains.* Boulder, CO: Paradigm.

Giroux, H. (2008). *Against the Terror of Neoliberalism: Politics Beyond the Age of Greed.* Boulder, CO: Paradigm Publishers.

Giroux, H. (2011). The disappearing intellectual in the age of economic Darwinism. *Policy Futures in Education, 9,* 163–171.

Goldberg, D. T. (2009). *The Threat of Race: Reflections on Racial Neoliberalism.* Brentwood, CA: John Wiley & Sons.

Goldberg, D. T. (2015). *Are we all postracial yet?* Brentwood, CA: John Wiley & Sons.

Gosse, V. (2005). Third World Liberation Front. In *The Movements of the New Left, 1950–1975* (pp. 127–128). New York: Palgrave Macmillan.

Hartley, M. (2002). *A Call to Purpose: Mission-centered Change at Three Liberal Arts Colleges.* New York: RoutledgeFalmer.

Hillman, N. W., Tandberg, D. A., & Fryar, A. H. (2015). Evaluating the impacts of "new" performance funding in higher education. *Educational Evaluation and Policy Analysis, 37*(4), 501–519.

Inwood, J. F. (2015). Neoliberal racism: The "Southern Strategy" and the expanding geographies of white supremacy. *Social and Cultural Geography, 16*(4), 407–423.

Iverson, S. V. (2006). Camouflaging power and privilege: A critical race analysis of university diversity policies. *Educational Administration Quarterly, 43*(5), 586–611.

Iverson, S. V. (2010). Producing diversity: A policy discourse analysis of diversity action plans. In E.J. Allan, S. V. Iverson, & R. Ropers-Huilman (Eds.), *Reconstructing policy in higher education: Feminist poststructural perspectives* (pp. 193–213). New York: Routledge.

Jayakumar, U. M., & Museus, S. D. (2012). Mapping the intersection of campus cultures and equitable outcomes among racially diverse student populations. In U. M. Jayakumar (Ed.), *Creating Campus Cultures* (pp. 11–37). New York: Routledge.

Kaeding, D. (2017). UW-Superior students protest move to suspend programs. *Wisconsin Public Radio.* Retrieved from www.wpr.org/uw-superior-students-protest-move-suspend-programs.

Keller, G. (1983). *Academic Strategy: The Management Revolution in American Higher Education.* Baltimore, MD: Johns Hopkins University Press.

Kezar, A. (2010). Faculty and staff grassroots leaders' beliefs about power: Do their beliefs affect their strategies and effectiveness? *International Journal of Leadership Studies, 6*(1), 84–112.

Kezar, A. (2012). Bottom-up/top-down leadership: Contradiction or hidden phenomenon. *The Journal of Higher Education, 83*(5), 725–760.

Kezar, A., & Eckel, P. D. (2002). The effect of institutional culture on change strategies in higher education: Universal principles or culturally responsive concepts? *The Journal of Higher Education, 73*(4), 435–460.

Kuh, G. D., & Whitt, E. J. (1988). *The Invisible Tapestry. Culture in American Colleges and Universities. ASHE-ERIC Higher Education, Report No. 1.* Washington, DC: Association for the Study of Higher Education.

LePeau, L. A., Hurtado, S. S., & Davis, R. J. (2018). What Institutional Websites Reveal About Diversity-Related Partnerships Between Academic and Student Affairs. *Innovative Higher Education, 43*(2), 125–142.

McChesney, R. W. (1998). Introduction. In N. Chomsky (Ed.), *Profit Over People: Neoliberalism and Global Order* (pp. 7–16). New York: Seven Stories Press.

McChesney, R. W. (1999). Noam Chomsky and the struggle against neoliberalism. *Monthly Review, 50*(11), 40.

Mitchell, D. (2002). Between books and streets, between home, mall and battlefield: The politics and pleasure of Cultural Geography. *Antipode, 34*, 335–339.

Mitchell, T. (1999). Dreamland: The neoliberalism of your desires. *Middle East Report, 29*(1; ISSU 210), 28–33.

Morrison, T. (1993). *Lecture and Speech of Acceptance, upon the Award of the Nobel Prize for Literature.* London: Chatto and Windus.

Muehlebach, A. (2013). On precariousness and the ethical imagination: The year 2012 in sociocultural anthropology. *American Anthropologist, 115*(2), 297–311.

Museus, S. D. (2014). *Asian American Students in Higher Education.* New York: Routledge.

Museus, S. D., Ledesma, M. C., & Parker, T. L. (2015). Racism and racial equity in higher education. *ASHE Higher Education Report, 42*(1), 1–112.

Patton, L. D. (2016). Disrupting postsecondary prose: Toward a critical race theory of higher education. *Urban Education, 51*, 315–342.

Pearce, C. L., & Conger, J. A. (2003). All those years ago: The historical underpinnings of shared leadership. In C. L. Pearce & J.A. Conger (Eds.), *Shared Leadership: Reframing the Hows and Whys of Leadership* (pp. 1–18). Thousand Oaks, CA: Sage.

Said, E. (1994). *Representations of the Intellectual.* London: Vintage.

Schein, E. H. (2010). *Organizational Culture and Leadership* (Vol. 2). San Francisco, CA: John Wiley & Sons.

Slaughter, S., & Rhoades, G. (2004). *Academic Capitalism and the New Economy: Markets, State, and Higher Education.* Baltimore, MD: Johns Hopkins University Press.

Smith, N. (2000). Afterword: Who rules this sausage factory? *Antipode, 32*(3), 330–39.

Solem, M. N. and K. E. Foote. 2004. Concerns, attitudes, and abilities of early-career geography faculty. *Annals of the Association of American Geographers, 94*(4), 889–912.

Tandberg, D. A., & Hillman, N. W. (2014). State higher education performance funding: Data, outcomes, and policy implications. *Journal of Education Finance,* 222–243.

Tierney, W. G. (1988). Organizational culture in higher education: Defining the essentials. *The Journal of Higher Education, 59*(1), 2–21.

Tierney, W. G. (1997). Organizational socialization in higher education. *The Journal of Higher Education, 68*(1), 1–16.

Umemoto, K. (1989). "On strike!" San Francisco State college strike, 1968–69: The role of Asian American students. *Amerasia Journal, 15*(1), 3–41.

Willis, J. (1996). Laboring for love? A comment on academics and their hours of work. *Antipode 28*(3), 292–303.

Wilson, J. L., Meyer, K. A., & McNeal, L. (2012). Mission and diversity statements: What they do and do not say. *Innovative Higher Education, 37*(2), 125–139.

14

DEVELOPING EQUITABLE WORK–LIFE POLICIES ON CAMPUS

The Importance of Addressing Power and Hierarchy

JAIME LESTER

Around 2010, I conducted a series of studies focused on work–life policy and cultural change on college campuses (Lester, 2013, 2015). The intent was to examine how colleges and universities underwent cultural shifts in order to support more work–life balance programs and policies for faculty or how they created a shared culture to normalize childbearing, childrearing, and caring for aging parents, among other work–life issues. The argument of external funders and institutions followed that policy change would lead to new social and cultural norms and eventually reduce stigma. What I found revealed the policy changes and accompanying institutional communication campaigns designed to promote the new policies and address stigma did not lead to cultural shifts. Instead, I uncovered evidence of how embedded historical power dynamics within universities—which include sociological, heteronormative, and cisgender notions of family and shifting organizational dynamics that exist at the local unit practices—prevented engagement in deeply held assumptions to create an equitable work–life culture. Without evaluating and changing deeply held assumptions, the work–life policies emerging from this environment perpetuated inequities.

The policies and practices that I was examining were intended to address systemic gendered inequities in higher education institutions that prevent the success of women and underrepresented faculty. Women accounted for only 33.2% of all faculty in 1987, increasing to almost half in 2013 (National Center for Education Statistics [NCES], 2015). The aggregate numbers of faculty by gender identify equal representation of women, but also mask the inequities across disciplines and employment contracts.[1]

In terms of rank, national statistics indicate that women remain concentrated in non-tenure-track roles at 54% and fewer women seek promotion to full professor; about 32% of full professors are women (NCES, 2015). In addition, women faculty remain segregated into specific disciplines with few changes over time. Hill, Corbett, and St. Rose (2010) found that women "made up less than one-quarter of the faculty in computer and information sciences (22 percent), math (19 percent), the physical sciences (18 percent), and engineering (12 percent)" (p. 15). More recent data from the National Science Foundation reports that women make up only one-fourth of full professors in science, engineering and health (National Science Foundation [NSF], 2015). For faculty of color, the numbers are decidedly worse. In 2016, faculty of color made up less than 25% of full-time faculty, and according to the National Center for Education Statistics (NCES), "6 percent were Asian/Pacific Islander males; 4 percent were Asian/Pacific Islander females; 3 percent each were Black males, Black females, and Hispanic males; and 2 percent were Hispanic females," with American Indian/Alaska Native and those faculty of two or more races constituting "1 percent or less of full-time faculty in these institutions" (NCES, 2018, p. 1).

The research explains that the lack of representation of women and underrepresented faculty is largely due to work–life issues, narrowly defined as an incompatibility of faculty work with motherhood. Research noted that women doctoral and postdoctoral students often opt out of the professoriate due to a belief that childrearing is incongruent with the expectations of tenure review (Mason & Goulden, 2002). Often, the tenure-track coincides with a woman's proverbial biological clock and a man's optimal time for childrearing, 30–40 years old, leaving many to think having a family and an academic career are incompatible goals. Those that do venture into academic positions develop strategies to create circumstances compatible with life responsibilities and faculty work. Armenti (2004) noted that many women aim to have "May babies," timing pregnancies to coincide with summer leave, thus not requiring any maternity leave during the academic year. Some women hide their pregnancies out of fear of colleagues' expectation around productivity (Armenti, 2004; Monroe, Ozyurt, Wrigley, & Alexander, 2008). Still others engage in bias avoidance behaviors, such as not using available institutional leave to avoid calling attention to their parental status (Drago et al., 2006). Studies have also found that men are likely to minimize the use of leave, fearing challenges not just to their careers, but to their identities as men (Sallee, 2014).

Work–life policies and subsequent communication campaigns to normalize the use of policies, such as stopping the tenure clock, were largely viewed as the solution to inequity. Although not systematically documented in the research, many college campuses have stopped tenure clock policies for family or medical leave and some offer paid leave for faculty. Yet, policy use remains low, with several studies noting that few faculty, both men and women, choose to stop the tenure clock or request semester leave (Bunton & Corrice, 2011; Mason, Goulden, & Wolfinger, 2006; Pribbenow et al., 2010; Quinn, 2010; Williams, Alon, & Bornstein, 2006). Higher education administrators and leaders cannot simply create new policies and programs that will deeply impact faculty, staff, and other higher education constituents to achieve work–life balance. Rather, organizational members must also be able to recognize participation in work–life policies as viable and legitimate courses of action.

This chapter aims to focus on and provide recommendations on changes to campus culture related to work–life balance to move beyond the expectation that policy development in an existing dominant culture will resolve embedded inequities. To do so, this chapter adopts a new approach to addressing work–life on college campus, one that derives from Gorski's (2016) work on equity literacy for K-12 schools to critique and to provide a roadmap for policy development around work–life. Importantly, equity literacy aligns with the discourse of social justice in education and in higher education. A long history of research on social justice in education identifies schools as places of social transmission where inequities in society are perpetuated and serve to support the dominant culture (Adams, Bell, & Griffin, 2007; Bell, Love, Washington, & Weinstein, 2007). The goal for social justice theories is to demand that schools unveil and transform oppressive policies and practices (Mthethwa-Sommers, 2012). Higher education scholars have also argued that colleges and universities have inequities deeply entrenched in institutional culture that make social justice work difficult (Osei-Kofi, Shahjahan, & Patton, 2010). The heteronormative and cisgender definitions of family, historical and current power dynamics across employment contracts, and the hierarchical structures and practices of higher education all lead to inequities in work–life practices.

WORK–LIFE BALANCE DEFINED

Work–life balance is a pervasive expectation on college campuses today. From well-being initiatives to a recognition of mental health concerns for students to health and exercise campaigns, colleges and universities are seeking to identify ways to promote more balance between work and life with an emphasis on more individual balance (American Council on Education [ACE], 2014). The pressure for such reforms comes from a variety of sources, including new research on the impact of sedentary work environments (Keenan & Greer, 2015); on blurred boundaries between work and life domains via organizational technologies (Currie & Eveline, 2011); and on the new generations of students and faculty who value life activities as much as work expectations (Trower, 2010).

While a sticky concept to define, work–life in the literature is generally considered conflict across the roles between life and work domains, with work–life balance being viewed as the satisfaction, saliency, and control of multiple, equitable roles across work and life with minimal conflict (Kalliath & Brough, 2008). Essentially, work–life balance is viewed as the ability for an individual to feel successful and meeting the demands in his or her work and home responsibilities. The research on work–life balance spans decades and disciplines, identifying relationships across a complex set of constructs including demographics (gender, socioeconomic status), organizational dynamics (turnover, job satisfaction, absenteeism), and individual consequences (role conflict, productivity shifts). Results from the research identify the relationship between organizational dynamics and culture in work–life as well as the impact of sociological views of family and gender.

WORK–LIFE BALANCE IN ORGANIZATIONAL AND SOCIAL CONTEXTS

Several researchers, including myself, have argued that higher education institutions continue to operate under the assumption of the ideal worker—the always available worker—derived from the work on gender and organizations (Acker, 1990, 1992; Lester, 2008; Lester, Sallee, & Hart, 2017; Martin, 1994; Sallee, 2012). The argument follows that universities were created by and for men, whereas heteronormative, cisgender family structures assumed a woman stayed at home and cared for the children. University policies and cultural norms relied on the idea that male faculty could work long hours and be available, because they had domestic support in the form of their wives (Sallee, 2014; Ward & Wolf-Wendel, 2004, 2012). Sallee (2014) found that academic fathers experience challenges when they attempt to be more available to their children as they are expected to work long hours.

Other organizational norms create challenges for faculty and staff to seek work–life balance. Several studies focused on the contemporary trend of institutions to seek the status as high research activity or what is often termed as a striving institution. Gardner (2013) found divisions of labor along the lines of gender, specifically in pay and labor inequities, with more women engaging in mentoring and informal relationships not included in productivity metrics aligned with research (i.e. number of publications and research grants). Gardner concludes that striving institutions place increased emphasis on the gendered nature of organizations.

Given the fact that the research environments to which these striving institutions aspire can foster culture that promote male-dominated social structures (i.e. "the old boy's network") as well as an emphasis on self-advancement, competition, and a lack of transparency (Becher & Trowler, 2001), the quest for status in the academic hierarchy can further such a gendered perspective. (pp. 363–364).

Wolf-Wendel and Ward (2006) in a study of faculty with young children at comprehensive institutions found that work–life among faculty was impacted by the shifting aspirational mission of the colleges who were striving to be more research-intensive and thus placing additional demands on faculty for research productivity. Faculty reported feeling overworked with high levels of stress. Having young children complicated their ability to meet the increasing and unreasonable demands and, thereby, created more frustration and stress. As another example, O'Meara and Campbell (2011) also found that the additive nature of faculty work, particularly in the case of striving institutions, constrains faculty agency to achieve any form of work–life balance. The participants in their study were regularly working over 50 hours a week, and female faculty felt more constrained than male faculty due to their status as the primary caregivers of children. Faculty felt that their ability to achieve work–life balance was constrained by institutional norms and expectations.

Issues of faculty productivity intersecting with gender and work–life is also evident in a focus on disciplinary differences. Wolf-Wendel and Ward (2015) in a study of work–life found that humanities faculty tended to have an easier time balancing work and family because their work tended to be individualistic and not place bound. STEM faculty, who worked in lab settings, noted that "the communal nature of the lab sciences made these women aware of their absences because the larger lab community relied on them for continuity" (p. 30). Male faculty also experience intense differences when it comes to work–life. Sallee (2012, 2014), in a study of academic fathers, focused on the ways in which divisions between genders do not just suggest divisions on campus, but divisions off campus as well. Men who wish to prioritize caregiving are often at a disadvantage as it is assumed that they have a wife to care for their children; these divisions are supported by institutional symbols that suggest that women are more nurturing than men. Sallee (2012) similarly found that these divisions and symbols were reinforced by interactions with other faculty and department chairs on campus. Some fathers received messages that family-friendly policies were meant to be used only by women and were reluctant to even consider learning about and using the policies. Without an understanding that work–life is a cultural value and social norm, faculty and staff in higher education institutions will not utilize these opportunities to attempt to achieve balance. The remainder of this chapter focuses on an equity literacy framework to assist college campuses to embed work–life as a cultural value *with* a set of policies and programs.

EQUITY LITERACY

Equity literacy is a framework and movement to cultivate "in teachers the knowledge and skills necessary to become a threat to the existence of inequity in their spheres of influence" (Gorski, 2016, p. 225). Equity literacy, as Gorski (2016) carefully describes, emerged from critique of multicultural education movements that take a cultural approach to change. Gorski describes the multicultural change efforts in K-12 schools, such as multicultural fairs and related campaigns that celebrate diversity through dance, food, and other cultural artifacts, as inherently flawed. These efforts, while well intended, fail to address intersectional identities, essentialize large racial or ethnic groups, and do not account for nor demand equitable distribution of power.

The equity literacy framework has four major tenets to assist educators, or leaders in the case of this chapter, to develop equity-based abilities. The four major abilities with examples of skills and knowledge and with application to work–life policies in higher education are outlined in Table 14.1. The first is the ability to *recognize inequity* with attention to subtle bias and microaggressions, and the second is the *ability to respond* immediately or in the moment. For example, and in the context of work–life balance issues in higher education, the first ability would be used to recognize that meetings held later in the afternoon or social activities held in the evening disadvantage those faculty and staff with significant parenting or elder care responsibilities. Responding to those work–life practices would include fostering conversation on the department or unit level to reconsider meeting times and social activities, acknowledging the inequity and creating new practices and policies. The third tenet takes a more strategic and long-term approach, with the ability to *redress inequities* through advocacy and professional development, "attending to the deeper cultural dynamics of the institution that make people believe it is acceptable to denigrate students' home languages" (Gorski, 2016, p. 225). Gorksi's quote is in reference to English-language cultural change efforts on schools but can also be applied to work–life practices. For example, redressing work–life would include developing equity-minded work–life policies that provide equal benefits to faculty and staff. Finally, the fourth tenet is the ability to create and sustain a *bias-free and equitable environment* though curriculum and professional development. Much of the research notes that faculty engage in work–life policies and practices due to department-level cultural and social norms (Lester, 2013, p. 205; O'Meara & Campbell, 2011; Sallee, 2014; Ward & Wolf-Wendel, 2004, 2012). An equity literate department chair or unit head would have knowledge of structural barriers and implicit biases that prevent work–life balance for faculty and staff and seek to redistribute opportunity with attention to the existing power dynamics. For faculty, examples of these activities could include department-level professional development workshops and activities that address the implicit biases that prevent faculty and staff from using leave policies. For staff, who are often seen as the individuals who must be present and available in the office to cover a front desk or to be present for student questions, an equity literate department chair could help organize hours for all staff and faculty to be present in the office to allow for staff to also have some flexibility during the work day. All too often faculty are the only group that has the privilege of flexible time and work from home or other locations. These individuals could also advocate for equity on the college and university level.

The equity literacy framework is a tool to assist college campuses in defining work–life as a cultural value, a core principle shared by the entire campus community. By doing so, individuals across the campus can begin to identify and practice work–life balance, such as using tenure leave or flextime policies, as acceptable behavior. Moving toward a cultural change also enables individuals and the campus community to become educated on the relationship between work–life and inequities. For example,

TABLE 14.1 Equity Literacy Ability and Associated Work–Life Knowledge and Skills

Abilities	Examples of Associated Knowledge and Skills	Work–Life Associated Knowledge and Skills
Ability to recognize even the subtlest biases and inequities	• Notice subtle bias in materials and interactions • Show curiosity of ways policy and practice disadvantage some • Reject deficit views • Broaden definitions of gender and family	• Conduct evaluation of policies and programs for bias and intentionally include respondents from across identity groups (parents, gender, race/ethnicity, employment contracts) • Challenge and change deficit views that suggest leave policies are unnecessary or are taken unnecessarily
Ability to respond to biases and inequities in the immediate term	• Develop facilitation skills and knowledge to intervene when recognizing bias • Cultivate recognition of bias in materials and curriculum • Foster conversations about equity • Examine disaggregated data • Identify key performance and outcome indicators	• Engage in professional development on microaggressions, conflict resolution, and work–life issues • Encourage and/or create professional development opportunities and learning communities on campus to gain knowledge of work–life issues and bias • Create inclusive language in programs and work–life campaigns that is sensitive to bias and power dynamics around work–life issues
Ability to redress biases and inequities in the long term	• Advocate against inequitable practices and for practices that advance equity • Define diversity, equity, and inclusion. • Teach about sexism, poverty, racism, ableism, transphobia, and heterosexism	• Advocate with human resources and other campus leaders for equitable work–life policies and practices • Create work–life policies that have basic standards while encouraging differentiation • Continuously include opportunities for discussion and knowledge about bias to accompany any policy or programming
Ability to create and sustain bias-free and equitable classrooms, schools, and institutional cultures	• Express high expectations for students through pedagogy • Consider communications with constituents with attention to access to resources (i.e., internet access) • Prioritize needs, challenges, and barriers experienced by marginalized groups in all areas of the educational institution	• Communicate success stories of work–life practices and reward/award supervisors that acknowledge and address bias in work–life • Place communications about work–life in prominent places in hardcopy and online sources • Include in all discussions about work–life the value of equity literacy

Note: Adapted from Equity Literacy Institute.

many campuses are committed to hiring more diverse faculty but often do not identify the relationship between faculty diversity and a burden of service expectations whereby diverse faculty have a higher workload due to service expectations of search committees and student mentoring, among other activities (Jayakumar, Howard, Allen, & Han, 2009). Valuing work–life balance and connecting to equity will help to reveal these very inequitable workload expectations directly related to gender and race and assist in creating workload plans and practices to prevent overload and assist with work–life balance.

RECOMMENDATIONS

Equity Literate Evaluation of Work–Life

The first area of the equity literacy framework is to recognize bias and to conduct evaluations being mindful of equity. Work–life balance in higher education is often operationalized as a set of policies and programs organized by human resources or provost offices with a focus on faculty development, rights, and protections. A major first step is for administrators to conduct a thorough evaluation of written policy to identify who has access to which family and medical leave benefits and systematically research if and when those policies are used. For example, many campuses have work–life policies that are available only for nine-month faculty in tenure-line positions. Staff and 12-month appointments only have access to the federal minimum of 12 weeks unpaid leave in accordance with the Federal Family and Medical Leave Act of 1993 (2006). These policies are not only inequitable across employment contracts, they also assume a heteronormative and cisgender family structure where one parent, often a woman, cares for the child. Colleges and universities will continue to create discontinuity and confusion about their support for work–life if they ignore the needs of contingent faculty and graduate students, give lesser policies to staff, and continue to propagate inequitable practices by viewing these issues through historically narrow and biased lenses. Policies serve an important symbolic role and can move institutions and individuals toward greater understanding and less discontinuity, if all constituent groups have access to support for family and medical issues. Broadening the policy to be more inclusive of medical issues (e.g. caring for aging parents and other definitions of family beyond just childbearing and children) and more cognizant of potentially embedded biases, is essential to bridging some of the discontinuities and inequities that exist and to better supporting all workers across their employment and life spans.

As discussed, another major issue identified in the literature is policy use with a pattern of evidence that suggests that department-level climates have a high impact on the perceived ability for faculty to use those policies. To remedy this issue, equity-literate administrators would need to commission qualitative studies to identify the department climates and the cultural norms that negatively impact work–life balance police use and program engagement. Examining current policies, seeking information on the needs of work–life, and establishing equitable, fair, and relevant policies across constituent groups that allow for great flexibility (and the ability for people to exercise agency) are needed to attempt to create a shared culture of equitable work–life. Examinations need to take into account the changing nature of work–life and how the cultural shifts and intersectional identities will impact individual perceptions of work–life needs and cultural values. This will include more uniformity and consistency across policies for faculty and staff and more collaboration between human resources and Provost offices to establish goals, benchmarks, and outcomes to consistently assess locations of inequity, such as a lack of use across a group or within a local academic unit.

PROFESSIONAL DEVELOPMENT FOR THE EQUITY-LITERATE LEADER

The evaluation of work–life balance will help to reveal and create knowledge and skills to recognize bias in work–life and across organizational culture, particularly inequities that are perpetuated in interpersonal dynamics, social norms, and cultural practices. Higher education administrators, and arguably all individuals in colleges and universities, need to consider engaging in their own professional development in equity-minded leadership, including understanding microaggressions, implicit bias, and other forms of racism and sexism on campus. College campuses, particularly student affairs and human resources, are awash with programs for staff and students to support our diverse environments; yet there are few campus-based or national leadership programs that provide the same level of education for leaders. A few organizations, such as the College and University Professional Association for Human Resources (CUPA-HR) conduct webinars and workshops periodically on topics related to conflict management, recruiting a diverse workforce, and strategic decision making, but do not engage in academic or student affairs. As already noted, work–life is often experienced in the individual units, which requires professional development for academic and student affairs leaders and not just those in human resources positions. In addition, responding to bias among a leadership cabinet or with other direct reports requires some development of conflict resolution skills. All too often, these skills are learned on the job, which is difficult when it comes to sensitive topics around race and gender, pertinent to work–life issues.

ADVOCACY FOR WORK–LIFE

Higher education leaders need to advocate for equitable and consistent work–life policies to establish both an equitable perspective within campus leadership and to encourage use of these policies amongst faculty and staff. Many higher education administrators and leaders are focused on the needs across constituent groups and may not be knowledgeable or continuously mindful of how generalized thinking or even deficit perspectives shapes how they develop policy, programs, and communicate with direct reports. Campus administrators should consider beginning all conversations about policy and program development with simple questions such as: who does this policy benefit; who is left out; what policies are in place for other employment contracts on campus; what are the barriers to policy use; what socio-historical dynamics intersect with this issue; and does this work address those dynamics? Other important questions consider who provided input and what forms of evaluation are in place to identify effectiveness. These questions require continuous opportunities for discussion and knowledge about bias to accompany any policy or programming. Structurally, higher education administrators could infuse in annual evaluations discussion of individual work–life and how supervisors are supporting work–life in others.

CONCLUSION

The outcome of equity literate work is to embed work–life as a pervasive campus value, not simply a policy and set of programs. This is not to suggest that policies and programs are not important, but they cannot alone address the power dynamics and inequities that pervade our histories, current practices, and disciplinary norms. Work–life needs to be infused with equity concerns that acknowledge and address gender, race and ethnicity, and other identities. As Gorski (2016) suggests, work–life needs to be seen through an equity literate framework that accounts for how institutional and societal inequities become perpetuated within institutional culture. Work–life equity requires a basic acknowledgement of socio-historical family dynamics, expectations of work based on gender, race, and heteronormativity, hierarchy of employment contracts, and the very ways that work–life policies and programs perpetuate, not address, inequity. Campus administrators would benefit from establishing their own commitment, gaining a deep knowledge about the work–life issues and policies on campus, engaging in professional development to learn about equity on college campuses and to promote knowledge in their direct report and colleagues. Also important are considerations of integrated resources across colleges, departments, and provost's offices. They need to constantly ask the question: how do my administrative efforts address and seek to remedy inequities inside and outside my educational institution that are present in work–life assumptions, policies, and practices? And, what can I do to integrate these efforts more fully across the organization and its sub-units?

QUESTIONS FOR REFLECTION AND DISCUSSION

1. What areas of my administrative practice would benefit from equity literacy? Do I recognize inequities on a regular basis? Think about the last week—what inequities did you document?
2. How often do I consider my ability or capacity to respond to and redress an inequity? If I identify I lack capacity, how am I building capacity?
3. How have I built equity literacy into key areas of work—professional development, hiring, mentoring, policymaking?

NOTE

1 National surveys only include binary definitions of gender and have no measures for sexuality, limiting what can be reported.

REFERENCES

Acker, J. (1990). Hierarchies, jobs, bodies: A theory of gendered organizations. *Gender & Society*, 4(2), 139–158.

Acker, J. (1992). From sex roles to gendered institutions. *Contemporary Sociology*, 21(5), 565–569.

Adams, M., Bell, L. A., & Griffin, P. (Eds.). (2007). *Teaching for Diversity and Social Justice* (2nd ed.). New York: Routledge.

American Council on Education (ACE). (2014). *National Challenge for Higher Education: Executive Summaries*. Washington, DC: American Council on Education.

Armenti, C. (2004). May babies and post tenure babies: Maternal decisions of women professors. *The Review of Higher Education*, 27(2), 211–231.

Becher, T., & Trowler, P. (2001). *Academic Tribes and Territories: Intellectual Enquiry and the Culture of the Disciplines* (2nd ed). Buckingham, UK: Society for Research into Higher Education and Open University Press.

Bell, L. A., Love, B. J., Washington, S., & Weinstein, G. (2007). Knowing ourselves as social justice educators. In M. Adams, L. A. Bell, & P. Griffin (Eds.), *Teaching for Diversity and Social Justice* (2nd ed.) (pp. 381–393). New York: Routledge.

Bunton, S. A., & Corrice, A. M. (2011). Evolving workplace flexibility for US medical school tenure-track faculty. *Academic Medicine*, 86(4), 481–485.

Currie, J., & Eveline, J. (2011). E-technology and work/life balance for academics with young children. *Higher Education*, 62(4), 533–550.

Drago, R., Colbeck, C. L., Stauffer, K. D., Pirretti, A., Burkum, K., Fazioli, J.… Habasevich, J. (2006). The avoidance of bias against caregiving: The case of academic faculty. *American Behavioral Scientist*, 49, 1222–1247.

Family and Medical Leave Act of 1993 (2006). 29 U.S.C. §§ 2601–2654.

Gardner, S. K. (2013). Women faculty departures from a striving institution: Between a rock and a hard place. *The Review of Higher Education*, 36(3), 349–370.

Gorski, P. (2016). Rethinking the role of "culture" in educational equity: From cultural competence to equity literacy. *Multicultural Perspectives*, 18(4), 221–226.

Hill, C., Corbett, C., & St Rose, A. (2010). *Why So Few? Women in Science, Technology, Engineering, and Mathematics*. Washington, DC: American Association of University Women.

Jayakumar, U. M., Howard, T. C., Allen, W. R., & Han, J. C. (2009). Racial privilege in the professoriate: An exploration of campus climate, retention, and satisfaction. *The Journal of Higher Education*, 80(5), 538–563.

Kalliath, T., & Brough, P. (2008). Work–life balance: A review of the meaning of the balance construct. *Journal of Management & Organization, 14*(3), 323–327.

Keenan, M., & Greer, A. E. (2015). Sedentary behavior and related factors among full-time, university faculty. *International Journal of Workplace Health Management, 8*(3), 206–213.

Lester, J. (2008). Performing gender in the workplace: Gender socialization, power, and identity among women faculty members. *Community College Review, 35*(4), 277–305.

Lester, J. (2013). Work–life balance and cultural change: A narrative of eligibility. *Review of Higher Education, 36*(4), 463–488.

Lester, J. (2015). Cultures of work–life balance in higher education: A case of fragmentation. *Journal of Diversity in Higher Education, 8*(3), 139–156.

Lester, J., Sallee, M., & Hart, J. (2017). Beyond gendered universities? Implications for research on gender in organizations. *NASPA Journal About Women in Higher Education, 10*(1), 1–26.

Martin, J. (1994). The organization of exclusion: Institutionalization of sex inequality, gendered faculty jobs and gendered knowledge in organizational theory and research. *Organization, 1*(2), 401–431.

Mason, M. A. & Goulden, M. (2002). Do babies matter? The effect of family formation on the lifelong careers of academic men and women. *Academe, 88*(6), 21–27.

Mason, M.A., Goulden, M., & Wolfinger, N.H. (2006). Babies matter: Pushing the equity revolution forward. In S. J. Bracken, J. K. Allen, & D. R. Dean (Eds.), *The Balancing Act: Gendered Perspectives in Faculty Roles and Work Lives* (pp. 9–30). Sterling, VA: Stylus.

Monroe, K., Ozyurt, S., Wrigley, T., & Alexander, A. (2008). Gender equality in academia: Bad news from the trenches, and some possible solutions. *Perspectives on Politics, 6*(2), 215–233.

Mthethwa-Sommers, S. (2012). Pedagogical possibilities: Lessons from social justice educators. *Journal of Transformative Education, 10*(4), 219–235.

National Center for Education Statistics (2015). *Full-time faculty in degree-granting postsecondary institutions, by race/ethnicity, sex, and academic rank: Fall 2009, Fall 2011, and Fall 2013 [Table 315.20].* Washington, DC: US Department of Education.

National Center for Education Statistics (2018). *The condition of education 2018 (NCES 2018-144), Characteristics of Postsecondary Faculty.* Retrieved from: https://nces.ed.gov/fastfacts/display.asp?id=61

National Science Foundation, National Center for Science and Engineering Statistics (2015). *Women, Minorities, and Persons with Disabilities in Science and Engineering: 2015.* Special Report NSF 15–311. Arlington, VA. Available at www.nsf.gov/statistics/wmpd/.

Pribbenow, C. M., Sheridan, J., Winchell, J., Benting, D., Handelsman, J., & Carnes, M. (2010). The tenure process and extending the tenure clock: The experience of faculty at one university. *Higher Education Policy, 23,* 17–38.

O'Meara, K. A., & Campbell, C. (2011). Faculty sense of agency in decisions about work and family. *Review of Higher Education, 34,* 447–476.

Osei-Kofi, N., Shahjahan, R. A., & Patton, L. D. (2010). Centering social justice in the study of higher education: The challenges and possibilities for institutional change. *Equity & Excellence in Education, 43*(3), 326–340.

Quinn, K. (2010). Tenure clock extension policies: Who uses them and to what effect? *NASPA Journal about Women in Higher Education, 3*(1), 182–206.

Sallee, M. W. (2012). The ideal worker or the ideal father: Organizational structures and culture in the gendered university. *Research in Higher Education, 53*(7), 782–802.

Sallee, M. W. (2014). *Faculty Fathers: Toward a New Ideal in The Research University.* Albany, NY: State University of New York Press.

Trower, C. A. (2010). A new generation of faculty: Similar core values in a different world. *Peer Review, 12*(3), 27–30.

Ward, K., & Wolf-Wendel, L. (2004). Academic motherhood: Managing complex roles in research universities. *The Review of Higher Education, 27*(2), 233–257.

Ward, K., & Wolf-Wendel, L. (2012). *Academic Motherhood: How Faculty Manage Work and Family.* New Brunswick, NJ: Rutgers University Press.

Williams, J. C., Alon, T., & Bornstein, S. (2006). Beyond the "chilly climate": Eliminating bias against women. *Thought & Action*, 79–96.

Wolf-Wendel, L. E., & Ward, K. (2006). Academic life and motherhood: Variations by institutional type. *Higher Education*, 52(3), 487–521.

Wolf-Wendel, L., & Ward, K. (2015). Academic mothers: Exploring disciplinary perspectives. *Innovative Higher Education*, 40(1), 19–35.

15

WORDS MATTER

Social Justice and Policy Discourses in Higher Education

MAGDALENA MARTINEZ AND DEANNA COOPER

The issues presented in this book underscore social justice and equity implications higher education has for individuals and society as a whole. Consider, for instance, research has suggested postsecondary education is a strong predictor of future opportunities, awarding higher earnings to those with degrees than those without (Carnevale, Rose, & Cheah, 2013). Likewise, graduates tend to live longer, are more apt to engage in their communities and politics, are less likely to commit crime, and tend to be less racist or sexist (Brennan & Naidoo, 2008). We propose that the policy discourses adopted by higher education administrators extend well beyond the institutional environment and are central to creating an equitable and just society.

Higher education leaders interface with a myriad of stakeholders, including policymakers. Whether as part of formal governing structures or legislative testimony on higher education issues, postsecondary administrators—in formal or informal institutional leadership roles—are frequently called upon to provide and speak about metrics, data, or context on critical higher education policy problems. The language that leaders use to frame problems and solutions matters. Language represents more than a mode of communication and is never neutral (Gee, 1999). Through language, "social goals are created, sustained, and distributed… people are harmed and helped" (Gee, 1999, p. 2). Word choices are seldom random. Cameron (2001) argues that language is based on ideological patterns and word choices serve particular interests. Take, for instance, word choices used to describe students' immigration status either as illegal aliens or undocumented which often frames how policy problems are defined and which solutions are pursued. Fischer and Gottweis (2012) assert that words and language, when combined with power, are important data for understanding policy problems, solutions, and analysis. We agree and draw on postmodern paradigms in this chapter to consider the critical role discourse plays in shaping higher education policy problems and solutions. According to postmodernists, "the world is made by, rather than mirrored in, language" (Hatch & Cunliffe, 2013, p. 13). Simply stated, language and discourses shape the world we live in. Hatch and Cunliffe (2013) stress that "power and communication are central phenomena within postmodernism because anyone who controls discourse can make something exist, or disappear" (p. 13). Moreover, since word meanings are negotiable not fixed, they can be manipulated to maintain and dismantle power and status (Bess & Dee, 2008). Given a world of higher education policy where discourses of efficiency, economics, competition and pursuits of prestige and excellence dominate, a postmodern paradigm provides higher education administrators a "revolutionary" leadership approach to espouse for just and equitable policies in their daily practices.

In this chapter, we seek to start a dialogue aimed at answering the following questions: How can higher education administrators, who espouse for just and equitable policies either internal or external to the institution, consider discourse analytic frameworks when interfacing with policymakers and other critical stakeholders? Additionally, what leadership practices can administrators adopt that align with their social justice beliefs? First, we provide a brief overview of our social justice framework. Then, we illustrate the ways in which language and discourse have shaped critical higher education policy. In the third section we argue how leaders need to be conscious of their language and its implications to ensure equity. Finally, we review how administrators need to rethink their view of leadership and offer several recommendations they may use to align their leadership practices with their social justice beliefs.

SOCIAL JUSTICE: A MULTIDIMENSIONAL LENS

Simply stated, social justice is the promotion of a just society by challenging oppression, and equity is the fair treatment of all individuals (free from bias and favoritism) in ways that produce equitable outcomes. We acknowledge the concept of social justice in the context of higher education is as complex as the "university" itself. Grounded in religion, philosophy, ethics, law, and politics, the meanings and uses of social justice are at times uniquely stretched, depending on how policy problems and solutions are designed and prioritized (Singh, 2011). Ultimately, we subscribe to scholars like Rawls (1999), Young (1990), and Gewirtz (1998) who together offer a multidimensional lens through which to understand social justice and equity. We agree with Rawls' (1999) conception of social justice as fairness, in which emphasis is placed on distributive justice and includes concerns about the distribution of material goods and non-material goods, such as cultural resources and social capital (Gewirtz, 2006). Justice depends on the promotion of equality of access to liberties, rights, and opportunities, which may necessitate the distribution of additional resources to individuals who are disadvantaged in order to achieve equitable outcomes (Rawls, 1999). However, as Patton, Shahjahan, and Osei-Kofi (2010) emphasize, higher education administrators and policymakers must be careful not to limit their view of social justice by focusing solely on distribution issues (e.g. numerical representation of minoritized populations across faculty, students, and administrators, college access, and curricula); otherwise, they may neglect to address the structures, processes, and institutional contexts that create these allocation issues in the first place.

Both Young (1990) and Gewirtz (1998) move beyond the distributive dimension and envision social justice more broadly by accounting for social structures and relationships. Young (1990) describes the five sides of oppression (i.e. marginalization, exploitation, powerlessness, violence, and culture imperialism) and suggests that oppression illuminates structural issues that act on social justice, such as decision making, divisions of labor, and culture. Similarly, Gewirtz (1998) defines a relational dimension of social justice as "the nature of relationships which shape society... [it is about] the practices and procedures which govern the organization of political systems, economic and social institutions, families and one-to-one social relationships" (pp. 470–471). She suggests that this dimension raises issues of power, privilege, and how people treat each other at the micro (individual) and macro (institutional) levels.

Being equitable and socially just within higher education means administrators are mindful of being fair when allocating resources, that they consider who benefits from their decisions, and that they respond to sources of bias and favoritism. Additionally, when called upon to provide and speak about metrics, data, or context on critical higher education policy problems, administrators thoughtfully consider how their language may frame policy problems and shape equitable and socially just policy solutions.

EFFICIENCY, ECONOMICS, AND EQUITY: TENSIONS IN HIGHER EDUCATION POLICY DISCOURSES

In the world of higher education policy, incongruities often emerge as various stakeholders, such as federal and state policymakers and institutional actors reinterpret and re-norm concepts of social justice and equity to meet the needs of dominant political and policy agendas (Singh, 2011). Today, discourses of efficiency and accountability, at the federal, state, and local levels, have largely overshadowed language aimed at social justice and equity considerations (Rivzi & Lingard, 2010). We briefly illustrate how dominant discourses on efficiency and accountability have steered policies and overshadowed social justice and equity goals.

Declining state appropriations, combined with increasing costs of higher education, have shifted the burden of financing college from the public to students and their families. This cost shifting has made the expense of college the dominant societal concern rather than access or quality of education (Humphreys, 2012). Public scrutiny over rising tuition costs has increased policy actors' and decision-makers' demand for greater efficiency and accountability. Consequently, higher education discourse has morphed from concerns of college access to student success to degree completion (O'Banion, 2010). For instance, the "completion agenda movement," which has sought "to collect more and better data about students' educational progress toward degrees, to enact new policies that incentivize increased graduation rates and improve the efficiency of degree production, and to tie funding to increased completion rates" (Humphreys, 2012, para.1) was designed by federal and state policymakers to address the call for greater efficiency and accountability from higher education institutions. As O'Banion (2010) suggests, major movements, especially those deemed urgent imperatives, usually have unintended consequences. Research has suggested the completion agenda may sacrifice college access for low-income, minority, and other at-risk students in order "to gain improvements in graduation rates without achieving meaningful increases in the number of students graduating from college" (Kantrowitz, 2012, p. 1). Pressures to increase graduation rates may cause some colleges to selectively admit students, and a simple way to increase graduation rates is to exclude high-risk students (Kantrowitz, 2012). To be sure, in a growing body of literature scholars examine how higher education rhetoric has shifted from language of colleges and universities as societal institutions for the public good, to postsecondary institutions in service of the capitalist enterprise (Bok, 2009; Deem, 2001; Giroux, 2002; Suspitsyna, 2012). Accordingly, policy discourse and priorities have focused on higher education as a commodity and a private good, with social justice priorities taking a backseat. In a poignant example, we need only consider the performance-based funding movement that has swept the nation.

Over the past decade, 21 states have implemented a performance-based funding model by tying institutional funding to completion rates rather than enrollment numbers (Hillman & Corral, 2017). This approach to funding higher education, which is intended to incentivize institutions to graduate more of the students they admit, has had mixed results. Although a two-year analysis of three states' (Indiana, Tennessee, Ohio) performance-based funding formula for public colleges provided evidence that outcomes-based funding has a positive effect on "a range of both interim and long-term outcomes for full-time students" (para. 5) in Indiana and Tennessee, on the negative side the study reported "performance-based funding effects were weaker or negative for part-time students in Indiana and Tennessee, and for disadvantaged students" (Fain, 2017, para 7). Similarly, another study found that on average, minority-serving institutions (MSIs) in states that adopted performance-based funding models lost significant funding per student when compared to MSIs in states that did not employ models of performance-based funding and non-MSIs in the same performance-based states (Hillman & Corral, 2017). Hillman and Corral suggest that with fewer state resources, MSIs could respond "by decreasing their faculty-to-student ratio, curtailing student and academic supports services, or by increasing tuition" (p. 1759). Further, they suggest that "each of these responses would make it more difficult for MSIs to improve retention and degree completion, which in turn would result in additional funding cuts in future years. If left uncorrected, pay-for-performance regimes are likely to generate the unintended consequence of worsening—rather than reversing—educational inequality" (Hillman & Corral, 2017, p. 1759). Once again, rhetoric situated in accountability and purported to improve student success left mainly low-income and institutions that serve them with fewer financial resources.

Just as discourses about demands for greater efficiency and accountability of postsecondary institutions have overshadowed social justice issues, dialogues of economic competitiveness imperatives and shortages of an educated workforce have seemingly eclipsed goals relating to fair access and equity in higher education (Singh, 2011). Higher education has experienced significant external pressure to increase the number of college graduates to meet global economic requirements (Humphreys, 2012). Carnevale and Rose (2014) suggest that "the United States (U.S.) is losing ground in postsecondary education relative to our competitors...increasing our supply of skilled labor is central to the vitality of the U.S. economy" (p. 13). Social efficiency, or the need to prepare individuals to fulfill necessary economic roles within society, has historically been at odds with other higher education goals, such as social mobility and democratic equality, both of which emphasize equity and social justice for individuals and society, respectively (Labaree, 1997). The argument has centered on whether or not higher education is a public good funded by the taxpayer and meant to serve employers and society, or a private good paid for by students and meant to improve their lifestyle and well-being (Labaree, 1997). To be sure, the call to increase an educated workforce has further inspired the completion agenda movement and revealed its unintended consequences.

WORDS MATTER: IMPLICATIONS OF POLICY VOCABULARIES

In the world of policymaking and politics, language is essential to defining policy problems and solutions. Dynamic storylines often drive policy deliberations and provide a window to understanding how policy problems and solutions are defined by individuals, coalitions, and decision-makers (Hajer, 1995, 2006). Problem definitions specifically are meant to explain, describe, recommend, and, above all, persuade (Rochefort & Cobb, 1994). Thus, use of language in framing problems may influence whether and how issues are acted upon (Rochefort & Cobb, 1994). Policy vocabularies consciously developed by policymakers to structure particular policies represent the dominant discourses (Hajer, 2003). Hajer (1995) has suggested dominant discourses provide policymakers with positions that define their social and power relationships in terms of acceptable narratives (as cited in Fischer, 2003). Once written into policy documents, policy vocabularies structure the implementation activities of policymakers by determining what can be considered as legitimate solutions (Carpenter & Diem, 2015).

As policy actors, higher education administrators are often requested to assemble, analyze, synthesize, and present data to help define policy problems and alternatives. According to Hajer (1995), speakers must situate their remarks in the recognized discourses in use at that time to be understood and considered relevant (as cited in Fischer, 2003). The challenge for higher education administrators is that they must be conscious of their policy vocabulary and its implications to their institutions' equity and social justice priorities. Their language may create categories, draw boundaries, and reproduce or reconstruct reality (Hatch & Cunliffe, 2013). To be sure, their language carries meaning and is "open to interpretation by legislatures, implementers, clients or policy 'targets', concerned publics or other stakeholders" (Yanow, 2000, p. 17). Ultimately, the metanarratives and storylines promoted by higher education administrators, can serve to position policy problems and solutions, draw clear distinctions between competing narratives, and sanction who is in and who is out and what arguments are valid or invalid (Hendriks, 2005). Thus, the language of administrators can serve to legitimize or delegitimize equitable and just policies within higher education. Language itself, however, is insufficient to create equitable policies. Leadership matters. In the final section of this chapter, we argue higher education administrators need to rethink their view of leadership, and we offer several recommendations they may use to align their leadership practices with their social justice beliefs.

LEADERSHIP MATTERS: MINDFULNESS ABOUT LANGUAGE IN ENACTING JUST AND EQUITABLE POLICIES

Kezar, Carducci, and Contreras-McGavin (2006) suggest the conceptualization of leadership in academic research and practice has revolutionized by "moving away from static, highly structured, and value-neutral leadership frameworks [to] dynamic, globalized, and processed-oriented perspectives of leadership that emphasize cross-cultural understanding, collaboration, and social responsibility for others" (p. 2). We believe this revolution continues today as the world becomes increasingly globalized and interconnected. A postmodern perspective on higher education highlights this leadership revolution and illuminates how administrators can be mindful of their language and actions as they embrace issues of social justice and equity.

Delanty (2001) and Hirschhorn (1997) suggest organizational leaders in a postmodern environment should: (1) take nothing for granted; (2) engage in deconstruction; (3) determine who benefits from particular ways of thinking about the organization; (4) give voice to traditionally silenced groups; and (5) embrace paradox (as cited in Bess & Dee, 2008). In this section, we individually address these five recommendations. To illustrate, we highlight Iverson's (2007) study of university diversity plans. Iverson examined 21 university diversity plans, often a formal means to advance and shape policy that affects underrepresented population. Rather than create a climate of inclusivity, Iverson found institutional leaders perpetuated, through diversity plans, biased views and reinforced practices that excluded populations the plans sought to serve. Iverson argues that the language included in the plans constructed images of people of color as "outsiders to the institution, at risk before and during participation in education, and dependent on the university for success in higher education" (p. 586). She concludes that well-intentioned institutional attempts to create inclusive campus cultures and practices "unwittingly reinforce practices that support exclusion and inequity" (p. 586). Iverson's findings are used as a starting point to illustrate how higher education leaders can incorporate Delanty and Hirschhorn's recommendations as they seek to enact just and equitable policies. Finally, we conclude this section by offering an additional suggestion from St. John (2009) that calls for the integration of moral reasoning into professional development and organizational intervention as a way to align leadership practices with social justice beliefs.

Take Nothing for Granted

In a postmodernist environment where multiple realities exist, uncertainty and chaos flourish, and change is inevitable, taking nothing for granted means higher education administrators are careful to avoid making assumptions. Organizational context, institutional culture, and societal influences are some factors worthy of their consideration during decision making (Kezar et al., 2006). For instance, as leaders seek to articulate their institution's commitment to diversity issues, they should be mindful of who is at the table and whose views are included or excluded on diversity framing and identifying institutional interventions (Iverson, 2007). Increasingly, postsecondary institutions are engaged in their local regions, appropriately local organizations and leaders can be included as key stakeholders to help frame diversity priorities.

Leaders Should Engage in Deconstruction

Engaging in deconstruction necessitates questioning assumptions and values. According to Hatch and Cunliffe (2013), "deconstruction is a way of reading and then rereading texts in the contexts of different discourses in order to expose their potential for multiple interpretations and thereby destabilize and undermine their authority to indicate or make particular meaning" (p. 44). They posited, "the purpose in deconstructing a text lies not in finding ultimate or essential meaning, but is to reveal a text's assumptions, contradictions, and exclusions in order to show that no text can mean what it says" (p. 44). For example, the word *diversity* can mean different things to different people, especially in terms of how diversity is defined and practiced. Through the process of deconstruction, administrators, collectively with various stakeholders, can identify the values and assumptions that underlie how diversity is used in the context of institutional diversity planning. For instance, in her study, Iverson (2007) found the embedded assumptions of university diversity plans were that students of color were outsiders, deficient, and in need of interventions to "fit" into the campus environment and culture. This discourse of disadvantage further constructed images of people of color as at-risk victims in need of rescuing. Similarly, as we discussed earlier, social justice is multidimensional, and at times its meanings are uniquely stretched, depending on how policy problems and solutions are designed and prioritized (Singh, 2011). By engaging in deconstruction, administrators can free themselves from the influence that a constructed reality may have on their thoughts and actions (Hatch & Cunliffe, 2013). Then, when called upon to provide their expertise, they can be more conscious of their choice of policy vocabulary, which may shape how policy problems and solutions are addressed.

Determine Who Benefits from Particular Ways of Thinking About the Organization

Martin (1992) suggests determining who benefits can also be a criterion in the process of deconstruction (as cited in Bess & Dee, 2008). Take, for example, diversity planning documents used to guide long-term activities and resource allocation of academic institutions. A postmodern lens demands administrators question: who participates in the planning process; how different voices can inform strategy development; and whose interpretation of the environment guides decision making (Bess & Dee, 2008). The concern is that such documents largely mirror the values that privilege upper management and reproduce conditions that favor the status quo, especially if stakeholders are excluded from the development process (Bess & Dee, 2008; Iverson, 2007). Similarly, mission statements communicate to a wide variety of internal and external constituents and provide institutions an opportunity "to lay claim to important terrain," (p. 459) such as being a designated MSI or Historically Black Colleges and Universities (Morphew & Hartley, 2006). Mission statements often signal organizational values and serve to, normatively and politically, legitimize institutional roles (Morphew & Hartley, 2006). Consequently, thoughtful consideration about who participates in the policy development process is essential to enable proper messaging to both internal and external constituents.

Give Voice to Traditionally Silenced Groups

This recommendation complements the third charge—"determine who benefits from particular ways of thinking." By providing space and voice to underrepresented groups, higher education leaders can avoid marginalizing their issues and empower them to become change agents (Bess & Dee, 2008). Giving voice to traditionally silenced groups also speaks to the concept of organizational diversity. Applying a postmodern lens, administrators should seek to highlight people's differences (e.g. race gender, sexual orientation, ethnicity) rather than kludging them all together. In doing so, individual and group differences can strengthen institutions by making them more creative and innovative (Bess & Dee, 2008). Iverson (2007) illustrates how the majority of diversity plans she examined contextualized the need for diversity plans based on efforts by governing board members or US Supreme Court landmark decisions (i.e. 2003 affirmative action) but seldom legitimized the local activism on the part of students, faculty or local communities who led efforts to expand equity-minded policies. To amplify the voices of traditionally excluded voices in the planning process, Iverson suggests diversity plans be co-authored through the use of counter-storytelling in order to incorporate and legitimize multiple stories and not just the dominant, institutional version and experiences. Iverson goes on to suggest that "the counter stories, uncovered by practitioners, also can be used to facilitate cross-difference dialogue" (p. 605). To be sure, diverse perspectives promote inclusiveness and better inform how policy problems and solutions are framed.

Embrace Paradox

Decision making in higher education can be paradoxical, or contradictory, in nature, challenging organizational leadership. Administrators may face a myriad of issues as they seek to meet public demands for efficiency, while maintaining their effectiveness, and as they strive to balance issues of equity, with aspirations for excellence and prestige. As Tierney (1992) emphasizes, "the dichotomous nature of higher education is evident on any number of fronts. We are called on to make painful budget cuts and increase services to diverse constituents. We want to lessen hateful speech on campus yet maintain academic freedom. We desire improvements in classroom teaching but find that our reward structure favors research" (2nd para.). We contend that administrators can learn to lead within the context of paradox, and that language can be a valuable tool in this effort. One approach is to move from either/ or binary categories to frameworks that accommodate both/and schemas (Bess & Dee, 2008). This suggests, for example, minority-serving institutions can serve their local communities through access and inclusive excellence while at the same time pursue prestige through greater research productivity and increased graduation rates. In fact, there is growing evidence that minority-serving institutions need not reject their MSI identity in order to achieve national recognition (Martinez, Cooper, & Henkle, 2018). Rhetoric on access and research productivity, when articulated by institutional leaders as complementary priorities, can expand support for institutions and create a greater sense of ownership and institutional commitment by traditionally excluded policy stakeholders and communities. Such an approach embraces the postmodern paradigm, which according to Baxter and Montgomery (1996) "seeks to preserve the interdependent relationships between oppositions" (as cited in Bess & Dee, 2008, p. 76). Rather than seeking to eliminate or resolve contradictions in favor of one side or the other like a positivism paradigm might suggest, administrators need to appreciate and learn to lead within the context of paradox given the dichotomous nature of higher education (Bess & Dee, 2008). These recommendations are a first step in moving toward more just and equitable policies. We suggest that purposeful leadership practice coupled with intentional policy discourse shapes how, when, and where socially just policies are pursued. Higher education administrators are often in privileged positions that are accompanied by power—whether formal or informal, resources, and the ability to influence colleagues and policymakers' understanding of higher education issues.

Integrate Moral Reasoning into Professional Development

In *Action, Reflection, and Social Justice,* Edward St. John (2009), offers a complementary lens for administrators and educators to consider as they have sought to advance and espouse just and equitable policies that align with their social justice beliefs. St. John's approach has called for an integration of moral reasoning into professional development and organizational intervention. He has suggested professional development should include development of a person's skills and knowledge along with one's values and moral reasoning. According to St. John, moral reasoning has been an essential part of professional action, and therefore, it should be integrated into professional education. Faculty should "create learning environments in which values can be openly discussed as part of the pedagogy of professional practice" (p. 2) rather than avoid questions of value (St. John, 2009). To be sure, he asserts that professional development is ultimately the responsibility of the individual professional over the course of one's career, yet he acknowledges that an organization's strategic interests may subvert this aim. Consequently, "professionals must keep an inner eye on their own moral and professional development and not abdicate this responsibility" (St. John, 2009, p. 224).

Similar to the leadership recommendations offered in Bess and Dee (2008), St. John has proposed key lessons for professionals, seeking to integrate moral reasoning into their development and actions. One lesson in particular suggests, "one's own value traditions—whether based on faith, justice, or both traditions—can be enhanced in communities of practice that also appreciate diverse value traditions" (p. 225). While it is essential for administrators and educators to hold values and act on them, it is also necessary for these individuals to address issues that arise in settings with people who possess different values (St. John, 2009). Because administrators are often in a position to lead groups or professionals, we agree with St. John that reflection on one's own values should be interrogated in order to "take nothing for granted" including our own biases and unchallenged assumptions about equity. Similarly, teaching professionals are often in positions to shape the development of students, colleagues, and other professionals who look up to them. By employing communities of practice that appreciate different value traditions, administrators and educators can broaden their ability to understand the moral aspects of a problem (St. John, 2009). Additionally, diverse perspectives can inform practice and policy well before solutions are designed (St. John, 2009).

Delanty (2001) and Hirschhorn (1997) have offered a framework for organizational leadership, recommending several ways administrators can be more mindful about their language and practices through the application of critical questions when planning, allocating, and interacting with multiple groups. Similarly, St. John has focused on moral reasoning and individual leadership, urging teaching professionals to create spaces of dialogue where values can be openly discussed and understood. This reflective practice, comparable to the approach of Delanty and Hirschhorn, holds the potential to move higher education as a community closer to understanding how the language we use can help or hinder our ability to achieve a more socially just society.

CONCLUSION

In this chapter we discuss the ways in which discourses on efficiency and economics have steered higher education policy and subsequent resources. We argue that socially just and equitable policies have been abandoned at a time when higher education institutions are seeking to serve a growing and more diverse population. The implications will be vast and long term, yet we believe higher education leaders are in positions to rearticulate the value and necessity of socially just policies that can benefit all. Doing so will require administrators' awareness and understanding that their words and leadership matters. We have outlined the multiple ways in which administrators can use language to reimagine and practice an inclusive leadership approach. A greater focus on higher education leaders' language (and their embedded assumptions) is an unexplored window to understanding how institutional issues of equity and justice (or inequity and oppressive practices) are framed (or perpetuated). Leaders' framing of problems inevitably influence the solutions they seek. Attention to language practices alone, however, is insufficient to bring about meaningful change. Mindfulness to leadership practices, we argue, is necessary to pursue a multidimensional approach to social justice and equity in higher education. As the social, political, and economic landscape of the United States changes and evolves, higher education leaders will also shape the future of (arguably) one of the country's most valuable resources—postsecondary institutions. The language used to shape higher education problems and solutions and how social justice leadership is practiced matters more than ever.

QUESTIONS FOR REFLECTION AND DISCUSSION

1. Why do language and discourse practices matter in a higher education policy context? What does equitable language look like? What does inequitable language look like? Think of examples you have encountered recently of each type.

2. How can higher education administrators consider discourse analytic frameworks when interfacing with policymakers and other critical stakeholders?

3. What leadership practices can administrators adopt that align with their social justice beliefs? For example, how might you engage in the process of deconstruction? Think about a particular policy or practice on campus—who benefits more from this policy or practice? Practice using several of the social justice leadership practices in this chapter.

REFERENCES

Baxter, L., & Montgomery, B. (1996). *Relating: Dialogues and Dialectics*. New York: Guilford Press.

Bess, J. L., & Dee, J. R. (2008). *Understanding college and university organization theories for effective policy and practice. Volumes I, the state of the system, and Volume II, dynamics of the system*. Sterling, VA: Stylus.

Bok, D. (2009). *Universities in The Marketplace: The Commercialization of Higher Education* (Vol. 39). Princeton, NJ: Princeton University Press.

Brennan, J., & Naidoo, R. (2008). Higher education and the achievement (and/or prevention) of equity and social justice. *Higher Education, 56*(3), 287–302.

Cameron, D. (2001). *Working with Spoken Discourse*. London: Sage.

Carnevale, A. P., & Rose, S. J. (2014). *The undereducated American*. Retrieved from https://vtechworks.lib.vt.edu/handle/10919/83052

Carnevale, A. P., Rose, S. J., & Cheah, B. (2013). *The college payoff: Education, occupations, lifetime earnings*. Retrieved from https://repository.library.georgetown.edu/bitstream/handle/10822/559300/collegepayoff-complete.pdf?sequence=1&isAllowed=y

Carpenter, B. W., & Diem, S. (2015). Guidance matters: A critical discourse analysis of the race-related policy vocabularies shaping leadership preparation. *Urban Education, 50*(5), 515–534.

Deem, R. (2001). Globalisation, new managerialism, academic capitalism and entrepreneurialism in universities: Is the local dimension still important? *Comparative Education, 37*(1), 7–20.

Delanty, G. (2001). The university in the knowledge society. *Organization, 8*(2), 149–153.

Fain, P. (2017, July 21). Study on performance-based funding in three states. *Inside Higher Education*. Retrieved from www.insidehighered.com/quicktakes/2017/07/21/study-performance-based-funding-3-states

Fischer, F. (2003). *Reframing Public Policy: Discursive Politics and Deliberative Practices*. Oxford and New York: Oxford University Press.

Fischer, F., & Gottweis, H. (Eds.) (2012). *The Argumentative Turn Revisited: Public Policy as Communicative Practice*. Durham, NC: Duke University Press.

Gee, J. P. (1999). *An Introduction to Discourse Analysis: Theory and Practice*. London and New York: Routledge.

Gewirtz, S. (1998). Conceptualising social justice in education: Mapping the territory. *Journal of Education Policy, 13*(4), 469–484. doi:10.1080/0268093980130402

Gewirtz, S. (2006). Towards a contextualized analysis of social justice in education. *Educational Philosophy and Theory, 38*(1), 69–81.

Giroux, H. (2002). Neoliberalism, corporate culture, and the promise of higher education: The university as a democratic public sphere. *Harvard Educational Review, 72*(4), 425–464.

Hajer, M. A. (1995). *The Politics of Environmental Discourse: Ecological Modernization and the Policy Process*. Oxford: Clarendon Press.

Hajer, M. A. (2003). A frame in the fields: Policymaking and the reinvention of politics. In M. A. Hajer, & H. Wagenaar (Eds.), *Deliberative Policy Analysis: Understanding Governance in the Network Society* (pp. 88–112). Cambridge: Cambridge University Press.

Hajer, M. A. (2006). Doing discourse analysis: Coalitions, practices, meaning. In M. van den Brink, & T. Metze (Eds.), *Words Matter in Policy Planning* (pp. 65–74). Netherlands: Netherlands Geographical Studies.

Hatch, M. J., & Cunliffe, A. L. (2013). *Organization Theory: Modern, Symbolic, and Postmodern Perspectives.* Oxford: Oxford University Press.

Hendriks, C. M. (2005). Participatory storylines and their influence on deliberative forums. *Policy Sciences, 38*(1), 1–20.

Hillman, N., & Corral, D. (2017). The equity implications of paying for performance in higher education. *The American Behavioral Scientist, 61*(14), 1757–1772. doi:http://dx.doi.org/10.1177/0002764217744834

Hirschhorn, L. (1997). *Reworking Authority: Leading and Following in the Postmodern Organization.* Cambridge, MA: MIT Press.

Humphreys, D. (2012). What's wrong with the completion agenda—And what we can do about it. *Liberal Education, 98*(1), Retrieved from www.aacu.org/publications-research/periodicals/whats-wrong-completion-agenda%E2%80%94and-what-we-can-do-about-it

Iverson, S. V. (2007). Camouflaging power and privilege: A critical race analysis of university diversity policies. *Educational Administration Quarterly, 43*(5), 586–611.

Kantrowitz, M. (2012). *The college completion agenda may sacrifice college access for low-income, minority and other at-risk students.* Retrieved from www.finaid.org/ educators/20120910completionagenda.pdf

Kezar, A. J., Carducci, R., & Contreras-McGavin, M. (Eds). (2006). Rethinking the "L" word in higher education. *ASHE Higher Education Report, 31*(6), 1–218.

Labaree, D. F. (1997). Public goods, private goods: The American struggle over educational goals. *American Educational Research Journal, 34*(1), 39–81.

Martin, J. (1992). *Cultures in Organizations: Three Perspectives.* New York: Oxford University Press.

Martinez, M., Cooper, D., & Henkle, J. (2018, November). *Urban universities' pursuit of top tier: Policy actors balancing institutional identity, urban social justice priorities and economic development goals.* Presented at the 43rd Annual Association for the Study of Higher Education, Tampa, Florida.

Morphew, C. C., & Hartley, M. (2006). Mission statements: A thematic analysis of rhetoric across institutional type. *The Journal of Higher Education, 77*(3), 456–471. doi:10.1080/00221546.2006.11778934

O'Banion, T. (2010, August 16). To what end? *Inside Higher Ed.* Retrieved from www.insidehighered.com/ views/2010/08/16/what-end

Patton, L. D., Shahjahan, R. A., & Osei-Kofi, N. (2010). Introduction to the emergent approaches to diversity and social justice higher education special issue. *Equity and Excellence in Education, 43*(3), 265–278. doi:10.1080/10665684.2010.496692

Rawls, J. (1999). *A Theory of Justice* (Revised edition). Cambridge, MA: Harvard University Press.

Rivzi, F., & Lingard, B. (2010). *Globalizing Education Policy.* New York: Routledge.

Rochefort, D. A., & Cobb, R. W. (1994). *The Politics of Problem Definition: Shaping the Policy Agenda.* Lawrence, KS: University Press of Kansas.

Singh, M. (2011). The place of social justice in higher education and social change discourses. *Compare: A Journal of Comparative and International Education, 41*(4), 481–494. doi:10.1080/03057925.2011.581515

St. John, E. P. (2009). *Action, Reflection, and Social Justice: Integrating Moral Reasoning into Professional Development.* Cresskill, NJ: Hampton Press.

Suspitsyna, T. (2012). Higher education for economic advancement and engaged citizenship: An analysis of the US Department of Education discourse. *The Journal of Higher Education, 83*(1), 49–72.

Tierney, W. G. (1992). Cultural leadership and the search for community. *Liberal Education, 78*(5), 16–21.

Yanow, D. (2000). *Conducting Interpretive Policy Analysis.* Thousand Oaks, CA: Sage.

Young, I. M. (1990). *Justice and the Politics of Difference.* Princeton, NJ: Princeton Press.

16

PRACTITIONER REFLECTION

Equity-Minded Leadership Perspectives for Community Colleges

LUCA E. LEWIS

Over the course of my higher education career, I routinely hear from colleagues' difficult and painful challenges of navigating community college cultures and a palpable fear, reluctance, and resistance to addressing and advancing equity. While there is a strong collection of community colleges that are making great strides in closing equity gaps, the great majority fall short in helping employees develop the needed confidence, competence, and deeper understanding to advance equity for the betterment of students—many who begin a postsecondary journey at a community college. The purpose of this chapter is to share my own experiences about the inherent conflicts and dilemmas that arise in navigating equity-minded leadership in community college, while working within and throughout structures that systemically produce equity barriers and that continue to erode the ability to critique the very system that perpetuates oppression in the first place. The goal of this chapter is to begin a conversation about the paradigm shifts needed to close equity gaps in the community college setting, and which have implications for other institutions as well. This paradigmatic shift requires resisting entrenched neoliberalism assumptions and practices which reinforce systemic oppression toward social justice. Lastly, I provide recommendations for leaders to explore their own understanding of social justice education in a community college setting.

THE EQUITY LANDSCAPE IN HIGHER EDUCATION AND COMMUNITY COLLEGES

Postsecondary completion reform has increasingly taken the national education stage and leaders in community colleges are being asked to demonstrate that high-quality higher education experiences can be delivered to students for a timely and relevant postsecondary credential or degree at a price that doesn't catapult students into debt, especially for low-income students, students of color, and first-generation students. Notable national data and best practice experts such as the Gates Foundation, the Lumina Foundation, the Aspen Institute, the Institute for Higher Education Policy (IHEP), and the Community College Research Center (CCRC) convey chronic equity, access, and completion gaps of students seeking and/or earning a postsecondary degree in order to thrive in a twenty-first-century global economy. According to the Lumina Foundation (2017), there is an economic imperative to get more students graduating with meaningful credentials: to stay globally competitive, the United States will need 16.4 million more graduates by 2025 and community colleges play a critical role in this endeavor. Expediting the need for community college leaders to implement comprehensive postsecondary reform, a critical student debt crisis has occurred and peaked for the very first time at $1.521 trillion in the first quarter of 2018, according to the Federal Reserve (Board of Governors, 2018). Alarmingly, student readiness, access, cost, persistence, and graduation rates are prevailing systemic barriers which permeate the community college landscape and don't appear to be subsiding any time soon. And community colleges enroll the greatest number of students and, in particular, first-generation, low-income and racialized minority students.

Yet, are community colleges leaders rising to this challenge that they provide equitable experiences for students from diverse backgrounds? In some instances campus can demonstrate progress, including the Achieving the Dream Initiative, American Association of Community College's Guided Pathways Project, and the Gates Foundation's Frontier Set. Yet, there are many unanswered equity questions, specifically as it relates to how Engle (2016) defines "post-traditional" students who make up transfer and completion gaps from community colleges to four-year baccalaureate programs (part-time, low-income, first-generation, students of color, adult, transfer) and how they progress toward timely completion, if at all. According to the National Student Clearinghouse (2017), with over 5.6 million students who attend community college annually, community colleges have yet to actualize overall significant gains in completion and graduation rates with approximately 29% of those students completing an associate's degree within six years (Shapiro et al., 2017). To further illustrate national transfer landscape challenges, in a study conducted by Jenkins and Fink (2016), of 720,000 degree-seeking students who entered a community college in fall 2007, only about 100,000 (14%), transferred to a four-year college and earned a bachelor's degree within six years. Community Colleges face complex equity challenges and leaders play a crucial role as stewards of policy and direction in order to successfully address these challenges. Given their significant equity mission, it would seem natural that critical conversations to understand systemic barriers that prevent students from achieving a timely degree or credential at an affordable price point, would be central among campus leaders and national stakeholders. In some cases this is happening, but often community colleges are not invited to national dialogues about reform equity-minded leadership practices.

My leadership experience drives me to the conclusion that the neoliberal environment on community college campuses shapes the slow progress toward equity in higher education writ large and community colleges in particular. So my journey will be described in relationship to this neoliberal context and how it creates challenges and tensions in doing the work of equity-minded leadership. Museus and LePeau (2019) explicitly challenge higher education administrators and faculty to deconstruct neoliberal ideologies expressed through institutional values, socialization, and enforcement that are all too often superimposed on social justice education efforts. Those who advance neoliberal ideologies and practices are often rewarded with promotion, tenure, and accolades, and those who critique, resist, and challenge are often characterized as disruptive, negative, and/or "not a good fit" for the institution. Such neoliberal ideologies create deep conflict between social justice and equity values and how institutions position diversity, equity, and inclusion values in rhetoric, contrasted with how an institution actually operates. For example, community colleges are characterized as "open access" institutions but fall historically and chronically short in advancing equity through disproportionate lower representation of faculty and staff of color (Moreno, Smith, Clayton-Pederson, Parker, & Teraguci, 2006), closing equity gaps for systemically non-dominate students (National Student Clearinghouse, 2018), and increase overall completion and graduation rates (Juszkiewicz, 2017). Additionally, these systemic inequities are then leveraged and exploited within a context where funding models are predominately enrollment driven and community colleges are receiving disproportionately less state and federal funding than their four-year college and university counterparts to effectively organize, fund, and support a greater number of underrepresented students.

OPERATIONALIZING SOCIAL JUSTICE AND EQUITY-MINDED LEADERSHIP

Like the authors of this volume, I adopt an anti-deficit view of students and hold institutions responsible for addressing equity. Institutions and the people that work within them are collectively responsible for the systems of educational inequities they create and perpetuate, not students. The context in which students navigate these inequities are deeply rooted in historical racism, sexism, classism, homophobia and additional systems of oppression and are responsible for today's inequities. I agree with the definitions that Kezar and Posselt posed at the beginning of this book regarding social justice. As a leader, I have intensely struggled to probe deeper awareness with colleagues and direct reports and to demonstrate a need to be co-conscious of how institutional norms, practices, and cultures work to perpetuate inequities and how their own identities, power, and privilege shape and influence decision making that impacts diverse student populations. Further, the Annie E. Casey Foundation (2014) states, "to be achieved and sustained, equity needs to be thought of as a structural and systemic concept." Inequities are often created and re-produced in language, behavior, policies, and procedures. Consistent with the works of Witham, Malcom-Piqueux, Dowd, and Bensimon (2015) to define and operationalize equity in a postsecondary setting is to interrogate practices that produce inequities through disproportional representation of gender, race, and ethnic groups, and those of different socioeconomic status regarding entry, progression, completion throughout the higher education experience, and specifically within the community college setting. For example, national best practice research openly criticizes the production of equity gaps of the entry and onboarding of racially minoritized students through sorting with standardized placement testing and the remedial education experience. According to Kolodner, Rancino, and Quester (2017) in a study conducted in the California Community Colleges, "only 1 percent of African-American students and 2 percent of Latino students who enrolled in the lowest level of remedial math in 2014 made it through an entry-level college math class within two years (the amount of time it's supposed to take to earn a full associate's degree)." Racial bias in placement testing is historically well documented (Steele & Aronson, 1995; Jencks, 1998; Bailey, Jeong, & Cho, 2010, Duffy, Schott, Beaver, & Park, 2014; Kolodner et al., 2017). Research experts have traced the source of this inequity to the standardized placement, sequencing, and progression experience by which several studies directly challenge the validity and reliability of standardized placement tests and underscore the dire need to address this inequity from a leadership perspective. However, without the deeper context and understanding of how standardized tests have been used to historically sort out and exclude students of color, administrators may knowingly proceed with decisions that serve to reinforce racist and oppressive practices without fully interrogating them. Witham et al. further define and operationalize equity-mindedness:

> As we defined it here, being equity-minded involves taking stock of the contradictions between the ideas of democratic education and the social, institutional, and individual practices that contribute to persistent inequities in college outcomes among different racial and ethnic groups and socioeconomic classes. Equity-minded individuals are aware of the sociohistorical context of exclusionary practices and racism in higher education and the effect of power asymmetries on opportunities and outcomes for students of color and students of low socioeconomic status. Being equity minded thus

involves being conscious of the ways that higher education—through its practices, policies, expectations, and unspoken rules—places responsibility for student success on the very groups that have experienced marginalization, rather than on the individuals and institutions whose responsibility it is to remedy the marginalization.

CHALLENGES OF EQUITY-MINDED LEADERSHIP

A colleague and I were first-time attendees at the American Association for Community Colleges (AACC) Annual Convention in spring 2018. The conference was located in Dallas, Texas and composed predominately of community and technical college presidents and leaders from all over the country—the majority of which were observably white. We co-facilitated a workshop and engaged with college leaders who wanted to sharpen their leadership skills and identify equity challenges on their respective campuses. Participants explored current forms of bias and culturally restrictive thinking manifested in their roles as leaders, with the central aim of cultivating equity-minded dialogue and strategies for community college leadership teams. One of the stark observations was a collectively expressed affirmation from executive leaders to engage and disclose experiences in a safe space and to share ideas that typically would not be shared at their respective campuses—to be more candid and vulnerable, and to some degree, to share more of their authentic selves in a space that offered support and trust. During our facilitated session, we asked participants to describe an equity challenge they were facing on their campus as leaders. We also asked them to explore and articulate why it was an equity challenge and why they were getting stuck. Responses to the two questions affirmed their desire to share insights from a leadership perspective and subsequently served as a humble reminder of intense equity challenges and neoliberal resistance rhetoric leaders face—both real and perceived—on their respective campuses.

Leaders in this session described what they believed to be high-risk equity-minded leadership dilemmas. They struggled with a desire to publicly declare an equity-minded agenda and an expressed desire in their roles as leaders to prioritize and advance equity for students and employees while simultaneously needing to unravel neoliberal values operationalized within their own campus and community cultures and with their respective board of trustees. Community colleges model similar operational make-up as the four-year experience where the key elements of the neoliberal apparatus are deeply embedded into the culture, structure, and function of higher education life and are amplified because of the more direct connection of community college experience to business, industry, and boosting local and regional economies.

As a leader who has become more aware of the systems of power that create inequities, I experience difficult conversations with colleagues. Campus leaders guided by neoliberalism often discount, distort, or don't know contextual histories, particularly racism, sexism, discrimination, and slavery or genocide, and focus exclusively on the current issues that favor data and institutional research to contextualized arguments. When needing to speak context and history into existence, these dilemmas often place me on the outside of a team dynamic through discussion exchanges that typically result in receiving feedback that I am a "difficult leader to work with," that I'm "not a team player," or that I "present as supportive, but often disagree with the work that the College has done for years." Challenging the neoliberal status quo affects my career and relationships with colleagues. I am consistently bombarded with subtle (and sometimes not so subtle) messages of my insights and perspectives viewed as resistance and in contrast with my colleagues' own unique understanding of intercultural competence, all framed upon the foundation of neoliberalism operationalized through assumptions, values, and practices.

Moreover and throughout my process of learning, I have become acutely aware of how culturally restrictive thinking and unconscious bias are both explicitly and insidiously manifested through leadership. These biases also carry a profound influence in who gets to experience higher education, and how they get to experience the teaching and learning dynamic (Witham et al., 2015). My journey to critical consciousness has allowed me to embrace the pervasiveness of how power and bias toward privileged identities (most of which I own) are manifested and reproduced within and throughout a community college experience. For example, I routinely observe and directly challenge faculty and staff who publicly declare that students are ultimately responsible for their success or failure in navigating college-going culture. I take on these challenges by questioning and clarifying assumptions which help deconstruct neoliberal arguments that place the responsibility of student success or failure on the student. In turn, assumptions are further clarified by repositioning arguments toward an understanding of how institutional inequities may present barriers that prevent students from navigating college-going culture. Corrected assumptions are then coupled with data that support and ground the need for understanding and how language and position power impacts students' ability to successfully navigate the community college experience paralleled with how programs, services, and practices are performed and evaluated from a leadership perspective. And, while I experienced these challenges personally within my own work experiences, I have also found that leaders nationally express this same dilemma.

How do we then challenge neoliberal tenants to advance equitable practices throughout a community college experience? It begins with community college leaders questioning their daily assumptions and values, as well as re-examining policies and practices and approaches to decision making. Leaders must understand how their intersections of identities informed power, privilege, and decision making at the institutional and student levels. Leaders must deconstruct neoliberal missions and reposition community colleges to close equity gaps with clear and explicit goals, outcomes, and key performance indicators. As part of job duties, responsibilities, and performance, leaders must enter and sustain conversations with curiosity and openness to be self-reflexive, to be open to critical feedback about how individual and collective decision making may be producing inequities, and to be willing to change their attitudes and behaviors in order to drive systemic change. Leaders must more heavily utilize shared governance structures to activate the voices of students, faculty, and staff throughout the decision-making experience. Leaders must develop, implement and measure experiential learning opportunities (through co-curricular activities, internships, and/or service learning) to broaden and deepen the experiences and learning outcomes for liberal arts education. Part of the community college mission constellates toward serving as economic engines for business and industry; equally important is the grounding of the community college experience to liberal arts education and to core workplace competencies that employers are seeking. And my own journey shows ways that leaders can grow as equity-minded leaders and engage in resistance—increasingly over time as one feels more empowered and confident.

MY CHANGING IDENTITIES AND JOURNEY AS A COMMUNITY COLLEGE LEADER

Throughout my career, I have had the privilege to serve in various leadership roles, knowing that my intersections of identities profoundly shaped (and continue to shape) my leadership identity development—some of which has changed over time. My intersections played a significant role in understanding how power and privilege are operationalized in my own daily work. My leadership identity development is shaped and influenced by my intersections of identity, critically illuminating the importance of defining equity-minded leadership as a process, and not simply defined by the positions held throughout my career (Kezar, Avilez, Drivalas, & Wheaton, 2017). For instance, it's a unique experience growing up in a community, leaving, and then returning 20 years later as an adult and working as an executive leader at a community college—a place that I grew up not as Luca, but as Alicia. I did not fully transition from female to male until I was well into my 30s and the majority of my transition took place on the job, while working in a community college. I identify as a white, 42-year-old transgender male administrator in the field of higher education, and specifically in the community college sector. I grew up working middle class, identify as white upper middle class, and am highly educated. I am one of the very few members of my immediate and extended family with an advanced higher education degree. Throughout my journey, my white identity continues to be an advantage and played a significant role in navigating microaggressions and bias with far less struggle and far more success. A significant portion of my gender transition journey, while personally and professionally rigorous and challenging, went smoothly. The campus community was generally supportive, compassionate, and respectfully curious about my existence and experience. I know I would not have experienced that level of support and compassion had it not been for the president who at the time and through her leadership, made social justice a core operating principle for the college. Coupled with my education attainment, my leadership position (I was a college dean at the time), my whiteness, and the contextual landscape made my gender identity transition less challenging because of my racial privilege situated within and intersecting my gender identity. It should be noted that I experienced the process of gender identity transition as "passing into more privilege" and how I navigated this world—both personally and professionally. I now identify with "he, him, his" gendered pronouns, and people who did not know how I identified often assigned a cisgender schema to my personal experience.

I am frequently asked questions about my gender identity. People who ask typically come from a place of curiosity and compassion for me. People often ask me why disclose that I am trans and why not just pass as a cisgender man? I find it critical that LGBTQ people see trans people in positions of power and influence, knowing that representation of trans people in positions of power and influence is rare, given the morbid contextual landscape of trans people in the United States. According to a report from the Human Rights Campaign and Trans People of Color Coalition (2017), since January 2013 at least 102 transgender people have been victims of fatal violence. I identify publicly as trans because it allows people around me an opportunity and choice to disclose their intersections of identity and serves as a useful way to demonstrate curiosity, inquiry, and connection. Yet I am conscious of context and share my identities to the degree I perceive people feel comfortable.

The continuous shaping of my intersections of identity—particularly gender, age, and social class—becomes significantly more complicated to navigate as I advance throughout my career. This is due to a persistent set of institutional and community norms and expectations which perpetuate cisgender and systemically dominant cultural identities in my role as an executive leader coupled with covert and insidiously conveyed messages that my identities are unimportant next to leadership. For example, prior to the advocacy of a new campus building, local legislators were upset and outspoken with college leadership over the college's decision to install gender-neutral bathrooms for gender non-conforming, queer, and transgender students. Institutional concern and anxiety prompted several discussions among college leadership (including myself) to avoid any reference to gender-neutral bathrooms in order to ensure legislative advocacy for building funding. Ethical and moral dilemmas can create a chilling effect to advance equity for the betterment of students, faculty, and staff who desire to exercise a basic human right. This particular context was an especially challenging personal and professional dilemma for me given my identity as a trans man and feeling compelled to not share my identity and censor my equity perspectives as a leader in order to reduce transphobic anxieties with colleagues and legislators (however real or perceived) that could have impeded the funding of a campus building. The building was ultimately funded, and while the prevailing circumstances resulted in a decision to not disclose my gender identity in order to leverage my position power as a leader for the betterment of students, the consequences of feeling a sense of loss with my identity as a human being was the ultimate cost—perhaps the same prevailing impact that students feel in navigating oppression, and where they do not see or experience their intersections of identity reflected in the very higher education experience that is supposed to eradicate these types of oppressions and advance equity in the first place. As I have continued in my career, I have developed a stronger awareness of equity-minded leadership and have been able to deploy this understanding to help lead student success efforts.

For example, as the vice president for student services at my current institution, I led the student services division through significant changes in organizational structure and function to enhance the way employees do their work with students. To activate institutional transformation, I incorporated language necessitating stronger partnerships with faculty and the community for over 50 position descriptions, coupled with integrating nationally recognized social justice and equity-minded frameworks into job duties and responsibilities. The work was daunting and came with different forms of interpersonal and cultural avoidance, minimization, and resistance to implement these changes due in part to differing group interests and a perception that already scarce resources needed to be protected (Kezar, 2008). This dynamic required me to seek input from and work closely with shared governance structures to leverage data, demonstrate transparency, and mobilize employees—new and established—to do their best work on behalf of students. Employees then took responsibility for and were motivated to implement culturally responsive practices that were attentive to students' sense of belonging. Equity and social justice competencies are connected to work plan indicators, performance evaluations and goal development, and institutional practices to improve performance and communication college-wide. Through my journey, I have developed a set of perspectives and leadership lessons that can help other equity-minded leaders in their work.

EQUITY-MINDED LEADERSHIP STRATEGIES AND RECOMMENDATIONS

My journey has led me to believe that equity requires a systemic shift from bureaucratic interactions with students toward intentionally and systemically removing equity barriers that are embedded in institutional habits. Exploring and identifying equity-minded daily habits and practices are one of the hallmarks of Inclusive Excellence (Asumah and Nagel, 2014) and should be leveraged to deepen understanding of intercultural competence. The following recommendations provide critical groundwork to expand understanding of social justice education from a leadership perspective in a community college setting and what it means to lead with equity.

EXAMINE ASSUMPTIONS

Automatic assumptions and values stem deeply in knowing that people come with bodies of knowledge, strengths, and experiences that we know nothing about unless we take the time and begin to ask questions with humility, curiosity, and a willingness to learn. This applies to the framework that we engage to work with students and employees more meaningfully as well—that every student and employee is motivated, and every student and employee possesses multiple intersections of identities and strengths. It is up to us leaders to create a context for inclusive practices so that students and employees can execute their best work. For example, entry and onboarding experiences for new community college students are typically packed with proscriptive higher education jargon, checklists, and didactic lecture—far from creating a sense of belonging and inclusiveness for students who possess identities and strengths oriented toward an empowering college journey. Thoughtful and critical dialogue and discussion with leadership teams who are willing to challenge automatic assumptions of what students do and don't know will lead to reimagined, shared values and assumptions that affirm students' identities, strengths, and motivations, thereby creating outcomes aligned with these ideas. As a result of these comprehensive and systemic changes, leaders (and their teams) are then responsible for and motivated to implement culturally responsive practices that are attentive to students' sense of belonging by building an experience that reflects students' individual contexts, intersections of identities, strengths, and goals.

DEFINE AND OPERATIONALIZE EQUITY, DIVERSITY, AND INCLUSION

What does it means to lead with equity? What does it mean to be an equity-minded leader? Begin the process of identifying equity challenges in your role as a leader and define both why you feel it is an equity challenge and why you feel you are getting stuck. Such questions are a prelude to habit-forming behaviors that become deeply embedded into equity-minded leadership skill building. Additionally, it is critical that community colleges take the time to define diversity, equity, and inclusion (DEI). Oftentimes, the context and meaning of these words are used interchangeably, or an executive-level group or a diversity committee defines these terms without having larger campus conversations or shared and inclusive decision making about DEI definitions. Comprehensively defining DEI creates a baseline by which goals and outcomes can be measured, performance is tracked, and effectiveness is demonstrated. Likewise, operationalizing DEI begins with individual employees and requires introspection of our own power and privilege perpetuated through language, behaviors, policies, and practices—driven by institutional values. For example, while consulting for a community college to help create an equity strategic plan, students, faculty, and staff were given the opportunity to participate in a series of planning forums by which diversity, equity, and inclusion were collectively defined, and a DEI visioning activity anchored these definitions to future goals, outcomes, and indicators of success. This process resulted in institutional clarity, clearer roles and expectations, and a collective understanding of why social justice and equity work is important.

IDENTITY SHARING AND STORYTELLING MATTERS

In contexts where I don't feel that my visibility as a transgender person is compromised by my own personal safety, I am explicit about narrating my identities of whiteness, gender, age, and social class. I believe we get to a very personal and vulnerable space through storytelling and sharing lived experiences to deconstruct our own power and privilege in ways that form stronger, more sustainable connections and bonds, particularly from a leadership perspective, thereby creating an institutional context and value where storytelling matters are essential to shaping and influencing college-going culture and the postsecondary experience. For instance, in meetings where people are gathering for the first time, I may lead with a prompt that asks people to what extent they feel safe and comfortable in sharing how they identify. Creating space for people to share their own identities outside of their roles and/or positions on campus reveals more about a person and opens up dialogue toward understanding, curiosity, and connection.

PROVIDE DIRECT AND CLEAR FEEDBACK

Oftentimes I am holding what feels like competing realities in working closely with colleagues and people that I manage and lead. Scott (2016) describes dynamic challenges that leaders need to compassionately and relentlessly face and navigate with their teams. Every day, I am thinking about and acting upon ways that I can demonstrate full confidence to my team that they can and will practice equity-minded leadership and that they can do the work. This confidence is expressed through direct feedback citing specific examples as to where and why they are thriving to address inequities. And yet, because institutional structures are fundamentally designed to manifest and produce inequities, our work and performance will fall short or incomplete in centering an acute and intense focus on closing equity gaps for students. It is my job and moral duty as a leader to call them out compassionately and offer direct feedback on what needs to change, providing a setting in which this type of feedback is both in the moment when it is needed most and also during a performance evaluation period—project-based, semi-annual, annual, or otherwise. Employee performance evaluations should represent equity-minded reflection, affirmation and acknowledgement, process improvement, and goals setting. This is a time to work with employees to understanding their job duties, responsibilities, and their role in advancing equity in addition to providing the necessary training and professional development opportunities and experiences to get them to a higher level of competency and understanding by consistently assessing the way they do and contribute to equity work for students. Leaders are responsible for creating the conditions to harvest the best ideas and strategies in order to advance equity and to create direct performance and communication feedback loops to track and assess effectiveness and change.

Community colleges within the postsecondary reform context require an expression of courage in ways that we've never had to do before. Our current context requires us to get closer, to learn, and to carefully listen to people whom we don't understand—people who are racist, sexist, homophobic, transphobic, xenophobic—people who, through social construction, neoliberal rhetoric, hate rhetoric, and conditioning, have hardened their hearts and minds. Our current context requires us to open our minds and hearts—fighting and softening at the same time—to understand perspectives that are different from our own, even when fundamental disagreement is imminent. Our current context requires transformational equity-minded leaders, who are willing to transform themselves, to do their own work, explore their own biases and blind spots, and to be vulnerable, introspective, and more self-aware—and explore deeply how oppression is operationalized in their everyday work and practice with diverse students.

QUESTIONS FOR REFLECTION AND DISCUSSION

1. As you engage with members of your professional community, do you discuss equity and social justice issues? If not, why not? How might you encourage more discussion?

2. How does your identity shape your views of administration for social justice and equity? How does your identity also shape your experience and journey as an administrator?

3. How do you define equity and social justice and how do you communicate this with the staff you work with? Do you use storytelling to communicate your beliefs? Might you use this strategy more?

4. When was the last time you called out a person for acting in ways that were inequitable?

REFERENCES

Annie E. Casey Foundation (2014). *Embracing equity: Seven steps to advance and embed race equity and inclusion within your organization.* www.aecf.org/m/resourcedoc/AECF_EmbracingEquity7Steps-2014.pdf. Date Retrieved: September 22, 2018.

Asumah, S. N., & Nagel, M. (2014). *Diversity, Social Justice, and Inclusive Excellence: Transdisciplinary and Global Perspectives.* New York: State University of New York Press.

Bailey, T., Jeong, D. W., & Cho, S. (2010). Referral, enrollment, and completion in developmental education sequences in community colleges. *Economics of Education Review, 29*, 255–270.

Board of Governors of the Federal Reserve System (2018). *Effects of demographic change on GDP growth in OECD economies.* www.federalreserve.gov/releases/g19/HIST/cc_hist_memo_levels.html. Date Retrieved: August 21, 2018.

Duffy, M., Schott, A., Beaver, J. K., & Park, E. (2014). Tracing the development of multiple measures for college placement across states and systems. *Research for Action.* Philadelphia, PA. http://8rri53pm0cs22jk3vvqna1ub-wpengine.netdna-ssl.com/wp-content/uploads/2016/01/RFA-Gates-Multiple-Measures-Phase-1-March-2014.pdf. Date retrieved: February 7, 2019.

Engle, J. (2016). *Answering the call: Institutions and states lead the way toward better measures of postsecondary performance.* Seattle, WA: Bill and Melinda Gates Foundation. https://postsecondary.gatesfoundation.org/areas-of-focus/networks/institutional-partnerships/. Date Retrieved: June 21, 2018.

Human Rights Campaign & Trans People of Color Coalition (2017). *A time to act: Fatal violence against transgender people in America.* http://assets2.hrc.org/files/assets/resources/A_Time_To_Act_2017_REV3.pdf?_ga=2.37050723.2134596731.1542721277-520849444.1542721277. Date Retrieved: November 20, 2018.

Jencks, C. (1998). Racial bias in testing. In C. Jencks & M. Phillips (Eds.), *The Black-White Test Score Gap* (pp. 55–85). Washington, DC: Brookings Institution.

Jenkins, D., & Fink, J. E. (2016). *Tracking Transfer: New Measures of Institutional and State Effectiveness in Helping Community College Students Attain Bachelor's Degrees.* New York, NY: Community College Research Center, Aspen Institute, and National Student Clearinghouse Research Center.

Juszkiewicz, J. (2017). Trends in community college enrollment and completion data. *American Association of Community Colleges.* Washington, DC.

Kezar, A.J. (2008). Understanding leadership strategies for addressing the politics of diversity. *The Journal of Higher Education, 79*(4), 406–441.

Kezar, A. J., Avilez, A. A., Drivalas, Y., & Wheaton, M. M. (2017). Building social change oriented leadership capacity among student organizations: Developing students and campuses simultaneously. *New Directions for Student Leadership, 155*, 45–57.

Kezar, A. J., Glenn, W. J., Lester, J., & Nakamoto, J. (2008). Examining organizational contextual features that affect implementation of equity initiatives. *The Journal of Higher Education, 79*(2), 125–159.

Kezar, A. J., & Posselt, J. (in press). *Administration for Social Justice and Equity in Higher Education: Critical Perspectives for Leadership and Decision-Making.* New York: Routledge.

Kolodner, M., Rancino, B., & Quester, B. (2017). *The Community College "Segregation Machine."* inewsource/Hechinger Report. https://hechingerreport.org/community-college-segregation-machine/. Date Retrieved: February 5, 2019.

Lumina Foundation (2017). *Strategic Plan for 2017 to 2020.* www.luminafoundation.org/files/resources/strategic-plan-2017-to-2020-apr17.pdf. Date Retrieved: August 21, 2018.

Moreno, J. F., Smith, D. G., Clayton-Pederson, A. R., Parker, S., & Teraguci, D. H. (2006). *The Revolving Door for Underrepresented Minority Faculty in Higher Education: An Analysis from the Campus Diversity Initiative.* San Francisco, CA: James Irving Foundation.

Museus, S. D., & LePeau, L. A. (2019). *Administration for Social Justice and Equity in Higher Education: Critical Perspectives for Leadership and Decision-Making.* New York: Routledge.

National Student Clearinghouse Research Center (2017). *Term enrollment estimates: Fall 2017.* Washington, DC. https://nscresearchcenter.org/wp-content/uploads/CurrentTermEnrollment-Fall2017a.pdf. Date Retrieved: November 26, 2018.

National Student Clearinghouse Research Center (2018). *Persistence and retention.* Washington, DC. https://nscresearchcenter.org/wp-content/uploads/SnapshotReport33.pdf. Date Retrieved: November 26, 2018.

Scott, K. (2016). *Radical Candor: How To Be a Kick-Ass Boss Without Losing Your Humanity.* New York: St. Martin's Press.

Shapiro, D., Dundar, A., Huie, F., Wakhungu, P. K., Yuan, X., Nathan, A., & Hwang, Y. (2017, September). *Tracking Transfer: Measures of Effectiveness in Helping Community College Students to Complete Bachelor's Degrees (Signature Report No. 13).* Herndon, VA: National Student Clearinghouse Research Center.

Steele, C., & Aronson, J. (1995). Stereotype threat and the intellectual test performance of African Americans. *Journal of Personal and Social Psychology, 69*(5), 797–811.

Witham, K., Malcom-Piqueux, L. E., Dowd, A. C., & Bensimon, E. M. (2015). *America's unmet promise: The imperative for equity in higher education.* Washington, DC: Association of American Colleges and Universities. www.washingtonpost.com/news/local/wp/2018/07/20/feature/crossing-the-divide-do-men-really-have-it-easier-these-transgender-guys-found-the-truth-was-more-complex/?noredirect=on&utm_term=.cf5639a1a6a0. Date Retrieve: November 17, 2018.

INDEX

Note: page numbers in *italic* type refer to figures; those in **bold** type refer to tables.

AACC (American Association for Community Colleges) 255

AAPI (Asian American And Pacific Islander) students: University of California, Los Angeles 34–35

AAU 135

AAUP 136; AGB/AAUP/ACE Joint Statement on Shared Governance (1966) 22, 23, 31

AAUP/AAU Joint Statement on Academic Freedom and Tenure (1944) 23

Abiola, U. 32

academic affairs: power asymmetry in 11–12; privileged status of 3–4

academic freedom 2, 136

ACC (Arkansas community colleges) 74, 79

access, and admissions decisions 53

access and engagement (EM³) 101, *101*

accountability, and policy discourses 240–242

ACE: AGB/AAUP/ACE Joint Statement on Shared Governance (1966) 22, 23, 31

Achievement Gap 75

Adams, N. A. 182

admissions 84; admission plans 149; affirmative action policies 147; claims on admission spaces 149; criteria 50, 149; decision making 50–53; merit aid and tuition discounts 150; non-cognitive competencies in 51–52; outcomes of decisions 53; processes 52–53; qualitative portions of applications 51; quantitative metrics in 50–51; recruitment decisions and demonstrations of interest 150; *see also* enrollment management, and social justice

African American students 198; Historically Black Colleges and Universities 114, 245

AFT 136

AGB/AAUP/ACE Joint Statement on Shared Governance (1966) 22, 23, 31

AHEE (Association for Higher Education Effectiveness) 202

AIR (Association for Institutional Research) 199

Albertine, S. 14

American Association for Community Colleges (AACC) 255

Annie E. Casey Foundation 254

anti-sexual harassment policies and practices 176–177, 191–192; biases 186–187; campus safety and sexual misconduct 178–180; community intervention programs 190–191; compliance approach to 180–183; criminal-like proceedings in 187; definition issues 184; federal policies 178; negative effects from reporting and referral policies 184–185; power, privilege, and administrators' assumptions 184–187; rape myths 184; sexual assaults in homosexual, bisexual and transgender encounters 186–187; social justice and equity-minded legal administration 188–191; trauma-informed care 189–190; values 189–190; victimization and trauma 185–186

Arkansas community colleges (ACC) 74, 79
Aronowitz, T. 186
Asian American And Pacific Islander (AAPI)
  students: University of California, Los Angeles
  34–35
Aspen Institute 200, 252
Association for Higher Education Effectiveness
  (AHEE) 202
Association for Institutional Research (AIR) 199
assumptions, examination of 260
avoided costs measure 74

Baime, D. S. 78–79
Baker, K. K. 187
Baker, Vicki 106
balance theory (Sternberg) 9–10
"Bargaining for the Common Good" 134
Barr, M. J. 77
Barrow, C. W. 24
Bastedo, M. N. 45, 52, 53
Baxter, L. 246
Bell, L. A. 27, 203
Bensimon, Estela Mara 121, 160, 254–255
biases 2; in anti-sexual harassment policies and
  practices 186–187; in community colleges 256;
  in decision making 45–46, 60; in hiring 56–57,
  115–116, 117, 126; implicit and explicit 45–46; in
  mentoring 96–97; in work-life policies 230, **231**
Bickel, R. D. 180, 181
bisexual women: sexual assaults 187
Blair, D. 202
Boards of Trustees/Governors/Regents 73, 219
Bolman, L.G. 15
bounded rationality 44–45
Bowman, N. A. 45, 52
Bradshaw v. Rawlings (1979) 180
"bread and butter" unionism 133–134
Brighouse, Harry 148
Brodsky, A. 185
Brown, K. M. 30, 34
budgeting see strategic finance approach
"business unionism" 133
Byars-Winston, Angela 104
Byrne-Jimenez, M. 27
bystander intervention 190–191

California Community Colleges 254
Cameron, D. 238
Campbell, C. 229
Campus Climate Survey Validation Study 2016,
  Department of Justice 187
Campus-based Aid programs 68

Cantalupo, N. C. 181–182
Carducci, R. 243
Carnevale, A. P. 242
Carolina Covenant (UNC) 152
CCRC (Community College Research Center) 252
Center for Improvement of Mentored Experiences
  (CIMER) 106
Center for Public Integrity 178
Centers for Disease Control and Prevention 187
centralized approach to budgeting 77
childrearing see work-life policies
Ching, Cheryl 12, 68, 87, 111–131
Cianni, M. 98–99
CIMER (Center for Improvement of Mentored
  Experiences) 106
Civil Rights Act of 1964 180
civil rights movement 211
Clayton-Pederson, A. R. 115
Clery Act 181
Coker, D. 186–187
COL (cost of living) 138
collective bargaining 15, 135–136, 138–139; complex
  context of 132–133; labor history 133–134;
  negotiating from a social justice perspective
  137–138; and shared governance 32
College and University Association for Human
  Resources (CUPAHR) 233
Collins, P. H. 13
colorblind ideology, and mentoring 99
Community College Research Center (CCRC) 252
community colleges, equity-minded leadership
  in 251; author's identity and journey 257–259;
  challenges of 255–257; equity context 252–253;
  operationalization of 253–255; strategies and
  recommendations 259–262
competition, and individualism 212
compromises 82, 83, 86–88
conflict mediation training 36
conscious public commitment, and shared
  governance 27, 28, 28, 29–31, 38
consultative approach to budgeting 77
consumerism 212
context, and wisdom 10
contingent faculty, and shared governance 31–32
Contreras-McGavin, M. 243
Cooper, Deanna 238–250
Cooper, M.A. 14
Corbally, J. E. 46
Corbett, C. 226
corporate-like management practices 4–5, 24
Corral, D. 241–242
correspondence bias 45

cost of living (COL) 138
cost per completer measure 74
costing, of proposals in collective bargaining 137–138
cover letters 116, 117
Creswell, J. W. 113
critical race feminism 117–118
cultural deficit perspective 166
cultural taxation 167, **168–169**
culture, and wisdom 10
Cunliffe, A. L. 239, 244
CUPAHR (College and University Association for Human Resources) 233
CVs *(curricula vitae)* 115, 116, 117
CWU 136

Danis, F. 186
Danowitz Sagaria, M. A. 117, 119
data: analysis and interpretation 201; as basis for policy 15–16; data collecting and reporting 200–201; ethnic data collection, AAPI (Asian American And Pacific Islander) students, University of California, Los Angeles 34–35; IR professionals as stewards of 202; and mentoring 106; *see also* data use, and racial equality; IR (institutional research) professionals
data literacy 203
data use, and racial equality 159–161, 171–172; craft of equity-minded data use 162–166; Equity Scorecard 160, 161–162; equity-minded leadership recommendations 170–171; racial literacy for disaggregated data use 166–167, **168–169**, 169
Davidoff, S. 186
Davidson University 152
Deal, T.E. 15
decision making 12, 43–44, 57–60, 87; admissions context 49–53; cognitive and social biases 45–46; context-specific nature of 47; criteria and process in 47; equity checks in 59; Framework for Equity in Decision Making 47–49, *48*, 84; hiring context 49, 54–57; intersectional positionalities in 59–60; multiple contexts in 57–58; and organizational culture 46; and power *48*, 48–49; priorities and preferences in 47; rational choice and bounded rationality 44–45
deconstruction 245–246
DEI (diversity, equity, and inclusion) 260–261
Dejean, J. S. 183
Delanty, G. 243, 244, 248
deliberative democracy 44
developmental relationships *see* mentoring
Di Angelo, R. 123

Di Ramio, D. 56
direct action 38
Direct Loan program 68
diversity: conflict with prestige and revenue issues 148, 150–151; DEI (diversity, equity, and inclusion) 260–261; diversity plans 244, 245, 246; and mentoring 94; slow progress on 146–147
Dizon, Jude Paul Matias 21–42, 84–85, 203
Dowd, Alicia C. 159–175, 254–255
Duke University 152
dynamic institutionalization, and shared governance 27, 28, *28*, *29*, 36–38, 39
dysfunctional relationships in mentoring 100, 102

Early Decision admission plans 149
Eastern Michigan University 178, 182
economic outcomes 74
economic pressures 214–215
economic principles in higher education institutions 4; *see also* neoliberalism
economics, and policy discourses 240–242
Education Amendments of 1972 *see* Title IX of the Education Amendments of 1972
"Education & Related" (E&R) expenditures 71–72
efficiency, and policy discourses 240–242
Elmore, Branden D. 159–175
employee performance evaluations 261–262
Engle, J. 252
enrollment management, and social justice 146–147; change leadership 151–152; demographic dividend 153–154; moral action 148; prestige 147–148; remedies 150–151; social justice 146–154; structural barriers 149–150; tuition revenue dependence 147; *see also* admissions
epistemology: Eurocentric epistemological ideals 117–118, 122, 124
equal opportunity 6–7
equity: definitions of 6–8, 68; DEI (diversity, equity, and inclusion) 260–261; framework for 6–17; historical and organizational barriers to 3–4
equity checks in decision making 59
equity literacy 227, 229–230, **231**, 232
equity measures 75
Equity Scorecard 160, 161–162; craft of equity-minded data use 162–166
E&R ("Education & Related") expenditures 71–72
ethnicity: and mentoring 94; *see also* race
Eurocentric epistemological ideals 117–118, 122, 124
evaluative storytelling 53
excess credit hours metric 86
exclusion, and admissions decisions 53

expenditures 70–72
explicit biases 45; in mentoring 96

facilitation training 36
faculty: and unions 135–136; *see also* hiring;
    mentoring; tenure policies; work-life policies
faculty of color, and systemic inequalities 225, 226
Fain, P. 241
Family and Medical Leave Act of 1993 (2006) 232
feedback 261
Feminist Majority Found. v. Hurley, 2018 176
finance *see* strategic finance approach
Fink, J. E. 252
first-generation students 96; mentoring 95; outcomes
    measures 74
Fischer, F. 238–239
Fisher v. University of Texas at Austin, 2013 147
fit, in hiring 54, 55, 56, 57, 112, 115, 117, 118;
    critical enquiry into search process 121–127, **124**;
    equity-based reconceptualization of 119, **120**, 121
Fortney, S. S. 188
Foucault, M. 13, 30
foundational courses, and equity measures 75
frame reflection 34, 35
Freeman, S. 56
Freire, Paulo 5, 11
FSA (Office of Federal Student Aid) 68
funding ecosystem *69,* 69–72, **71**; *see also* strategic
    finance approach

Gallagher, S. K. 186
Gardner, S. K. 228
Gasman, M. 32
Gates Foundation 252
gateway courses, and equity measures 75
Gee, J. P. 238
Geertz, C. 213
gender and gender identity: biases 46; equity and
    justice 6; hiring 56, 117–118; mentoring 94, 95, 96,
    97; power 12; Title IX protection 176–177, 179;
    see also work-life policies
gender-neutral bathrooms 258–259
genocide 256
gentrification, by campuses 4
Gewirtz, S. 240
GI Bill 147, 153
Gorski, P. 227, 229, 230, 234
Gottweis, H. 238–239
governments, as source of revenue 70, **71**
GPA (grade point average) metrics in admissions
    50–51, 52, 149
graduation rates 241

Gratz v. Bollinger, 2003 147
Griffin, Kimberly A. 12, 93–110
Grubb, A. 184
Grutter v. Bollinger, 2003 147
Guinier, Lani 166–167
Gutiérrez, R. 74

Hajer, M. A. 242–243
halo effect 55
Hatch, M. J. 239, 244
Heckman, D. 181, 182
Hernandez, Theresa 9, 12, 43–66, 84
Higher Education Act 1974 147, 153
Hill, C. 226
Hillman, N. 241–242
hiring 12, 54, 84, 87; biases in 56–57, 115–116,
    117, 126; criteria 54–55; equity-minded
    reconceptualization 119, **120**, 121; homophily
    in 118; interview protocols 125–127; job
    announcements 123, **124**; limited diversity
    113–114; merit and fit in 54, 55, 57, 112,
    115, 116–118, 119, **120**, 121–127, **124**; myths
    about racially minoritized candidates 114–115;
    outcomes 57; processes 55–56; racial inequality
    55, 111–127; *see also* search committees
Hirschhorn, L. 243, 244, 248
Hispanic Serving Institutions (HSIs) 87, 123
Hispanic students: outcomes measures 75; *see also*
    Latinx students
Historically Black Colleges and
    Universities 114, 245
Hodges, C. R. 171
Hoekema, A. J. 34
holistic review 53, 58–59
homophily: hiring 118; mentoring 95–97, 102
homophobia, and mentoring 94
Honeyman, D. S. 78–79
HSIs (Hispanic Serving Institutions) 87, 123
Huff, Darrell 201
human capabilities 14; institutions' duty to
    promote 7
Human Rights Campaign & Trans People of Color
    Coalition 258
humanities, and shared governance 32
Humphreys, D. 241

IAT (Implicit Association Test) 116
ideal 82, 83–84, 88
identity (EM³) 102
identity sharing 261
IHEP (Institute for Higher Education Policy) 252
Implicit Association Test (IAT) 116

implicit biases 45–46; hiring 115–116, 117; mentoring 96
inclusion 7; DEI (diversity, equity, and inclusion) 260–261
Inclusive Excellence 259
income level, and outcomes measures 74
incremental value measure 74
Indigenous students 196; and discrimination in standardized testing 198; *see also* Native American students
individualism, and competition 212
information: information needs, identification of by IR professionals 199–200; informational approach to budgeting 77; *see also* data
Institute for Higher Education Policy (IHEP) 252
Institutional Effectiveness function 202
institutional precarity 214–215, 216–217
institutional racism 112
institutional research professionals *see* IR (institutional research) professionals
Integrated Postsecondary Education Data System (IPEDS), National Center for Education Statistics 68, 70, 200, 202
intergroup dialogue 35
intersectionality: decision making 49, 59–60; mentoring 106
interviews: admissions 51; hiring 125–127
IPEDS (Integrated Postsecondary Education Data System), National Center for Education Statistics 68, 70, 200, 202
IR (institutional research) professionals 196–198; data analysis and interpretation 201; data collecting and reporting 200–201; definition of institutional research 198–199; educating data users 203; identifying information needs 199–200; social justice in higher education 203–204; as stewards of data 202; strategic planning and evaluation 202
Iverson, S. V. 244, 245, 246
Ivie, Jennifer L. 196–205

James, E. H. 182
Jenkins, D. 252
job announcements 123, **124**
job descriptions 43, 54–55, 103; *see also* position descriptions
Johnson, W. B. 96
Julius, Dan 15, 132–145

Kahneman, D. 126
Kerr, Clark 140n4
Keynesian economic theory 211

Kezar, Adrianna 1–18, 21–42, 84–85, 203, 243, 254
Kolodner, M. 254
Konrad, A. M. 113, 115

labor management relations *see* collective bargaining
Lake, P. F. 180, 181, 182
Lambert, C. A. 186
Land Grant colleges and universities 147
language 238–239; implications of policy vocabularies 242–243; linguistic violence 161, 167, **168–169**, 170; *see also* policy discourses
Latinx students 198, 254; *see also* Hispanic students
legal administration *see* anti-sexual harassment policies and practices
Lepeau, Lucy A. 203, 209–224, 253
Lester, Jaime 12, 225–237
letters of recommendation, in admissions 51
Lewis, Luca E. 251–262
LGB people, and mentoring 94, 96, 97
libraries, identification procedures for access 28–29
Liera, Roman 12, 57, 87, 111–131
linguistic violence 161, 167, **168–169**, 170
listening 35
"living wage" 138
local communities, relationships with campuses 4
logic of appropriateness 45
logic of consequences 44–45
low SES students, admissions processes 52–53
Lucido, Jerome A. 146–155
Lumuna Foundation 252

Major, T. 14
majoritarian discourse 166
Malcolm-Piqueux, L. E. 254–255
Mannix, Tom 138–139
March, J. G. 44–45
Martin, J. 245
Martinez, Magdalena 238–250
Mauzy, D. L. 186
McClennan, G. S. 77
McDonald, N. 14
McGee, Richard 104
McNair, T.B. 14
medical school interviews 51
men: sexual violence experienced by 187; *see also* gender and gender identity; White males; work-life policies
men of color: and mentoring 95, 96, 97
mentor and mentee identities (EM^3) 102
mentoring 12, 93–95, 106–107; access to mentors 95–97; assessment, reporting, and accountability

in 105–106; biases in 96–97; and diversity 94; dysfunctional relationships 100, 102; EM³ (Equity-Minded Mentoring Model) 100–103, *101*; formalizing expectations in 103–104; homophily 95–97, 102; imbalanced distribution of labor in 97–98; incentivizing participation in 104; inequality reduction and outcome improvement strategies 103–106; power dynamics 99–100; professional development and identity awareness 105; professionalization of 104–105; relationship quality 98–99

merit, in admissions 149; merit aid 150

merit, in hiring 54, 55, 57, 112, 115, 117, 118; critical enquiry into search process 121–127, **124**; equity-based reconceptualization of 119, **120**, 121

Michigan State University 25, 84

microaggressions 167, **168**

Milkman, Katherine 46

Miller, C. W. 58

mindfulness, in administrative practice 8–9; routinizing of 15–17

Minor, J.T. 23

minoritized identities, individuals with: and mentoring 94, 96, 98–99

minority-serving institutions (MSIs) 241–242, 245, 246

mission statements 215–216, 219–220, 245

Montgomery, B. 246

moral reasoning 247–248

morality, declining 212

Moreno, J. F. 115

Morrill Act 147, 153

MSIs (minority-serving institutions) 241–242, 245, 246

Mullin, Christopher M. 67–81, 84, 85

"multifocal lens" for leadership 171

Museus, Samuel D. 203, 209–224, 253

Myers, S. L. Jr. 113, 114

National Center for Education Statistics *see* NCES (National Center for Education Statistics)

National Crime Victimization Survey 186

National Institute for Transformation and Equity 209

National Institute of Justice 178

National Labor Relations Act 135

National Postsecondary Student Aid Study, United States Department of Education 75

National Research Mentoring Network (NRMN) 105

National Science Foundation 226

National Student Clearinghouse 252

Native American students 202; *see also* Indigenous students

NCES (National Center for Education Statistics) 226; IPEDS (Integrated Postsecondary Education Data System) 68, 70, 200, 202

NEA 136

neoliberalism 4, 84–85; community colleges 253, 256; decline of shared governance 24–25, 26–27; higher education culture 213–219; neoliberal psyche of administrators 4–5; organizational cultures 209–211, 221; origins and core tenets of 211–212; as a paradigm 210–211; strategies to advance social justice in 219–221

new managerialism 24

New School for Social Research 135

Nonaka, I. 10

norms 82, 83, 84–86, 88

Northwestern University 104

NRMN (National Research Mentoring Network) 105

Nussbaum, Martha 7, 14

Obama Administration 178–180

O'Banion, T. 241

OCR (Office of Civil Rights), Department of Education 178–179

Office of Federal Student Aid (FSA) 68

O'Meara, K. A. 229

oppression, five sides of 240

organizational culture 83, 86–88, 228–229; decision making 46; faculty hiring process 56; *see also* work-life policies

organizational structures and dynamics (EM³) 102–103

organized crime, and unions 134

Orr, M. T. 27

Osei-Kofi, N. 240

othermothering 98

Parker, S. 115

participative approach to budgeting 77–78

participatory governance 33

Patton, L. D. 240

Pell Grant program 68

Penn State University 25, 84

people of color: diversity plans 244, 245, 246; mentoring 98–99; myths about racially minoritized candidates 114–115; *see also* men of color; race; racism; women of color

performance evaluations 261–262

personal and professional outcomes (EM³) 101, *101*

personal statements, in admissions 51

Pfeffer, J. 113, 115

PhD students 52, 56

Pifer, Meghan 106

policies: and race 37; reversing of 37–38
policy discourses 238–239, 248; efficiency
    and accountability tensions 240–242;
    leadership matters 243–248; policy vocabularies'
    implications 242–243; social justice framework
    239–240
political pressures 214–215
Pompelia, S. 75
position descriptions 44, 58, 87, 123, 259; *see also* job
    descriptions
positionality 13–14; decision making 49, 59–60
Posselt, Julie 1–18, 43–66, 84, 254
postmodernism 239, 246
power: anti-sexual harassment policies and practices
    184–187; critical consciousness about 11–13;
    decision making *48*, 48–49; labor management
    relations 132; mentoring 99–100; neoliberalism
    210–211, 219; postmodernism 239; redistribution
    of 33–34; relinquishing of 32–33; self-knowledge
    and positionality 13–14; shared governance 22,
    26–27, 32
precarity 212; institutional 214–215, 216–217
prestige 147–148, 214
Princeton University 216
private sources of revenue 70, **71**
privilege, and anti-sexual harassment policies and
    practices 184–187
professional development: equity literacy 233;
    mentoring 105; moral reasoning in 247–248;
    work-life policies 233
protest movements 38
public good, higher education as 24–25
Pusser, B. 24–25

quality, and revenue 216–217
Quester, B. 254

race: biases 46; data use and racial equality 159–172;
    discrimination in standardized testing 198; equity
    and justice 6; hiring 55, 111–127; mentoring
    94, 95, 96, 97–98; outcomes measures 74; policy
    processes 37; power 12–13; racial composition in
    leadership 32; *see also* people of color
race-neutral policies 12
"racial audits" 122
racial literacy 166–167
racial tokenism 167, **168**
racialization, and decision making 49
racism 256; anti-racist leadership stance 170–171;
    institutional 112; mentoring 94, 97–98; "words
    that wound" 161, 167, **168–169**
Rancino, B. 254

rape: rape myths 184; *see also* anti-sexual harassment
    policies and practices
rational choice, decision making framework 44–45
Rawls, J. 239
references 116, 117
reflection: and mindfulness 8–9; *see also*
    self-reflection
Rege, R. 182
Rein, M. 34
relationship quality (EM³) 101, *101*
religion: equity and justice 6; mentoring 94
resistance 38, 220, 221
retention data 163, 164
return on investment (ROI), and equity 72–75, *73*
revenue 70, **71**; performance-based funding model
    241; and quality 216–217; revenue-generation
    pressures 5
Rivera, L. A. 117
ROI (return on investment), and equity 72–75, *73*
Romberger, B. 98–99
Rose, S. J. 242
Ross, L. E. 199
Ross v. University of Tulsa, 2017 189
Rutgers University 135

Sable, M. R. 186, 189
Sacchetti v. Gallaudet Univ., 2018 176
Salem International University 182
Sallee, M. W. 228, 229
San Francisco State University 215
Schein, E. H. 46
Schon, D.A. 34
Scott, K. 261
screening interviews *see* interviews
search committees 54, 55, 84, 232; biases 56–57,
    115–116; equity 119, **120**, 122, 123; interview
    protocols 125–127; limited diversity of 113–114;
    merit and fit 116–118, 124–125; race 114–115;
    see also hiring
Sedlacek, William 51–52
SEIU 136
self-knowledge 13–14
self-reflection 13, 87; and shared governance 27–28,
    30–31
Sen, Amartya 7
Sensoy, Ö. 123
Sergiovanni, T. J. 46
sexism 256; and mentoring 94, 97, 98; *see also* gender
    and gender identity; Title IX of the Education
    Amendments of 1972
sexual harassment *see* anti-sexual harassment
    policies and practices

sexual identity: equity and justice 6; mentoring 94
Shahjahan, R. A. 240
shared governance 12, 21–22, 39, 84–85, 87; decline
    of 22, 23–24; history of 22–26; power 22; social
    justice and equity based model for 27–39, 28;
    transformation of 26–27
silence, and oppression 167
Simpson v. University of Colorado Boulder, 2007 189
SJTI (Social Justice Training Institute) 36
slavery 256
Smith, D. G. 54, 115, 121
Smith, W. A. 37
SMU (Social Movement Unionism) 140n2
social class: equity and justice 6; power 12
social justice: collective bargaining 132–134,
    137–139; definition 210; higher education
    203–204; policy discourses framework 239–240;
    shared governance model 27–39, 28; strategies
    to advance in neoliberal environment 219–221;
    see also enrollment management, and social justice
Social Justice Training Institute (SJTI) 36
Social Movement Unionism (SMU) 140n2
social movements 210
social network analysis 106
social sciences, and shared governance 32
socialization 217–218, 220–221
socio-emotional competencies in admissions 51–52
Solorzano, D. G. 37
Spencer Mentoring Award (Spencer Foundation) 104
St. John, Edward 244, 247, 248
St. Petersburg College 78, 79
St. Rose, A. 226
stakeholders, students as 27
standardized test scores 197–198; GPA (grade point
    average) metrics 50–51, 52, 149; racial bias in 254
Staples, J. 167
stereotypes, in hiring 117
Sternberg, R. J. 9–10
Stevens, Mitchell 53
Stoner, E. N. II 189
storytelling 261
strategic allies/alliances 76
strategic finance approach 67, 79, 84, 85, 87; actions
    to rectify injustices 75–79; definitions of equity
    68; economic outcomes 74; equity measures 75;
    expenditures 70–72; funding ecosystem 69, 69–72,
    71; inclusive budgeting approaches 77; outcomes
    measures 74; revenue 70, 71; ROI (return on
    investment), and equity 72–75, 73; strategic
    budget cuts 78–79; strategic plan 72
strategic planning 72, 76, 202
structural barriers in institutions 75

student affairs: lower status of 4; power asymmetry
    in 11–12
student identities, diversity in 16
Student Right-to-Know Act 200
student-centeredness 14–15
students, as source of revenue 70, **71**
Sun, Jeffrey 176–195
SUNY Buffalo 135
SUNY Stony Brook 135
surveillance 212
Swing, R. L. 199

Takeuchi, H. 10
Task Force on Admissions in the 21st Century 151
tenure policies: negative impact on women 22;
    widening the circle in shared governance 31–32;
    work-life policies 226
Teraguchi, D. H. 115
test scores *see* standardized test scores
Third World Liberation Front 210
Tienda, Marta 153–154
Tierney, W. G. 23, 25, 46, 214, 246
Title IX of the Education Amendments of 1972
    176–177, 179, 180, 183, 184, 185, 189, 191
Title VII of the Civil Rights Act of 1964 180
Torres, Vasti 82–89
Toyama, R. 10
trans people: Lewis's identity and journey 257–259;
    and mentoring 94, 96
transformative discourse, and shared governance 27,
    28, 28, 29, 34–36, 38–39
Travers, C. 32
Tribal Colleges 114
Trump Administration 179, 180
"trust builders" and "trust busters" 170
tuition discounts 150
tuition revenue, dependence on 147
Turner, C. S. V. 113, 114–115, 124
Turner, E. 184

UAW 136, 138
UE 136
unions 15; conscious public commitment in shared
    governance 29; and organized crime 134; union
    leaders 134; *see also* collective bargaining
University of California 138
University of California, Los Angeles: AAPI
    (Asian American And Pacific Islander) students
    34–35
University of Florida 135
University of Illinois: anti-sexual harassment policies
    and practices 188–189

University of Michigan: Centre for Research on Teaching and Learning 105
University of North Carolina at Chapel Hill 152
University of Notre Dame 178
University of Oregon 135
University of Southern California *see* USC (University of Southern California)
University of Virginia 152
University of Wisconsin 104, 214
upfront costs measure 74
USC (University of Southern California): Center for Enrollment Research, Policy and Practice 153; CUE (Center for Urban Education) 7–8; resistance 38; sexual abuse scandal 14, 25–26, 84

values 215–216; anti-sexual harassment policies and practices 189–190; and wisdom 10–11
Villarreal, Cynthia D. 9, 12, 43–66, 84

Wake Forest University 152
Wampler, B. 33
Ward, K. 228–229
weighted average instructional cost per credit hour measure 74
weighting, and wisdom 10
Weiss, K. G. 186
Welch, O. M. 171
Whinnery, E. 75
white leadership 32

White males 3, 12, 55, 96, 118, 197; White, male, Eurocentric epistemological ideals 117–118, 122, 124
widening the circle, and shared governance 27, 28, *28*, 29, 31–34, 38
wisdom: in judgment 9–11; and mindfulness 8; routinizing of 15–17
Witham, K. 254–255
Wolf-Wendel, L. 228–229
women: mentoring 94, 95, 96, 97, 98–99; negative impact of tenure policies on 22; systemic gender inequalities 225–226; *see also* gender and gender identity; work-life policies
women of color, and mentoring 95, 98
Wooten, L. P. 182
"words that wound" 161, 167, **168–169**
work-life policies 12, 225–227, 234; advocacy for work-life balance 233–234; definition of work-life balance 227–228; equity literacy 229–230, **231**, 232; organizational and social contexts 228–229; professional development for leadership 233; recommendations 232–233
writing samples, in admissions 51

Yanow, D. 243
Yeshiva University, New York 135
Yosso, T. J. 37
Young, I. M. 240

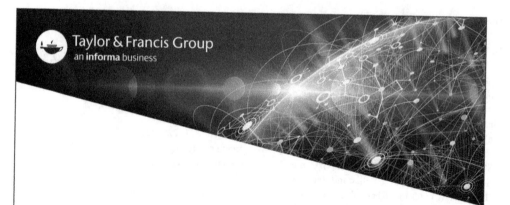